HISTORY OF
THE HOUSE

HISTORY OF THE HOUSE

With a foreword by

SIR ROBERT MATTHEW

C.B.E., M.A., M.T.P.I., F.R.I.A.S., P.P.R.I.B.A.

Edited by

ETTORE CAMESASCA

Translated by

ISABEL QUIGLY

G. P. PUTNAM'S SONS New York

FOREWORD

The history of the house is the history of civilization. It would require a sizeable library to maintain it in full. The editors and contributors, from many countries, with one volume at their disposal, had the difficult task of preserving comprehensiveness through selection.

Ranging from the dwellings of pre-history to the landmarks of Wright and Le Corbusier; from the tools and materials available, to interior furnishings, decorations and equipment, the inter-action of climate, technical knowledge, social custom, economics and the allied arts upon building and town-planning is described in immense detail, and beautifully illustrated.

The elusive, timeless qualities of the vernacular in building come alive in these pages, equally with the recurring, sometimes eccentric, impact of formulism. The effect of the one upon the other in every country and in many periods can be appreciated by the comparative method used, and by the parallel inclusion, as part of the total phenomena, of the vast range of artifacts, arts and facilities that, in life, mark the difference between a house and a home.

ROBERT H. MATTHEW

First American Edition 1971
This edition copyright © 1971 by Wm. Collins Sons & Co. Ltd.
Originally published in Italian as STORIA DELLA CASA,
copyright © 1968 by Rizzoli Editore.

Library of Congress Catalog Card Number: 73-141310

Printed in Italy by Rizzoli Editore, Milan.

CONTENTS

Frontispiece: Old and new in São Paulo, Brazil.

Opposite page: A house sandwiched between the Ardighelli towers in San Gimignano, Italy.

Ettore Camesasca - Gianni K. Koenig

WHAT IS A HOUSE?

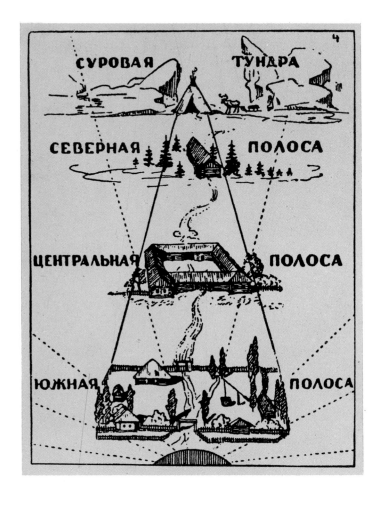

Nineteenth century Russian drawing which illustrates the types of dwelling found in the frozen tundra and the northern, central and southern regions. The dwellings shown are, from north to south (top to bottom): the tent; the wooden house; the large house, also of wood with several rooms; the mud and straw house, part of a complex of buildings within a protective wall. The dotted lines indicate the angle of the sun's rays, shorter in the south than in the north. By contrast, the size of the dwelling increases as one travels south, as the lines of the large triangle show. The drawing is intended to illustrate the importance of climate, of the availability of building materials and of tradition and economy in the development of the dwelling house.

House is probably one of the most frequently used words in a number of languages. Its function is to be a dwelling-place and a refuge for men, and under this description come palaces and castles, mansions and mud-huts, cottages and caves, anything with four walls and a roof. In the history of architecture more attention has been paid, naturally enough, to the grander buildings, the palaces, abbeys, cathedrals and castles. Such great monuments are given frequent mention in the chronicles of the Middle Ages. However, despite the fact that the life of adjacent town and country areas revolved around the activities of such buildings, most of these references have an architectural rather than sociological slant. Little may be said about the stonemasons and original inhabitants, although a few well-chosen words about the castellan may be found. In later centuries, when the architect's name began to be included in the historical records, the construction of a palace might be fully documented. Some of these records may reveal the arguments inherent in the relationship between architect and client.

But the wooden houses of the medieval cities that sheltered craftsmen, workmen and their families, the thatched roofed cottages of agricultural labourers, shepherds, herdsmen, gardeners, and the rest, do not on the whole feature in the chronicles. Their builders have no known names. The employment of architects on the design of working class houses is a very recent phenomenon, hence little has been written about the history of the ordinary house. To redress this injustice to some degree is the object of this book.

The historian of the ordinary house is at a disadvantage, however. Time takes its toll of every building but more noticeably of the cottage than of the castle. Stone and metals are the materials of great buildings: builders used bronze, marble, iron and granite not merely because they looked well but because they lasted. Simpler buildings of

Further examples of the extent to which the structure of a building may be dictated by external influences. (Below) A building with an earthquake-proof iron framework (1877). During the nineteenth century iron was often used to reinforce the framework of buildings and in this it replaced wooden beams. This form of strengthening can be seen (above) in this Turkish house; the photograph (right) shows the same house in the course of construction by a technique traditional to Anatolia.

House at Pescocostanzo in the Abruzzi, built between the sixteenth and eighteenth centuries. The projecting roofs necessary to protect the house from the strong prevailing winds, require very stout supports. They shelter the external staircases, their landings and the small windows and narrow doors.

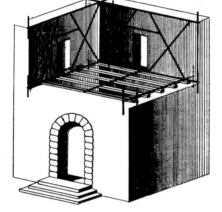

mud and wattle and brick — whether sun-dried or baked — were less resistant to the erosion of time and climate. The Emperor Augustus boasted that he had found a Rome of brick and left it a city of marble. It was not, however, entirely transmogrified and the brick residuum was to prove a hazardous problem to the city fathers in later reigns.

Both castle and cottage, however, are in a sense living organisms. They change, they adapt to the demands made on them. Additions are made to them which may entirely alter the appearance of the original structures or, eventually, almost completely conceal it. The process is more easily appreciated in the case of churches where a Gothic cloister may be added to a Romanesque building, a classical porch may be added to a Norman nave, a baroque façade may be added to an early basilica. In the case of a dwelling house, the changes may be more haphazard, less easily visible at a casual glance and are, almost certainly, less well-documented. Successive owners may have added one or more storeys or blocked up doors and — in Britain during

the eighteenth and early nineteenth centuries, in order to evade Window Tax — windows. More recently, the introduction of electricity and central heating has in some cases drastically altered interiors more than half a century old. In the seventeenth and eighteenth centuries, both large and small buildings were converted from single family to multiple dwellings and the process continues today in the central residential areas of cities, as the town houses of noble families and great merchants are divided into flats. But of these divisions the exterior of the house may give little or no indication.

In the belief that there is a connection between a great man and his environment, the houses of Shakespeare, Goethe, Mozart, Leopardi and others have been lovingly preserved. Later generations can thus see faithful reflections of the customs and tastes not of an age perhaps, but at least of some of its most famous sons. These houses are of the greatest assistance to students of domestic architecture but they are few in number and the majority of them belong to the last two centuries. For earlier

periods, restoration – that most demanding and contradictory of tasks – may depend on inspired guesswork based on whatever information is available.

With modern buildings, the problem presented by time is even greater since present-day building techniques allow for more rapid obsolescence. The society envisaged by Mies van der Rohe and Le Corbusier never materialised (Nazism, in fact, arose in its place), so that masterpieces like the Tugendhat house at Brno in Czechoslovakia and the Villa Savoye at Poissy near Paris were soon abandoned and quickly became pathetic ruins. The Kaufmann house built by Richard Neutra in the Colorado desert is already submerged in sand and will have to be dug out before it can be restored.

None of this bears any relation to the merits of Mies van der Rohe or Le Corbusier or Neutra. Here we touch on the question of function and meaning in a building. Théophile Gautier said that the truly beautiful is always entirely useless. Architecture has not only rejected this idea but has sought to combine both and yet remain mainly functional. When, therefore, the function of a building is lost, so is its meaning. Two hundred years from now, when trains no longer exist, what will be the point in preserving a railway station, however fine?

Yet people have successfully disproved Bacon's claim that houses were not for looking at but for living in. They have argued, moreover, that buildings which are pleasant to look at may also be the most comfortable – essentially a functionalist viewpoint.

With considerations of comfort we come to climate. Its importance in determining the forms of domestic architecture is agreed. Though the houses on the Italian side of the Alps are built with the same wood and slate as those in the French and Swiss valleys, they appear more open for they possess natural protection against the cold north winds; they have larger windows and even balconies on which to dry hay and cereal without great danger of frost. Northern Europeans, indeed, spend so much time shut up in their houses that these have developed into warm, gleaming refuges. Southern Europeans have come to value indoor comfort too although the Mediterranean climate more easily allows for outdoor living. Northern Europeans have a word for home: neither Latins nor Russians have such a word.

At its simplest, the whole history of the house is embraced in the necessity of finding protection from sun or snow by the ever-improving use of the materials available for its construction. Widely separated peoples often reach the same solution to the problem. The Patagonians shelter in something more

Time and accident are not the only elements to alter the appearance of a house. This may be changed by deliberate design. On this page and the next are two views of the Casa Isolani in the Strada Maggiore in Bologna, one of the finest surviving examples of thirteenth century domestic architecture in Italy. On this page we see the building as it appeared after the restorations of 1877; on the opposite page as it appears now with the intrusive brick pillars built to help carry the weight of the projecting upper floor and reduce the strain on the three oak beams, 29½ feet high. An effort has been made to match the pillars to the base of the beams, which are almost certainly original: unfortunately, however, the pillars detract from the appearance of the house as do the gutters and lights.

Even in the western world, belief in magic — or a reluctance to take any chances with it — may crop up in domestic architecture. The eye in the roof of this particular house is a case in point. Its circumstances, however, explain it: the house was built in America during the nineteenth century Gold Rush.

like a windbreak than a tent: the summer shelter of the Eskimos is very similar. The *beit* of the nomad in the Sahara resembles that of the tribesman on the high plains of Tibet.

Of course, other considerations than those of protection have conditioned the shape of a house. In some areas of, for example, Asia, primitive superstitions still influence the design of the house to some extent. Nor have the elements been the only enemy from which a refuge was sought: the need for protection against enemy attacks, both human and animal, has in some instances dictated the form of the house.

In the end, the house — the history of which is inseparable from that of its owner — disappears; it is demolished or it crumbles from neglect; either way it is as if it had never been. It leaves no reminder of itself. We know a great deal about the pyramid at Sakkara and nothing at all about the house of the great Imhotep who conceived it. The dome of the cathedral in Florence tells us much about Brunelleschi but how did he himself cope with the routine of everyday living?

The study of dwellings needs patience, an intuitive reading of written records, and a creative

ALTRA VEDVTA DELLA FACCIATA PRINCIPALE DEL PALAZZO DELL'ECCELLENTIS.CASA ALTIERI VERSO IL GIESV
Architettura di Gio Antonio de Rossi

The three illustrations above show how insistence on legal rights can affect the design of a house. (Left) The southern aspect of the Palazzo Altieri in Rome — according to the plans drawn up for Cardinal Giambatista Altieri by Giovanni Antonio de Rossi about 1650. (Centre) The door and window of the house traditionally said to have been inhabited by an old woman called Berta on the site of the palazzo; she apparently refused to allow her house to be demolished so that it had to be incorporated in the palace, thus seriously affecting the architect's design of which the illustration (right) shows a detail.

— and disciplined — imagination. With these tools to hand we have set about writing this book. Basically its plan is chronological. Sometimes, however, it has proved necessary to play around with history. From time to time, moreover, the decision as to what is typical has been a difficult one — understandably so, even if we think no further than the homes of our friends.

A great many paintings, engravings and drawings have been used as well as photographs. Artists are, indeed, among the most valuable of assistants to the historian. The help they afford, especially during the Middle Ages and the early part of the Renaissance period, is often unwitting. The houses, castles, palaces, rooms and their furnishings are merely incidental backgrounds to their paintings of the Annunciation, of the Adoration of the Magi, of episodes from the lives of the saints and similar themes, but since they painted what they knew and what they saw around them, they tell us much about the material background to everyday life and even the greatest of them succeed in conveying something of the atmosphere of their period. An example is Benozzo Gozzoli's *Procession of the Magi* in the Palazzo Medici-Riccardi in Florence in which the three kings ride through a gay and lovely Tuscan landscape on a spring morning. Study of the backgrounds of medieval and Renaissance paintings can be very rewarding for in them we see the walled cities and towers of the Middle Ages, the rounded hills of Tuscany or the wide plains of the north of Italy, peasant huts with the peasants themselves minding their animals or tilling the ground. The windows of interiors are, in some cases, the windows on to an age. Examples in

this book are the paintings by Giovanni Mansueti (on page 87) and by Robert Campin (on page 113).

Artists of the Dutch and Flemish schools are more deliberate in their recording of the interiors of their period. Here the households and their treasures are set out for our inspection and admiration: here, we are informed, are prosperity and security embodied in splendid table covers, fine china and silver, paintings on the walls and substantial furniture. And here too we learn, from the paintings of Vermeer and de Hooch, how the work of the house was carried on.

Plans have been included which demonstrate the long, gradual process whereby the lay-out of the house has become more complex. These show the gradual allocation to particular rooms of particular functions and how this has affected the relationship between the main entrance and the principal public rooms; how access to upper floors has been contrived and what divisions have been raised between the public and private rooms of the house. They show what additions have been made and often why. Where they are available, contemporary sketches are also invaluable in this respect, and have been reproduced in this book.

Anton Ivanov (1818-1864). The boat of the Cernetsov brothers at the time of their voyage on the Volga *(oil on canvas, 1838: Leningrad, Russki Museum). This interior is less typical of a boat than of an ordinary dwelling-house. The idea of the comfortable houseboat with most of the amenities of a house on land is not so recent as we tend to assume.*

Entrance to the cave at Font-de-Gaume near Les Eyzies in the Dordogne, one of the most famous of the painted caves of the Palaeolithic Age. It is probable that climatic conditions during this period drove man to shelter in caves. Where and when, conditions were less rigorous, shelters or windbreaks such as that shown (right) were probably used.

ETTORE CAMESASCA

A ROOF OVER MAN'S HEAD

PREHISTORIC CIVILIZATIONS

We use the term *caveman* with a mixture of superiority and indulgence when we refer to our most distant ancestors. The miserable creature, it is usually believed, could find nowhere better to shelter than a cave. He preferred one to which entry was difficult although he would settle for a jutting rock that gave him the sense of having a roof over his head. But in fact, neither caves nor rock shelters seem to have played an important part in any of the very earliest cultures.

In particular circumstances of climate and soil, the cave became a dwelling but this must certainly have happened in less mistily remote times. And once he had taken up residence, the cave-dweller was not content to accept it as he found it. He improved his home, widening an entrance here, blocking up another there, or, more ambitiously still, he might dig out a completely new cave.

On the whole, however, we should not imagine our ancestors groping about in the rocky recesses of caves or perched in the unsophisticated forerunners of the tree dwellings of India and Malaysia, so much as crouched behind windbreaks, branches or twigs clumsily heaped or plaited together or large pieces of tree bark. These are the simplest form of dwelling, still in use today by the natives of central Australia and the bushmen of southern Africa.

The period during which these shelters were used represents by far the larger part of man's history. It took many thousands of years to evolve the windbreak and to adapt the cave. Of the events of these millennia, little remains in the material sense save the tools that man used to help himself to adapt and conquer his environment: the stone axes, scrapers, arrowheads and spears, with which he hunted the animals that supplied him with food and clothing, with which he dressed their skins, and with which he fashioned shelters for himself from branches and animal skins. Very slowly, the tools improved in sophistication and efficiency: a spearhead of flint, exquisitely balanced and fashioned, is a beautiful implement. Thus the users of these tools early turned their attention to ensuring that the supply of game on which their life depended was maintained: to their attempts at a form of insurance by means of probably magical rites, we may owe the magnificent paintings of the Palaeolithic caves of France and Spain with their extraordinarily lively, in some cases cinematic, representations of animals.

Contemporary aboriginal societies

In the tropics today, a single wall with two supports to shore it up may be the only form of shelter. It suffices, for example, the Veddah in Ceylon, the pygmy-type natives of Malacca, the Andaman islanders, the Negritoes of the Philippines, and certain nomad tribesmen in South America. Prehistoric man may have lived in a dwelling of this kind which particular conditions have allowed to survive. Thus a number of primitive peoples still live in a *lean-to* type of building, the construction of which involves no great inventiveness or skill and this too may be a survival from prehistoric times.

What is rarer is the continued use of caves or rock shelters, although *cave-dwellers* do exist in North Africa, southern Europe and North America. Practical cave-dwelling is defined, unexpectedly, by Daniel Defoe in *Robinson Crusoe*. Crusoe took some trouble to find 'a proper place' for his dwelling. 'I found a little plain on the side of a rising hill, whose front towards this little plain was steep as a house-side, so that nothing could come down on me from the top; on the side of this there was a hollow place worn a little way in, like the entrance of the door of a cave, but there was not really any cave or way into the rock at all.' It did not take him long to improve his environment by digging into the rock behind to create an artificial cave.

The dwelling which resulted, however, from deliberate construction rather than from improvisation of a natural phenomenon such as a cleft in a rock face, is the *hut*. Its object was, clearly, to isolate a certain space. The space itself was chosen carefully to suit the demands, usually those of security, of the builder. Where leaves or branches of trees were available, its construction was simple enough: the branches were stuck in the ground and their tips were then tied together. The main ribs of the hut might then be covered with smaller branches, leaves or grass. A slightly more sophisticated plan involved planting both ends of the branches used for the framework in the ground; the row of parallel arches thus created might be covered with smaller branches, leaves or grass. It was a primitive form of barrel-shaped roof: some Australian aboriginal tribes still use this form of construction.

The shape of the hut based on a framework of branches depended, of course, on the flexibility of the branches available. If they were sufficiently pliable to curve easily, the form that evolved was that of the rounded *cupola* hut. If they were rigid by nature and did not bend, the builder constructed a conical house. And since the branches of trees tend on the whole to be rigid at the end next to the trunk and pliable on their outer extremities, huts evolved which were neither conical nor cupola-shaped but egg- or beehive-shaped.

Attempts have been made to link the flexibility of the materials used in the skeleton of the house to the level of civilization achieved by the builders. It has been concluded that less developed tribes are content to live in raised *conical* dwellings. Admittedly, the entrances to these huts are usually narrow so that the incomer has to slip in sideways. Inside, the lack of space has restricted the amount of furnishing. But this, it may also be argued, has made the conical house not more but less popular among primitive peoples while more highly developed tribes, nomads in particular, like it and turn it

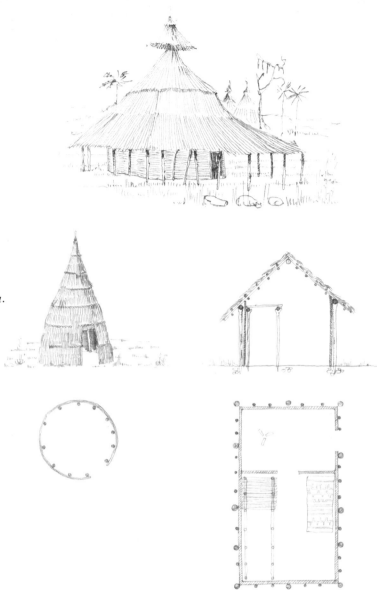

(Above, left) Hut with radiating arches of the cupola type, common among the Cumana peoples of Venezuela.
(Above, right) Hut with conical roof found in western Sudan.
(Opposite page) Large hut built on piles on the island of Sumatra.
Cupola hut of the Waganda at the source of the Nile.

into a wide tent. Animal skins or the bark of trees cover the stout poles of the Siberian *cium* or the Indian *tepee*. Skins alone form the summer tents of some of the Eskimo tribes, and for the wanderer on the steppes and plains of Asia and America there are great advantages in a conical structure which defies the plucking of the wind.

More primitive peoples in South America and Africa are tenaciously attached to the *cupola* form which the nomads of these regions have translated into tents with ribs of wood and mats or skins: these bear a resemblance to the much more elaborate Mongolian *yurt*.

The forms of the *beehive* hut are, perhaps, the most persuasive reason against the relating of a dwelling's design to the level of civilization of the builder. For these can range from the small huts of the Winnebago Indians, which are seldom more than about six feet wide, to the massive houses of the Waganda in Uganda, 30 to 36 feet across and as much as 24 feet high, with their roofs of straw firmly set on a framework of heavy tree trunks. Both are beehive huts but whereas the first is only a precarious shelter against the rain, the second is almost completely rainproof. More than ever the materials available and the physical environment condition the result. Grass and small branches in the steppes or savannahs; bark and stout sticks further north or south in the temperate forest zones; banana or palm leaves in the tropical rain forest; mats among shepherds, skins among hunters, straw among growers of cereals; these are the elements that decide the size and strength of a hut.

In desert regions in, for example, Colorado or

(Above, left) Entrance and plan of a conical hut built by nomads on the western bank of Lake Chad: it is 14¾ feet high. (Above, right) Section and plan of a hut with a ridged roof of the western Bangala, Congo. (Below, left) Framework, seen from the side and from above, of a Nigerian cupola hut. (Below, right) Raised circular hut and its floor, of the Sokoto at Baro on the River Niger.

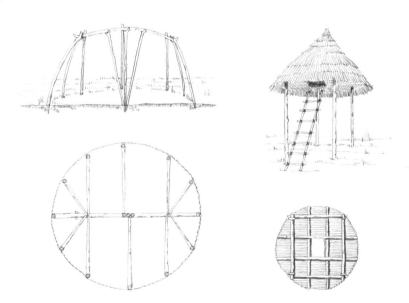

most of North Africa and the Middle East, the dryness means that huts can be covered with earth or mud, effective protection from heat and cold. The cupola-shaped hut with a roof of clay may be the ancestor of vastly more ambitious edifices. Round the shores of the Mediterranean, the Syrian *gubabs*, the *trulli* of Apulia, the Saharan huts of earth and pebbles differ only in size from the prodigious shell that Michelangelo designed for St. Peter's in Rome.

Cut off at a certain height, the supports of a *cupola* hut form a cylinder: when a roof like a sugar loaf is placed on top of this, one of the commonest types of dwelling encountered in tropical or subtropical zones is obtained, one which determines a rich variety of forms from Oceania to Asia, from Africa to America. The *toqul*, as the cylindrical hut with a conical roof was called by the Arabs, still predominates in the vast spaces of the Sudan, in the savannahs to the south, and in the Ethiopian highlands as well. Often the roofs jut out to form a wide

gutter which may be propped up by posts. Clay, used in South America as a light covering, is in Africa used to produce a complicated pattern when a clay paste is pressed between two concentric wooden moulds: mixed with straw, it reduces to a minimum the need for a framework to carry it.

The rudimentary lean-to also has its descendants. Two of these sheds placed side by side form a single ridged roof, a quadrangular hut open on two sides. But there is little space to spare in a dwelling of this kind. For various reasons, the transition to a quadrangular form with a ridged roof and vertical walls must have depended on the presence of piles; that is, on the need to live in places which were undesirably damp. At the same time, of course, a heavy rainfall dictates the need for a sloping roof. In wide areas, from Malaysia to Melanesia, where it may have originated, the quadrilateral hut occurs at every stage of its development, from the rudimentary lean-to shed to the gigantic club house. But even there, the type that stands on the ground without an intervening platform is found only in the more highly developed forms – introduced, in fact, by Europeans.

Here again we are reminded of the frequency with which widely separated peoples have arrived at similar solutions – by whatever methods – to similar problems. Thus the rural houses of eastern Europe or the Alps, with walls made of roughly hewn planks or tree trunks laid one on top of the other, with roofs of thatch or shingles, the spaces and gaps in the walls plugged with moss or mud and straw, show affinities with dwellings scattered along the southern foothills of the Himalayas. The advent of corrugated iron, in use from the Hebrides to the Himalayas, has made the affinities if anything even more striking. The Russian *izba*, the Alpine hay-barn houses, the Himalayan *blockbau* are the results of using similar materials in similar conditions: they indicate that the demands of similar ways of life – however great the superficial differences – are met in approximately the same fashion; even though several thousand miles separate the Swiss farmer from his counterpart in Nepal or Sikkim, they have found comparable solutions.

In the same way, the primitive hut with its ridged roof arose in every corner of south-east Asia and Oceania, in Central America and central Africa, to shelter the inhabitants of those regions from the rigours of heavy seasonal rainfalls. Where economic considerations or the requirements of security demanded it, the huts were raised on piles above swamps or on river banks: building on piles in this way was an ancient craft as the *crannogs* or lake dwellings of prehistoric man in Europe indicate. It was also a long-lasting one: *crannogs* were still in use in Europe in the Middle Ages and the city of Venice is still, of course, the largest and most splendid of all lagoon-dwellings.

In the early quadrangular huts, in houses of the Alpine or *blockbau* type, wood was not, in some areas, used for long. Clay was more easily worked and stone, though less manageable than clay or timber, was more durable. In the drier parts of India and China, accordingly, clay and stone took over from the branches and tree trunks of the most primitive buildings.

The shape of a pitched roof gives, obviously, great variety to huts of the same form. In the primitive type, the vertical walls are low while the steeply sloping roof is very large with eaves extending almost to the ground. The original plan of two sheds leaning against one another is still recognizable here. The roof became smaller and the walls higher in the temperate zones. In the oldest rectangular forms, the entrance is placed on one of the short sides and this is the type which survives in

(Opposite page) Ruanda Urundi: hut under construction. Its lower part is cylindrical and its roof will be conical; this is one of the commonest types of hut in the tropics. The scaffolding is rudimentary but sufficient.

(Below, left) Two types of subterranean dwelling. Plan and section of a cave used at Mopti in the western Sudan: note the staircase with a single support. (Centre) A half-buried hut, seen on the surface and in section, of the Salish in Canada. (Below, right) Example of a hut with parallel arches – framework and complete – built by fishermen near Bamako on the River Niger.

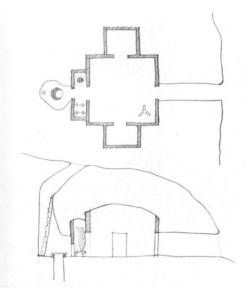
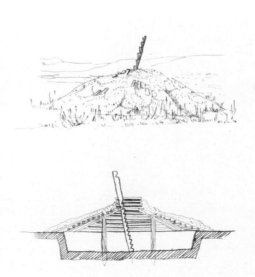

the tropics. In the more highly developed forms, the door opens from one of the long sides, a feature which produced important changes in the house's interior.

In dry regions, however, there was no need of pitched roofs. In the desert and semi-desert areas of Asia and Africa, therefore, the pattern is the flat roof on buildings constructed – for lack of timber – of clay or stone. These we find from Spain to China, carefully planned refuges from heat and hot winds. Another means of combating a hot, dry climate was to set the house underground, either wholly or partly. In the desert regions of Africa, China, and America some peoples have buried their houses in search of the coolness which the earth retains from winter. For reasons of safety, a long underground passage was sometimes built – this is the

Trulli, typical dwellings in Murgia in Apulia, built singly or in large groups, as in the town of Alberobello (Bari) where there are more than 1000 of them. Above the low dry-stone outer walls, either square or circular in plan, are the high, conical roofs, often of grey limestone with stout chimneys protruding from them. At the highest point of the roof is a limestone pinnacle which (unconfirmed) tradition alleges held the rope with which people could pull down the house if they wished to avoid paying taxes on it. The contrast between the vertical walls and the dark grey roof is sometimes heightened by whitewashed inscriptions or religious symbols on the roof. On the street side of the house, the lower edge of the roof rises to form a pediment over the entrance. The interior consists of a main room directly under the conical roof (two-storeyed trulli, about 50 feet high, are extremely rare) with four archways opening from it, one to the entrance, the others to the kitchen and other rooms. (Above) A rare view of trulli at Alberobello, under snow. This type of trulli may be no older than the fifteenth century but its origins are very ancient.

case with the *tembe* of the Sudan. And while the earth retains its winter coolness in one part of the world, it may also retain its summer heat in another and for this reason use is also made of underground dwellings in the icy sub-Arctic wastes.

In brief, depending on the climatic conditions, a house may be found several feet below ground or several feet above it. Until only a few decades ago in the peninsula of Kamchatka in eastern Siberia the inhabitants combined both ways of life: they lived underground in winter and in tree houses in the summer.

To us, the concept of even a single-storeyed house being divided into several rooms and of more than one room communicating with the exterior through doors and windows is entirely normal. But primitive houses are, as a rule, unicellular; even if they are very large, the walls enclose only one room without permanent divisions. The only exception worth noting is found in the cylindrical huts found in parts of Africa, but like all primitive houses these have a single door through which are admitted people, light, and often smoke, from the cooking fire outside. Some primitive people ran the risk of having a hearth in the middle of the hut, but very often the cooking fire was situated immediately outside in order to avoid the danger of setting the house alight and to afford protection from insects and wild animals.

The rectangular hut also began with a single opening (a low one to retain coolness and discourage unwanted incomers, among them mosquitoes). It had no internal divisions. Several huts were sometimes put together to make what was not so much a house with several rooms as an apartment of several houses. The concept of floor or storey preceded, unexpectedly, that of the room and was brought into being by the simple expedient of setting one hut on top of another.

But before the idea of interior division was developed, there came that of increasing the number of doors and windows. The Malayans may have led the way in both cases, although windows made more progress in cold climates than in tropical ones. The winter houses of tree-dwellers are seldom without them and very often they are found in the igloo as well, for windows are most needed where there is little light and where the need for heating inside the house means that the smoke thus produced is allowed to escape.

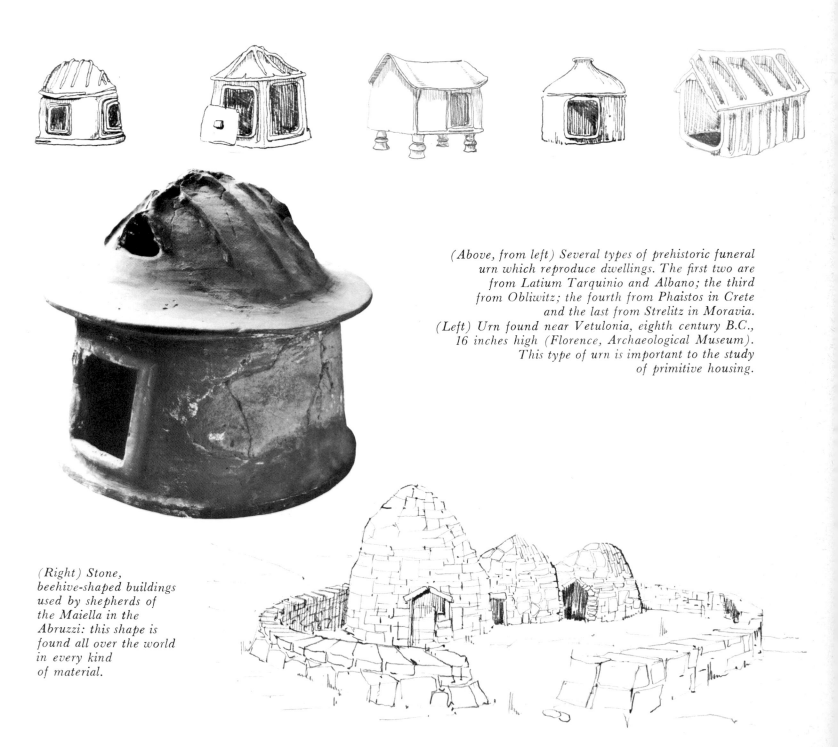

(Above, from left) Several types of prehistoric funeral urn which reproduce dwellings. The first two are from Latium Tarquinio and Albano; the third from Obliwitz; the fourth from Phaistos in Crete and the last from Strelitz in Moravia.
(Left) Urn found near Vetulonia, eighth century B.C., 16 inches high (Florence, Archaeological Museum). This type of urn is important to the study of primitive housing.

(Right) Stone, beehive-shaped buildings used by shepherds of the Maiella in the Abruzzi: this shape is found all over the world in every kind of material.

PRIMITIVE SETTLEMENT

We do not know with any certainty if early man had a fixed dwelling place. All that we can say is that half a million years ago, human or nearly human creatures were sheltering under projecting rocks and that they occupied caves where they left unmistakeable traces of their existence.

But does shelter and occupation imply any degree of permanence? Some of the paintings in the palaeolithic caves of France and Spain may represent huts or tents. This in turn may suggest that they spent the summer in tents or huts. But this can be no more than surmise although it has been agreed that where no natural shelters were available, early man did build for himself and what he built was probably not so very different from the shelters constructed by his remote and undeveloped descendants.

The cultural development of primitive man is measured in tens of thousands of years. His learning of the skills of house-building began, arguably, in the caves or rock shelters of a hundred millennia ago. Fifty thousand years later, mammoth hunters in what is now Czechoslovakia had taken to sheltering during the winter in ditches covered with boughs, tree-trunks and earth: in summer, their homes were tents of skin.

Twenty-five millennia passed and the prehistoric inhabitants of what is now Württemberg devised for themselves small, oval houses or huts. A group of 38 such huts has been found, with the remains of wooden frames consisting of small posts which had been obviously covered with branches. These may have been summer shelters like those made of birch branches found in the Pennines or at Seamer in Yorkshire where a floor has been found, also made of birch branches.

From almost the same period comes the first known European hut on ground level, discovered at Bochum in Hanover. Its framework consisted of posts, each about three inches in diameter, and the hearth was of shingles. Contemporary with it is a group of huts at Farnham in Surrey where the floors were of shingle and the walls must have been covered with leaves. What is significant about these huts was the discovery of more than 15,000 flints, which indicates a more permanent dwelling than has been encountered so far.

The speed of development began to increase.

By about 8000 B.C. in Europe, besides cave dwellings and half-buried huts, there now stood ground level dwellings. In some places they were raised on piles. Man had settled down and was learning to till the soil. He learned, too, to make pots and to dig out of the earth valuable minerals. He created villages composed of as many as 40 huts. As he extended his control of his environment, he extended the size and strength of his house.

In the neolithic period, between 4000 and 3000 B.C., the *rectangular* building appears. Tombs of the period tell us what they looked like as do several hut-shaped urns, since the homes of the dead were almost certainly faithful reproductions of the houses of the living. The new form came from the Near East. In Europe, it is probable that the round and rectangular types co-existed, for the urns which represent them both are contemporary with one another, although it is also likely that hut types which were no longer in use continued to be reproduced in the urns.

In Italy, huts of the neolithic age were nearly always circular whether or not they were partly sunk in the ground or raised on piles. North of the Alps, traces of horse-shoe-shaped huts have survived near Michelsberg, Baden. Huts on floating rafts have been recorded in the island of Sjalland in Denmark. Further north again, a more ambitious complex has been uncovered at Uppland in Sweden where three buildings were found side by side, one apparently serving as a kitchen, one a living-room, and one a rest room or bedroom.

All this indicates that the form of the neolithic hut is immensely varied. In the Portuguese fortress of Sabroso a round one was found, more than 15

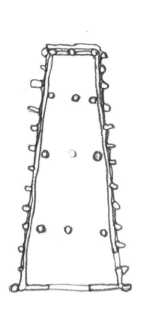

(Left and above) Plan and reconstruction of a late neolithic hut. This was found in Westphalia but similar forms were typical of villages of the same period in Poland.
(Opposite page) Plan of a rectangular dwelling of the Stone Age found at Schussenried in northern Sweden.

feet wide, and set on a horse-shoe of stones. At Parazuelos in Spain, it was rectangular with rounded corners. In central and eastern Europe, it was four-sided with a *cupola* roof. In France and England it was both round and oval. Variety of form was maintained into the Bronze and Iron Ages. Rectangular huts were sometimes divided into two rooms with the sleeping-room raised over the other. In southern Germany and the north of Italy they developed into a building like the Greek *megaron* with a projecting hallway and a stone base.

The idea of furnishing a hut grew gradually. The neolithic settlement at Skara Brae in Orkney, once rescued from the accumulation of blown sand and refuse that concealed it for centuries, produced some built-in furniture consisting of dressers with shelves, box beds, wall cupboards and fish tanks, all fashioned out of the fine-grained sandstone that was readily available locally. Other settlements of the same period were probably less well-equipped and like many Bronze Age huts may have offered little more than stones as seats and skins and leaves and grass as bedding. The hearth was formed of a large stone. But during the neolithic period the potter had begun to extend his skill. He won greater control over fire and constructed simple kilns. During the Bronze and later ages, pottery of considerable sophistication of design and of some delicacy of form was produced. It was decorated at first with the finger or nail prints of the potter, or with the impress of a piece of rope or string; later again it was painted and the process was set in motion whereby there were fashioned, ultimately, the splendid vases of Greece.

As we know, human progress is not achieved at the same rate in all areas. While the inhabitants of the northern shores of the Mediterranean were still learning the more elementary skills in house-building and furnishing, the inhabitants of Egypt and Mesopotamia were already living in houses made of fired brick incorporating windows with grills and doors on stone hinges.

(Left) Plan of a prehistoric house at Melsungen in Cassel. (Below) Sectioned reconstruction of a stone hut of the fifth millennium B.C. found at Khinokitia in Cyprus.

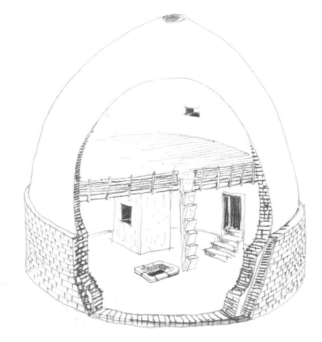

Everyday life
in a
neolithic village

In Val Camonica, about 20 miles north of Lake Iseo in the hills above Brescia, a series of striking rock carvings tells the story of an Alpine people during the second millenium B.C. They depict horsemen of all kinds, engaged in interminable skirmishes; hunters chasing bear and buck and doe; boys minding geese; women weaving; ploughmen at work; fishermen with their nets; smiths, sorcerers, gladiators; pious folk in procession and very important persons in carts. In thousands of carvings, they come to life before us and, more important for our purpose here, several hundred of these lively rock drawings also show buildings.

Some are of ritual or industrial buildings – small temples, chapels, booths, haybarns, stables, and storehouses. A number are of actual dwelling places with people inside or just entering or even with the workmen still constructing them. They contribute greatly to our picture of a neolithic settlement as the remains that emerge from excavation seldom amount to more than the stone circle of a hut's foundation: if we are fortunate, there may be a fragment of wall. On this the informed imagination must work. Drawings such as those of Val Camonica provide a useful stimulus. From them it can be established that these far-off inhabitants of this valley lived in quite small houses intended for various family groups. The houses were often raised on piles and were divided into

an upper and lower storey. The lower was used as a storehouse and the upper as a dwelling house reached from outside – as the drawings indicate – by a wooden ladder. The whole was covered by a sloping roof.

Within this basic type, however, there was a large number of variations (on a single rock, there are drawings of as many as twenty different houses), as befitted the pretensions of a variety of owners. The chieftain, the rich man and the priest had better houses than the peasant or the artisan. But what is surprising is the variety in the arrangement of quite modest houses which suggest that a fond-

A carving from one of the caves at Val Camonica, a house on stakes. The sloping sides of the roof may end in discs of symbolic importance, more clearly visible in other carvings: a building such as this may be a chapel or other religious building.

ness for the home was widespread at every level of society. It appears in the marked individuality of the treatment of the house as each man tried to improve his own home and to distinguish it from that of his neighbour.

The carvings of Val Camonica are of particular interest to town planners for they preserve the layout of the village with the position of houses; granaries, stables, enclosures, vegetable gardens, fields, waterfalls, hills and fortifications, and it is possible from this to trace the development of the community. These neolithic maps are indeed so faithful that the course of a stream and the lie of the rocks are still recognizable in today's landscape, where the low wall or the small field of the Bronze Age can still be detected.

(Left) Shepherd's hut of the type used until a few years ago and in rare cases still surviving on the plain round Rome. (Above) Modern house-hut in the region of the River Cavalli in Liberia: the form of the house and the exterior decorations recall prehistoric buildings.

HOUSES AND HUTS

By a curious reversion of a cultural process, the huts of today often imitate the forms and materials of the architectural house which is the descendant of their remote predecessors. At the same time it is not unusual for them to preserve archaic elements which have vanished from later buildings. In some areas the archaic form itself is preserved. The circular hut with the conical roof persists in many rural areas of Europe. The beehive form is, by contrast, rare though an exception may be found in the more rudimentary of the *trulli* in Apulia.

The most usual European hut has a rectangular plan and a ridged roof. Some of them, with steeply sloping roof, the entrance under the ridge of the roof, no windows, and the walls made of horizontal planks, have shown extraordinary powers of survival as a type. But more extraordinary still are the *trulli* in which a square structure is surmounted by a conical roof; or the large oval huts, with one short closed side and the other open under the extension of the roof, which have been found in central Italy; or the strange, oval, stone-walled buildings with low thatched roofs and their entrances on the longer side which are typical of mountains round Arunzo in north-east Italy. Their distant predecessors should be sought in the wilds of Asia and Africa.

The importance of the hut in European history should never be forgotten. Huts or small wooden houses huddled together form the beginnings of

(Opposite page) Gerolamo Pennachi da Treviso, called 'il Vecchio' (c. 1455-1497): Resurrection with Calvary in the background (detail) (Treviso, Civic Museum). A rare example of the survival of huts in a Renaissance city – with washing hanging out. Near them are a stable and hayloft apparently built of wood and thatched with straw

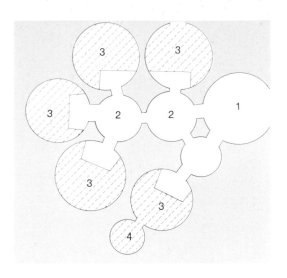

(Right) Plan of a group of igloos between November and
January, the period of heavy snowfalls and fierce gales.
The shaded areas indicate banks of snow which
often have side cavities for storage. The main hall (1),
which is sometimes open, leads to the next room (2)
by a covered passage, to permit ease of movement,
and from there to another room (3). Each of these
rooms usually accommodated an Eskimo family group.
This complex has a private storeroom (4) but the stores
were sometimes held in common in a room next to the hall.

(Left) Stone dwellings at Graoun-Loto in the Upper Volta
region. (Below) Drawing of Red Indian tents, better
known as tepees: the raised edge of the tent
in the foreground shows the framework of stakes.

medieval cities, often with the massive stone walls
of Romanesque or Gothic cathedrals already over-
shadowing them. Often flimsy, of wattle and daub
and with thatched roofs, prone to sudden and disastrous fires, they could be quickly destroyed and as
quickly rebuilt. They were expendable in war and if
they survived in peace were liable to fall down eventually through neglect. For centuries, such huts
housed the majority of the populations of the cities
of Europe. London in the fifteenth century and
Moscow in the seventeenth were still cities of small
wooden houses – or huts. Giovanni Villani, a native
of Florence (1275-1348), refers quite casually to the
'houses and huts' destroyed by fire at the end of a
siege. Another Villani – Matteo – writing of the
rebuilding of houses in Florence, refers only to 'huts'
and this is in the middle of the fourteenth century.
The majority of the 13,000 houses destroyed during
the Great Fire of London, that broke out in Pud-
ding Lane in the City in September 1666, were small
houses, replacement of which is rather less well
documented than the building of the Wren churches. But if they were the chronic victims of fire,
war, civil disorder and similar events, such houses
and huts were also tenacious: they rose again, from
the ashes if need be, and to prove it there they are
in the background of innumerable paintings.

House of a Hausa chief in Nigeria. Its masons have so shaped their material, mud, as to make a piece of sculpture.

THE UNPREJUDICED EYE

A dwelling at Ksar-el-Barka in Mauritania in which the window grills – simple means of ventilation – reduce the horizontal emphasis of the façade by their well-balanced design.

To express an opinion on a hut or on any primitive building, we must bring to it the same judgment that we would to any other building – as well as a certain openness of mind. There is no point, for example, in condemning the use of stone for the roof of a *trullo*. And it would be unwise to echo the first reaction of the Florentine merchant, Filippo Sassetti, to a strange style when he travelled to Goa in 1583. He was not impressed by his first sight of the palace of the local ruler or by Goan architecture in general. 'Their homes are more like pigsties than houses,' he wrote disapprovingly. 'I am not saying this in order to deprecate what belongs to another country but just consider – they are below ground level and a man cannot stand upright inside them. The walls and the roof are entirely of palm leaves and so are the doors and windows. I never saw anything uglier.'

This he wrote soon after his arrival. But he lived to change his mind for he was a cultured man with an alert intellect. At the beginning of 1585, he was already saying in another letter that he had realized that Indian houses were 'among the best and worst' and that in particular, at Cochin in Travancore, 'the beautiful palaces and charming houses' made him exclaim what fine views the buildings offered. He even compared them with the balconied houses of the Piazza Santa Croce in his beloved Florence where 'the windows are full of fine ladies.'

He had had another look – that was all. Or perhaps he had just bothered to look carefully.

House at Laimy, in the former French Sudan; the massive projections of the exterior create an effect of impressive strength.

This bas-relief of the first millennium B.C., found at Susa in Sumeria (now in the Louvre in Paris) is a valuable document of domestic life. It depicts a woman of high rank spinning while a slave fans her. She sits cross-legged on a stool and before her is a small table. Both pieces are solidly made, with little ornament save on the feet. They may have been of wood or even of bronze.

ETTORE CAMESASCA

MUD
AND
GRANITE

THE EARLIEST EMPIRES

That period which is the end of prehistory and the beginning of historic times is gradually but constantly receding through time as written records of increasing antiquity are discovered and deciphered. They reveal the development from neolithic village to the town, a unit larger than what had gone before, stable and densely populated.

These towns were prosperous trading centres, perhaps with a shrine as an added attraction, and in them industry and commerce thrived. They provided scope for enterprise and craftsmanship that was not purely utilitarian. The advent of bronze and iron widened this scope while it also provided the materials for the arms which allowed tribal leaders to unite, by force if necessary, groups of towns and even cities into kingdoms and then empires. Unification meant organization and the creation of a bureaucracy. The accumulation of technological experience, whether for purposes of peace or war, made it desirable that such experience should be recorded. For both of these reasons a record of some kind was essential and such a record was devised.

It was devised, most notably, on the banks of the Tigris, the Euphrates and the Nile. The methods of writing used were very different but the impetus behind their evolution was similar. The circumstances of these two heartlands of civili-

zation were also very different. By the banks of the Nile the Egyptians, guarded by the deserts on either side of them, were grateful for the gift of the river, for the regular inundations that produced bountiful crops and, in time, a highly organized civilization.

In the land between the two rivers, Mesopotamia, the rivers also overflowed their banks and the floods were duly noted and regulated. But the inhabitants of this territory, unlike the protected Egyptians, seem to have lived with a sense of constant menace ever about them which created in them a harshness and restlessness foreign to the self-sufficient Egyptian.

Our knowledge of these empires in the Near and Middle East is, however, of comparatively recent date. No longer ago than 1904 when he published the text of his *General History of the Plastic Arts*, Salomon Reinach could not extend his treatment of Egypt, Mesopotamia and Turkey beyond 12 pages with illustrations. A century before that, all that was known about the Assyrians was what was said in the Bible, while the Sumerians, the Hittites and the Akkadians were unknown names. The discoveries that have been made since the beginning of this century have been greeted with enthusiasm and rightly so, for the story is never less than fascinating.

*Discoveries such as this at Byblos in Lebanon do much to increase
our knowledge of the history of the house. The trapeze-shaped outline in the
foreground is that of a house: the other two groups of buildings
are the temple of Rechef (in the middle distance) and
the so-called temple of the obelisks (right, in the background).*

Brick by brick

In the 1870's the French resident at Basra, M. de Sarzec, was ambitious to add to the Louvre's collections of antiquities. Happily, he was able to realize his ambition from 1877 onwards, and in doing so, he uncovered the culture of the Sumerians. Several decades earlier Paul Botta, the French consul at Mosul, had discovered a magnificent series of Assyrian reliefs at Khorsabad. Fortunately these were recorded in Eugene Flandin's drawings, for these reliefs, hundreds of feet long, later either vanished or were damaged beyond repair.

Neither Botta nor de Sarzec were in the least interested in housing. They were indifferent, indeed, even to palaces and temples. It was only towards the end of the century that a study was made of temples and the period of the great excavations was initiated. Archaeology had by then progressed beyond the indiscriminate picnic dig and digging for treasure.

(Above) Reconstruction by Viollet-le-Duc of an Assyrian dwelling. The base is of stone and the walls of unfired brick. There is a terrace roof and an external staircase. Excavations have, unfortunately, not always confirmed these details.

At the beginning of this century, a party of German architects was dispatched to Babylon to examine the site of Semiramis' hanging gardens. The walls of the towers which they inspected were made of brick. Accordingly, when they reported back to the Kaiser, on every carefully drawn map every single brick and every fragment of stone was meticulously recorded.

Increasing precision was brought to bear not merely on surface remains but also on the trenches cut down through layer after layer of civilization. Finds, even the smallest and apparently least important, were detailed. Gradually the total picture of an ancient site was built up. Today the archaeologist looks not only at the plan of the temple but also at the site of the hut of the man who helped to build it, and at the workshop where the man's tools were made; he studies a king's throne-room, a workman's latrine and an official's haybarn.

It is a slow process. It produces a vast quantity of fragments which must be fitted together like a jigsaw, but, now at any rate, few pieces of treasure. Instead of splendid reconstructions in the style of Viollet-le-Duc with fluttering curtains and cedarwood staircases, it gives us drawings often long on question marks and short on details. But they tell us what is known and not what is surmised.

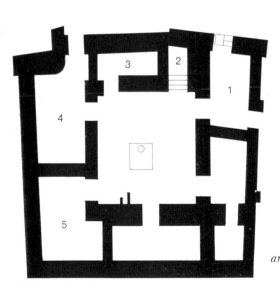

(Above) Remains – and a reconstruction of them –
of a farm of the fifth millennium B.C. found
at Hassuna, south of Mosul in Iraq. This is the oldest
known example of an architectural dwelling.

SUMER AND BABYLON

During an excavation in north-east Iraq in 1955, R.J. Braidwood identified at M'lefaat 'the most ancient Mesopotamian village', older even than the village of Jarmo in Iraqi Kurdistan, discovered in 1948 and dated by the radiocarbon method to about 5000 B.C.

The ancient craftsmen of Jarmo, using stone tools, fashioned small figures of animals; they were the first of the marvellous animal sculptures of Mesopotamia. Not many centuries later and over one hundred miles to the west, men settled down as farmers in the land between the two rivers and found time to decorate the objects they used daily. More important, they built houses with rooms arranged after a functional plan. In these dwellings we can detect the beginning of architecture.

While the design of houses developed in sophistication, huts continued to be built. The same primitive forms were used and, indeed, both types of dwelling were built of the same materials. Their builders had very little choice in the matter and were compelled to use mud since neither stone nor timber was readily available in the region. As time went on, the mud was prepared in a more easily usable form in that it was dried as bricks.

At Ur of the Chaldees during the third millennium B.C., moreover, an improvement was made on the sun-dried brick with the development of the

Plan of a house found at Ur. The lower side is about 40 feet long. The arrangement is typical of Sumerian dwellings of the patriarchal age. The narrow entrance opens on to a hall (1) which leads to the courtyard in the centre. The staircase (2) may have led to an upper floor. The washroom (3), kitchen (4) and storeroom (5) open from the courtyard.

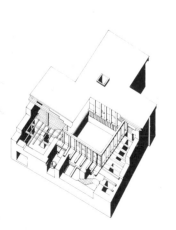

(Far left) Reconstruction (by Sir Mortimer Wheeler) of one of the principal houses at Mohenjo-daro in West Pakistan with rooms grouped round a courtyard and roof terraces.
(Left) Houses at Kairouan in Tunisia they repeat ancient eastern patterns.
(Opposite page) Plan of a house of the Akkadian period at Assur south of Nineveh (end of the third millennium B.C.) Recent reconstruction of the interior of an ancient Assyrian house: left, an alcove or oratory for religious observances; in the foreground, a bed with a pillow; in the background, stools and floor cushions.

baked brick. Mud fired in an oven or kiln, it was noticed, became as hard as stone. These baked bricks with their convex surfaces were bonded together with bitumen. The technique is mentioned in the Book of Genesis with regard to the building, on a plain in the land of Shinar, of the Tower of Babel; the builders 'had brick for stone and slime (bitumen) had they for mortar.'

The Sumerians of the third millennium B.C. limited their use of baked brick, however, to the foundations of buildings, to the arches of doorways and vaults, and to floors. The unfired bricks were still used, even in some temples. These had flat roofs with sequences of rooms round the outside walls: they opened on to internal corridors which formed a cloister. On one side of the cloister was placed the shrine of the god and beyond it were the rooms of the priest, which formed another courtyard. A number of the architectural features of these 'houses of the gods' were used in the houses of wealthy citizens.

Basically, the houses of ordinary citizens differed little in lay-out from the temples. They were no less carefully built on the same rectangular plan with a single entrance, a hall and courtyard, around which were arranged the other rooms. As a rule the houses consisted of a single storey, though in some cases there may have been an upper storey. The foundations were usually of fired brick as were the floors of the rooms and the courtyard. The walls were of unfired brick. Sanitation was simple but satisfactory and efficient.

According to Herodotus, the mounds of grey, crumbling brick, eroded by the winds of centuries – all that remains of that great city of Babylon – must originally have belonged to houses three or four storeys high. Whether these did exist is doubtful. What we do know is that it did accommodate immense temples and luxurious palaces sprawling through the city, the activity of which their inhabitants might watch from the terraced roofs. The internal arrangements, however, seem to have been very similar to those in use from that day to

this in the Near and Middle East; that is, the house was made up of three parts. One was reserved for the men of the family, one for the women and one for the family servants. The men's part of the house contained the public rooms. The women's part of the house was the centre of its family life to which the prince or merchant retired with his wife, or wives, concubines and children. The servants' quarters served the others. Each section of the house was separate from the others but linked to them by the main courtyard.

The same lay-out has been found at Ur and on Sumerian sites, and it is probable that the Babylonians and Assyrians followed the example of their predecessors in the planning of their dwellings. They adhered to the single-storey plan with a single opening to the street and with, perhaps, a gallery above the inhabited storey, with a flat roof supported by pillars on which earth might be spread, to sustain a modest version of the hanging gardens of Babylon.

But the greatest innovation of all, the achievement which guarantees the empires of Sumer and Babylon their place in architectural history, is their use of the vault and their knowledge of how to construct a curved or hemispherical roof, a science which was later to spread throughout the western world.

In contrast with the wealth of historical treasures of Egypt, we have few reminders of the ancient civilization that flourished on and around the banks of the Tigris and Euphrates. What there is attests to a high degree of artistic achievement which reached its peak between the eighth and seventh centuries B.C. in the Assyria of Sargon, when furniture reached a level of luxury that has seldom been surpassed. Gold and silver were applied to a framework of bronze or brass and the resulting chair or couch might be covered with cushions in painted or embroidered fabrics. The most popular decorative motifs were of animals, the same imperious menagerie which we encounter on Assyrian monumental reliefs.

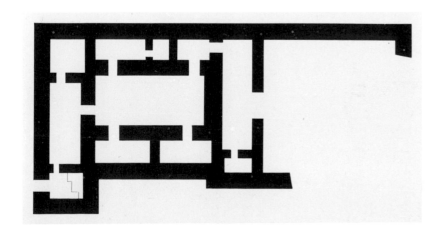

Linen chest (19 inches long) now in the Egyptian Museum, Turin, found at Deir el-Madina in the tomb of Cha, who lived in the reign of the Pharaoh Amenhotep II (1450-1415 B.C.). The dead man appears on the right with his wife, both sitting on high-backed black chairs: under the woman's chair are some toilette articles. Before the couple is a pedestal table with food on it; standing, are two of Cha's children.

EGYPT

For information about the dwelling house in ancient Egypt, we shall look first at two sites, one in the Fayum, the great oasis to the west of the Nile in middle Egypt; the other at Tel el-Amarna, further south on the eastern bank of the Nile. Both were for a time the capital of Egypt, the first in the reign of Sesostris II, one of three Middle Kingdom pharaohs of the same name, and the second in the reign of the heretic pharaoh Amenhotep IV or Akhenaton, in the fourteenth century B.C. Both were abandoned on the deaths of their founders.

The city of Sesostris II at what is now Illahun was divided into two parts by a main road over 30 feet wide. On one side was the fashionable residential area in which wide avenues lead to spacious houses; on the other were the smaller, closely-packed dwellings of the working class district.

Akhenaton's city, which he called Akhetaton 'The Horizon of Aton', rose out of the desert north of Thebes in response to the pharaoh's ambition that a city should be dedicated to the god he had chosen, Aton, on soil that had never been dedicated to any of the old gods of Egypt. On a more political level, it may have originated in his wish to break the power of the priests of Thebes. In this new city, the houses of the nobles were built cheek by jowl with the smaller, more modest dwel-

lings of palace employees, craftsmen and merchants. The temple of Aton and the royal palace, with their satellite buildings, occupied a complex of their own. It is from these buildings that we derive our knowledge of what is now known as Amarna art, of which the outstanding characteristic is an atypical naturalism. The floors and walls of the royal palace were decorated with paintings of animals, birds and flowers: there are paintings too of the royal family, that is, of Akhenaton and his queen, Nefertiti and their daughters. The beauty of Nefertiti is known from the painted bust in Berlin as well as from an unfinished head in the Cairo museum; the strange appearance of the Pharaoh – the elongated head, long neck and thick lips – is almost equally well known. His experiments in monotheism and town planning lasted in all probably less than 20 years. After his death in 1354 B.C. his temples were destroyed and the palaces crumbled away.

But these two cities of Sesostris and Akhetaton cast a remarkably clear light on Egyptian methods of town planning. Had these new capitals not been abandoned so soon after their foundation, they might have evolved into the unplanned chaos of Memphis, Thebes, or any of the other Egyptian cities, in which temples, palaces, the houses of offi-

(Opposite page, left) Plan of a rich man's house in Egypt during the Second Empire, similar in dimensions and structure to that shown in section on page 38
(Centre) Plan of a middle class house with two bedrooms (1,3), dining-room (2), kitchen with stove (4) poultry-run and dovecote (5,6), latrine (8), and storeroom (9), the latter rooms being set in the garden (7)
(Right) Plan of small houses of from two to four rooms, found during excavations at Tel el-Amarna

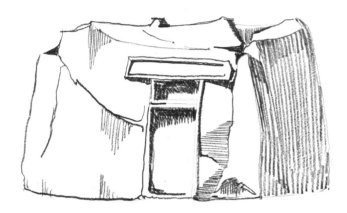

cials of the kingdom and the hovels of workmen, shrines, bazaars, fountains, parks, offices, guard-rooms, workshops and wells are huddled together in what is to the present day typically eastern confusion. At Tanis, on the delta of the Nile, the city expanded over gardens and carefully planned avenues. At Athribis, also on the Nile delta, overspill overwhelmed even important burial places such as the tombs of the sacred falcons which, according to priestly record, were covered by a house built over them.

This house at Athribis was a hut of unfired

bricks, built after a very ancient pattern. As was the case elsewhere, the earliest attempts at house-building in Egypt took the form of rough shelters. From the Merimdean culture of the delta, we know that they devised roofs held up on poles and possibly covered with mud and that they dug their hearth several inches deep into the rock. They learned how to construct houses of unfired brick, houses consisting of a single rectangular room with a doorway on one of the shorter sides. The doorway was surmounted by a wooden lintel. On the wall opposite was a small window for ventilation. Houses

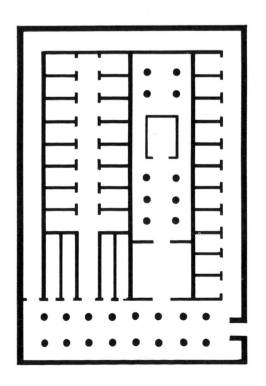

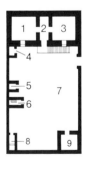

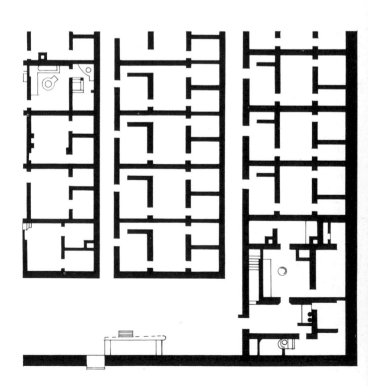

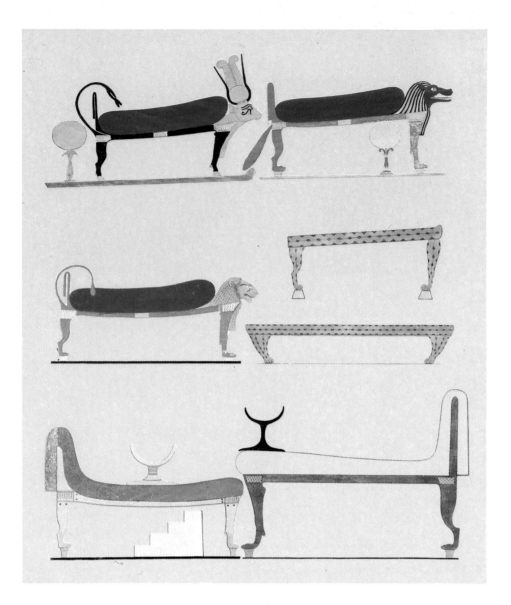

Types of Egyptian furniture: a stool, a linen chest (seen from the short side) with handles, an armchair with arms in the shape of a lion, a bed, an armchair without arms. (Opposite page) A chest and a stool, again with an X-frame. The finest pieces were so well made and with such carefully designed and skilfully fashioned joints that the furniture found in the tomb of Tutankhamen, for instance, showed very little sign of its great age.

like these were the homes for generation after generation of peasants in Egypt between Nubia and the delta.

For wealthier Egyptians, the pattern was more complex. Near El Faigum, which is a wooded region, we find traces of houses on several floors built of fired brick. Their size depended, obviously, on the resources of their builders. One, more than 200 feet long and 150 feet wide, consisted of 70 rooms. Like other houses of its type, it probably resembled a small temple with its portico of papyrus-shaped columns and its stone architrave decorated with palm leaves.

A still more elaborate plan surrounded the building with a colonnade covered by a projecting

(Opposite page) Egyptian beds. The first three are decorated with, respectively, carvings of a bull, a jackal and a lion. The next two suggest a panther. The last two are supported on cats' feet. Animal legs and feet are common on the beds that have survived. What looks to us like a headrest is in fact the foot of the bed; the ivory or ebony headrest was, as two drawings show, at the other end. The framework of the most luxurious beds might be of ebony with gold or ivory ornaments.

roof. At the front of the house, the portico gave on to the hall which in turn led to a reception room; the interior of the house was thus protected from the curious gaze of casual passers-by. The rest of the main body of the house consisted of rooms for the serving of food and drink, bedrooms, bathrooms, storerooms and wardrobes. At the side and back of the house a series of smaller buildings

housed the servants and slaves and here too were the kitchens, bakehouses and stables. The lay-out was always completed by a garden.

Such a house as this would be the home of a senior official of the palace, a general, a prosperous landowner, or an important priest and in essence the outline of the house is the same as that of the pharaoh's palace.

On a more modest scale, a middle class house might have several floors on which the master both lived and conducted his business. Like the house of the general or the landowner, to which we have already referred, it contained an almost completely self-sufficient community of family and slaves. Under one roof most of the needs of the household could be met and this involved not merely the maintenance of the house and the preparation and serving of food but also the weaving of cloth, the making of pottery, the fashioning of furniture, all those occupations, in fact, which are depicted with such vividness in tomb paintings.

It was on the ground floor of such a house that the food was prepared. Only the door and a few small windows lit the interior. On the next floor was the sitting-room of the master of the house with its ceiling supported by graceful columns. On the second floor the everyday life of the house was conducted. Here the master was washed and shaved, listened to the reports of his scribes and supervised the work of his servants. The disposition of the stores depended, of course, on the nature of the business of the master of the house. In the house of a certain Mahu at Tanis, for example, a cache of weapons was discovered. These turned out to be the spoils of Mahu's trade however, for he was the chief of police.

A terrace occupied the flat top of the house. In some cases it was surrounded by a trellis, possibly to safeguard childen and almost certainly to afford more privacy to the house's occupants, for at certain seasons of the year the terrace was the centre of the life of the household. Tomb paintings indicate that on some roofs there were what look like triangular weather vanes for what might have been windmills, not so very different from those still in use today in India and parts of the Levant.

Furniture was comfortable and elegant as was appropriate to a civilization of refined and delicate taste, which was at the same time able to draw on the work of highly skilled craftsmen. At its finest, it is superbly rich in material and varied in design. Unlike many inhabitants of the Near and Middle East, Egyptians did not sit on the floor but preferred to sit on chairs or stools. The basic shape of the

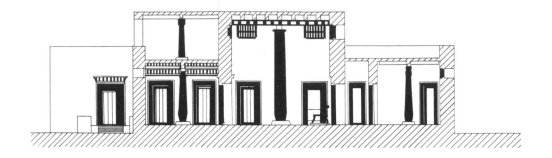

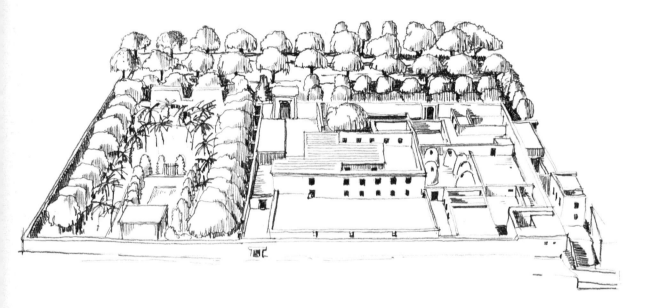

stools made by their craftsmen was simple – a spare or rectangular box set on straight legs or X-frames. However, there was nothing simple about the workmanship in the richest of the stools – with, for example, tortoiseshell inlays, heads of animals and birds carved on the feet, and ivory and ebony decoration on the sides of the stool.

Their armchairs were basically stools with backs. The legs terminated in carvings of lions' or bulls' feet. The cushions on the seat and the back were gaily coloured. Dining-room furniture consisted of large and small tables – the former used as sideboards – and stools. Beds for rich and poor alike were made of a rectangular wooden frame with interlaced cords or strips of leather as a support for the mattress, if any, laid on top of it. The whole was supported by four feet, undecorated in the more modest examples; carved, painted and inlaid in the more opulent models. For storage, Egyptians used coffers, often shaped like a house or a temple and nearly always brightly painted. As always, the richer the household, the more abundant and splendidly decorated the furniture, but a few possessions went a long way in the matter of prestige. A respectable assembly of pottery vessels, some mats, a couple of tables and a wooden chest found in a house are sufficient to indicate the comfort of its inhabitants.

CARTHAGE
AND JERUSALEM

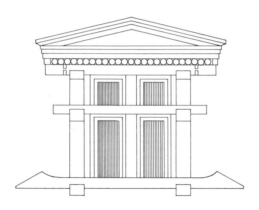

Front elevation of a cave tomb at Xanthos in Lycia which very accurately reproduces a private house.

Along the coast of North Africa and round the shores of the eastern Mediterranean, there were close trading and diplomatic links with the empires of Egypt and Mesopotamia. Roads connected the Tigris and the Euphrates with the territory of the Hittites in Asia Minor. The sea-faring enterprise of the Phoenicians linked areas as remote as Carthage and the Levant, Sicily and Jerusalem. In their ships they brought the products of one end of the Mediterranean to the other, and thus one finds examples of Egyptian exports in Sicily and Etruria (modern Tuscany).

The cities of the Phoenicians were compactly planned and built within stout defensive walls. For lack of ground space, they built upwards so that their houses were several storeys high. Their stone-masons were the finest in the then-known world and in their greatest colony, Carthage, they probably built as high as six storeys. This is uncertain, however, for the Roman legionaries who obeyed the elder Cato's bidding that Carthage must be destroyed performed their task so thoroughly that our knowledge can hardly be more than a supposition of the city's tall houses or wide loggias, their spacious courtyards, or their capacious water cisterns. The Greek geographer, Strabo, estimated the population of the city at the time of its destruction as 700,000 inhabitants, but this probably included the inhabitants of surrounding settlements in what was a very thickly populated region. During the period of the wars with Rome, the majority of the male inhabitants were probably employed in armaments factories and naval workshops, turning the metals brought in from the Carthaginian colonies in Spain and Sardinia into weapons of war.

At an earlier date, however, when the Jews had wanted to carry out a major architectural undertaking – for example, the construction of the temple of Solomon in Jerusalem – what more natural than that they should have turned for advice to the Phoenician craftsmen? For the Jewish public buildings were made of stone in a similar style to those of the Phoenicians, yet their houses were, by contrast, made of unfired brick no more than a single storey high. Their rooms were arranged round a central courtyard which was often gay with flowers but which also contained basins for ablutions. The terraces on the roof were supported by beams of palm or sycamore and the domestic furniture was likely to be Egyptian, which was also influenced by Phoenician designs.

In ancient Persia too, the style of furniture recalls that of Egypt. But its environment differed; for here again we encounter in houses at a fairly exalted social level, the rooms with domed or barrel-vaulted ceilings of which we saw the beginnings in the civilizations of Sumer and Babylon.

P. M. Bardi

AMERICA BEFORE COLUMBUS

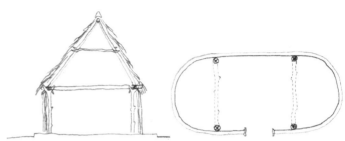

An early attempt by a European — Theodore de Bry (1528-1598) — to depict the kind of villages in which the natives of America lived from Canada to Argentina. The hut in the foreground is that of the chief. On the right ritual dances are in progress. In the middle distance, between the tobacco field on the left and the sugar and maize fields on the right, a banquet is being prepared. Beyond it are more huts and, in the background, a pool that is probably the village's source of water.

When the Spaniards landed on the continent of America they found the civilization of the Mayas, the Aztecs and the Incas in decline but still astonishingly impressive. The priestly caste, profoundly versed in astronomy, architecture, science and the techniques of agriculture, was in control. A rigid system of religious rites reinforced their sway. In these civilizations, discoveries had been made relating to the laws of astronomy, the idea of zero, complex methods of recording, the cutting of hard stone with jade — but not, curiously enough, the principle of the wheel.

History has provided illuminating glimpses of the life and customs of pre-Columbian America which are reflected in our own time. We hear of 'houses across the threshold of which a witness carried the bride to her husband for the marriage ceremony' and of, more legalistically, 'the conjugal roof'. Yet for the majority of the population, *house* meant a hut with walls of mud and reeds and a sloping thatched roof. It had no windows and only one door set low in order to keep out cold. The furnishings consisted of some pots, a few mats of rushes or hides, and perhaps one or two objects whose use would be religious or devotional.

The more prosperous native lived in a house made of sun-baked bricks, sheltered by a rain-proof roof of close-fitting planks; its furniture included chairs with backs, painted vases and stone mortars. In America, as in Europe and Asia, business and domesticity were closely allied: the craftsman's workshop was beside or part of his hut. The merchant's stores were safe under his own roof. In some areas there are indications of early exercises in town planning. Don Fernando Columbus tells of his father, the explorer, leaving the island of

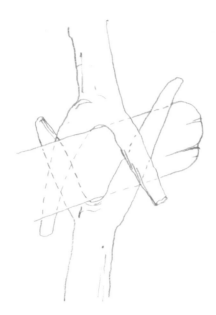
Guadeloupe and mentions 'some houses that were
well-built according to their custom with an open
space and a doorway facing the sea, and a very
wide street with towers made of reeds on either
side'.

While the ordinary people worked at their
crafts, cooked their meals at the fire before their
hut doors, and shared their huts with chosen items
of livestock and certain unwanted insects, the princes and kings of these American empires enjoyed
the luxuries appropriate to their station. And the
luxury was such as to astonish the Spanish conquistadors. When Hernando Cortes entered the
palace of Montezuma, the spectacle left him
breathless; 'I walked till I was tired out and
never managed to visit the whole of it,' he said.
Walls lucent with marble, richly decked with paintings and fabrics, carpets of skins and birds' feathers,
the incense-laden smoke of the constantly burning
braziers, flowers, jewels and everywhere the gleam
of gold – not even Cecil B. de Mille in all his glory
could surpass the splendour presented to Cortes.

To this same palatial category probably belong
buildings attributable to the Tulha-Olmec period
(the first and second centuries A.D.) and to the
Toltec period (fifth and sixth centuries A.D.), which
are the most ancient of their kind so far to be studied. In each group the complex of building was
in three sections. The main section, occupied presumably by the owner of the house and his family,
was composed of parallel rooms that ran the length
of the building. The other sections were set at either
end of the first and at right angles to it and may
have been the servants' or slaves' quarters. The
space enclosed by the three buildings was used as
a courtyard. This was probably in turn used for
meetings and ceremonies since the rooms even in

the main body of the building were very small.

Like the pyramids, temples and other monuments of pre-Columbian America, these buildings
were built of massive stone blocks which were then
either painted or further veneered in stone. Stone
slabs lined the rooms which rarely measured more
than 10 feet either way. A distinguishing feature of
ancient American architecture is, indeed, the dis-
proportion between the amount of interior space
and the exterior display.

Above and around the entrance projected a
kind of porch, also in stone, supported by moulded
brackets. The decoration of the brackets as of the
rest of the building was rich and complex so that the
walls seemed to be patterned with a deeply cut
network of hieroglyphs and geometric figures. Windows were few and small so that the interior was
lit almost entirely from the doorway: a terrace
occupied the roof.

All this made a deep impression on the Europeans who arrived to conquer this new world.
When Juan de Grijalva arrived in the territory of
the Mayas in 1518, he saw there 'a great civilization, especially as far as architecture was concerned... astonishing buildings of extraordinary
size, solid, made of stone and lime.' To him, and
to us, it seems incredible that these temples and
palaces were built by people who had no knowledge
of the wheel.

Uxmal (Yucatan): detail of the decoration on the western
building of the so-called Las Monjas (the
Nunnery Group) by Stierlin. It consists of four
buildings round an open court.

South of the palace of Knossos in Crete, the group of buildings usually thought to have been the dwellings of nobles or officials, beside the South-West House at the end of the Corridor of the Procession, includes this house with rooms on three floors. The entablatures and columns are painted red; the capitals are green. The unravelling of the history of this enormous palace complex – the construction of which took several centuries – begun by Sir Arthur Evans in 1900, still continues.

THE POWER OF REASON

THE CLASSICAL WORLD

From the golden age of Greece we have received an enormous heritage of religious architecture. Of private building we have little more than a few fragments of paved streets in Athens. Not one domestic building has survived, nor is there a complete picture of one. We may suppose with reason that the houses of the Greeks were endowed with the same virtues as the temples they have left to us, but we do not know for certain and can do no more than conjecture.

The best of Greek architecture possesses a marvellous unity and harmony among the various parts. The aesthetic success of the greatest of Greek buildings lies in the care with which their construction was planned. The ability to make the necessary calculation, and the definition of the rules governing the enclosing of space in buildings, were only achieved by stages. The oldest buildings lack the absolute perfection that was attained later and that in the western world is summed up in the word *classical*.

It is doubtless correct to attribute some of this perfection to private dwellings as well as to public buildings, in spite of the witness afforded by some of their inhabitants. 'My house,' Xenophon wrote about 354 B.C. in his *Oeconomicus*, 'is not beautified by this or that ornament: the various rooms were built with a single object — to be useful containers for what is put in them so that every place holds what it should. The cupboard, placed in a secure part of the house, contains anything precious, fabrics, valuable pieces of furniture; the dry storerooms hold the grain; the cool ones, the wine: those which are well lit, whatever needs light, and the utensils.' But even while Xenophon was thus preaching functionalism, the temple of Aphaia in Aegina was already embodying classical ideals in architecture.

Xenophon mentions too that the women's quarters in his house were separated from the men's by a locked door 'so that no one could take away what he should not.' In this, he observed the oriental tradition of a house divided into public and private rooms. It was an idea which surprised the Romans. 'To us,' Cornelius Nepos remarks, 'things which they [the Greeks] consider indecent, are not at all improper. What Roman would be ashamed to take his wife to a banquet? What mother of a family does not, in a Roman house, occupy the place of honour or enter the most crowded room? It is very different in Greece where she may be admitted to a party only if the guests are drawn from the family, where as a rule she stays in the inner part of the house — what are called the women's quarters — where no one may enter unless he is a close relation.' The Etruscans would have agreed with Cornelius Nepos. But as time passed and it became fashionable in Rome to imitate the customs of the Greeks, the differences in household customs between the two nations became less marked.

By the first century B.C., Terentius Varro in his treatise on agriculture was complaining: 'No one nowadays thinks he has a proper house unless the various rooms are given Greek names; that is, if it has not a *procoiton* (hall), an *apodyterion* (dressing room), a *peristyle*, an *ornithon* (aviary), etc.' The mixture of style is perceptible in the houses at Pompeii and Herculaneum and the result, while pleasing, is not entirely classical in character.

THE WORLD
OF THE AEGEAN

Since a great deal of attention has been devoted to the study of the houses and their contents – often works of art – of the well-to-do, villas such as those of Pompeii and palaces such as those of the Minoans on Crete have come to be regarded as the typical dwellings of the classical world. In these, certainly, Pompeians and Cretans alike lived comfortably. But what was the home of the ordinary citizen like?

In Crete, for a while the centre of the Aegean world, the royal palaces of the Minoan civilization

apartments and they may have been the houses of officials. They have a central hall with a hearth in the middle. The roof, held up by four columns, is open to let out the smoke. Drawings on tablets show houses with rooms on several floors.

At Gournia, east of Heraklion on Crete, the houses are simpler again, with stone floors and painted and plastered walls; they are connected to one another by alleyways and steps and two paved roads. Their furnishings would include a wide range of pottery, from the elegantly shaped and brightly coloured jugs that have been found on the island, to the enormous storage jars used to hold grain and oil.

For the Cretan, whose business was flourishing either on land or sea in the centuries between 3000 and 2000 B.C., it was a pleasant life. Wall paintings tell us quite a lot about it, about the athletes and dancers who performed before the prince, the reapers singing on their way home from work, about the wide-eyed ladies of fashion, the flowers and animals which gave pleasure to Cretans and the cult of the double axe and the serpent goddess.

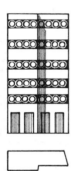 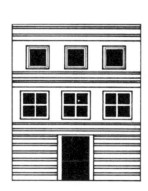  

were for long the focus of archaeological research. Destroyed several times and rebuilt, the intricate organization on several levels of public rooms, bedrooms, storerooms, courtyards and passages entered into Greek mythology to give rise to the legend of the labyrinth. In each urban community, moreover, the palace which gave employment to a large section of the population was an important energizing force.

But there existed too, of course, and excavations and drawings on tablets bear this out, a substantial number of more modest houses belonging, for example, to the enterprising merchants who two thousand years before our time established the frontiers of Crete's maritime empire in the farthest corners of the Mediterranean. A few houses have been discovered – at Knossos and Haghia Triada – that go back to the second millennium B.C. Their plans are similar to those of the royal

In one sense this sunny civilization ended about the end of the second millennium B.C. – yet in another it lives on in the pages of Homer. The world that the poet describes in the *Iliad* and the *Odyssey* is that of Crete and Mycenae. Homer's heroes had seen such chairs as the so-called throne of Minos with its high back and sculptured decoration, and slept on beds the heads of which were inlaid or adorned with filigree. But were those exquisite vessels of fine pottery or of precious metals that have been found intended for use? Or were they ritual vessels fashioned only for religious ceremonies?

In mainland Greece, domestic architecture derived from the neolithic and Bronze Age hut in its several forms, circular, oval and rectangular. The rectangular hut proved more adaptable than the others. A porch was added to the front and one or more rooms to the back. This unit of two or three adjacent rooms, usually without a courtyard (although it might have had a very small one) and only occasionally extending to an upper storey, changed slowly through the centuries. But the changes that did take place were characteristic of Greece in that they were directed at achieving a more systematic plan for the house. System in the design of the house was accompanied by an interest in interior decoration. We know from Plutarch that Alcibiades had his house painted by one Agatarchos. For whatever reason he kept the unhappy man under lock and key until the job was finished, when he 'let him go with rich gifts.'

The logical consequence to planning one house was the planning of a group of houses – town planning. Olynthos, south of Thessalonika, is an example of early Greek town planning. Athens was not. There, houses were huddled together at the foot of the Acropolis and their poverty surprised some visitors, although Demosthenes defended them eloquently. The citizens of the past, he said, 'built so many public buildings for us and so many temples of such beauty that they left no room for their

the living-rooms, used in particular by the women of the household. Vitruvius took note later of the arrangement. 'The Greeks do not use a hall nor do they build one,' he wrote. 'From the front door they build smallish passages. On one side they have the stables and on the other the rooms for the porters who open the doors leading to the interior. The space between these and the entrance is called the *thuroreion* (hall). From this you enter the *peristyle* which is open on three sides. Behind it are large rooms where the mother of the family sits spinning and weaving with the women. On the right and left are the bedrooms, one called the *thalamo*, the other the *amphithalamo*. Around the portico are the dining-rooms, some small bedrooms, and the slaves' quarters.'

The Athenian spent most of his day in public places, in the *agora* and the *areopagus* where he contributed to public debate, and in gymnasia and places of entertainment. His need, therefore, for homely comfort in his own house was not great. 'My house is on two floors,' Euphiletos wrote, 'the arrangement being the same above and below, in

A series of small faience tablets (one or two inches broad) in the Archaeological Museum in Heraklion show the variety of façades in Cretan domestic architecture. They varied in structure as well as ornament. Some of the houses seem to have had attics with windows in them, some had a tower on top (anticipating the fashion in medieval Italy), some had very few windows, some had quite a lot; some windows were large, some small, and a few seem to be double windows.

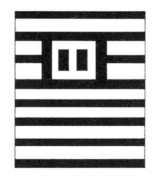

descendants to do better'. But in private they were so modest and adhered so strictly to the rules of the state that if anyone had asked which was the house of Aristides and which that of Miltiades or of any other well-known man of the time, he would have seen that it was no richer than that of his neighbour. Heraclitus the Critic, a foreigner to Athens, noticed the modesty – or poverty – of the houses too. 'The city is dry and lacks water,' he wrote, 'the division of the districts is bad because it is old. Most of the houses are worth little and few are worth much. At first sight, a stranger might be forgiven for doubting that this was the much-lauded city of Athens.'

In the fifth century B.C., when Pericles administered Athens and the Parthenon was rising on the Acropolis, the house of a well-to-do family would be composed of about ten rooms grouped round a courtyard. On the northern side of it were

the women's part and in the men's. When my son was born and his mother was nursing him, I moved up to the first floor and sent the women down to the ground floor to avoid the risk of her falling downstairs when she had to come down and wash him.' The house mattered only during some special gathering when it was enlivened with conversation. Plato described a gathering of sophists in the *Protagoras*: 'As we came in, we stopped in the hall to talk... inside, we found Protagoras walking up and down the portico behind it... Hippias of Elis was sitting on a high seat on the opposite side; around him on benches were Eriximaco and Phaedrus... Procidus of Ceo was in a room which had served as a store for Hipponicus but which Callia, because of the large number of sophists who had come to visit him, had turned into a bedroom. Procidus was in bed, wrapped in sheepskins and blankets. Beside him, on beds next to each other, were

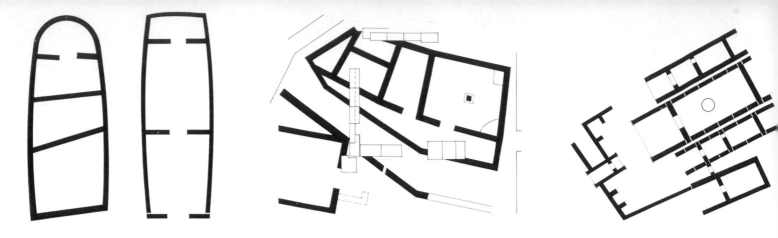

(Below, top) Greek houses with a well-defined plan have been found at Olynthos near Thessalonika, the city destroyed by Philip of Macedon in 348 B.C. The main hall (1) leads to the colonnaded courtyard (2) from which open a number of public rooms (4 to 8). There is a second entrance (3) and the staircase (9) leads to the upper floor used by guests and servants. (Below, bottom) This house with a regular plan found at Mallia in Crete may have belonged to a rich merchant and is typical of its period, the second millennium B.C. The vestibule (1) leads to the main corridor (2); on the left are small storerooms and a bathroom (3); on the right larger rooms which may again have been stores. At the end is the room (4) used for eating and sleeping with a stone floor and no windows and adjoining a pilastered reception room (5) from which it derives its light. The remains of a staircase (6) points to a possible upper floor.

(Above) In the Homeric epic, a fairly complex type of dwelling is described with a hall, a colonnaded courtyard, a reception room, a nuptial chamber and an apartment for the women, and the description is a reflection of the royal palaces of the civilization of Mycenae. The houses of ordinary people may have more closely resembled those of the eighth and seventh centuries B.C. in Greece and Asia Minor: they may have been huts, either oval or rectangular or a combination of the two (as in the first two plans, left), in wood or unfired brick with the straw roof supported by a row of posts. At Eleusis (third plan), a house has been found that more closely resembles the Greek dwelling of historic times with the rooms opening from a hall; the portico foreshadows the temple porticos to come. At Troy, at the second stratum (fourth plan), these structures of unfired brick of the third millennium B.C. have been found and represent a number of primitive houses side by side.

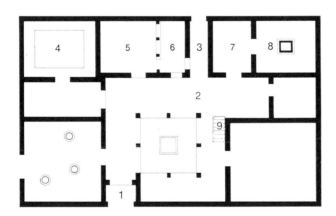

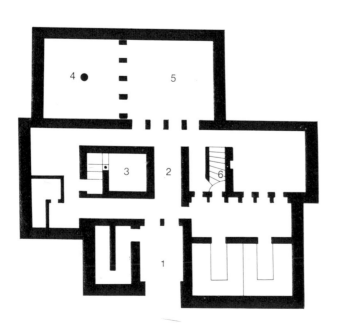

Pausanias and a boy.'

From these brief remarks, we can gain a fairly accurate idea of the furnishings of a Greek house. There were the indispensable stools or chairs, some with straight legs, some on a folding X-frame like their Egyptian originals. The back, if any, was slightly inclined; the seat was generally plain with an animal skin stretched over it, by way of upholstery. There were a few tables. Beds were made of planks on trestles and covered with blankets; for a mattress there might be a sack filled with leaves or wool. In place of cupboards there were a number of chests which were used as seats. The Greek approach to furniture and interior decor was, probably, practical. There was as much furniture as there needed to be and what there was, was well designed: we can still admire it in the drawings on Greek vases.

At a slightly later date, however, between the fourth and second centuries B.C., the house and its furnishings assumed more importance in the life of the Greek. Significantly, it was the period in which the individual's importance as a participant in political affairs diminished. From sites on mainland and Hellenistic Greece it is possible to acquire an idea, fragmentary at best, of what domestic archi-

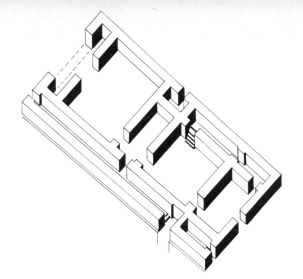

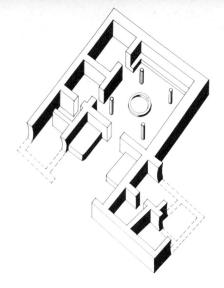

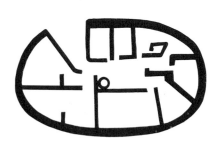

(Above, left) Plan of the House of the Tiles *(about 2000 B.C.) at Lerna in the Argolid. The building which is more than 66 feet long owes its name to the abundant remains of its terracotta roof tiles and this is a very ancient example of this kind of roof.*
In the complex arrangement of the great palaces at Knossos, Phaistos, and Tiryns, the megaron *or primitive brick house is the nucleus as in this building (right) at Kültepe in Anatolia. The roof, often open to let out smoke and let in light, is supported on pillars.*
(This page, left) Plan of an ancient house in Crete where buildings with curved external walls were common.
(Below) The rules of town-planning drawn up by Hippodamus of Miletus in the fifth century B.C. were widely applied in the cities of Greece and Asia Minor. At Priene, near Miletus, as at Agrigento in Sicily (see plan) groups of houses were laid out in rows along the main roads with narrow streets, along which were laid the drains: the apparent monotony of the arrangement was relieved by the bright paint on the house fronts.

tecture of this period was like. The houses found at Priene, a wealthy trading city in Asia Minor at the mouth of the valley of the Meander, were laid out tidily and followed a very regular town plan with the streets intersecting at right angles. The buildings were not large and the arrangement of rooms was that accepted in Greece itself.

In the Macedonian capital of Pella, the birthplace of Alexander the Great, splendid palatial villas have been recovered, richly decorated in marble and mosaics. These were probably, however, princely residences. More typical of an ordinary Greek house of this period would be the kind of house built on the island of Delos. This would generally be on two storeys, with the rooms grouped irregularly round a small courtyard, the object being to make the best use of the limited space available in the narrow streets.

Overseas, notably in Sicily, Greek colonists also built in the style of their homeland. The town plan of Agrigento, for example, is similar to that of Priene. Thus the peristyled house was constructed beyond the shores of mainland Greece, not merely in Asia Minor but far to the west. And as can be seen from page 50, the pupils of Greek architects and builders included the Romans.

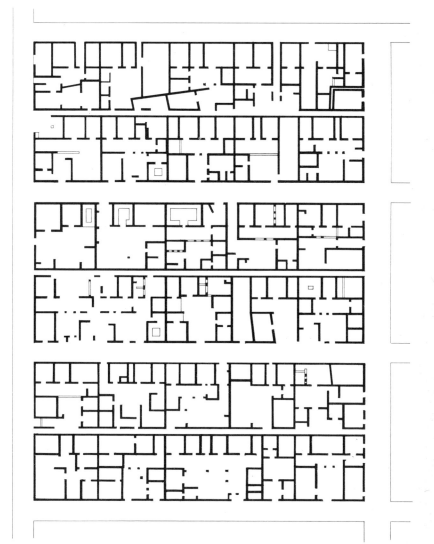

ETRURIA

We know little directly about the Etruscan house although the most important element in it, the *atrium*, also formed the nucleus of the Roman house. Excavations at Marzabotto, Veii and Vetulonia have yielded little more information than that the houses may have consisted of several rooms round a central courtyard, of two or three rooms or, in some cases, a single room without a courtyard. The plan of Marzabotto, an Etruscan town near Bologna, has been uncovered to show broad streets intersecting at right angles. The bases of the walls seem to have been built of stone and it is possible that the rest of each wall was constructed of wood and unfired brick.

It is from tombs and funerary ornaments that we learn most about the houses of Etruria. The funeral urns show us what they looked like when the Etruscan civilization was at the height of its powers during the sixth and fifth centuries B.C. – rectangular with a ridged roof and on occasion with an upper loggia as well. Etruscan tombs reveal even more. The rock tombs of Blera, Norchia and Sovana show buildings under construction, while the underground tombs of Tarquinia and Orvieto and the *tumulus* graves at Cerveteri afford us a vivid idea of what the rooms in an Etruscan house were like. The entrance passage which leads to the main room of the tomb corresponds to the vestibule of the house which opens into the *atrium*, the central apartment of the house. The *atrium* which Vitruvius called Tuscanic – that is, Etruscan – had a central opening in the roof but, as a rule, no windows to the outside.

The furnishings of the tombs closely reproduce those of the houses of the living. The houses of the dead contain, accordingly, the *triclinium* on which the Etruscan banqueted or rested, the things he used every day, and his cherished possessions. On the walls are paintings depicting banquets, hunting scenes and the dancers and jugglers who entertained him (and the women of his household who, clearly, were not isolated in their own quarters). The theme of the dead contain, accordingly, the *triclinium* on elusive people. And elusive they will remain until the secret of their language has been broken.

(Opposite page) Burial room in the Tomb of the Bas-Reliefs, also known as the Grotta Bella, at Cerveteri. The structure as a whole is that of other tombs of the same period (fourth to second century B.C.) with two pillars supporting the pitched roof. Its unusual feature is the reproduction in painted relief of the household utensils, the armour and clothing – shields, helmet, sword, shoes, cups, jugs, knives, axes, and the rest – of the dead. On the panel supporting the bed are a demon with a fish's tail and the three-headed dog which guarded the underworld.

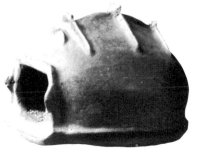

(Right) Plan of the Tomb of the Shields and the Chairs, also in the necropolis
at Cerveteri. Apart from the small thrones, funeral beds, and shields carved
in the tufa with the customary vigour of the Etruscans, the tomb is important in that
its plan probably resembles the plan of an Etruscan house more closely than
that of any other tomb. It is rectangular with a hall from which two side rooms
open and which leads into a large central hall or atrium.
smaller rooms open into it.
(Opposite page) Etruscan urns in the shape of huts, now in the
Gregorian Museum in the Vatican.

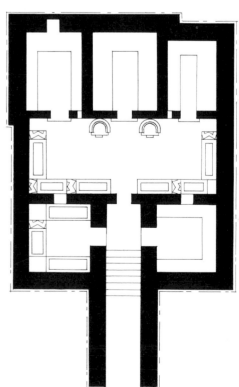

ROME

The record of domestic architecture during the period of the Roman Republic and Empire is more complete than that of any domestic architecture that preceded it and, in some ways, than that of much of the architecture that followed. Every aspect of it is open to our examination, from the hut in Latium to the magnificent palaces of Imperial Rome, from the Roman tenement to the villas that Roman colonists scattered about the empire. We can see how the Roman adapted himself to different surroundings and climates, how he endeavoured always to improve his living conditions, and — most noticeably — the importance he attached to two essential matters, water and heating. Water he controlled first by collecting it in cisterns and later by leading it through aqueducts from springs to private houses, fountains and public baths. He diminished the rigours of cold climates by an efficient under-floor heating system. All this involved changes in the design of the house.

In the eighth century B.C., which traditionally saw the foundation of Rome, the commonest type of dwelling was still the Bronze Age hut, generally egg-shaped and built of wood, straw and mud. Funerary urns in Latium are models of them. By the fifth century B.C., however, rectangular huts were being built. Here a low base of tufa chips supported walls of wood and unfired brick and on top, a tiled roof. The interior was divided into several rooms with mud floors or, as has been indicated by the remains of a house of this period found on the Palatine Hill in Rome, floors of pebbles or beaten tufa.

By the third century B.C. we begin to find the house with an *atrium*, that is, with a central roofed courtyard. Whether the Romans took over this style from the Etruscans after having defeated them or whether the style developed independently in Roman territories at the same time, it is difficult to say, but literary tradition confirms, as we have already noted, the close links in this field as elsewhere between Rome and Etruria.

In Campania, the Tuscan-Roman house with an *atrium* met and fused with the *peristyle* house of Hellenic tradition. Examples of this fusion have been found in Pompeii and Herculaneum. The result was a single large dwelling with the *atrium* house as the front part — linked to the street through the vestibule — and the *peristyle* house as the back portion where it took the place of the garden of the old Roman house. It was a plan which, at the back of the house at least, allowed more privacy and at the same time more scope for luxury than had been possible in the Roman houses that had gone before. Internal arrangements were, however, affected by the site. In a house set on a hillside the peristyle was often replaced by a terrace commanding a view of the valley.

The house with the *atrium* and *peristyle* became traditional in Rome and continued as such until the third century A.D. Testimony of this is contained in a fragment of the great marble plan of the city made in the reign of Septimius Severus. It was principally, of course, the house of the noble families. The ordinary citizen lived in more modest quarters – small rooms and a courtyard as at Herculaneum. But often these houses had a pleasing upper storey, one side of which projected over the street in a wooden balcony where a family might dine or enjoy the fresh air.

Different circumstances dictated different plans for Roman houses in the sometimes unruly and frequently chilly provinces of the empire. Set at the heart of a large estate in a colony, the villa was equipped with towers for defence and, in cold climates, with central heating in the rooms most frequently used.

The development of new building techniques in Rome at the end of the republican period was accompanied by several problems for the administration of the city, chief among which was control of the height of buildings – less from any aesthetic concern than from fear that the buildings would collapse, as they sometimes did. New building methods introduced at this time, such as the use of cement, allowed builders to build upwards. During the Punic wars against Hannibal, buildings were sufficiently high for Livy to mention the plight of an ox in the Foro Boario which 'went up to the third floor of a building on its own initiative: there, terrified by the noise of the inmates, it threw itself to the ground'; the date was 218 B.C.

During the Republic laws were passed to control building. They were reinforced during the reign of Augustus by the *lex Iulia de modo aedificandae urbis* which limited the height of houses to 69 feet. Legislation proved on the whole unsuccessful. Martial pokes fun at the glutton Santra laden with provisions which he carried 'up two hundred steps to his home'. Santra may have lived in an ancient building older than the *lex Iulia* or, as is quite likely, in a tall house illegally erected by one of the many speculative builders who flourished at that time in Rome and charged exorbitant

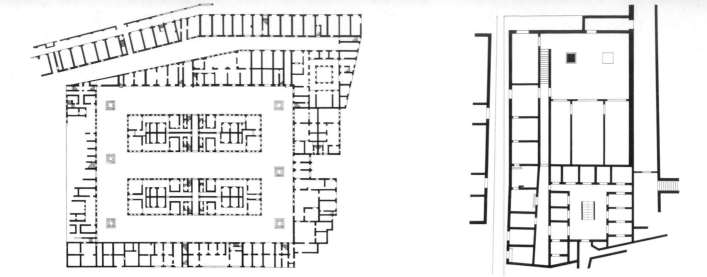

(Left) In Ostia there are still many examples of multi-family housing on several floors. This new factor in building affected the capital from the second century A.D. These buildings often included large inner courtyards, within which were accommodated minor buildings with colonnades. The apartment consisted of an entrance hall which led to the main rooms; to the side of it were secondary rooms. In a corner were the kitchen and service rooms (water closets were often shared). Water was drawn from wells and rainwater tanks placed in the courtyards.
(Right) Plan of the House of Livia on the Palatine, famous for the paintings that decorated its interior: but, without ornaments of marble, it seems to have been quite an average house of its period, the end of the Republic. The hall, top right, opened into the atrium *which in turn led to three large public rooms with brick arches. The dining-room may have been the separate room beyond the five small rooms. A staircase led to the floor above.*

rents – Cicero denounced the good-for-nothing Clodius Pulcher for asking 10,000 sesterces for a small apartment in an *insula* (tenement) he owned.

At the end of the first century A.D., houses still tended to collapse and the Emperor Trajan reduced the permissible height to just over 56 feet. Rome had, indeed, a serious housing problem and the cost of repair after collapse, fire, flood or earthquake was generally conceded to be excessive. It did not help that, according to Vitruvius, the law limiting the height of buildings also limited the thickness of the outer walls. 'The large size of the city and the enormous number of its citizens meant that the number of dwellings had to be increased,' he wrote, adding that as the levelled

area could not accommodate the houses of so many people, it became necessary to build upwards. Buildings which were already very tall were often increased in height by adding attics, and even the lofts were considered useful. So by increasing the height of their buildings, the inhabitants of Rome had no difficulty in finding excellent homes for themselves.

On a more impressive scale were the houses built at the end of the first century A.D. for family groups. Their plan was rectangular and they occupied the sites between intersecting streets. They consisted, of course, of several storeys and the apartments within them were reached by a number of staircases. As well as dwelling houses, more-

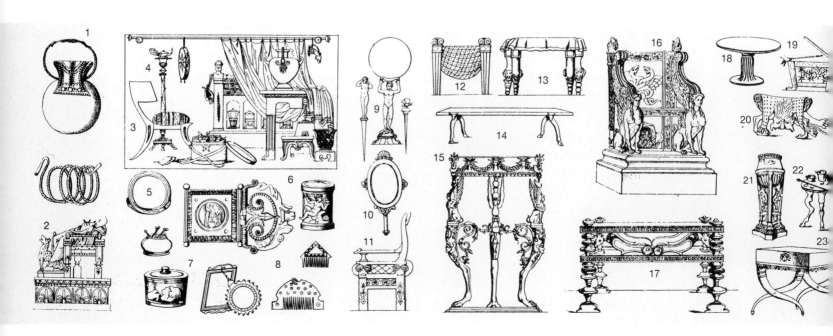

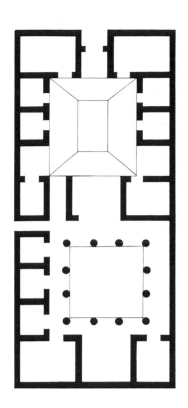

(Left) The House of the Red Columns at Herculaneum. The intense colours found on pillars, capitals, and other structural features of the house, are typical of buildings of the ancient Mediterranean countries. (Right) Many houses at Pompeii have a plan similar to this which was common during the Republican period in Rome. The main entrance, at the top, opens into the entrance hall which is flanked by two rooms, often used as shops. Beyond this was the atrium which connected with several small side rooms; at the end of it was a living-room with a peristyle behind it. One of the rooms facing on to this colonnaded courtyard was the dining-room with a marble table in the centre. The service rooms – kitchen, water closets, stables and the rest – were tucked into unimportant corners of the building.

over, these buildings accommodated shops, offices and baths. Otherwise, as at Ostia, the rooms were grouped round a courtyard which in style foreshadowed that of the Renaissance and which has little connection with the Roman *atrium* or Greek *peristyle*. In this new type of house, the idea took shape of a dwelling which shut out the prying eyes of strangers, where the family – the extended family covered by the Roman *gens* – sheltered, governed by the *paterfamilias*.

This architectural development reflected a series of social changes in Rome. At the height of the power of the empire, the city's population numbered a million, most of them crowded into a few districts such as the Suburra, the district by the Forum; here peoples from every province of the empire swarmed in company with the native Romans. The rich in turn abandoned the Palatine which was occupied by Imperial residences, and withdrew to palaces on the Esquiline, the Quirinale, and the Pincio which had the advantages of comparative peace and privacy.

In his *Annals* Tacitus records an attempt by Nero to improve the lay-out of the city. After the notorious fire of 64 A.D., the emperor ordered that 'the houses destroyed in the fire should not be rebuilt but that the districts should be planned with wide streets, that the height of buildings should be limited, and that open spaces and porticos should be added to protect the fronts of the

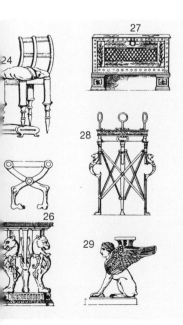

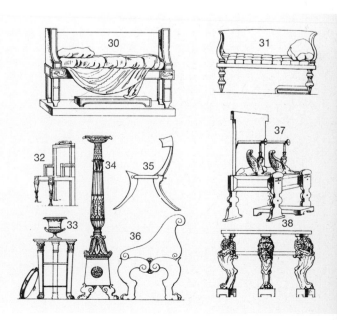

In Graeco-Roman houses articles in use included toilet articles, mirrors, combs, cosmetic holders and so on (1, 5, 6, 7, 8, 9, 10). Furniture included stools (12, 13) which were often folding or on an X-frame (20, 23, 25) and could be very elaborate (17); chairs with a high back and cushions (3, 24, 32, 35), and armchairs of marble or wood with bronze decoration (2, 11, 16, 36, 37); marble tables, mostly round and supported on a pedestal (18) or with three legs in the shape of animals' feet (14, 22, 26, 38); bronze holders for basins and other receptacles (15, 28); lamp or torch holders (4, 21, 29, 33, 34); beds (30, 31) often with a high back and like ours, equipped with mattresses and pillows; and chests (19, 27).

insulae.' The emperor went so far as to offer to build the porticos at his own expense and return the restored areas to their owners. Some parts of the buildings, he further laid down, should be strengthened with stone and tufa and not with timber because 'these stones would not catch fire... They should not have walls in common', he added, 'but each building should be surrounded by its own walls'.

In the design of their houses during the centuries of the Empire, Romans were concerned with more than structural problems. The conquest of Egypt, Palestine and Asia Minor (the latter held somewhat uneasily) was followed by increasing orientalization of the way of life of an influential

of the ridiculous Heliogabalus. It wanted only the transfer of the capital of the Empire to the east: this took place in the reign of the emperor Constantine during the fourth century. He chose a city within convenient reach of the industries of Asia Minor and the grain supplies of Egypt – Byzantium, which he renamed Constantinople.

The chairs, seats and tables used by the early Romans were simple in design. They combined the style of similar Greek pieces with the heavy solidity of Etruscan furniture. Typical of Etruscan furniture is a chair with a high, curved back and a slightly curved seat, a shape that lasted for centuries without perceptible alteration. From the Etruscans too the Romans adopted the *triclinium*:

(Opposite page) Roman sarcophagus (now in the National Museum of Antiquities in Leiden) the interior of which reproduces the interior of a Roman house

Wall painting of a house on the Esquiline, known as The Marriage of the Aldobrandini *(Vatican Museum). It shows a nuptial chamber; the bride seated on the bed in her ceremonial dress, attended by Venus, awaits her husband. On the right is Hymen, god of marriage. The bed is a typical Roman one with mattress, pillow and bedclothes.*

section of Roman society. Traditionalists disapproved but could hardly restrain the resultant love of luxury and display. The more enterprising inhabitants of the provinces at the eastern end of the Mediterranean took up residence in Rome the better to further their businesses. 'For years now', Juvenal lamented, 'the Orontes has poured its sewage into our native Tiber'. But still those Romans with money to spend spent it on the silks of Cos and – even more expensive – of China itself, on the soft dark wool of Laodicea, on the works of Asian metal-workers, on the sculptures of the studios of Aphrodisias, and on Levantine slaves. Rome's gold reserves slipped eastwards out of the Empire. During the third century A.D. Rome acquired an Emperor from the east, in the shape

depending on the taste or wealth of the owner, it was either richly ornamented or austerely plain. The table used for meals, again often decorated, repeated a pattern used in Greece: three-legged or four-legged, square or rectangular, polygonal or round, its top of marble and the legs terminating in griffin's or sphinx's feet. Bronze was a favourite material for decoration and smaller pieces of furniture were made of it entirely. In Rome as elsewhere, the most commonly used type of seat was the stool with rigid or folding legs. As the empire expanded, so did love of ostentation. The elder Pliny writes indignantly of the prices paid by furniture lovers and of the ridiculous sums paid for the wood alone. Comfort and convenience also became more important. The storage coffer was

This house, on the slopes of the Capitol
is the only example so far known in Rome
of a large building of the period of the Empire.
Like those at Ostia, it has several storeys
and the remains of four floors have survived
apart from the ground floor with its shops.
The row of windows above the shops
belonged to the mezzanine floor where the
shopkeepers and their families lived. When,
as in this case, the building was set
on a hill, the upper floors at the rear
were at ground level.

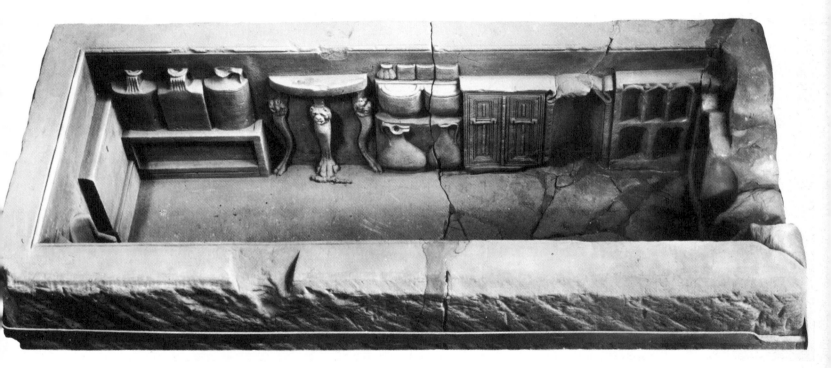

replaced by the cupboard with shelves inside it.

In the early Christian period, reaction against luxury was accompanied in Rome by a recapturing of the more sober and more delicate designs of earlier furniture. But in the Byzantine world, silks and embroideries, gold, silver and mother-of-pearl inlay added magnificence to the house's furnishings. Visitors to the great city stood amazed at the richness of the exterior ornament and the interior luxury, and at the wealth on show in the bazaars. One traveller gave up in despair the attempt to record his impressions: 'It would be wearisome', he concluded, 'to tell of the abundance of all good things... Ships are at all times putting into this port so that there is nothing that men want that is not brought hither.'

Reminders of Rome grew more faint. Even in the furnishing of the house, so important a piece as the *triclinium* changed its form and was eventually superseded altogether by seats, often three-legged, sometimes with backs, or by benches and stools. The bed itself rose higher and higher on its four legs until it stood several steps off the ground, or else it was lowered until its legs disappeared altogether. It was at this time, too, that there developed in the monasteries the small study furnished with a simple table and chair or a rudimentary desk in which a few necessities were kept.

Mario Bussagli

THE ASIATIC TRADITION

The most powerful influence on the development of the house in Asia has been the extreme variations in climate and local conditions. From the Arctic to the tropics, these range through the tundra, forest and steppes of the north to the deserts, semi-deserts, mountain chains, high plateaux, well-watered plains and finally the jungles of the Equatorial belt of the south-east. On the fringes of the continent are the islands and archipelagos that used to be and still are centres of flourishing civilizations. Circumstances of such extraordinary variety have produced social and economic organizations of equal variety. They have dictated, too, widely varied attitudes to the idea of the house, of its function, and of what may be described as the art of living.

They have done so, moreover, over many thousands of years. During more than five millennia, the people of this vast continent have – to meet their particular needs and conform with their particular beliefs and customs – excavated homes for themselves out of rock, dug them into the ground, or built them high upon piles or trees. They have used, as has already been noted, the materials that came to hand. In some cases their homes were mobile, for example, the felt tents of the nomads of the steppes. In others – in the Indus civilization of the third millennium B.C. – they conformed to a more definite plan.

Each of the great civilizations made its contribution to the design of the house; each offered its own solutions to the problems this raised; each developed a rich tradition of decoration and ornament. In the Indian sub-continent, for example, which was dominated for many thousands of years by a peasant economy in which the population was dispersed in villages rather than concentrated in towns, the problem of integrating a single isolated house into a landscape did not arise, as it did in Japan.

Throughout the history of the countries that make up Asia, two factors have exerted a very great influence. One is tradition; the other is contact with Europe. The two have, on occasion, come into conflict, though more recently attempts have been made to combine European influence with Asiatic tradition. The traditional elements that have persisted in the design and building of a house – as elsewhere – are frequently very ancient in origin, a factor that in no way diminishes their strength. Included in this reverence for tradition is a regard for certain magical and religious beliefs which affect the choice of site and in some cases, elements in the house's construction. Geomancy and astrology decide the right site and time of building. The wrong site and the wrong time might bring misfortune to the inhabitants of the house. The beliefs of society also affected the structure of the house. In India and Iran the house was closed in on itself: in China it was open to heaven

Villa Aldobrandini at Frascati near Rome. Detail of a room with Chinese wallpaper made towards the end of the eighteenth century. It depicts a landscape with a number of domestic and other buildings as well as picturesque scenery and inhabitants.

An alleged reconstruction of the transport of Tartar or Mongol tents with the help of a sizeable herd of oxen: its accuracy is open to a great deal of doubt.

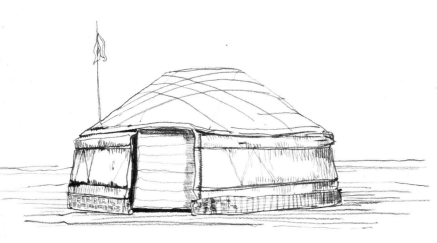

Typical Mongol yurt of felt. The framework is a wooden trellis; at the top is the opening by which smoke escapes. Its shape is calculated to resist the winds of the steppes. By the entrance is a war banner. Dwellings of this kind figure in ancient engravings.

The house of a prosperous inhabitant of Siberia in the eighteenth or nineteenth century. Basically, it is a tent of wood on an octagonal base. The floor is slightly raised. Its central entrance recalls the approach gallery of the semi-subterranean dwellings that are its precursors.

– and to the lower regions – in the belief that the family consisted not merely of the living but also of the dead.

An exception to Asian reverence for tradition and sentiment for one's own place seems to have been the civilization that flourished on the banks of the Indus at Mohenjo-daro five thousand years ago. It was almost certainly a trading civilization, the products of which travelled far throughout the ancient world: a jewel from a workshop in Mohenjo-daro turned up in a tomb at Ur and there are indications that there was communication at least with Egypt. Their metal-workers and potters produced work of great sophistication, and such statuettes as that of the famous dancing girl are extraordinarily lively and beautiful. Their city was, for all that, peculiarly utilitarian and notable absentees among the buildings excavated are temples. This does not mean that the Mohenjo-daro people did not worship gods – their seals commemorate several, in particular a horned god – it merely means that we do not as yet know how they worshipped them. Their principal claim to fame is, however, their competence as town planners and water engineers. The city was carefully laid out to take advantage of the prevailing wind while their drainage system has been described as the most ingenious and complete known to antiquity and one which could be put into use again at any time. Their water supply, derived from reservoirs outside the city in which rainfall was gathered, was distributed by brick conduits to wells in the houses: the poorest houses did not have wells of their own but had access to those of their more

Greenland: Eskimo winter dwelling.
The walls of the building are of alternate layers of stone and turf or peat. The roof, on which the skin boats are stored to keep them out of the jaws of the dogs, is made of driftwood gathered on the sea or lake shore.

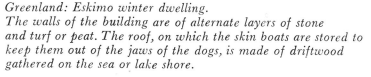

privileged neighbours. But, and here again we come to another apparent contradiction in the story of this civilization of the third millennium B.C., fine and ingenious craftsmen though they were, the people of Mohenjo-daro do not seem to have taken the trouble to decorate their houses. Industrious as ants, they seem to have been entirely devoted to industry and it is probable that the house in this civilization did not occupy the position of importance that it did elsewhere.

Contacts between Europe and Asia have not always been happy, especially in the field of architecture. Japan has probably been most noticeably affected by the introduction of European and American styles. In India the monuments of the Raj bespeak the influence of Europe — though here there has been a two-way traffic as can be seen from the introduction of the bungalow to the British Isles. The attempt to combine the two cultures was made by Gandhi in his village of Sivagram near Wardha in central India where he tried to adapt a peasant's hut to modern needs and methods of construction, using brick and reinforced concrete. Although he condemned everything the machine stood for, he was aware of modern needs and of the desirability of taking advantage of natural surroundings. The houses he built satisfied both these demands. The same use of landscape is found in Le Corbusier's Chandigarh, the new capital he designed for the post-partition Punjab, which is both functional but also characteristically Indian in its use of light in the houses. Nevertheless, Chandigarh remains a western interpretation of Indian social needs and traditions.

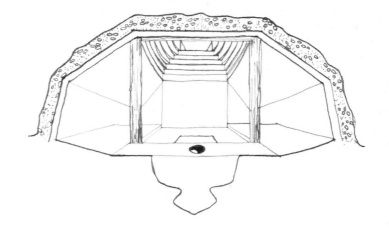

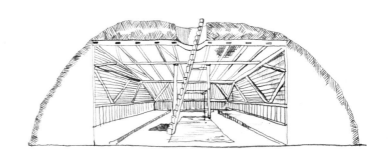

(Above, top) Winter houses — in section — of the western Eskimos and the Eskimos of Alaska. Both types are half-buried, covered with earth with an entrance from above to the middle of the room near the hearth: the entrance also serves as window and chimney.
(Centre) Kamchatka dwelling, similar to the others but rectangular inside. The entrance at the top was used by the men of the tribe (the ladder is of a type also found in Africa); women and children used the underground passage.
(Bottom) Tent of the reindeer herdsmen of western Siberia, very similar to the Mongolian yurt.

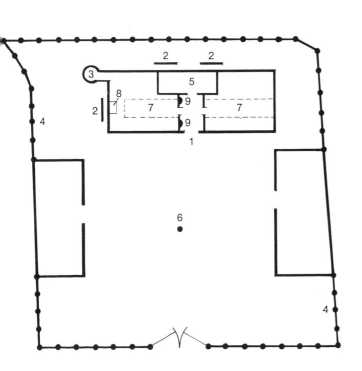

Plan of the temple and residential complex of a Mongolian shaman or wizard. The outer wall (4) defines the consecrated area controlled by the magic power of the shaman. The entrance (1) led past two hearths (9) to the living-room (5); to the left and right were two reception rooms (7) in one of which was an altar to the ancestors (8). Near the altar was the fireplace (3) and on the outer panels of this building were hung certain liturgical objects (2). The centre of religious ceremony was in the open (6).

CHINA AND JAPAN

In China, recognition of the importance of the family unit is of very great antiquity. From earliest times, the concept was preserved of the family as a self-contained entity, even though that entity more closely resembled a clan than the restricted group now comprehended by the term 'family'. By the period of the Chou dynasty (the tenth to the third century B.C.), these groups were living together in great family houses. Records of the Chou dynasty affirm that the king's residence and almost certainly those of his nobles were orientated on a north-south axis and contained three court-yards. The buildings were rectangular with double sloping roofs. The central courtyard was, in a royal household as elsewere, 'the well of heaven' in which rituals were conducted in the presence of the earth gods and the ancestors. On the fringes of such a resi-dential complex were the houses of the craftsmen, officials and labourers. The tradition of the court-yard house was not, however, universal in China during this period. In north China, the house with-out a courtyard but with a central chimney devel-oped, possibly for climatic reasons.

Less sophisticated forms of the same idea are found in Siberia, Tibet and – here we trace move-ments of population – down the American Pa-cific coast as far as Central America. In Europe, of course, the Roman house also accommodated a central courtyard, the *atrium*, but with a very differ-ent purpose; for the courtyard of a Chinese house expresses beliefs profoundly alien to the Roman mind.

The Tibetan house, like the Chinese, is closed to the outside world. The heart of it is the room with the hearth in it and, a necessary refinement, the chimney or opening to the sky. The house is constructed on several storeys which themselves reflect a vertical hierarchy of rooms – similar, it has been alleged and, indeed, borne out by written texts, to the arrangements of the celestial worlds.

In houses throughout Asia, life is conducted at or only slightly above ground level. To this cir-cumstance we owe the widespread use of carpets and the special forms of furniture devised. In Ja-pan, the practice is seen in its most highly devel-oped form, the pleasing one of gleaming floors and *tatami*, the mats of standard size.

The Japanese house resembles the Chinese in many ways and the building techniques are similar.

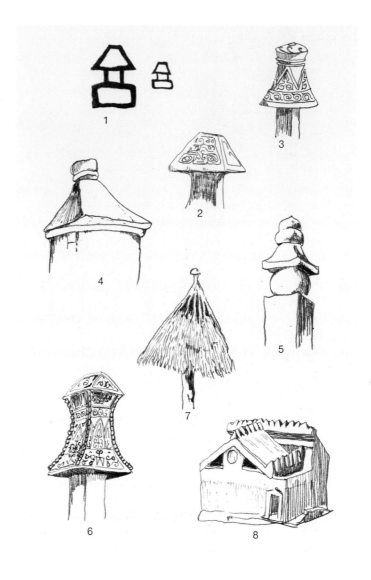

They differ, however, in the care taken by Japanese builders to integrate the house into a landscape, to create the impression that it is a natural growth and that nature is part of the house. The impression is achieved partly by the use of sliding walls, partly by the lowness of the roof, partly by the fact that the framework of the house is seen to be on a low platform. Japanese feeling for nature, which does not exclude a profound sense of the intimacy of the house, is derived in part from the country's Buddhist heritage: Buddhism reached Japan in the sixth cen-tury A.D. During subsequent centuries and espe-cially during the Heian period from the eighth to the twelfth centuries A.D., the peculiar artistic genius of Japan developed, which allowed it to create a sense of the infinite out of nothing and to

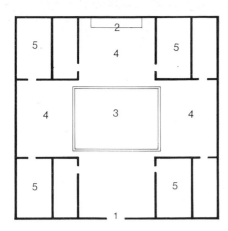

Plan of a wooden Hakka dwelling in Canton. The plan probably derives from central China. It shows the 'well of Heaven' (3) in the middle, the entrance through a hall (1), the reception rooms (4) communicating with the private rooms (5) and the altar to the ancestors (2).

Model in coloured ceramic of a Chinese house connected with the cult of the dead dating back to the Han dynasty (202 B.C. to 220 A.D.) and found in Thank-hoa, Vietnam. The structure is similar to that of upper middle class houses of the Chou dynasty as described in the Erh-ya, one of the most ancient of Chinese records (Kansas City, Atkins Museum).

(Opposite page) It was from the archaic Chinese character signifying a house (1), according to Carl Heutze, that the so-called ornamental bosses of Shang-Yin vases (1400-1057 B.C.) were derived. These might show the four aspects of a pitched roof, or be bell-shaped (3). Small wooden funerary objects, either Mongolian (4) or Japanese (5), show a similar type of motif. The motif of which the hut is the symbol (7) is still found today on the island of Flores in Indonesia, accompanied by a legend which betrays its Chinese origin. An intermediary form of boss with a stem is a recurrent element in ancient Chinese bronzes (6) and an echo of it seems to be contained in the small model of an ancient Peruvian house (8), the remote ancestors of which should perhaps be sought in eastern Asia.

achieve exquisite elegance from delicate forms and simple materials.

The traditional Japanese house took advantage of the fact that, for safety, the kitchen was always placed outside the building and a charcoal brazier was the only means of heating. There were no staircases. The habitable area was extended by a verandah (supported like the rest of the house on posts) facing the sun. In the Momoyama period (sixteenth and seventeenth centuries A.D.) the tea ceremony, an essential part of Japanese life, took place in buildings outside the house. These looked rustic but were in fact very delicately constructed. The garden was a landscape in miniature in which moderation was sought, excess was avoided and an incomparable elegance was achieved.

In planning their towns and cities, China and Japan preserve even today a tendency to develop along a vertical, north-south axis rather than to radiate from a central point. But the relationship of house to street in the two countries is very different. In Japan, the street is in general the shortest distance between two points. In China, where there is more room to spare, the street meanders in and out of whatever space is available, regardless of distance or direction.

The most obvious characteristic of both Chinese and Japanese houses, familiar in the West from drawings and photographs and also from the patterns on china and pottery, in particular the Willow Pattern, is the wide, projecting roof with upturned edges. The roof, which rested on

pillars and a combination of mainbeams and crossbeams, sometimes so skilfully contrived that it appeared to be floating, was traditionally the most important part of the Chinese house. By the thirteenth century A.D. those timbers exposed to view were carved and painted in bright colours. The practice of making upturned roofs is probably several centuries older and may date back to the Tang dynasty of the seventh to tenth centuries: an architect of the eleventh century who writes of his admiration for Tang architects cannot forbear, however, to add that they had not quite mastered the trick of curving their roofs upwards. Originally such curved roofs were reserved, by imperial de-

cree, for the enrichment of the houses of people of high rank and of government buildings. Similar attempts were made to restrict the use of ornaments in the shape of dragons, phoenix and other pleasingly decorative but mythical animals.

Throughout the Sung, Yuan and Ming dynasties in China – which correspond roughly to the Middle Ages and early Renaissance in Europe – the importance of the house increased as a factor in society, and despite overcrowding in the cities and various sumptuary regulations, each generation seemed determined to improve on the decorative achievements of their forebears. During the thirteenth century a wealthy household in a

This section of a Tibetan house, by the scholar Jen Nai-k'iang, shows the lay-out with, on the ground floor, the stable (1); above it, the living-room (2) and the latrine (3); then the threshing floor (4) and the chapel (5); on top is the ritual brazier (6) and the totem (7).

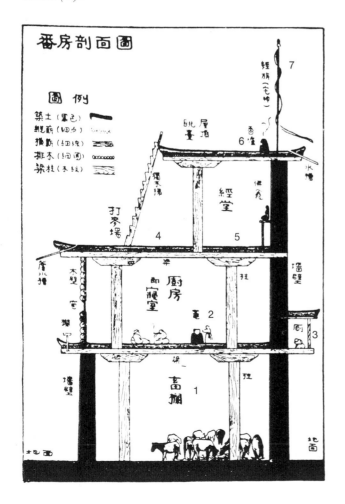

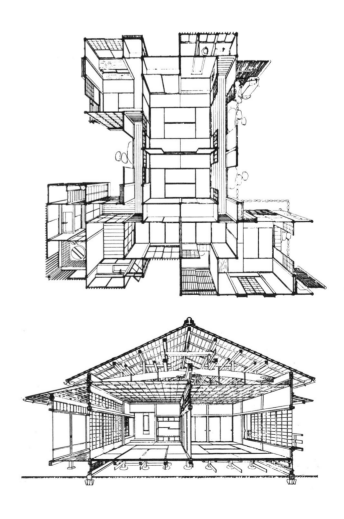

Left) Tibetan tent – exterior and section. Though it is necessarily movable,
he basic elements are those of the Chinese house; the pole in the centre symbolizing the axis of
he world; the hearth, the sacred fulcrum of the dwelling, also centrally placed;
bove this, the opening to heaven – and to let the smoke out.

city like Hangchow would occupy a complex of buildings set at right angles to one another or positioned in parallel lines. The whole stretched back, in an intricate arrangement of porches and roofs, from the front gate with its protective gods set on either side to prevent evil spirits from entering the house. The separate buildings of the house served separate functions. These were not, however, the mundane offices of bedroom, dining-rooms and so on. One room or pavilion might be designed for listening to music or for admiring the moonlight or for banqueting or, its walls possibly painted with snow scenes, for enduring the hot weather.

(Above) Modern Japanese house at Kyoto, built after a traditional plan though glass has been substituted for paper. The prominently projecting roof protects the outer walls and at the same time co-ordinates the house's design. Emphasis is placed on the use of natural materials, for example, bark on the roof.

Left) View from above and section of
traditional Japanese house with outer walls and interior
liding walls of paper in wooden frames; these screens
re skilfully and delicately made. The floor is
overed with tatami, *closely woven straw mats often*
vith borders of darker straw; they are a standard
ize – about one yard by two – and thereby
orm the unit of measurement for the house.

(Left) Rich Burmese house of a traditional type which betrays both Indian and Chinese characteristics.
(Above) Tibetan house at Lhasa, the home of a townsman of the middle class. It is a much more elaborate building than the largely rustic dwelling on page 62; the roof carries gilt ornaments and the windows are curtained.

INDIA

In India the structure of the house and the importance accorded it are influenced by the demands of a rigidly organized society dominated by religion. In this the most significant part is played by belief in Karma and in the continuous cycle of birth and rebirth.

The individual in classical and medieval India belonged to three great social organisms – his caste, his clan and his family. The family was the basic cell in the social framework. It was linked to the caste, in which its special position was defined, in the same way as the position of the caste in relation to other castes was also defined. The system allowed no social mobility.

The Indian world was also a world of villages in which the house consisted in essence of a hut, either rectangular or round, with a roof of palm leaves or straw. If the hut was rectangular, the roof was ridged; if round, the roof was conical or ogival. The timber framework was driven into the floor of beaten earth. To the three rooms of the house was a single entrance and a single window. The bedroom lay to the north, the living-room to the south, and the kitchen in the middle. The walls were of beaten earth and cow dung. The roof was reasonably waterproof. There was little furniture and even fewer utensils: indeed leaves often took the place of pottery.

The Indian town house was more complex in plan and, depending on the income of the owner, better furnished. It was often several storeys high; its outer face looked to the street, its inner face to the garden. The curved roof of terracotta tiles was supported by bamboo beams and in some cases a terrace occupied part of the roof area.

A staircase with handrails of brick, stone or marble, or with banisters of wood decorated with coloured stones, led to the upper floors. On the first floor a verandah ran along the front of the house. On the upper storeys too there were balconies on stout supports. The top floor, lit by skylights, was used as the main storeroom of the house. These windows in the roof which were formed by an arch called a *kudu*, like the Greek letter *omega*, were made of wood and decorated with coloured mouldings. Since the roof curved up they

were visible from the street. The other windows, wooden-framed with heavy shutters and with blinds and curtains on the inside, were fitted with carved or latticed shutters on the outside.

Within the house the rooms were often divided by coloured curtains or wooden partitions. The floors might be of coloured mosaic. In the walls there were niches to hold statues of ivory or metal. And somewhere in the house, sometimes occupying the space of a room, was the family's strong room in which valuable possessions were preserved.

Space, comfort and colour – these were the basic features of an Indian town house and they were created by the carved balconies, the mouldings of the skylights, the handling of stone, brick and timber and by the brightly coloured bird cages hanging near the windows. It was above all in the use of colour that the Indian house differed from others in Asia, especially from those of the Far East. The use of materials clearly betrayed the conception that a house was a deliberate architectural creation and not an urban accident.

In Indian cities as in western ones, houses grew upward rather than outward. The building space in a city centre was, accordingly, densely populated. *City centre*, is, however, a term which meant something rather different from what it does today. Both village and town houses in India depended for their situation on the outcome of magicoreligious rites which determined whether or not a certain piece of land was favourable for the building of a house. An unlucky site was, automatically, an unsuitable one. The area of a city was likewise limited not merely for defensive or organizational purposes but for magical and religious reasons: a limited area was magically favourable and religiously consecrated.

So far we have considered the Indian house constructed within the framework of Hindu tradition. To a considerable extent, Islamic domestic architecture resembles it. But one of the most significant events in the architectural history of the subcontinent and one to which the artistic tradition of Islam is related, was the advent early in the sixteenth century of the descendant of Tamerlane and Genghis Khan, Babur, the first of the Mogul

emperors of north India. Until the end of the seventeenth century, when their long drawn-out decline into impotence and foolishness began to manifest itself, the Moguls were dedicated builders. The greatest of them was probably Akbar, whose finest and strangest achievement was the city of Fatehpur Sikri, west of Agra, which Akbar designed as his capital and abandoned in 1584, fourteen years later, when the water supply gave out. It contained palaces, pavilions, courtyards, mosques, a temple and offices, the splendour of which rendered almost speechless English envoys from the court of Queen Elizabeth. It is still an extraordinary monument, the intricately carved red sandstone of which is as sharp in outline as on the day when Akbar deserted it. Better known, however, are the buildings raised by his grandson, Shah Jehan, during the second quarter of the seventeenth century in Agra and Delhi. Here we find the exquisite inlays in precious and semi-precious stones, in mirror glass and mother-of-pearl, the decoration with gold and silver leaf, the flower patterns reminiscent of Persian art, all facets of Mogul art and architecture. The flowers of the inlays were those of Mogul gardens, for the Mogul emperors cherished a fondness for gardens and fountains. One of their most lasting gifts to the country of their adoption was their formal gardens in which flowers, shrubs, water and, under a night sky, lamps were combined to afford delight to them and their court. There is, however, one curious omission from this *mise-*

(Above, left) The hut of a Naga chief in Assam. The roof slopes steeply for this is a region of heavy rainfall. A typical feature of the hut is the decoration of the outer walls.
(Above, right) Dwelling at Ayutthaya, the ancient capital of Thailand on the lower reaches of the Menam river. Piles are used in construction and the gracefully curving roof is of a type frequently found in Thai architecture.
(Left) Houses at Katmandu dating from the seventeenth to the nineteenth centuries. Elaborately carved ornament on façades is a common feature of Katmandu houses.

en-scène; though they and their craftsmen used painted brick in their buildings, they seldom incorporated the beautiful enamelled tiles common in Iran and throughout the Moslem world. Only two palaces, one at Gwalior, south-east of Agra, the other at Chitogarth in Rajasthan, made use of such tiles for ornament. Even so, apart from the fact that their use is very limited, those at Gwalior belong to a slightly earlier period.

The smaller houses were often simple huts and repeated the plans of the village houses. Usually they were huddled below the walls, both inside and outside the city. Or, as in Rajputana, now Rajasthan, they gathered round the fortresses of the Rajput nobles who opposed the Moslem invaders. The main characteristic of these fortresses was their framework of columns and stone beams strengthened at the joints and cemented with marble lime on strips of copper or lead. The windows were slim arrow slits. The single entrance was guarded by a massive gatehouse. In this castle – as in the house-fortresses of fired bricks and beaten earth of the Maratha to the south of Rajputana – the people of the villages or, perhaps, of more than one village could take refuge with their belongings in time of danger. Such a shelter was the great fortress of Chitogarth to which reference has already been made, one of the most important monuments in Rajput history, besieged three times – once in the fourteenth and twice in the sixteenth century – each time with disastrous loss of life to the Rajput clans, women as well as men.

More than fifteen centuries before, however, the area of India that was for long most exposed to foreign influence was the north-west. Here contact was maintained, with varying degrees of success, with the Greek kingdom of Bactria, carved out of the Persian empire of Darius, and one of the many legacies to Asia of the campaigns of Alexander the Great. Here too there developed the style of art now most often described as Gandharan, in which Greek and Indian elements merge; there are, indeed, Gandharan friezes that are more reminiscent even of Rome than of classical Greece. Architecture was affected by this fashion from the west; the columns depicted on the friezes, for example, are markedly Greek. The incipient Greek talent for town planning also travelled east to what is now northern Afghanistan and the structure of some towns in this region seems to betray a Greek or Hellenistic origin.

On the northern and eastern fringes of India and within the region influenced by Indian styles and traditions, we find that these combine with styles that are Chinese in origin. Frequently, styles were adapted to suit another material. In the mountain state of Nepal, for example, wood is used extensively and it is probable that the designs fashioned in it, especially decorative designs, were originally intended to be translated into stone. Over the centuries, however, timber took its place. The carved wooden sculptures of porch pillars, balcony rails, architraves, brackets, skylights, windows, gratings and doors of all sizes among the older houses in Katmandu are recognizably Indian in origin. But the building of which they form so decorative a part may have a carved, projecting roof of a pattern more common futher east.

In the great cities of the Khmer empire in Indo-China, such as Angkor Wat and Angkor Thom, public monuments such as temples, monasteries, libraries, galleries and sacred towers have survived to prove their artistic debt to India. They were built of stone and have resisted the attempts at annihilation by the engulfing jungle. But ordinary houses were of wood and earth and have left no trace of their existence: of the people who inhabited them we know little or nothing and, while it is easy to romanticize about the vanished Khmer empire, what kind of people were they who lived in the shadow of the incredible mass of the temple of Bayon?

Upper class Indian house at Jaipur in Rajasthan in India, in which balconies, loggias, terraces, rich in ornament, proliferate in tropical profusion. The splendid luxury of the effect is enhanced by the contrast between the painted walls and the natural tones of the woodwork. Such a house is an integral part of the thronging street life below even while it preserves the privacy of its inhabitants.

THE WORLD OF ISLAM

West of India, Iran, the frontiers of which reach out from central Asia and Afghanistan to Iraq or Mesopotamia, has few ordinary buildings of pre-Islamic date. The splendid remains of Achaemenian, Parthian and Sassanian buildings are monumental in character whether they commemorate gods or kings. Their value was the symbolic one of celebrating power; but of the majority of the people to whom the symbol was directed, we know little.

City life existed in Susa as early as the fourth millennium B.C. It was probably organized on very much the same lines as in Syria and Mesopotamia and some of the buildings were of brick and wood. Excavation of the fortress of Hasanlu, which was

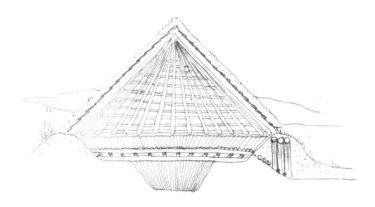

Section – after Vitruvius – of an underground hut in Colchis at the eastern end of the Black Sea. Excavations in this region have not, however, uncovered a dwelling to confirm this plan which, with its conical outline, differs from that of the subterranean houses commonly found.

very much later and can be dated to about the tenth century B.C., provides a hint of the appearance of a middle-class Iranian house of this period. The ground-floor walls of what have been called the House of Pearls and the House of the South have been uncovered. In each were two rooms. In prosperous districts, houses had more than one storey.

By the Sassanian period, from the third to the seventh centuries A.D., a preference had developed for the arch and dome which was to be maintained throughout the Moslem world. They occur again and again not only in public buildings and palaces but in dwelling houses in both town and country, and from then on throughout the east the white

outline of the *cupola* became characteristic of the landscape.

Although Islam owes much to the traditions in the decorative arts of Iran, it assimilated elements from elsewhere as the armies of the Prophet marched on their campaign of conquest. During this period of expansion, governors, caliphs and generals built for themselves castles and palaces, for use and for display.

These castles in Syria and palaces in Spain have been carefully studied and recorded, but little attention has been devoted to the houses of less exalted persons; to the dwellings, for example, of the merchants and craftsmen. The first

Afghan house at Kabul with the living-room at the top of the building. It may have been built as late as the eighteenth century, though its defensive appearance would indicate a date closer to that of the Mongolian invasions of the fourteenth century. The ornament is pre-Islamic in style and as such fairly common in central Asia. This is only one type of tower building: the variety is very great as the following pages show.

67

More examples of Afghan tower houses. In some cases they are military buildings which have been adapted as domestic dwellings. High on a city wall (above, right) a house is perched on the original structure. Elsewhere the upper part of the tower itself has been adapted to domesticity by the simple expedient of knocking windows in the wall (below, background). More often, however, an aggressive appearance is deliberate as in the octagonal tower (above, left). The upper living area has the air of a watchtower, set as it is above these massive walls. The tower (below) is a less coherent structure with its apparently clumsy combination of round and square walls.

flourished on the trade routes of Europe and Asia. The second prospered as a result of the skill and delicacy of his work which, in certain fields, surpassed that of his European contemporary. There were, too, the small farming communities, dependent for their markets on the towns and cities, of which traces have been found.

In the large cities, the working people lived in cramped, windowless houses and spent the greater part of their lives on the streets, in the *suks* or markets, in the shadows of the great mosques, in the public baths, or on the broad squares. Here they transacted business, were entertained, met friends, watched games, processions and parades. A picturesque effect was caused in many cities by the lack of town planning; in one or two instances this effect has survived, although in many cases the combined demands of traffic and hygiene have encompassed its destruction.

Cairo during the Middle Ages exemplified the Moslem arrangement of citadel, residential area and suburbs. In the shadow of Saladin's great citadel, houses were built, often as high as five or six storeys. They were built for defence and turned a blank face to the street, although the ground floor frontage was often let out as shops. But behind this daunting exterior were courts and gardens with flowers, trees and fountains. From the main court, at ground floor level, there opened the principal reception room as well the *selamlik*, the room where male visitors were received. A staircase led to the women's quarters, the *harem*, on the upper floor. There were no bedrooms or dining-rooms as such. Meals were

Even in those areas of Afghanistan which suffer less from the attentions of bandits, domestic architecture
still has a closed, defensive appearance, the outcome of a basic and justifiable sense of insecurity. It is lightened,
however, by hints of the country's Hellenistic past. The pillars and loggias of the buildings (above right)
belong to a tradition that goes back to the campaigns of Alexander the Great: a similar tradition has influenced
the decoration of some of the more heavily fortified houses (above).

(Below) Houses at Konya in southern Turkey. This nineteenth century building is typically Turkish
with its projecting upper storeys which introduce light and air to the upper parts of the house.
Wood was widely used as a building material throughout the Turkish empire and the older parts
of Turkish towns indicate how skilfully it was worked.

Bedroom and living-room of a nineteenth century house in the
southern Caucasus. The central hearth is built of flat stones; above
it, suspended from the chimney, is the chain on which pots were
hooked. The chimney is shaped like the base of a pyramid; it is
very similar to that of the semi-subterranean dwelling in the Hunza
territory (page 65).

eaten wherever the head of the house wished, and bedding stored during the day in wall cupboards, was unrolled at night in any room. Furniture was minimal – chests for clothing and valuables, braziers, candle-stands (so fashioned as also to form little cupboards) and stands for the large trays from which the household ate their meals.

In similar fashion, elements from Iranian private houses of the Sassanian period survived into some of the more important middle class houses of the Ommayad and Abbasid dynasties. The use of the *liwan*, the recessed portico that later spread through western Islam, is part of this older tradition.

In the noble Ommayad house, three spacious rooms with an alcove gave on to one side of the large central courtyard. In an Abbasid house of similar standing, in the area of Samarra, there were several courtyards with many rooms opening from them. On one of the shorter sides of the house, there was always a large, rectangular reception room with a *liwan* at the end of it. During the hot season, the inhabitants of the house remained as much as possible in the coolness of the interior.

In Spain the mingling of Islamic architecture with Spanish produced a variety of styles that are usually grouped together as Hispano-Mauresque. The most noticeable change involved here was the use of the patio which was later to achieve great popularity in America, especially in Central America.

The hold of Islam upon Europe lasted longest in the Turkish empire. The Turkish house in those parts of south-east Europe that were formerly Turkish, as well as in European Turkey, differed from the traditional classical or Byzantine house of the region in its use of wood. As a rule, the rectangular, often windowless ground floor, made of brick reinforced by wood, forms a base to the light, well-ventilated living floor above. This wide-windowed upper storey projects beyond the ground floor to afford a view on two or even three sides. Where a second storey has been added, it may have a completely open loggia or gallery and there are tiled stoves for heating. The Turkish house thus reflects the practical spirit and capacity for organization of its builders.

Houses of some of the more prosperous residents of Sana, capital of the Yemen. (Working class houses consist, for the most part, of single, square rooms). They are built of unfired brick, ingeniously decorated with motifs some of which belong to a tradition older than Islam.

OCEANIA

Although Oceania is not part of Asia, its houses are very like some types of Asian houses and some may derive from south-east Asian models.

Dwellings of a very primitive kind are still found in Oceania. Aboriginal tribes, such as the Wonkonguru who live on the shores of Lake Eyre, still make use of such shelters today. They still build beehive-shaped huts about 3 feet high. In their settlements, the chief's hut, which faces north, dominates the group by being sited on higher ground than the rest. The wooden frames of the huts are covered with mud, canes or pieces of bark. The village's supplies of food and water are safeguarded from predatory dogs by being placed on a platform high in the midst of the houses. A little distance off, a windbreak of two walls set at an angle protects the villagers from the worst of the prevailing wind and heat.

But the most characteristic dwellings of Oceania are those built on poles. The reasons for this type of construction are many – protection from reptiles, rodents and other wild animals; from enemies or thieves, from damp or floods. The poles, formed from tree trunks on top of which the houses are built, may be no more than several inches high or as much as 10 feet. As a rule the huts are rectangular with two rooms in one of which there may be a

Canachi hut in New Caledonia. That it belongs to an important family is indicated by the totemic designs of the central pole and the wooden panels set on either side of the doorway.

fireplace. The verandah gives light to the house and also serves as a meeting-place for the men, a playground for the children and a working-place for the women. Where the hut is at some distance from the ground, an access ladder is provided which can be pulled up for security at night.

In Melanesia, though use of the quadrangular hut, probably imported from Malaysia, is widespread, there are also conical buildings, often reserved for 'the man who has been given breath', that is, the wizard or *shaman* of the community. In New Guinea and the Caroline Islands, wooden houses are found again, often built on a stone base. In New Zealand among the Maoris the wooden house possesses a special grace, not just because of the beautifully carved pillars but because of the elaborate harmony of the plan itself.

(Left) Upper class house in the village of Obulaku in the Trobriand Islands off Papua.
(Below) House roofed with palm leaves in the Fiji Islands. The shape of the roof is reminiscent of those of the Far East.

(Above) An evident hybrid is the batak *house of Indonesia in which Asia combines stylistically with Oceania. Even in its humblest forms, this house is well planned and beautifully balanced; the carved and painted ornamentation is always lively and skilfully executed. The plan varies little: the house rests on piles even where water is not an important factor. It has a single living-room and above that is the granary, covered by a densely thatched roof, pointed in order to discourage evil spirits.*

REASON AND BEAUTY

THE MIDDLE AGES AND THE RENAISSANCE

During the centuries when Rome was mistress of the world and Roman legions maintained the *pax Romana* from the Euphrates to the Tyne and from the Nile to the Danube, small outposts of individualism persisted. The advantages of the Roman villa were generally acknowledged but it was not the only type of dwelling erected during the period of the Empire. Here and there, in parts of Gaul, for example, the habit continued of building in wood. It continued actively through what used to be known as the Dark Ages — too much light has recently been thrown on them for this misnomer to be allowable — encouraged, rather than otherwise, by the prejudices of invading barbarian tribes from beyond the old boundaries of the Empire.

It is probable that for centuries both types of house were erected, in some cases side by side — the villa or a recognizable adaption of it, and the timber-framed hall. Their occupants would enjoy a considerable measure of luxury, would reap again the advantages of trade with the east (the Crusades, above all, re-forged Europe's links with the Levant), and might even have begun to take an interest in the world outside their own four walls. For a period in the early Middle Ages, houses were built with doors and windows facing onto the streets. Their comfort was maintained and even enhanced, but the outward-looking design in housing was short-lived, at any rate in Italy where political disorder persuaded house-owners of the desirability of a return to the ancient pattern of blank street walls.

The medieval city was cramped, dirty, pestiferous, smelly, confusing, ill-lit, not so much badly planned as completely unplanned; and authors of many nationalities have been at pains to commemorate in the most unflattering terms the principal disadvantages of their least favourite towns. Occasionally, they praised a city in which they did not have to live: William Dunbar, the fifteenth century Scottish poet, scarifying Edinburgh and lauding London, is an example.

For most of the inhabitants life in these cities was brutish and almost certainly short, and they were in no position to realise that it was nasty. At the top of the social scale, however, the quality of life improved as the Middle Ages lumbered on towards the Renaissance. House furnishings improved in design. The kind of furniture fashioned for a medieval house was still, for the most part, substantially the same as that used in a Roman or post-Roman house — chairs, tables, beds and chests. But by the beginning of the Renaissance period, the assigning of separate roles to separate rooms had begun. The consequence was an elaboration of the furnishings required for these rooms. It was a slow process. For many centuries and even well into the modern period, rich and poor alike in certain parts of Europe used one room only for eating, sleeping and for the general business of living.

Detail from the Finding of the Body of St. Ercolano, *one of the series of frescoes painted by Benedetto Bonfigli about 1460 in the chapel of the Prior's Palace in Perugia, now the National Gallery of Umbria. The rest of the painting depicts Perugia besieged by Attila and the composition as a whole is dominated by an impressive view of the city. Here we see the city walls and the church of St. Ercolano with massive wall broken by romanesque arches. Behind them are tower houses and other, smaller dwellings: the curved Roman tiles are still in use.*

ITALY
From the ruins of Rome

The oldest records we have of the medieval house in Italy are vague and often contradictory. When the Roman Empire fell and central government, already enfeebled, abandoned control, and the rule of law was suspended, for a while the social life of the people was drastically affected. In a sense, the situation that faced many of them was a reversion to a more ancient society than that of Rome, to a more primitive way of life, in which each family fended for itself, hunted and fished and foraged for its own food, built its own shelter and tended its own livestock. Refugees from the cities fled to the countryside for safety, or, in the case of refugees from Aquileia and other cities in the north-east of Italy, to a group of islands in a lagoon which later became the city of Venice. The word for *house* underwent a change in meaning in Italy. The Latin *domus*, the substantial stone-built dwelling, was not the precursor of the medieval Italian house. It was from the hut that the later house evolved. Italy has seen, indeed, the abandonment of many forms of housing. Their remains are still visible in the countryside, especially in the more remote areas where ancient dwellings are used as byres, stables or toolsheds. There are the deserted heaps of rubble in Istria that in a more developed form are the *trulli* of Apulia, the forlorn haybarns that sometimes house animals, and the thatched huts built of wood or branches which are sometimes found in the fishing villages.

Until the fifteenth century, Italian towns were no more than a huddle of huts about a group of important public buildings. The large house illustrated here is an example of a more ambitious type of dwelling. The portico, the original nucleus of the building, serves as a covered barn. It is, however, separate from the other rooms – kitchen and bedrooms – all of which are upstairs and reached by a ladder. The house has progressed sufficiently from the primitive hut to permit of a more efficient and comfortable dispersal of smoke from the cooking fire; it is emitted not through the door or through a hole in the roof, but through a chimney which the builders have placed between the outer and inner walls or contained in an earth and brick structure.

In the Middle Ages as in earlier periods, climate and available materials influenced the planning of the house. In the south of Italy, the traditional house was designed to catch every breath of coolness and every drop of rain. In the north the object was to ensure protection against rain and even flood. The raising of Venice out of the waters of a lagoon has been achieved by the use of piles as foundations. Through the stormy centuries of Venetian history, moreover, the lagoon itself with its shifting sandbanks and uncertain tides was the city's ultimate deterrent and indeed it was never taken by storm by an enemy. The son of Charlemagne, Pepin, early came to grief in it. Attacking the city which then occupied the islands in the centre of the lagoon, the Rivo Alto, or Rialto, he required to find a way

One of the casoni *or rustic houses still to be found on the plains west of Venice, especially on the lower River Brenta. The walls originally made of reeds are now of stone but the thatched roof remains to hint at the antiquity of this type of house. Comparatively few of them survive in use as permanent dwellings though they are often used by fishermen, especially in the delta of the Po, as temporary houses (or bothies) or as storehouses. Often they are brightly painted.*

through for his ships. One old woman, according to one story, was found to direct him. 'Sempre diritto', she pointed. And Pepin's fleet duly ran aground to the delight and advantage of the Venetians. Secure, the Venetians proceeded with the building of their city, with the government of their small but expanding republic and with their exploitation of those markets, especially at the eastern end of the Mediterranean, from which they derived the wealth to make the city one of the wonders of the world.

The availability of certain materials has had, of course, obvious effects on the houses built. It has occasionally created confusion for archaeologists and historians. Throughout the Middle Ages and indeed even later, the ruins of ancient Rome itself and the ruins elsewhere of Roman cities, towns and villas have proved a convenient source of easily worked building material. They provided dressed stone and timber. If the materials had to be moved, this was not too difficult, for the buildings were usually close to a road or river. In many cases the new huts were built up against the more imposing of the remaining ancient monuments – monuments which were, moreover, rather too large to be easily dismantled. In this fashion, for example, medieval Rome was built in the shelter of the ruins of ancient Rome: it is probably also true to say that it was largely built with the ruins of ancient Rome. And on the outer rim of Rome's former empire, the barbarians who had presided over its downfall plundered Roman walls to build shelters for themselves. It was a practice that persisted for more than a thousand years. Stones that were first dressed by the builders of Hadrian's wall are even now part of north country and border farmhouses and steadings.

Wooden house near the old quay on the San Trovaso Canal in Venice. It is a rare surviving example of a kind of dwelling that demonstrates clearly how builders in the Middle Ages made use of their materials, and how access to upper floors was gained – by external ramps and staircases – before the technique of building internal staircases was developed.

House on the slopes of Mount Vesuvius at Boscotrecase. Since Boscotrecase was almost certainly destroyed by lava in 1631 and again in 1906, the house is not old but its plan is: houses like it have been built for several millennia on the shores of the Mediterranean.

The ruins of the Theatre of Marcellus in Rome, begun by Julius Caesar and finished by the Emperor Augustus in 13 A.D. It rose to two and possibly three storeys and could hold 20,000 spectators. In the fourth century it was partly demolished and during the twelfth it was turned into a fortress. In the sixteenth, the Savelli and later the Orsini family took it for a palace which later passed to the Sermoneta family. Its career is typical of the way in which ancient public buildings were adapted as, or formed the basis of, private dwellings during the Middle and later ages.

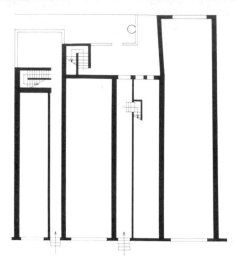

Elevation and plan of medieval tower houses at Lucca. In this type of house, the wall at street level is unusually thick but is less solid on the upper floors of which there may be as many as four or even more. The form and purpose of the building did not, however, prevent the use of the ground floor as a shop or store: the living-rooms were above.

Castle and city

In the period that succeeded the fall of Rome, traditional methods of land tenure in Italy were weakened and in some areas disappeared. They were replaced, however, by the feudal system. It was not indigenous to Italy but was an importation from countries north of the Alps, rendered necessary by widespread need of protection from marauders and made possible by the advent of the feudal lord, a man with sufficient resources to provide that protection.

Detail of the series of frescoes painted by Ambrogio Lorenzetti (c. 1290-1348) in the Sala della Pace in the Palazzo Pubblico in Siena: it is taken from the famous fresco on good government and supplies us with a view of the towers, palaces, shops and streets of Siena itself.

Detail of the Raising of Tabitha *in the Brancacci chapel in the Church of the Carmine in Florence. This fresco, it is now agreed, was painted by Masolino da Panicale shortly after 1425 though it is also claimed that his pupil, Masaccio, had a hand in the lay-out of the townscape reproduced here. It seems likely that Masaccio, whose interest in people and their houses may have been greater than that of Masolino, would have found room in a religious painting for these middle class houses, usually neglected by painters of the period.*

In Viterbo, during the Middle Ages one of the most important cities of Latium in which several popes took refuge from Rome, a medieval quarter survives near the church of San Pellegrino. It includes towers, working class houses and middle class houses. These last form an interesting group with their arched, barred and romanesque mullioned windows, and their entrances on to narrow alleys. One of the best examples is the small palace of the Alessandri (below), an excellent example of fourteenth century private building with its austere façade relieved by the wide arch and balcony of the upper floor.

Self-sufficient communities were established in which each man had his part to play; his position in society, as a vassal of the feudal lord, was clearly defined. The earliest type of feudal castle, a primitive tower, developed from the fortification of a mound or 'motte' with a timber palisade and ditch. In this tower, keep or donjon, the ground floor, usually windowless, was most often used as a store. On the first floor were the living quarters of the lord and his family, though in some cases this might be given over to the garrison of the castle, and the living quarters were then accommodated on the floor above with, where it existed, the chapel. A courtyard or bailey separated the keep from the outer walls. Around the walls of the castle were the huts of the lord's dependents who, in time of peril, took refuge with their belongings within the fortifications and reinforced the garrison. From these simple beginnings there developed the massive fortresses of Britain and France, for, as the art of war grew more complex and sophisticated, so did the art of fortification. Some were so heavily defended that they could not be taken by force but only by treachery or, in a few cases, by starvation. In Britain, comparatively few early castles survive in their original simplicity. However, those of Windsor, Edinburgh, and Caernarvon exist today to demonstrate the complexity of medieval castellated architecture with its succession of walls and courts, its multiplicity of towers, and the consummate skill of the medieval mason who dressed the massive stone blocks and fitted them together to defy an attacking enemy – until the advent of gunpowder defeated them. Walls and, in particular, towers were crowned with battlements and, a slightly later development, with machicolations, a technique the Crusaders brought home from the Levant which involved the projection of the battlement on supporting corbels, a feature which facilitated the discouragement of invaders with boiling oil or lead.

At the heart of the castle there remained, however, the keep, which still housed the lord and his family and from which the defence of the fortress was directed. And, since the castle as a whole was built not for comfort but security, even the lord's quarters were not, by modern standards, lavishly furnished. There were tables, chests, stools, a chair for the castellan himself, perhaps another for a guest, the 'state' bed, and tapestries on the walls.

Houses in the towns and cities also developed in complexity as the wealth of these communities increased and greater thought was devoted to house design and town planning. The structure of a house was still liable to alteration as a result of accident, whether political or natural: the interiors of some of the older houses in Italian cities have been drastically altered during periods of political disorder. Or, as in the case of the Palazzo Davanzati in Florence, the accepted pattern has been simply abandoned: here the palazzo, built in the local fashion of dressed and undressed stone, lacks the battlements generally found on such a building. Instead there is a beautiful open loggia, sheltered by a generously overhanging roof that protects the front of the building and anyone walking below it.

During the period of the free communes in the twelfth and thirteenth centuries, when the cities took to themselves a greater measure of independence, an impetus was given to the framing of statutes which had as their objective the good and order of the community. It was a period that was to influence the formation of modern Italy six centuries later, for in it was emphasized that love of freedom which reached fruition in the united Italy of the nineteenth century. It was, however, this same love of independence and fear of losing it that persuaded the communes to look to the building of their city walls.

That there was a building boom all over Italy during the fourteenth century is indicated in the laws then promulgated relating to the building of brickyards, to the improvement of town planning and in particular to the control of the appearance of those buildings which fronted the city's main streets. The fresco by Ambrogio Lorenzetti in the Sala della Pace in the Palazzo Pubblico in Siena, executed in the first half of the century and dealing with the effects of good government, shows what is probably a typical medieval townscape. There are the tower houses with their battlements, the houses with projecting eaves, the plastered walls and the walls of dressed stone, the loggias jutting out over the street, the windows with their pointed arches, the balconies, the narrow streets.

The artist has focused his attention clearly on the most important buildings of the city. For information about the buildings inhabited by ordinary people, we must look elsewhere. From time to time they appear in the background of miniatures; more often they feature in documents recording lawsuits. Their style was almost certainly much the same as that of their more ostentatious contemporaries.

Some typical examples of fourteenth century houses have, however, survived on the Ponte Vecchio in Florence. In Perugia and Viterbo as well, it is still possible to acquire a satisfactory idea of

Palazzo Davanzati, in the old centre of Florence, takes its name from the family who lived in it from the sixteenth to the nineteenth centuries. The building itself is fourteenth century and its defensive appearance bears out Stendhal's comment that those houses made one understand the dangers of the streets about them. The Palazzo Davanzati's solid masonry and massive doors present an appearance of security. Within, the hall itself is like a guard-room; beyond it, however, the rooms of the palace possess both elegance and charm.

the appearance of a fourteenth century house and shop. On the ground floor is the workroom, shop or tavern which gave directly on to the main road or street. At the back of it was the storeroom and the stair to the upper floor. In fourteenth and fifteenth century houses one room was usually reserved for living and eating while the other rooms served as bedrooms for the master of the house, his family, his servants and his apprentices. The methods of display of the goods for sale downstairs added, as it developed, to street furniture, for merchandise was set out in front of the shop and protected by a moveable wooden trellis. This shelter projected over the street and protected the customer too. A row of shops, each with its protective shelter, created a kind of gallery; in effect, a shopping arcade. There was nothing novel about the arrangement: the same feature was found at Pompeii.

In Florence a distinction was drawn between shops where the owner lived and the 'house with a small dwelling space' in which, in all probability, the owner did not live at all. In one document in the Florentine archives, the type of building that combined the function of shop and house was called a *laborerium*. The owner of a *laborerium* was, it is clear, a pillar of the community.

Merchants and craftsmen

According to a custom most widely observed in the eastern Roman Empire and in part perpetuated by the medieval guilds, all craftsmen who practised a particular craft were compelled to live in the same district. In the Italian communes they were able to co-operate to improve their individual skills and their products. House building techniques improved too. By the dawn of the Renaissance, moreover, wealthier citizens were in a position to employ such craftsmen. Many cities retained their medieval towers. In parts of Tuscany the castle remained a fortress, formidable and warlike, within the fortified city itself. The towers of San Gimignano still stand to show us what a fourteenth century city may have looked like, at a period when families and groups of families looked to their own defence.

But in Bologna, for example, the porticos supported by octagonal columns, which shade the streets of the late medieval centre of the city, showed the shape of Italian cities to come. They indicate the increasing importance of commerce and with it the growing affluence of the people.

As the middle classes grew richer, as the conditions under which they lived achieved at least a measure of stability, they began increasingly to concern themselves with the comfort, convenience, and appearance of their houses. City administrations framed legislation compelling the straightening of streets – Lorenzetti's painting gives us some idea of how tortuous these could be. Limits were set to the projection of upper storeys – these could darken the streets almost completely. Regulations were issued about the removal of rubbish from the inhabited sections of the town. Fires and furnaces were strictly controlled, for the enduring nightmare of the medieval town was fire. Lamps, it was also directed, should be set in front of shrines. This was a most practical form of piety, for at night these lamps also provided street lighting.

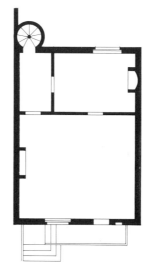

Plan of a medieval Italian house. At the front (below) beside the entrance was the shop: behind this lay the large room, the storeroom, which led to a courtyard on to which the stable faced: the dwelling house was on the upper floors.

Another plan of a medieval Italian house. The building may not have included a shop. Here, the passage to the staircase is at the back, behind the main family living-room.

Façade of the Ca' da Mosto on the Grand Canal in Venice. In spite of the restorations and additions that have been made, this remains one of the most interesting and characteristic examples of the Venetian-Byzantine house of the fourteenth century. Especially worth noting are the first floor windows with their arcades of six arches and the marble capitals and cornices, the decorations of which recall the importance of the da Mosto family in Venetian history as navigators and explorers.

...etail of a fresco by Domenico Ghirlandaio (1483-1486) from ...e Sassetti chapel in the church of Santa Trinità in Florence, with ...e portrait of Pope Innocent III confirming ...e rule of St. Francis. In the background is a middle class ...ouse with shops on the ground floor.

The Palazzo della Giudecca, now the Casa Ciambra in the old ghetto of Trapani in western Sicily. This is a late fifteenth century building in which a number of decorative traditions combine, among them the Gothic Catalan of the windows.

In the district of Rome where, during the Middle Ages and later, the city's inns were concentrated, was the Albergo dell'Orso where Rabelais, Montaigne and Goethe stayed – and Dante too, according to tradition. The building has been extensively restored but sufficient remains to indicate the appearance of a medieval building.

(Preceding page) The east side of the Piazza d'Armi, the courtyard of the Castello Sforzesco in Milan. Fragments of ancient buildings have been built into the walls of the courtyard: on the left, part of a Renaissance house from the Via Porrone. Beside it is part of a fifteenth century house from what is now the Via Torino.

The new frontiers of the Renaissance

In the background of Mantegna's *Martyrdom of St. Sebastian* (c. 1481) in the Louvre, there are houses of a kind that are still found in every corner of Italy. There, among the ruins of ancient buildings, shopkeepers have settled with their families. On an almost inaccessible crag is the castle of the feudal lord. Beneath it, scattered over the countryside, are the houses of his dependents. The characteristic structure of these buildings speaks of a past and a tradition that must be understood, if we are to comprehend the nature of Italian architecture during the Renaissance.

The new architecture was based, above all, on an awareness of the classical world. At the same time, windows of perception were being opened on new wonders. The barriers imposed by distance and outworn prejudices were being overthrown. Men were beginning to look out at the world beyond their own villages or towns or cities. They examined the products of other countries and found them desirable. They looked – either directly or by hearsay – at other ways of life and speculated on imitation. Like the Romans before them, they were enthralled by the east, by the luxury that came from the countries of the Levant. From there they bought furniture, leather goods, fabrics and metalwork with which to adorn their houses. This process was and is most noticeable in Venice whose ships carried these splendid cargoes to the west. Venetian merchants maintained depots all over the eastern Mediterranean. First the merchants themselves acquired a taste for the customs and styles of the east. Then, when they went home, they took with them the exquisite fabrics, the works of art, the furniture, to beautify houses in Venice, to which were added the oriental characteristics that would make them a suitable setting for these trophies.

The Ca' da Mosto on the Grand Canal, with its porticos and loggias still reflected in the water, is a typical example of the house of an enterprising Venetian merchant. This *domus de statio* – that is, dwelling house – belonged to a famous navigator who like his more celebrated compatriot, Marco Polo, faced dangerous journeys and unknown hazards for the sake of trade. His house was his office and his warehouse. The portico on the ground floor was used for the loading and unloading of goods. Nevertheless it is elaborately decorated, for Venice did not subscribe to any pretensions of equality as regards housing. Only one building in the city, admittedly, was allowed the name of *palazzo* – that of the Doge – and only one square qualified for the name of *piazza* – that of San Marco. But for the rest, the principal families of the Serene Republic did not suffer from false modesty. They were rich, and the world should know it and acknowledge it. They covered the façades of their houses with coloured marble and added splendidly decorated windows and balconies from which they could watch the passing show of life in the city, and keep an eye on the competition. The character of the ornament of these great 'palaces' betrays the close contact of the city with the east. It is, however, also pointed out by certain scholars, Patzac and Ackerman among them, that more than any other, the Venetian house long preserved in its structure traces of the Roman house. In the social structure too of the city, something of the ancient Roman pattern was preserved. The Venetian citizen with full rights enjoyed the same prestige as the Roman *civis* did in the Roman Empire.

Venice was not, of course, the only community in Italy to be influenced by eastern styles. Other cities sent their trading fleets to the Levant and brought home more than merchandise. In Sicily, moreover, Europe, Asia and Africa met, and their differing artistic traditions combined to affect not only the artistic future of the island but also that of the south of Italy. The people of Amalfi, south of Naples, first fought against – for their resistance to the Saracens, the city's rulers were entitled Defenders of the Faith – and then traded with the Levant. The relics of their commerce are still visible in the city's architecture. One of Amalfi's satellites, Ravello, was influenced meanwhile by the Norman-Moorish styles of Sicily, most notably in the Casa Ruffolo which, with its courtyards and gardens, most clearly betrays Arab fondness for running water and greenery.

But in Milan, the city that was Venice's rival in northern Italy, architecture developed on quite different lines during the Renaissance. During the reign of Ludovico 'il Moro', Duke of Milan, at the end of the fifteenth century, the city underwent enormous changes, largely as a result of the presence in it of the great architect, Bramante. In the interest of the beauty of the city, huts and hovels of medieval origin were demolished to make room for the splendid new buildings with their double loggias, spacious courtyards and broad halls. Of the pre-Bramante period, one of the few houses to have survived is the Casa Borromei which belongs to the beginning of the fifteenth century. It is probably characteristic of Lombard architecture of the time with its plastered and painted walls and finely decorated plasterwork.

In Milan, as in other cities in Italy, the more prosperous citizens were beginning to think about comfort at home and about the possibility of efficient heating. In practice, the structure of the new houses depended on the placing of the chimney, and an accurate guide to the social and financial standing of a family was the number of rooms in the house that were either heated or capable of being heated.

The same citizens also considered separation of

Elevation and plan of the ground level of what used to be the Casa Cocchi and is now the Casa Serristori in the Piazza Santa Croce in Florence. The design of the building is attributed to the architect Bartolomeo Baglioni, better known as Baccio d'Agnolo (1462-1543). This remarkable house has two upper storeys divided from each other by heavy cornices and each floor is decorated with pilasters. The plan shows the importance of the entrance hall and the wide staircase leading to the upper floor.

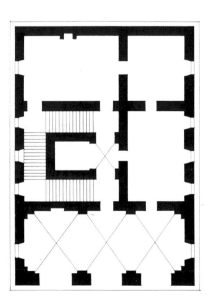

Built on the site of an earlier Venetian-Byzantine building for Marino Contarini, the Ca' d'Oro may have been designed by Marco de Amadio and built first by Lombard workmen under the direction of Matteo Reverti, then by Venetians under the supervision of Giovanni and Bartolomeo Bon. It was finished by 1440. Its name, the 'House of Gold', probably derives from the rich gilding and paintings that once decorated the canal façade.

(Opposite page) Detail of a painting by Giovanni Mansueti probably of 1506, depicting the miraculous healing, in 1414, of the 'little girl of Benvegnudo' who, paralysed from birth rose from her bed at the touch of three candles which her father had set near a relic of the Cross (Venice Accademia). The cure takes place in a richly furnished room, reached by an external staircase. This interior, that of a Renaissance house, gives a strong impression of a stage set.

Plan of the ground level of the Ca' d'Oro on the Grand Canal in Venice. The canal is at the front. Here too is the portego or portico. At the opposite end is the beautiful courtyard with a well and an open staircase to the upper floor: it gives, via a Gothic doorway, on to the calle at the side of the building.

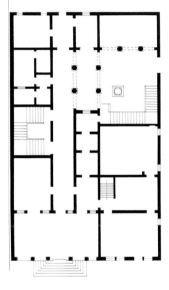

the functions of certain rooms. The custom was disappearing of having all-purpose rooms in which the family ate, drank, slept and worked. But before separate rooms could be planned, houses had to be built with staircases and passages to allow the division to take place. In the north of Italy, the problem of heating and, later, limitations of space and the consequent high cost of land presented difficulties in the separation of rooms. A solution was eventually devised for humbler buildings in the shape of galleries running along the front or round the inner walls from which apartments opened. In richer houses, external staircases made each floor independent of its neighbours. The *Bovolo* attached to the Palazzo Contarini in Venice, a spiral staircase shaped, allegedly, like a snail, is one of

the finest examples of this kind of staircase (see p. 354). The staircase was, in fact, the only part of the Palazzo Contarini that was actually built at that time and why the building was left unfinished at that stage is unknown.

To the south, in Rome, the re-planning of the house was begun at an earlier date. An example is the Albergo dell'Orso in Rome, which was already standing in Dante's time and which provided fairly comfortable lodgings for the large numbers of pilgrims and ambassadors who came to the papal city. Travellers enjoyed there the comparative comfort of lodgings in inner rooms while the porticos and arched loggias outside them sheltered their servants. This design was later modified and while the open loggias survived on the upper floors, the porticos gradually disappeared.

To know what a noble house in Venice looked like at the period of its greatest splendour during the Renaissance, we must look again at a painting, this time at the *Miracle of the Cross* by Giovanni Mansueti. The room is, clearly, a reception room, reached by a broad staircase and facing on to the front of the house. In the other walls, doors open into the family rooms. Like other interiors of this and later periods, it has the appearance of a stage set.

The Ca' d'Oro, too, displays the fundamental characteristics of a Venetian house with its portico, courtyard, outside staircases that lead to the mezzanine and upper floors, the loggias, the reception rooms, balconies, battlements, the well with its parapet, and the cistern in which rainwater was collected. All the decoration is, typically, restricted to the façade while the side walls remain plain, and even today the profusion of marble, bas-reliefs, statues, columns and the gilding which gives the building its name, still draw the eye.

The opulence of the Ca' d'Oro was, of course, very Venetian. More typical of the Italian Renaissance as a whole are the civic buildings of Florence. By the time that Brunelleschi came to design the marvellous dome of the cathedral, the Florentine house was already enriched with porticos, loggias and decorated façades. In the fifteenth century, the city's noblest families deserted the fortified towers of their ancestors and began to build in dressed stone. When Leon Baptista Alberti designed the Palazzo Rucellai in the middle of the fifteenth century he created what is perhaps the most noble example of civic architecture of its time. The projecting roof slopes away into the sky; a splendid open loggia accommodated ceremonies and receptions; the many windows, even on the ground floor, bear witness to peace and stability.

In Florence and in other cities throughout Italy, professional architects designed houses and palaces that grew ever richer and more complex. The Dario family in Venice commissioned Pietro Lombardo to build them a house several storeys high on the right bank of the Grand Canal. It was faced with marble and delicately decorated with coloured stones. Front, rear and corner windows commanded views of the canals for the house faced on two sides on to waterways and there were doors to both, each with its own landing stage. The door on the landward side opened beyond a tiny garden on to a very narrow alley. Over all rose the tall, elegant chimneys which the Venetians – for practical as well as aesthetic reasons – preferred. The house was worthy to be dedicated *genio urbis* – to

Fresco by Domenico Ghirlandaio from the series painted between 1485 and 1490 in the sanctuary of Santa Maria Novella in Florence. The birth of St. John the Baptist is shown as taking place in a plain, stone-walled Renaissance room with a coffered ceiling; the bed is surrounded by chests which took the place of wardrobes and were used as seats.

A Tuscan chair or a stool with a back (Vienna, private collection) which bears the crest of the famous Strozzi family of Florence. Tradition alleges that it was carved or designed by the celebrated sculptor Benedetto da Maiano: it certainly dates from the fifteenth century.

the genius of the city – the words inscribed on one of its cornices, especially if, as is likely, the interior included such a room as the one depicted by Carpaccio in his *Vision of St. Augustine* – a beautifully fitted private oratory and study with desk, tools and a collection of books and antiques.

Rainer Maria Rilke told the story of an old sailor whose great joy was to watch the sea from his own house. Unfortunately, the houses around him grew higher and higher so that in order to retain his view, he had to add one storey after another to his own. It was the kind of thing that happened fairly often in the coastal cities of Italy. In Genoa, for example, like Venice the heart of a mercantile and maritime empire, the houses seem to reach out towards the sea. There is often a theatrical air about the palaces of the city's great families such as the Dorias, about the multiplicity of courtyards and the broad, sweeping staircases,

but in the background there is always the sense of the sea and ships.

The theatricality betrays a later development in Renaissance taste: Mannerism. When it was not over-classical or foreshadowing Baroque over-emphasis, Mannerism elicited from architects some very strange but often pleasing works. Elegance and a kind of humorous ingenuity sometimes produced delightfully unexpected results. Consider the setting of the Corsini house in Florence beside the Ponte Santa Trinità, with the beautiful fountain and small open loggia on the first floor; or the many other Tuscan and Roman buildings of the period with their gardens and fine decorations, and the amazing freedom of imagination combined with harmonious discipline which they show so plainly.

Another strain influenced Italian architecture at this period. It derived from the oppressive solemnity, almost bombast in some cases, of the Counter-Reformation on the one hand and Spanish occupation on the other. A wish to escape from a depressing present into an apparently golden past nourished a taste for the architecture of that past. At its worst and most ostentatious this escapism produced monumental buildings without interest and without the grave good sense of the originals.

Between the fifteenth and seventeenth centuries, the marriage chest was painted, carved or inlaid, or decorated by a combination of the three. Earlier chests were plainer, such as this from Terracina and dating from the eleventh to the thirteenth century (Rome, Museum of the Palazzo Venezia).

Artists at home

Painters, sculptors and jewellers were considered in the Middle Ages as craftsmen, and like all craftsmen they were grouped together in their particular districts of the cities. There most of them lived and worked in surroundings which, though often cramped, had, by the dictates of guild statutes, to be sufficiently lit not only for the artist to be able to see well but for his customer to be able to inspect him at work. In fourteenth century Florence, painters occupied two narrow streets – the Corso degli Adimari and the Via San Bartolo, now a single street, the Via Calzaioli. As in the jewellers' shops on the Ponte Vecchio, the ground floor was lit from the door and shop window. The family usually lived on the upper floor although in Florence, from the fourteenth century onwards, artists' families tended to move to the outskirts of the city, whereas in Siena and Venice, for example, they continued to live in the same building that housed the workshops.

At that period shop rents were fairly high. Masaccio, who made do with part of a shop, paid two florins a year (about £23 or $55 today). He was however, an unlucky painter for all his genius and when he died he was deeply in debt. One of his creditors, the otherwise unknown painter Niccolo di Lapo, spent seven florins a year on his studio and this was the usual amount. Sculptors who needed more space might pay as much as 15 florins for their premises.

From 1450 onwards, Ghiberti's studio in Florence faced the church of Santa Maria Novella; a hundred years later the historian Vasari was still in time to see the enormous furnace that had been used to cast metals. The studio was occupied by Ghiberti's sons who were goldsmiths. At the end of the century it was rented by Perugino. Later it was used by Bonaccorso, the nephew of Ghiberti, who was also a metal-worker. From him it passed to his son, a sculptor and painter. Equally well-documented records of other houses exist in the city.

Painters and sculptors of the Renaissance, like painters and sculptors of today, took care to find studios suited to their exact needs and in some

Palazzo Pandolfini in Florence, designed by Raphael about 1520 and built by the Sangallo family for Gianozzo Pandolfini, Bishop of Troia. It was probably left unfinished as the doorway without any superstructure seems to suggest.

Palazzo Uguccioni in the Piazza della Signoria in Florence, built by Mariotto Folfi about 1550 after a plan sent from Rome and variously attributed to Michelangelo, Raphael and Sangallo. (Below) The delightfully mannerist building designed for himself by Federico Zuccari when he left Rome to live in Florence in 1578.

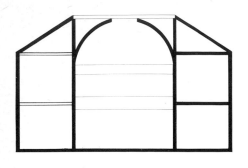

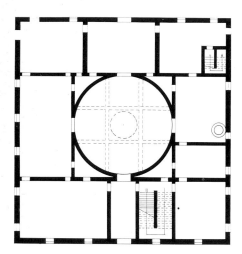

Section and plan (left) and bird's eye view drawing (right) of Mantegna's house at Mantua, as its designer, almost certainly Mantegna himself, intended it to be: it has been much altered by restorers. It was probably a round villa, a villa rotonda of a type that, under the influence of classical ideas, was becoming increasingly popular in Italy in the closing years of the fifteenth century. It may have been intended that the central courtyard should be closed by a dome similar to that of the Pantheon in Rome.

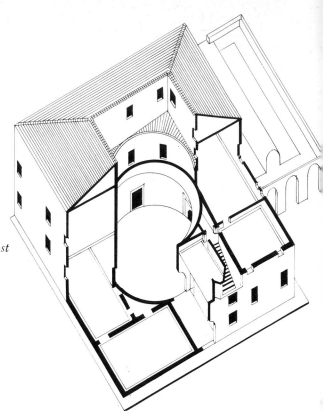

As proof that the villa rotonda *had increased in popularity as a town house, here is a plan similar to that of Mantegna's house, found among the designs drawn up by Francesco de Giorgio Martini for his treatise on civil and military architecture (1482).*

These interesting plans of houses for artists and artisans are also by Francesco de Giorgio Martini.

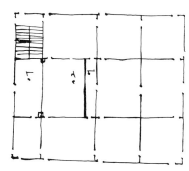

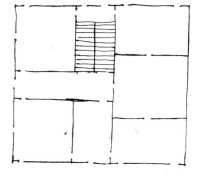

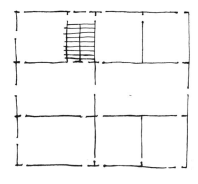

points, such as the direction of light, their needs were the same. One or two artists, such as the medieval painter Cennino Cennini, otherwise so careful about their professional affairs, did not concern themselves about good lighting. It was Leonardo da Vinci who stipulated that the artist's workroom should face north, should have windows that could be opened as required, and should have walls painted grey to assure a proper diffusion of shadow. He also recommended that the room should be small so that the artist could concentrate in peace. Unfortunately for us his studios in Florence, Milan, and also in France, have all disappeared.

Raphael's house in Rome was also destroyed and the loss is doubly distressing, in that it seems to have been built by the great Bramante. (His father's house at Urbino survives but has been rather spoiled.) The houses of other Renaissance artists have also been either destroyed or so drastically altered that serious examination of them as studios in which these painters worked is hardly possible. Mantegna's house in Mantua tells us little or nothing about the painter's studio despite the lengthy debates that have taken place about the house's function as a dwelling and a gallery. The house has been altered since the time of Mantegna and has also been subjected to rather unwise restoration.

Artists have fared badly on the whole, as regards the survival of their houses. It may or may not be true that Michelangelo's famous house in Florence, the Casa Buonarotti, was bought for his

nephew, but it is certainly the case that what we see of it today is almost entirely the result of early seventeenth century restorations. In the same way the house of Giulio Romano in Mantua suffered later transformation, and that of Vasari, better known as an art historian than as an artist, was in part put to other uses.

But their works survive and in the case of Michelangelo these include masterpieces of architecture such as the new sacristy in the church of San Lorenzo in Florence, the buildings on the Capitol in Rome, and, of course, the magnificent dome of St Peter's. While he was the greatest Renaissance architect, there were lesser figures who still left behind them buildings of outstanding quality, among them Sansovino, Alberti, Palladio, Scamozzi, and Vignola. They confirmed that architecture was no minor art.

(Above) View of the small house, often referred to as Raphael's House, in the grounds of the Villa Borghese in Rome, painted from the Villa Medici by Ingres (1780-1867) during his stay in Rome. The painting is 6½ inches in diameter. (Now in the Musée des Arts Décoratifs in Paris).
(Below) The same house painted from a different angle, this time by a painter in water-colours whom a pencilled note identifies as 'Giacomo Romano'. The date given is 1814. The house owes its name to the tradition that Raphael occasionally stayed there but there seems to be no suggestion that he designed it. It was an excellent example of the less than palatial urban villa. It was demolished in 1849.

GOTHIC AND MOORISH SPAIN

During the greater part of the Middle Ages, house design in Spain underwent no substantial change; it was still based on Roman patterns. Within the walled cities, space was so precious that town houses were usually small. As a rule they were rectangular with a courtyard or a small light well in the centre or towards the back. In the houses of the richer families, a staircase led to the first floor while the other floors were reached by internal stairs.

Few examples remain now of this kind of house and most of those that do have been radically altered. Windows have often been added to them, thereby changing the house's appearance and character, and changes in the way of life of the inhabitants have necessitated reorganization of the house's internal structure. Documentary evidence of the appearance and plan of a medieval dwelling is also often unsatisfactory, and is rendered even more confusing than the passage of time would lead one to expect, by the imprecision of the terms used.

By the early Middle Ages, however, the rulers and nobles of Spain were already beginning to abandon their earlier austerity. The process was fostered by the richness of the booty brought back in the campaigns against the Moors. Furniture and other objects in daily use improved in quality and design and the lay-out of the house, especially among the middle classes, who probably enjoyed more stability in their daily lives than the largely itinerant kings and nobles, gradually evolved towards greater comfort and convenience.

Among many examples of Romanesque building, there is a thirteenth century house known as the 'house of the Dukes of Granada' in Estella in Navarre, which preserves the characteristic pilasters and round-headed arches of the period on the ground floor. On the upper floor are double windows with small arches supported by columns enriched by remarkable decorated capitals. In Segovia, twenty modest houses in the 'canons' quarter' near the Alcazar have survived, again with the round-headed arches of the period as part of the façades. In Leon, the remains of a house of the late twelfth century are contained within an Augustinian convent. Fragments of a number of houses of this period, or a little later, also survive in the mountain districts of Aragon and Catalonia.

In Catalonia, several private houses of the thirteenth century show a mixture of Romanesque and Gothic elements in their design. Others from the last decade of the same century show in fully evolved form the regional style which was to appear to such advantage in fourteenth and fifteenth century architecture. These are fine buildings with sober façades of dressed stone, each stone being of moderate size. Sometimes the façades are adorned with towers and with twin or three-light windows flanked by slender columns with characteristic and undecorated capitals. On the upper floors a gallery is supported on fine pillars or columns. Above it again is a large projecting cornice. Some of these houses accommodated small shops at street level which opened to the front through arches that served as show cases.

The internal plan of the houses varied. The

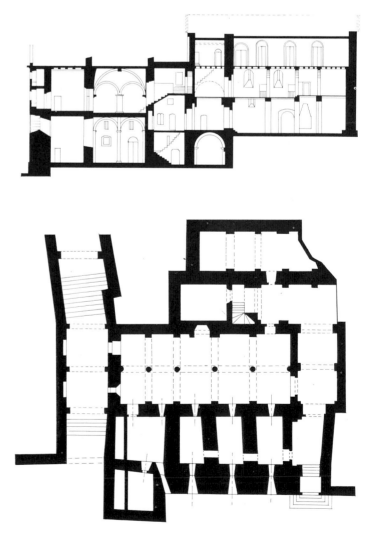

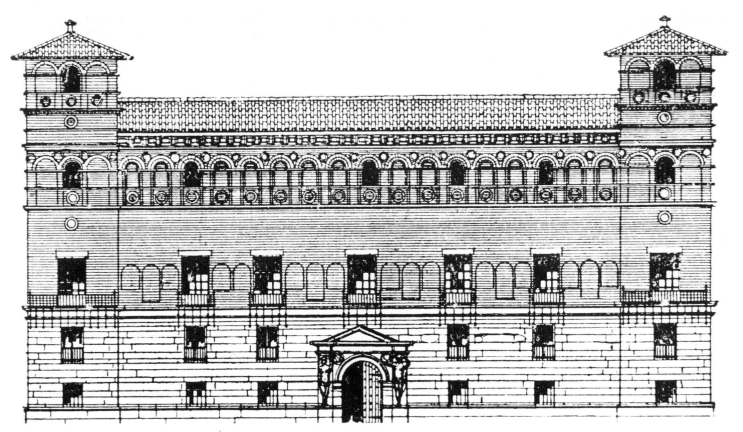

House of the Counts of Luna at Saragossa (today the Court of Appeal), built about 1550 by the architects Juan de Amezcueta and Juan de Albirtu. The main entrance, flanked by caryatids and adorned with a relief depicting the entry of the anti-Pope Benedict XIII (a member of the de Luna family) into Rome, was by the French artist Guillaume de Brimbez. As in many sixteenth century buildings in Aragon, the lower part is of stone and the upper of brick.

simplest were about 16½ feet wide. Others, slightly larger, were built round a small courtyard. In the grander houses, this courtyard assumed a more important role and was surrounded by galleries and arches supported by slender columns. On the ground floor were the stables, storerooms, servants' quarters and, as a rule, the kitchen kneading trough and oven; the kitchen also sometimes served as the dining-room. Another staircase led from the courtyard to the upper floor on which were the principal reception room and several bedrooms; these bedrooms often had ceilings supported by stone arches. Above this floor was the attic and the terrace or loggia. At the back of many of these houses was a garden or, more usually, a kitchen garden.

There are a number of examples of this kind of house in Barcelona, among them one of the thirteenth century in the Calle del Correu Vell and several in the Calle Montcada. The Casa Berenguer de Aquila belongs to the fifteenth century

(Left) Section and plan of the Archbishop's Palace at Santiago [d]e Compostela which dates in its present form from [th]e seventeenth century. The original building, [th]e residence of Don Diego de Gelmirez, the first Archbishop [o]f the city in the twelfth century, is still, however, [id]entifiable (in the section, lower part, right.)

and the Casa Padellas, the house of the archdeacon Luis Desplá, shows signs of Renaissance taste in its detail.

In Valencia domestic architecture was influenced by Catalan styles although, for historical reasons related to the reconquest of the south of Spain, these were modified by Aragonese forms. In the city of Valencia itself a few middle class and aristocratic houses remain, among them the remarkable *Admiral's House*. They have, usually, an open staircase in the courtyard, large windows with two or three lights divided by small columns: in the public rooms the beams are exposed and painted. All this follows the Catalan style but the gallery with its small arches running along the top of the façade suggest the fashions of Aragon. There, despite a dynastic connection with Catalonia which lasted for several centuries, Catalan Gothic was not particularly popular. Only a few examples of pre-sixteenth century domestic architecture remain in Aragon to show us its principal characteristics. There is a recently restored house in Saragossa, the house of Rodrigo de Mur at Huesca, and a group of dwellings at Teruel. The Palace of Ayerbe already betrays Renaissance influences.

To the south, in the Balearic Isles, the architectural reconquest was as complete as the military and Moorish styles disappeared under the onslaught of Catalan Gothic.

In the northern part of the Iberian peninsula we find a mixture of Gothic and Romanesque. In Santiago de Compostela, one of the most important centres of pilgrimage in Europe in the Middle Ages and as a result a very rich city, the thirteenth century nucleus of the bishop's palace survives, basically Romanesque in style. So too do a few houses in Gothic style. Asturia is richer in Gothic architecture of the Middle Ages. It includes the large Casa de Valdecarzana at Avilas (fourteenth century) with its mullioned window with two lights; the fifteenth century Rua house at Oviedo; and another, undoubtedly the finest, at Salas where the change to sixteenth century styles is foreshadowed.

To the east, near Santander on the northern coast of Spain, the oldest remains of civic architecture are thirteenth and fourteenth century tower houses. Square, low, heavy, with few windows, their appearance is deliberately forbidding. In most cases, all that remains standing are the stout outer walls. The tower of the Merino family at Santillana del Mar retains, however, its inner structure of wood. Towers of the succeeding fifteenth century

tend to look less formidable. The tower of the Infantado at Potes and that of the Borgia family at Santillana were more comfortable than their predecessors. In the same region, some merchants' houses remain in good condition, among them that of the Portalon at Vittoria, built of wood with a framework of bricks.

Though many Gothic dwelling houses were built in Castile and Leon during the Middle Ages from local materials – mud blocks, wood, fired and unfired bricks – few are left. The buildings that have survived are those which were constructed of dressed stone, such as the so-called *priest's house* at Aguilar de Campo (Palencia) and another at Aranda de Duero (Burgos), both of them middle class houses. More splendid than these, however, is the house of Dona Maria la Brava at Salamanca, probably the most beautiful house in Castile of its period – the end of the fifteenth century – and certainly very characteristic of it.

In a number of cities in Castile, among them Guadalajara, we find several buildings of the sixteenth century built after similar patterns. They are usually constructed of small mud blocks, bricks, plaster and timber. The façades are generally of brick and they are decorated with high pediments and sometimes a series of blind arches. Behind them are wide courtyards with, on two sides, porticos two storeys high; the public rooms take their light from the porticos. The interior is ornamented with moulded plasterwork and coffered ceilings.

Buildings in Gothic style are rare in Andalusia save near Jaén which was reconquered from the Moors as early as the thirteenth century. In this frontier area we find, accordingly, buildings similar to those of Castile; such houses exist at Baeza and Ubeda. To the west in Extremadura, we find again houses in the same style though two different forms may be distinguished. In one, the houses – such as those in the ancient city of Caceres – are still basically fortified keeps. The other type is entirely non-military in character: an example is the palace of the de la Roca family at Merida – despite the towers that flank its front.

The expulsion of the Moors was the event that dominated the medieval history of Spain. The long campaign culminated in the conquest of Granada in 1492 when Ferdinand and Isabella received the

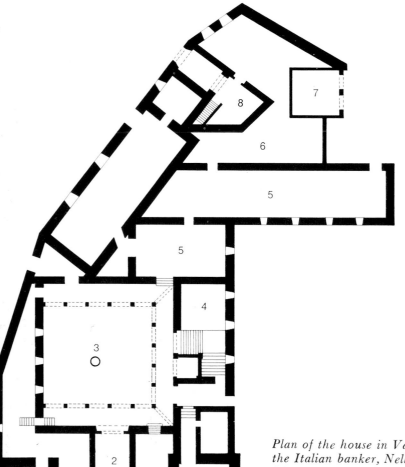

Plan of the house in Valladolid built from 1576 by the architect Juan de la Lastra for the Italian banker, Nelli. Two towers (1) were added to the front in 1594 by Pedro de Mazuecos; the main door is by Diego de Praves. The hall (2) leads to the patio (3). On the left are narrow stairs to the cellar and on the right the winestore (4). Behind this are the stable (5), and beyond them are the servants' quarters (6) and a shed (7) with a small courtyard (8).

keys of the city from the last of the Moorish sultans. But though the Moors had been defeated, they left behind them an enduring architectural inheritance.

Both in palaces and small town houses, the basic element of the Spanish Moslem house is the courtyard. From it the rooms received light and air. The outside of the house presented a blank face to the narrow winding streets. The plan of the oldest type is shown in a group of huts at Alcazaba (Malaga). These eleventh century dwellings are cleverly arranged to make the most of the limited space available. The patio, almost square, is reached through a hall which connects with the street, the two doors being unaligned. On either side of the patio is a portico from which open small rectangular rooms. The latrine was always placed as far as possible from the rest of the house and particular care was given to the draining of water. In the case of a Moorish house on two storeys, the upper floor, reached by a staircase, repeated the lay-out of the one below. No room was set aside as a kitchen since moveable stoves were used.

The fourteenth and fifteenth century architecture of the Alhambra in Granada repeats this structure. Two innovations appear here, however, the porticos on the shorter side of the patio, and the alcoves set in the far walls of the inner rooms, the floor before them being slightly above the level of the rest of the room. These alcoves, which are not found in the east, may derive from Hispano-Roman or Visigothic houses.

Moslems who submitted to the Christian kings and became their vassals were called *mudéjares* and *mudéjar* is the name given to the particular form of art executed by Moslem artists and craftsmen or by Christian artists and craftsmen trained in the Moorish south. It produced a certain type of dwelling planned round the nucleus of the patio, with two porticos, and rooms on all sides. There is no element of defence about the building and there are no monumental staircases, but behind the richly decorated main door, there are bathrooms, then unknown in Christian houses and palaces. The rooms were decorated with ornamental stucco and coloured tiles, especially on the lower part of the walls and on the floors below the coffered ceilings.

In Seville where no Moorish houses have been

Patio of the Palacio de Aguilar in Barcelona, now the Picasso Museum. The building seems to have been the work of Juan de Berenguer de Aguilar and is probably fifteenth century in date though it incorporates elements from the fourteenth and sixteenth centuries. It is one of the most important buildings in the old part of the city.

Patio of the Casa de las Conchas — *the House of the Shells* — *at Salamanca, so called because of the shell reliefs which decorate the façade. The patio with its double gallery is richly decorated with lions' heads surmounting shields bearing the fleur-de-lis above the first row of columns: above the second, the arms are set within shells. The building is an excellent example of early sixteenth century Spanish architecture.*

found, an important group of *mudéjar* buildings still exists. These range from the Alcazar built by Pedro I, King of Castile, to the fourteenth century house of the Count of Palma which is now part of the Carmelite convent of Ecija. In Toledo, mudéjar craftsmanship challenged the hold of Gothic and in Seville and Granada, its influence continued well into the sixteenth century. In Granada a beautiful group of houses built in 1570 by *Morisco* craftsmen survives; these were Moors who had been compelled to become Christian. The post-conquest buildings of Seville include too the palaces '*de las Dueñas*' and '*de los Abades*' and the extraordinary house of the Pilato family in which are mingled not only Moorish and Gothic elements but also Plateresque (literally 'silversmith-like'), the name given to the profuse and delicate decoration which closely resembled the work of silversmiths.

In Andalusia, towards the end of the sixteenth century, the design of the house became more severe, but the Moorish traditions were not entirely abandoned. This is clearly seen in the house of the Valenzuela family at Ronda in which the patio is typically mudéjar. Other houses that display similar characteristics can be found in Aragon and Extremadura and even in the Basque provinces.

Mudéjar influence is perceptible too in Portugal, for example, in the palaces and mansions of Lisbon and the Alemtejo where it is evident in the ornament lavished on windows and doors.

After the re-conquest of Spain and the discovery of America, the art of architecture developed quickly in Spain in the sixteenth century. New wealth flooded in from the New World and important new buildings were raised in the largest cities. Styles were introduced from elsewhere, with varying success. In Aragon, the Italian Renaissance style was interpreted with variations that crystallized into a completely recognizable local fashion. In the Basque provinces and in the north around Santander, importation merely laid the foundation for later development.

In Castile and Leon it was the period of their greatest splendour, and a fine example of the magnificent architecture produced is the *Casa de las Conchas* (the House of the Shells) built, it seems, in 1512 by Dr. Talavera Maldonado, university professor and city magistrate. In Burgos, though the houses of the rich merchants have virtually disappeared, one is still preserved, albeit sadly altered, the house of the merchant Andres de Maluenda in the Calle de las Coroneria. At Valladolid three houses command attention; the first built in the last quarter of this prosperous century by the banker Fabio Nelli de Espinosa; the second built a few years earlier for the lawyer Butron; and the third built for the great Castilian sculptor Alonso Berruguete. In Avila, the local granite imposed its own conditions, and many houses there indicate the harmony achieved between the material available and Renaissance taste. Several buildings at Toledo belong to this period, among them the house that is said to have belonged to El Greco. At Alcala de Henares there is the house of the physician Francisco Valles and at Almagro, near Ciudad Real, the house of a banker, one of the German

Fugger family. And finally, at the heart of the Spanish Empire, in the Escorial, there is the Gardener's House, charmingly built to the designs of Francisco de Mora.

In Galicia and the Asturias, the new styles were confined to certain towns. In Santander and the Basque provinces regional forms of architecture, modified by local climatic conditions, were beginning to evolve. In Extremadura, the region from which many of the early colonizers of America came, houses of remarkable richness in design are found in the towns of Cáceres, Trujillo, and Plasencia. The same towns were also enriched by the building of splendid Renaissance-style houses.

Andalusia, too, is rich in Renaissance buildings. During the sixteenth and for most of the seventeenth century, Seville expanded enormously and a number of examples remain of that housing 'boom'. Their lay-out is a development in Renaissance terms of the mudéjar models, the magnificent palace *de las Dueñas* and the house of the Pilato family, to which we have already referred. It consists, in most cases, of a wide hall with stables and storerooms on one side and the servants' quarters on the other. At the far end an iron gate led to the central patio. Around this on the ground floor were the kitchen, the summer dining-room, and the garden. On the floor above were the public rooms, small and large; bedrooms; the winter dining-room and the great richly decorated reception room of the house.

Another type of Andalusian house shows a closer kinship with the fashions of Castile. It is found at Baeza and Ubeda. At Ubeda, for example, a house

in the Calle Montiel built between 1510 and 1515 bears traces of Gothic influences but is nevertheless one of the first Renaissance buildings in the town. In the same town is the house of the Emperor Charles V's secretary, Francisco de los Cobos. At Cordova, the house traditionally believed to have belonged to the humanist Hernan Perez de Oliva was probably built about 1540; its façade is finely ornamented. An interesting sidelight is cast on the Andalusian style in the houses built in the Canary Islands. In Las Palmas many buildings survive which show clearly the adaptation of late Spanish Gothic to the decorative themes of the Renaissance.

In Aragon, as we have already noted, Renaissance architecture took on a character of its own. There we find buildings with simple façades, decorated with small towers at the corners and equipped with large arched doors, balconies with wrought iron railings and upper galleries with small arches and wide wooden cornices. Good stone was in short supply so that brick was used for the outer walls and for the ornamental sculptures. The plan of the house is centred on a large courtyard reached through a wide hall. On the ground floor, as elsewhere in Spain, were the service rooms – stables, storerooms and servants' quarters. Above, there was a series of spacious drawing-rooms with coffered ceilings. The widely spaced stone columns of the courtyard supported lengthy wooden beams. On the upper floor, small columns supported a row of arches, the whole being surmounted by a projecting wooden cornice. The staircase, usually divided, was often handsomely roofed by a Gothic mudéjar vault

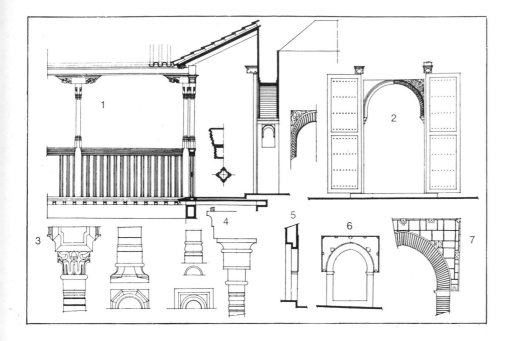

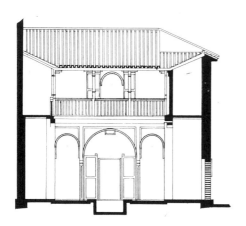

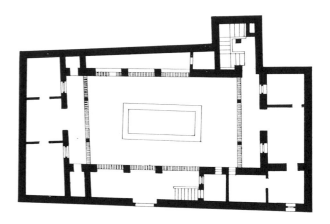

or by a coffered ceiling. Examples of this kind of house include the one that the banker of Saragossa, Miguel Zaporta, had built after 1546; an outstanding feature is its richly decorated courtyard. Another such house is the magnificent mansion of Barbastro where the poets Bartolome and Lupercio de Argensola were born.

In upper Aragon, houses built in regional style are found side by side with dwellings in which are incorporated elements of Renaissance design which suggest French rather than Spanish origins. An example of this is the palace of the Ribagorza family at Benasque.

Catalonia retained a preference at this period for the older Gothic tradition of lay-out and decoration, even in buildings which contain Renaissance elements. The new forms appear only in decorative detail; the façades are more richly decorated with sculptures; windows lose their small columns and gain pediments above the mainly square openings. These pediments may contain medallions in bas-

relief. Main doors take on additional importance with columns and projecting entablatures. But comparatively little building from this period remains. One of the most typical is, however, the Casa Judice at Barcelona which belonged, significantly, to a family of merchants of Genoese origin.

The Italian influence also emerges to the south, in Valencia, where a number of sixteenth century houses faithfully follow Italian patterns. But in the same region other houses adhered to the example set by Castile and Aragon. In the Balearic Islands, links with France and Italy as well as Catalonia and Valencia produced a characteristic architecture, quite unlike that of the rest of Spain.

Throughout the century Portugal remained faithful to the sophisticated, heavily decorated form of late Gothic architecture known as *Manueline*, so named after King Manuel I (1495-1521). This florid style was not, however, used at every level of society; until late in the seventeenth century even noble houses remained comparatively modest.

JOHN DRUMMOND

FROM SAXON
HUT TO TUDOR MANOR

*(Above) Fish House of the Abbots of
Glastonbury in Somerset, a stone building
of the early fourteenth century.
(Below, from left to right) Plans of the ground
and upper floors and a drawing of the façade
of the Manor House at Boothby Pagnell
in Lincolnshire, built about 1200.*

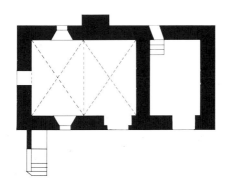 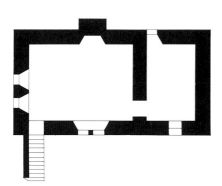 

Romanesque and Gothic architecture spread throughout England in the wake of the Normans and during the reigns of their Angevin successors. The buildings that survive from that period, however, are almost entirely cathedrals, castles or monastic foundations. *The Jew's House* in Lincoln and the manor house of Boothby Pagnell are rarities which probably remain because, unlike other dwellings of their period, they were built of stone.

Saxon thanes lived in halls which were, quite simply, enlarged huts, rectangular in shape, built of wattle and daub on a timber framework and with a thatched roof. Under this roof were gathered the lord, his family, his servants and his livestock.

A primitive method of construction involved the use of *crucks*, naturally curved trunks of trees. Two of them set in the ground and joined at the top formed a Gothic arch. A horizontal beam joined the tops of the arches and other horizontal beams sustained the weight of the roof. The walls were wattle and daub panels. Huts were built after this pattern

*(Right) Fifteenth century house
at Canterbury with its wooden
structure visible.
(Below) The Jew's House
in the Strait in Lincoln which dates
from the twelfth century; this
is one of the oldest houses in one of
the most historically interesting
cities in the United Kingdom.*

The cottage said to have belonged to Anne Hathaway, Shakespeare's wife, at Shottery, near Stratford-on-Avon in Warwickshire. The cottage, a picturesque Tudor building flanked by a charming garden, may be considered an example of the ordinary house of the sixteenth century. The ground level walls have probably been reinforced within modern times and the bricks on the first floor may replace earlier wattle and daub. The roof is thatched with straw, then the cheapest material and today, because of the scarcity of thatchers and the level of insurance premiums, an expensive luxury.

(Opposite page) Ockwells Manor at Bray in Berkshire, buil about 1465. As in Anne Hathaway's Cottage, the framewor is of timber but this being a manor house, the walls are o brick laid in herringbone pattern. An outstanding feature o the house is the large windows and here we see the begin nings of bay windows. The individual panes of glass are sti small and incorporate heraldic motifs.

(Left, above) The basic elements of the cruck-framed building, the two lengths of curved timber, the crucks, joined at the top by a purlin. As can be seen from the building (left, below), the height of which was about 19 feet, the crucks form the framework and carry the weight of the building from the ridge-pole to the base where the crucks stand on stone bases.

for centuries. Refinements such as the use of stone or brick were occasionally made. But the introduction of the roof truss which allowed greater areas to be spanned did not materially affect the popularity of the cruck-framed house.

At manor house level, however, building design did change. The dwelling of the feudal lord derived from the Saxon hall. Basically it consisted of a large rectangular room with a raised portion, perhaps at the end farthest from the door, for the high table

Elizabethan house at Mayfield in Sussex, built about 1575. It still has features in common with Ockwells Manor though only the second upper storey projects beyond the rest of the building. The magpie effect of black and white lath and plaster is splendidly Elizabethan.

100

of the lord and his family. A slightly later type of hall placed the lord's room on the first floor for reasons of safety – as at Little Wenham Hall in Suffolk, built about 1260.

The addition of a small two-storeyed house to the upper end of the lord's hall and the consigning of the kitchen and storerooms to a separate area wrought further changes in the design of the house and created the H-plan dwelling. Pitched roofs were set on the wings and the finishing touch was the addition of gables. Another gable was sometimes set over the main entrance. A good example of this ar-

space within the house. Or the demands of safety may have necessitated this method of building, in which the ceiling beams projected beyond the wall and were counterbalanced by the walls of the projecting storey above, the effect being to balance the weight of the upper storeys of the building in such a way as to cause the least possible movement of the framework.

A feature of building in England, which has become associated with Tudor architecture but is medieval in origin, is the mullioned window. It is very similar to the Italian Renaissance mullioned

rangement is Ockwells Manor in Berkshire. A fourth gable was added now and again in the interests of symmetry, although the desire for a symmetrical façade was rare before the seventeenth century. The country house often grew in haphazard fashion as extensions were added to accommodate a chapel, more living-rooms and storehouses.

In the towns, the wooden house on several storeys with a shop at street level was common throughout the Middle Ages. The most notable and picturesque feature of English medieval towns was the projection of the upper storeys, one above the other, over the narrow streets. It has been suggested that this was a survival of the porticos of Romano-British buildings, which were designed to protect the merchandise set out for sale below. It may also have been, it is argued, a means of creating more

and transomed window although the lights tend to be narrower and there may be several transoms or horizontal bars. The head of each light was often arched and the whole might be surmounted by a heraldic embellishment.

Under Henry VII and Henry VIII, a number of Italian artists and craftsmen worked in England. They left to us the splendours of Henry VII's chapel in Westminster Abbey and traces of Italianate decoration at Hampton Court but their stay had little effect on domestic architecture as a whole. Not until the reign of Elizabeth I in the second half of the sixteenth century, when the new Tudor aristocracy, enriched largely by the dissolution of the monasteries, were building their enormous, astonishing houses – to which they welcomed their queen during her endless progresses – did the influence of

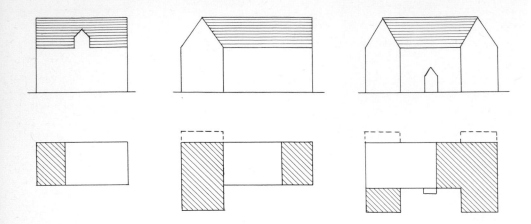

Plans and elevations of 'average' English houses in the sixteenth century. The H-plan house developed from the hall (left) by the acquisition of first one wing (centre) and then a second wing (right).

Italy bulk large in English architecture. And even then, the Englishman did not take to academic classicism with enthusiasm. Many Englishmen had travelled to Italy – and to Holland where mannerist motifs had achieved great popularity – and had inspected Italian buildings for themselves. But at home, haphazard use was made of Renaissance detail with results which are to the purist interesting rather than admirable.

The blame has been laid at the door of English conservatism, the same which persuaded William Langland to look on chimneys with distrust in the fourteenth century, and which provoked the Reverend William Harrison two centuries later to regret the loss of the old-fashioned English hearth, set in the middle of the hall – and filling it with smoke. This, the reverend gentleman said, was the kind of fireplace that Englishmen had used until the reign of Henry VIII, and smoke was really very healthy. (The adoption of the fireplace in England was apparently attended with the same reluctance as is its abandonment today.) But the fireplace, set in one wall of a room with a properly constructed chimney, was an innovation essential to the comfort and convenience of the house. It did not, however, become the focal point of the room until the Elizabethan age was well advanced. The bay window too was a Tudor innovation which, despite a period of eclipse in the eighteenth century, has retained its popularity to this day.

Much of the splendour of sixteenth century interiors lay in the fabrics used – the magnificent tapestries, the carpets (used as table and floor coverings), curtains and cushions. Furniture was still rather scanty and confined to benches, stools, chests and tables. The most luxurious piece in the house was probably the four-poster bed with its embroidered hangings. Chairs with backs were rare and

Grevel House, in Chipping Campden, Gloucestershire, built about the year 1400. In this ancient Cotswold wool town houses similar to this, once the homes of wealthy wool merchants, still survive.

reserved for ceremonial use; even at the end of the sixteenth century, Queen Elizabeth's courtiers were complaining of the discomfort of sitting on backless stools.

Floors were covered with straw or rushes or ferns renewed as often as the prejudices of the household dictated; Erasmus of Rotterdam found the practice unhygienic. Walls were limewashed or, in wealthier households, wood-panelled, often in oak; the panelling was often carved to resemble folded linen or *linenfold*. Such panelling or wainscot might be capped by a moulding and above it would hang a tapestry or arras, possibly imported from Arras. Staircases were af first spiral, or straight and narrow and steep until the technique was developed of inserting a staircase of more impressive dimensions without endangering the stability of the house.

Woodcarving in England at the end of the Middle Ages and at the beginning of the Tudor period achieved, as we can detect from details like *linenfold* panelling, a high degree of delicacy. During the Elizabethan period, styles and decorative detail, strongly influenced by Flemish originals, were heavier but in their vigour they reflect accurately the spirit of that age of exploration.

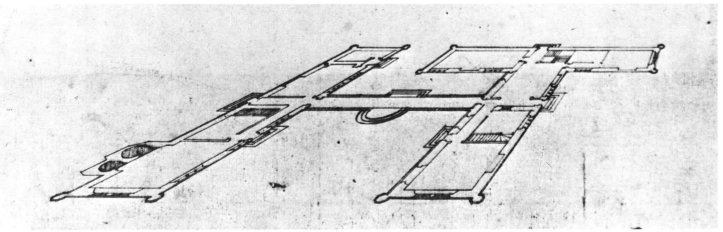

John Thorpe (1568-1620), land surveyor and possibly architect, was employed in the Office of Works from about 1583 until 1601. He is remembered, however, by reason of the book of designs preserved in his name in the Soane Museum in London; it contains plans for a variety of Elizabethan and Jacobean buildings, most of them domestic but there is no reason to believe that he designed them. Here perhaps he did design one, a house with the outline of his own initials.

DANIEL ALCOUFFE

COMFORT AND DISCIPLINE IN FRANCE

At the end of the eleventh century in France towns were no more than haphazard clusters of houses. Their heritage of Roman buildings was exhausted; the buildings had collapsed or were on the edge of ruin. New dwellings were being erected which contained more than a single storey but were usually built of wood.

But after more than a century of the Capet dynasty, growing political stability during the twelfth century encouraged the development of the country's economic life. The population of the cities began to increase and, indeed, new towns were established. The people of the cities took part, moreover, in their government, betraying as they did so a nostalgia for Roman tradition. They recalled too their memories of Roman building and out of the recollection there evolved the medieval French house.

Its builders took the best that tradition had to offer and combined it with the techniques and tastes that suited current needs and satisfied current preference. The result was a functional building, economically constructed from local materials, simple in plan, appropriate to the climate: and its decoration was restrained.

Stone and timber were plentiful in France in every region and were the principal building materials until the end of the eighteenth century. Some stone houses have survived from the twelfth century but few wooden ones pre-date the fifteenth century. But, whatever the building process, the plan was substantially standard and hardly changed until the sixteenth century. The house, roofed with thatch or curved Roman tiles, faced straight on to the street and consisted of one or two storeys above the ground floor. In the more crowded cities it might run to three storeys in addition to the ground floor. The large, well-lit room on the ground floor served as kitchen, dining-room, reception room and bedroom. Other smaller rooms either adjoined the large all-purpose chamber or were placed on the upper floor with the servants' rooms, wardrobes and latrines. In houses where the various rooms did not communicate with one another, they were reached from a side passage or an open gallery on the outside of the building. This gallery, possibly a survival from Roman practice, often faced on to the courtyard at the back of the house and some-

times there were galleries on several floors. In some cases a passage joined the main house to another group of buildings at the back of the courtyard.

During the fourteenth and fifteenth centuries, the plan of the French house continued to improve. Attention was devoted to lighting and heating – in particular to the position of windows, chimneys and staircases. The end of the Hundred Years' War in the fifteenth century was naturally accompanied by a greater feeling of stability and security. The middle classes set about building for themselves houses that were larger, more comfortable and better furnished; more important still, the arrangement of rooms was made more convenient. They began to decorate the exteriors of their houses. The ornament chosen was, for the most part, in the by now declining Gothic style but it was handled with admirable discipline.

But with the taste for ornament came the concern for fashion. Travellers to Italy brought back Italian fashions. There appear, accordingly, on buildings constructed after traditional patterns and decorated in the Gothic style, the classic motifs beloved of Renaissance artists – vines, candelabra, putti and medallions. Juxtaposition of these disparate elements provoked speculation on the nature of style. Artists from Italy came to work in France. Architecture became a subject of systematic study, the results of which were abundantly visible in the official buildings erected in the reigns of Francis I and Henry II. They indicate very clearly a growing interest in the imitation of the antique.

In the course of the development of this academic classicism, the old master builders of the Middle Ages were replaced by architects equipped by their studies to theorize on architecture, such as Jacques Androuet Du Cerceau. In his *Livre d'Architecture* (published at Paris in 1559) – 'contenant les plans et dessaigns de cinquante bastiments tous differens; pour instruire ceux qui desirent bastir, soient de petit, moyen, ou grand estat' – he describes a plan for a house for a person 'in the middle estate'. The building, he suggests, should extend over an area twelve-and-a-half tese (80 feet) wide and five-and-a-half tese (33 feet) deep, including the thickness of all the side walls: in other words, the building should be measured on the outside but without including the courtyard

(Above) Group of medieval houses in Strasbourg which even today, in its oldest quarter, preserves in the narrow winding streets the appearance of a town of the Middle Ages.

(Below) Romanesque house in the Rue de la République at Cluny. This district was built in the shelter of the famous Benedictine abbey after the disastrous fire of 1159. The house is built of the most readily available building material, stone, with a pitched roof, moderately thick walls and large windows. Like the other houses that were crowded into this area at Cluny, it had two doors at ground level. The main one, with the wide pointed arch found in many buildings of the period, particularly in Burgundy, opens on to the shop or workshop. The smaller, narrower and plainer door leads to the passage that runs the length of the house and gives access to a staircase to the upper floor: the staircase, as in other houses of the kind, whether stone or wood, rises straight up from ground level. As a rule, the houses in this district are not decorated on the outside or at most carry a few simple motifs on the upper part of the façade. This house's upper windows form a small, beautiful loggia with rounded arches resting on short columns. The arches themselves are decorated and the area above them is also ornamented with rosettes and arches in shallow relief.

or outer walls. The building is arranged as follows: from the ground level of the courtyard up to the cornice is three tese (18 feet) in height; from the ground floor itself down should measure two tese (12 feet) including the foundations. This makes a total of five tese (30 feet). For the lower floor, one goes down 6 feet under the entrance steps. The list goes on, implacably, pedantically accurate, conceding nothing to those eccentricities that make medieval architecture inimitable.

Fortunately, in the larger cities and especially in Paris, they succeeded in building houses without paying too much attention to the finer points of the theorists who found more sympathetic audiences in the provinces. There each region took what suited it and so the regional styles developed. The differences between them increased gradually; one was the size and placing of windows, hitherto strictly functional but now subject to fashion and the desire for symmetry. Certain aspects of the house remained the same throughout. The climate demanded pitched roofs and pitched roofs continued in use:

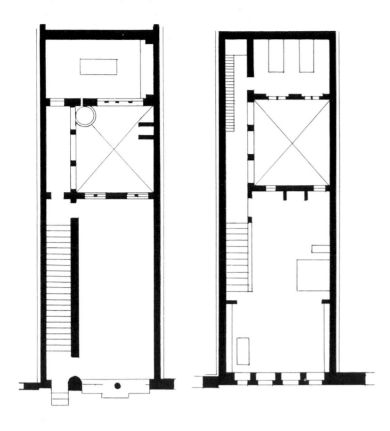

Plans of French Gothic houses. As in other medieval cities and towns of Europe, their builders built backwards and upwards from the narrow frontage (lower part of the drawings). As in the house at Cluny (page 105), the house on the left has two doors to the street, the smaller of which leads to the staircase. That on the right is similar; in both there is a vaulted room behind the shop or store that faces the street.

The present state of the Hôtel de Vauluisant (see opposite page). The arrangement of doors and windows, as in that of the house at Cluny, illustrates the practicality of medieval builders who placed them according to their needs. Here too we have an entrance surmounted by a wide pointed arch, the narrow secondary door, and the expanse of windows at upper floor level; the window arches are, however, more Gothic in style and incorporate trefoil windows. On the floor above them, the roof soars very steeply.

terraces in the Italian style were not practical.

Just as it had eschewed the excessively flamboyant decoration that was widespread at the end of the Gothic period, the French Renaissance house avoided the rigid classicism and ornamental extravagances characteristic of the period elsewhere. At the same time, however, it welcomed, with an enthusiasm probably unknown even in Italy, the variety that the new age added to furniture and furnishings.

This emerges from a number of contemporary inventories. In one ground floor bedroom of the house belonging to Henry II's chaplain, Gaston Olivier, the following items were listed after the death of their owner in 1552: a table four feet long and its trestle with turned legs; four walnut chairs variously upholstered in morocco leather or petit point; three stools, also walnut with turned feet; a cupboard and a cabinet of oak; two wooden bedsteads with any number of pillows, mattresses, quilts and blankets; a Turkish carpet; a framed oil painting on the story of Joshua; a walnut chessboard with its pieces; eight tapestries from Tournai of the *millefleurs* design; copper utensils for the kitchen; and 'in the dressing-room next door', a wardrobe and four chests that contained the chaplain's clothes and linen.

(Opposite page) Miniature of the school of J. Bourdichon o the late fifteenth century (Paris, École des Beaux-Arts showing the workshop of a furniture-maker and his tool still familiar in appearance.

The type of wood available encouraged French builders to use it as the framework for their buildings of stone or brick. They built the skeletons of their buildings with linking posts or struts and horizontal beams and filled in the walls with stone or brick, or a mixture of clay and straw. At first, the vertical posts were as high as the building, as they are here, in the house at Sens called 'Abraham's House' which belongs to the early fourteenth century. Then they were reduced to the height of a single floor and the upper floor was added above them.

(Below) Courtyard of the house of Pierre du Puy at Tours (about 1490). The structure and plan repeat those of earlier centuries but new details are added which are conducive to greater comfort and dignity. Brick and stone were used and, laid in either English or Flemish bond, were found to be strong enough to carry considerable weights and strains. The small tower on the right encloses a spiral staircase, also of brick.

French wooden chair, carved, with arms, and covered in fabric, sixteenth century. It is 58 inches high, 24 wide and 16 deep (Paris, Musée des Arts Décoratifs).

Early fourteenth century oak chest (68×32×27 inches) (Paris, Musée Carnavalet): one of the oldest known pieces of French furniture. It was made of thick planks (the technique of cutting wood thinly was not yet mastered) with sharp corners and covered with spirals of finely wrought iron. Originally it was painted: others of the same period were often covered with gilded leather.

Sideboard or buffet (62×43×24 inches) of the second half of the fifteenth century (Paris, Musée des Arts Décoratifs). In the fifteenth century, the closed chest was superseded by a style that was lighter. Here the framework is of solid supports and crossbars into which have been set thinner oak panels, so placed as to allow for shrinkage and expansion without cracking.

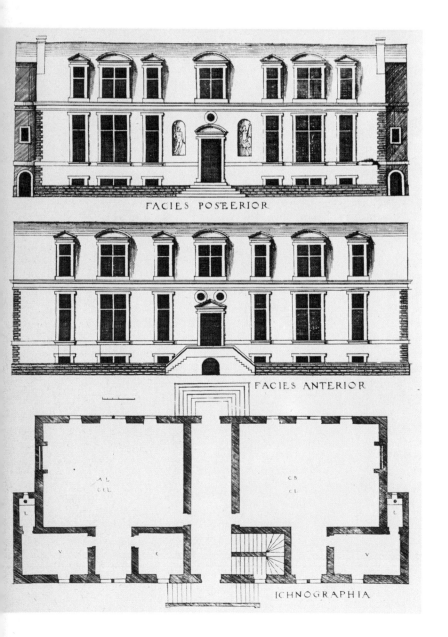

FACIES POSTERIOR

FACIES ANTERIOR

ICHNOGRAPHIA

Plate from the Livre d'Architecture *by Jacques Androuet Du Cerceau (c. 1510-1585). The rear elevation of the building (top) is interesting in its betrayal of Italian Renaissance influence in the classical lines, the symmetry and the niches with statues.*

ANNE BERENDSEN

DUTCH AND FLEMISH MEDIEVAL INTERIORS

The evolution of those gleaming spick and span interiors, with which we are familiar from the paintings of Dutch and Flemish artists, began towards the end of the fourteenth and beginning of the fifteenth century. As in other countries, the first essential was a more convenient arrangement of the rooms of the house.

In both Dutch and Flemish cities space was scarce. Street façades were, accordingly, narrow and builders built up and back. From a single, undivided room Dutch houses soared upwards into several storeys and, as a further refinement, the storeys were divided into separate rooms. There were usually two rooms on each floor, one behind the other, the front part of the house being known as the *voorhuis*. The main entrance opened straight on to the front room of the ground floor, which was high-ceilinged and well-lit. In some cases this *voorhuis* was used as a shop or workshop although, as the householder's prosperity increased, there was a tendency to divorce business from domestic premises.

But while he still lived at if not always above the shop, the room at the back, divided from the front room by a wooden wall, was usually the sitting room of the house. When an upper floor was added, the lower back room accommodated the kitchen and the stair to the cellar, and the sitting-room moved upstairs. A spiral staircase at the back of the shop linked the two floors. A *hangkammer* or hanging room was in some instances added to the back of the shop: this was then enlarged until it turned into a mezzanine floor occupying the depth of the *voorhuis*. The whole was covered by a tiled roof in obedience to local edicts, which dictated the use of tiles on wooden buildings as a precaution aginst the ever-present danger of fire.

In details of construction and even more in details of decoration, certain local differences developed in the regions of Flanders and the Netherlands. In Bruges, for example, we find that win-

The Bethlehem House in the Gasthuisstraat in Gorinchem between Rotterdam and 's-Hertogenbosch, built in 1566 and now used as a museum of local history. The façade is surmounted not by crowsteps as in an earlier Gothic period, but with elegant swan-neck curves, Renaissance in influence.

(Above, left) House of the Borluut family at Ghent (1175), one of the few surviving Romanesque houses in Flanders; the horizontal division of the façade is characteristic. The steps of the gable are ridged. (Centre) Gothic house at Bruges behind the Town Hall. The elegant mouldings on the upper windows and the unified fenestration are typical of buildings here. (Right) Van 't Sestich house at Louvain (1445). As in the house at Bruges — and in contrast to that in Ghent — the façade is divided vertically. The two windows on the second floor were a later addition for which two rose windows with their decoration were sacrificed. It is typical of the medieval architecture of Flanders and the Netherlands that a middle class dwelling like this, though richly ornamented, should be decorated with mouldings in brick rather than stone.

(Below) House on the Luttik-Oudorp Canal in Alkmaar from the first half of the sixteenth century. The decoration of the façade shows Renaissance influence; at ground level is a wooden framework.

dows are treated as a single decorative unit on the façade which is recessed around them. In Ghent there was a fondness for crow-stepped gables decorated at the pinnacle and on both sides; this style was rivalled by the pointed arch gable which was common throughout central and northern Flanders.

The common feature of architecture in the Low Countries in the Renaissance period, however, was the use of warm, red brick façades decorated or strengthened by inserted courses of, in most cases, cream-coloured or yellowish stone. Colour, against a grey northern sky, was important to the people of the Low Countries, and during the sixteenth and subsequent centuries was used with growing ingenuity.

The interiors of the houses of the Netherlands and Flanders were as splendid and elegant as those

of France and Italy. Colour was used with care and imagination, as paintings of interiors indicate. Light walls contrasted with dark oak beams and provided an admirable background to the carved furniture, the tapestries and embroidered hangings, the curtains, the polished copper household utensils, the cherished dishes and the brick or tiled floors. When the shutters were closed to keep the heat in and the winter storms out, the remaining light that filtered through their small glass panes took on the golden or green light of the glass.

In the furniture of this late Gothic and early Renaissance period we see examples of the Dutch talent for handling wood. They knew how to cut it so as to extract from it the latent beauty of grain and texture, and how to carve it into, for example, *linenfold* panelling so successfully that Dutch woodcarvers did a flourishing trade in carving imported wood and re-exporting it. In making furniture they were aided by the skill of their country's metal-workers in wrought iron.

As the demand for furniture in all its varieties increased during the Renaissance period in the Low Countries, so the work of the craftsmen developed. It became lighter in style than it had been a century earlier and could be more easily moved about. It was also adaptable in that a chest could be used as a table or a seat. Chairs were still, for the most part, ceremonial pieces of furniture and the high-backed chair, almost a throne, was reserved for the use of the head of the house or for a guest of overwhelming importance. There were two other important pieces in a Dutch or Flemish house. One was, as in France and England, the bed with its hangings. The other – and this is associated peculiarly with the Low Countries – was the dresser, first used by the Flemish to display the wealth, in the shape of plates, jugs and cups, in silver or even gold, of the householder.

Fashions in design from the world beyond the Low Countries had their effect, admittedly slight. Cornices were decorated in the Italian style. Metal fittings were reduced in size and became more functional. But the Flemish and Dutch retained their affection for light walls and dark oak, though they added to them a taste for Spanish leather tooled with gold. An important change took place in their treatment of shutters. By the end of the sixteenth century these no longer opened into the room but opened outwards to be folded back against the façade of the house, where their colour, often green, contrasted pleasingly with the red brick. Their inner sides were also painted in bright colours. The Dutch interior as we know it had arrived.

From the records of one of the houses illustrated here, it is possible to learn at first hand a little of life in the Netherlands in the sixteenth century. The house is the *Scots House* (see opposite page) at Veere in Zeeland which was the headquarters of the trade between Scotland and the Low Countries during the sixteenth and seventeenth centuries. As it now stands it is in fact two houses, the older of the two being the House of the Lamb: its neighbour is the House of the Ostrich. The *Lammeken*, the House of the Lamb, played an important part in the career of one Thomas Cunningham who settled in and traded from Veere. He is on record as paying a tax of thirteen Flemish shillings in 1588, for 'four chimneys' in the town. By 1595 he was paying tax on the *Lammeken* though there is some doubt as to whether it was also his private residence. He became very wealthy, married five times and left behind him a family that was considered large even by sixteenth century standards. In his will he bequeathed sums of money to his wife and children and to the poor of Veere, both Scottish and Dutch, and a quantity of silver goblets, gilt cups and plates, cut diamonds, rings and costly cloaks. Thomas Cunningham's dresser was obviously richly furnished.

Dutch oak table, about 1570 (private collection). The brackets and design of the legs show the influence of the designs of Vredeman de Vries.

(Opposite page, left) The Zudenbalch House at Utrecht (1467-1468), the town house of a noble family of the time. With its battlements, it is a rare example of a fortified house of the period.

(Right) Dwelling house near the Zaadmarkt in Zutphen, Gelderland. Built in 1547, the gable was originally finished with pinnacles and the windows of the lower storeys were decorated in the same way as those of the upper floors.

(Below) The Scots House at Veere in Zeeland, the headquarters of the Scottish wool trade with the Netherlands during the sixteenth and seventeenth centuries. The house on the left is the House of the Lamb (Lammeken) so called from the plaque over the door; that on the right is the House of the Ostrich, for the same reason. The latter is the older of the two, built in 1561; the Lammeken was built in 1639. Both houses possess the unusual feature of stone mouldings.

Zwolle, the capital of the Province of Overijssel: this house, built in 1571, is characteristic of Dutch architecture in the mannerist style with its rich ornament and gracefully curving gable.

WOOD AND WARMTH IN GERMANY

Differences between German and French or Flemish houses in the late Middle Ages were not substantial. So much we learn from paintings which show fairly accurately what German interiors were like. The modest house of the servant or peasant was almost always of wood and the squire's or merchant's dwelling (*Herrenhaus*), which usually possessed on a smaller scale the characteristics of a castle, was easily distinguishable from it. The middle classes, as the term is understood today, arrived rather late in Germany so that the bourgeois house of the period which today occupies the centre of German towns was also late in developing. (The first interior – albeit Flemish – of typically middle class character can be seen in the van Eyck portrait of Jan Arnolfini and his wife, painted in 1434.)

Little remains of the smallest houses of the Middle Ages partly because of their inflammable wooden construction and partly also due to their adaptability to growth and change. Rooms were frequently added to them so that their plan was often altered. In the case of stone-built houses a glance at the outline of the plan will often show the original nucleus, usually recognizable by the greater thickness of the original walls. With the wooden house, however, such recognition is difficult and in many cases virtually impossible as the outer wall was not noticeably different from later construction.

A considerable gap separated these buildings from the squire's house which was large, usually stone-built and much less adaptable. It was divided into a few spacious, sparsely furnished rooms lacking in the comforts and refinements not merely of the twentieth century but of even the earlier centuries of Rome and Byzantium. The main reception room, which served as living-room and dining-room, occupied most of the upper floor of the house. The ground floor was used for storerooms, stables and the armoury. The local Council Chamber, the *Rathaus*, which began to appear in the thirteenth century, was built on the same plan. The upper floor was often directly accessible from the outside by way of a most impressive external staircase which even today is one of the finest features of these buildings.

The furniture of the squire's hall was very simple. The most important item was the table of honour, fixed, often raised on a dais and placed so that anyone sitting at it could survey the whole hall at a glance. Other tables in the hall were moveable, laid on trestles. Other moveable pieces were chests, which often served as seats as well as containers, and stools. Chairs, where they existed, tended to be of the folding variety, of iron or wood and leather on an X-frame, a very ancient pattern which is now, however, frequently called the *Savonarola* chair. Collapsible chairs like adaptable chests were designed for mobility. The upper classes in the Middle Ages led an itinerant life as they followed the court or the hunt. Being prudent, they took most of their belongings with them for the sake of security and comfort, and this meant carrying not only clothing and bed linen but dishes, pots and pans, tapestries (accommodation, especially in hunting lodges, must have been extraordinarily draughty) and even chairs. Most of their luggage was packed into chests and carried by mules or on carts.

During winter at home, the noble lord's hall was heated by a large stove and warmth from the kitchen below helped to combat the cold. Entertainments were simple and occasionally blood chilling. In the absence of public theatres or similar gathering places, they were held in private houses. The most important houses in a town or city – such as the one we describe – looked on to the main square and from time to time the occupant and his guests were offered the spectacle of a public hanging or the burning of a heretic.

In the bedroom of this medieval squire's house, the furniture was as simple as in the hall. The most important piece was, of course, the canopied bed; around it were some chests, stools and perhaps some tables set against the walls to hold jugs and basins. The hangings round the bed served at least two useful purposes. They provided a measure of privacy in a society in which personal servants often slept in the same room as their masters. They also gave at least the illusion of warmth in rooms which must have been almost intolerably cold; and if they did not provide much warmth, they did ward off the worst of the draughts – for nightgowns were not worn at this period. In some cases the beds were encased by wooden walls so that they became, in effect, wardrobes and in this form they continued to be made and used until efficient forms of heating were evolved.

This way of life was most unhygienic and the

smell was almost certainly powerful, for bathing was a complicated operation and, therefore, a luxury. Buckets of water had to be heated in the kitchen below, and then carried upstairs and poured into the wooden baths or, rather, tubs. The bath or tub was often elliptical in shape thus following the lines of the seated human body. Some sybaritic households possessed double tubs in which married couples could bathe together (see p. 390). Having a bath together was one of the preliminary rites of marriage in which the erotic and hygienic combined. During the fourteenth and fifteenth centuries, fashion did more to encourage cleanliness than it did in the complicated modes of dress of a later age.

The development of the separate functions of the rooms of a house and of the appropriate furnishings was slow. Two centuries elapsed, for example, before chests finally resigned their secondary function of seating and were opened up to become cupboards. It was during the Renaissance period that the cabinet – that is, a piece of furniture that opened in front to reveal a number of shelves inside – became common. Such a cabinet was used to hold small valuable objects, but chests were still used to store linen and the chest of drawers did not become fashionable for some time.

During the fourteenth century, however, a discovery was made in Bavaria which was to affect profoundly the manufacture of furniture. This was the invention of the water-saw. Very heavy handworked pieces, which were prone to warping and splitting in damp conditions, were gradually replaced by furniture in which a framework of a light, stable wood, such as pine, was faced with a thin layer of a more valuable wood like walnut. These veneered pieces were delicate compared with their predecessors and could not be subjected to the same removal from place to place and room to room. And so furniture began to settle down, to find a permanent place in the room and in the house.

Certain pieces of furniture always tended, however, to stay in the same place in the house for practical reasons. One was the country version of the chest, the kneading trough in the kitchen. The dough was kneaded on the flat top of the chest – its sides rimmed to prevent loss of the precious flour. The trough itself held the rising dough and protected it from the omnipresent draughts which

Detail (enlarged) from The Holy Conversation *by the Swiss painter Konrad Witz (Naples, National Gallery of Capodimonte). Witz was a disciple of Van Eyck and in this fragment of a townscape he affords us a vivid glimpse of a mid-European town in the fifteenth century, with its steep-roofed houses, one of them decorated by a pair of antlers and, perhaps, a sign or painting on the house opposite the open doorway.*

would prevent rising. It was a disastrous day in the kitchen if the dough failed to rise.

A manoeuvre in the long battle to keep warm was the introduction of wooden floors. This had clearly taken place by the time that Jan Van Eyck painted Jan Arnolfini and his wife. At first the floors were rough planks or beams, laid, as it were, in imitation of the deck of a ship. As flooring it was not as clean as stone or brick and it was also an additional fire risk. But it was warm, especially in the bedroom.

It was to protect the feet from cold that wooden floors were frequently laid in studies or in any room used for meditation, study or business. In the well-known portrait by Antonello da Messina of *St. Jerome in his Study* (like the van Eyck, in the National Gallery in London), painted in the second half of the fifteenth century, the study is a room within a room, the elements of which – apart from a small armchair and a chest or two – form a single architectural whole: it is the kind of unity that many centuries later Frank Lloyd Wright was to create in his buildings. The idea of a small room within a large room is, however, Italian rather than German: in Germany rooms were smaller, anyway, even in wealthy houses.

In two prints by Dürer of *St. Jerome in his Study*, one a woodcut (1511) and the other a copper

engraving (1514), two different rooms are shown and the difference between them is the difference between two ways of life. In the woodcut, the room is noticeably more archaic, almost as if the medium had imposed its own limitations. The study has a barrel-vaulted ceiling, fairly lofty but slightly wider than the small bed which the saint is using as a seat. A curtain divides this tiny alcove from the rest of the room and the only furniture, apart from the bed, consists of shelves on brackets; on these, in studied disorder, are jugs, books and candlesticks. Strips of linen and leather, nailed to the walls, hold papers, scissors and pens. The same system of leather straps decorates the front of the desk-lectern which also serves as a bedside table. The large chest in the foreground, equipped with a couple of soft cushions, served as a seat of honour for visitors.

It is a very cramped interior. If poor St. Jerome is working with his hat hanging down his back, it is only because there is nowhere else for him to hang it without recourse to acrobatics unsuitable in a saint. His unfortunate lion crouches in the only free space, being too well-trained, presumably, to sit on the chest. Certainly the most is made of very little room: the learned father of the church does seem to survive in the *Existens-Minimum* that Walter Gropius was to describe centuries later.

Dürer returned to the subject of St. Jerome in his Study in this etching of 1514. Despite the memento mori on the windowsill, the saint is now more comfortably accommodated in a house which probably has an upper floor. The lion, apparently more somnolent, now has company.

An engraving signed 'M.Z.', presumably produced in or before 1508 since it depicts a ball at the court of Duke Albert III of Bavaria who died in that year. The artist may have been Matthäus Zasinger. The room's most splendid piece is the ornate table, heavily carved and probably gilded: the cup standing on it seems to match it in style. The table is placed in the Erker, the covered balcony characteristic of central and northern Europe; an exaggerated version, in a sense, of the bay window from which the house's residents might derive the advantages of sun and light without the disadvantages of wind and cold.

In the other print, the saint has moved house. The study, freed from the necessity of serving as a bedroom, has become as attractive as a sitting-room and the heavy beams in the ceiling indicate, indeed, the presence of an upper storey where the saint might rest more comfortably. The room is well-lit with several neatly aligned chests and even a bench with a back to it, rather like a divan. In the background, the hat has at last been hung up beside the hour-glass. A skull is lying on the windowsill; not, perhaps, a suitable place for a *memento mori*; and the lion, no longer alone, lies smiling in the sunshine that floods into the now welcoming room through the large windows.

A whole world, a whole way of life, divides the two rooms. The first is monastic, the second middle class. That the second was becoming generally established is shown in a later portrait of *St. Jerome* painted by Cranach in 1525 (now in the Hessische Landesmuseum, Darmstadt). The furniture of Dürer's engraving is faithfully copied and made to look even more comfortable and charming, as befitted the environment of Cardinal Albert of Brandenburg who appears as the saint (see p. 404). Mario Praz in his *Philosophy of Furnishing* remarks that this painting 'opens up the way for the Biedermeier painter of interiors.' In fact, once the spatial unity of Dürer's first *St. Jerome* had been broken, the painting was no more than a collection of still-lifes, each composed in a distinctive unity in which the human figure was balanced by the basket of fruit or the cloth perfectly laid on the table.

It was during the sixteenth century that the house was deliberately opened to the events of the street. In Italy, it was only in 1517, when Michelangelo opened up the 'kneeling' windows in the already existing Medici Palace in the Via Larga that the ground floor became an integral part of the life of the house. These 'kneeling' (*inginocchiate*) windows, protected by stout, projecting bars, allowed a limited view of the street. Some time earlier in Germany this same view had been obtained, though not from the ground floor, through windows projecting from the face of the house (in Italy the English term *bay window* was used, for the windows were rare). A room within a room was created – the *Erker* – usually an octagon with three windowed sides, two of them at an angle of 45 degrees. This small, man-sized room, which was the precursor of the generally small Elizabethan bow window, was an ideal place for work and conversation, especially when the windows caught the mild winter sunshine. In Italy, however, while the climate allowed the use of an open but sheltered loggia for work and conversation, this was rarely found in northern Europe at this particular period.

119

Wooden houses

The tradition of the wooden house is, as we have seen, an extremely ancient one. Where there were forests men built in wood; and today throughout Europe we can still see proof that this tradition has been maintained from Spain to the Balkans, from Norway to Italy. The decorative possibilities of timber were, indeed, acknowledged at an early date. Tacitus mentions, with some surprise, the unexpected gaiety of the brightly painted wooden buildings of Germany: the colours were obtained from bulls' blood, yellow ochre and rust.

The oldest wooden houses were of the type still common in Sweden, Norway, Russia and the Alps; tree trunks were laid one on top of the other and roughly planed on the two opposing sides so that one trunk fitted into the other. But this rudimentary technique had some defects, the principal one being the difficulty of sealing the building which was subject to the natural movement of the timbers. A reserve of moss or rags was kept at hand in each house, with which to stop up the gaps that opened between them. Wood had other disadvantages as well. It had a tendency to rot from exposure to weather and it offered a comfortable home to insects and animal pests. The cost was also very high and still is, because of the large amount of raw material needed to produce suitable timber for building; in flat regions, such as north Germany, where the land was required for other purposes, the natural reserves of wood were quickly exhausted. In the Middle Ages, as the spread of the plague

Wherever the raw materials exist for them, there are wooden houses in Europe. Climate, social conditions and tradition have produced, however, a variety of types. In Scandinavia and the Alps, the living-rooms are raised above ground and snow level. In central Europe we find the tall, complex, handsome houses of Germany; in south-east Europe, the shuttered houses, divided internally into the public rooms and the women's quarters, betray the influence of the long Turkish ascendancy.

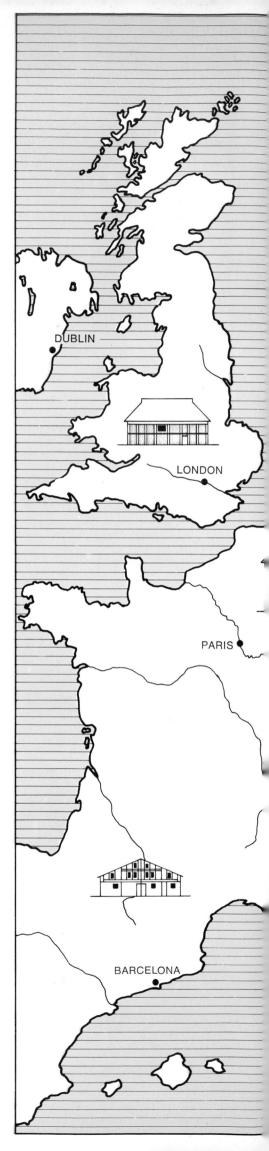

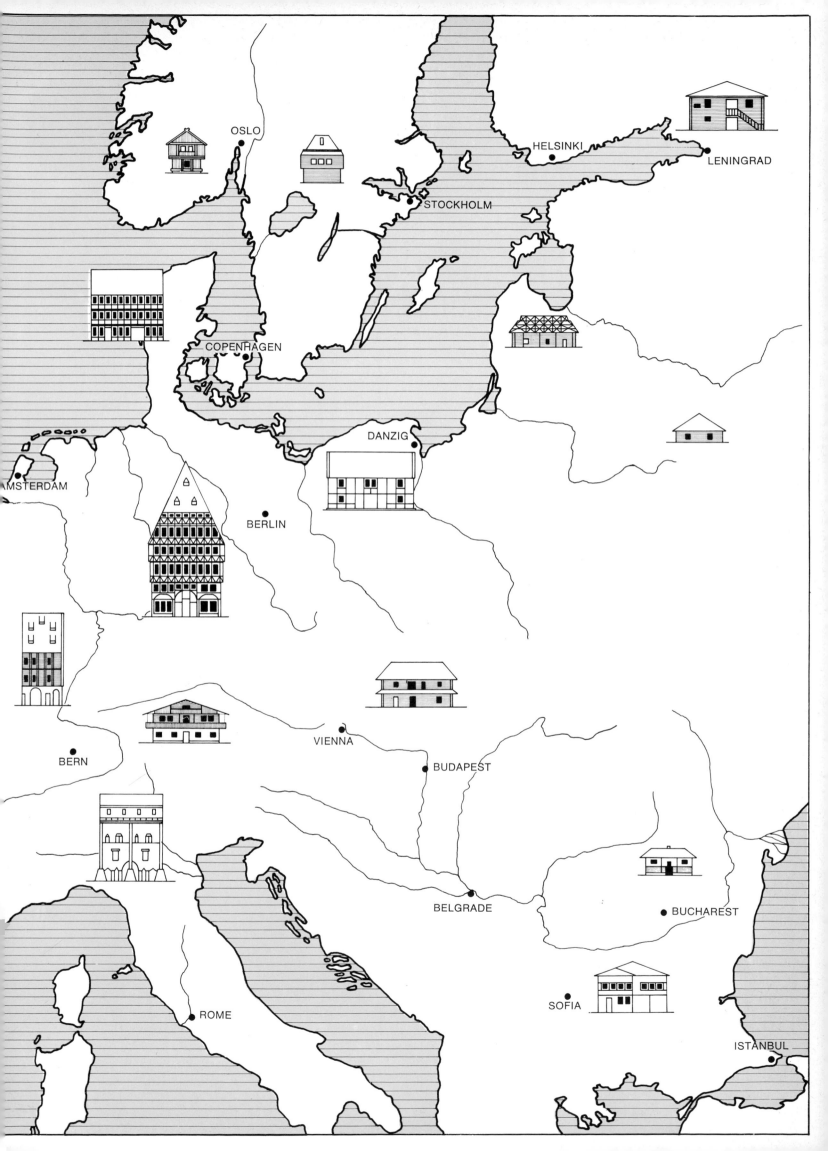

OSLO

HELSINKI

LENINGRAD

STOCKHOLM

COPENHAGEN

DANZIG

AMSTERDAM

BERLIN

BERN

VIENNA

BUDAPEST

BELGRADE

BUCHAREST

ROME

SOFIA

ISTANBUL

was attributed to the propinquity of woods, whole forests were razed to the ground by burning.

Wood became, therefore, a valuable material, to be used economically. Moreover, as forests close to water were exhausted, its transport, mainly a matter of floating logs downstream, became difficult and expensive. The consequence was a building technique of a type still in use. In this, wood formed only the framework of the building; the spaces in between were filled with other materials which were more stable, more efficient as insulators, more weatherproof and more easily sealed.

In every part of Europe and from every period of its history we find buildings constructed in this way. Some are very crude, but with the acquisition of greater skill, wood was used more effectively, its decorative possibilities were exploited, and in some cases, it was even used to imitate stone buildings.

An example of one of the oldest ways of constructing the framework of a half-timbered house survives near Belfort in Alsace. In the type of house shown here, tree trunks were cut in half longitudinally and placed at right angles within a rectangular frame. They were set at irregular angles for strength and the spaces between filled with a mixture of a muddy marl strengthened with small twigs. It made a solid wall and a good defence against the elements. In addition, it was realised by the builders that a rigid structure – that is, one that would stand up not only to frontal but also to side attacks by the wind – could be created by the insertion of diagonal beams that would strengthen the whole house. But they handled them timidly at first, as if struggling to free themselves from the dominance of the idea of the vertical.

Although the technique is rudimentary, the house in Alsace (and several others like it) has a certain delicacy of composition. It is obvious, above all, that a symmetry was sought based on the central vertical axis. This was quite easy to achieve. The trunks were sliced in half and both parts used, set opposite one another, the one the looking-glass image of the other. The arrangement of the upper and lower trunks is unlikely to have been a matter of chance with the upper ones coming close to the roof's vertical supports. The builders of this house, it is clear, had learned, whether consciously or not, the structural lesson of the great Romanesque and Gothic cathedrals, the essentials of which can be found popularized, almost parodied, in its constructions.

Structurally less rudimentary than this is a house at Schlitz near Cassel, two details of which

are worth considering. The beams are deliberately regular in their arrangement and the strengthening cross-beams seem to have been reduced to a wide all-embracing X. What is interesting is the absolutely arithmetical exactness of the horizontal and vertical beams: the building process was obviously governed by the varying lengths of wood that the builders had at their disposal and this produced something organic rather than geometric. The wall-filling inserted during successive centuries consisted first of a mixture of marlish mud, then brick, and lastly small blocks of cement that came into use quite recently. Technically, of course, the use of the later materials is nonsense: it is wasteful to use bricks and cement as neutral elements carried by old wooden beams much less strong than they are. But this shows how traditional techniques survive beyond the life of the material on which they are based. Many of our houses today are, for that matter, not much more sensibly built than the one at Schlitz: the excellent bricks, which are carefully arranged for show in houses that are really concrete cages, could be eliminated without any structural weakening of the house.

Another striking feature of the house at Schlitz is the harmony of colour and the precise rhythmical arrangement of the whole building. As in a painting by the Dutch artist, Piet Mondrian, thick vertical and horizontal lines divide the surface into rectangles of different colours.

In the large cities of Europe in the Middle Ages, building land was as scarce as it is today and costs were proportionately as high. In Florence, Bologna and Venice, for example, an attempt was made to solve the problem of site costs by building houses with upper storeys projecting over the street. These became very common and local legislation was framed which stated the maximum size permissible of such projections – contravention could be punished by demolition of the house – and their minimum height above ground level as a protection for pedestrians.

Houses with projecting upper storeys were built in Germany but the methods were rather different. Instead of a single, large projection supported on a stone bracket, German householders added small projections all the way up the building with the storey above supported on small brackets. It was a technique well suited to building in wood. It was also typically Saxon and various examples can be seen in Schlitz. The example here recalls a point worth making about wooden houses. Wooden buildings lose their shape permanently and noticeably: they become 'out of plumb', that is, they no longer square up with the vertical. People unaccustomed to them tend to think they are on the brink of collapse – quite reasonably, for if a stone building showed such abnormal signs of subsidence it would indeed be in a dangerous condition. But wooden buildings do lean or cant, so much so that when an old building has been restored or even entirely rebuilt, the process is obvious because the angles are too regular. In the expressionist films of the early twenties – Wegener's *The Golem* designed by the great architect, Mans Poeling, was an example – the twisted buildings with their contorted arches and doors askew were regarded as brilliant fantasies. In fact they were merely interpretations of buildings that had existed or still exist, their eccentricities exaggerated in the interests of drama.

The brackets supporting the upper storeys of the house were a characteristic element in Saxony's urban architecture. Elsewhere, as in Scandinavia, for example, such supports are rare and a more sophisticated structure, one less liable to subsidence, was typical. It was characterized by diagonal beams which formed with the vertical supports of the house's façade an upward or downward pointing arrowhead. This allowed the vertical supports of the house to be set more widely apart.

It was a technique which sometimes achieved remarkable elegance, as in the Abbey of Beben-

hausen near Tübingen. Here, in an inner courtyard, the double arrowheads or tridents create irregular octagons on the ground floor façade and the windows, in turn, their sills and architraves lengthened to reach the building's main supports, create others. This is a rhythmical use of surfaces that has become quite common in modern architecture. In spite of the formality, however, there is still great freedom; for instance, in the trapezoid segments of wall beside the windows, not one is equal in size to the others. The permanently unstable balance between what is organic and what is abstract.

(Below, top) Front of a house with a wooden structure in the market place at Helmstedt in Magdeburg. On the horizontal beams at ground level are inscribed: 'SAMUEL MEIER. MARIA PAUSTS. 1648'.
(Bottom) Inner courtyard of the Cistercian Abbey at Bebenhausen near Tübingen. Founded in 1187, it was subject to frequent alteration until in 1807 it became a royal residence.

between freedom and order, rhythm and line, is nearly perfect in these fifteenth century wooden buildings. The building at Tübingen reveals an unforced rhythm at once structural and aesthetic, that is mercifully free of the repetitive regular arrangements that appeared when too much order and too little imagination were set to work to justify too much decoration.

In a beautiful house on the Pegnitz at Nuremberg, the Swabian structure with its trident or arrow-shaped beams has Saxon-style projections, one above the other, on its flanks. The floor beams,

House at Schlitz near Cassel (Hesse). Detail of the brickwork and the wooden framework. The variegations of the bricks resulting from alterations at various times, and the timber framework, create a colourful effect.

which are under very great stress, are doubled but are not placed side by side. They are 12 inches apart and connected by blocks. This method of building meant that horizontal lines took on greater importance than the vertical which had so far dominated, and this had an immediate aesthetic effect. The lower part of the house is of stone, proof against dampness and flooding from the river. The loggia, which faces on to the river, is protected by vertical timber facing. Under the enormous roof alone there is abundant room for three storeys, two of which were meant to be used as dwellings. These are lit by long lines of dormer windows characteristic of houses of this kind, as well as by windows on the two façades or gables of the building. In the largest buildings of this type, there may be as many as four rows of dormer windows strung out along the immense spreading roof.

One of the finest groups of wooden houses in the whole of Germany were those at Hildesheim, which were unfortunately destroyed by fire in the closing days of the Second World War. Many of them dated back to the sixteenth century and the illustration shows a detail from the lower part of one of the survivors of the group. It displays the irregularity usual in such buildings, and the type of decoration used. The latter – the coloured carvings under the windows, the carved beams and brackets and the denticulated cornice – is very rich and the structure clearly takes second place to it. It is indeed the kind of decoration that had so far been confined to the interior of the house, where it had enriched chests and cabinets; we find it beginning to be used on exteriors at this period.

Now two seventeenth century examples. The first – and more modest – is a row of houses typical of the charming city of Helmstedt in Magdeburg where a vice-chancellor of the local university during the seventeenth century was the Italian philosopher, Giordano Bruno. He found lodgings in a small house which still stands and which was similar to that in the illustration (p. 123). The structure of the house is more regular than that of houses in the previous century, but what is remarkable about it is the simple and controlled quality of its decoration, with its fan shapes, stars and intertwined ribbons. The dormer windows, now placed on the front of the house, extended the rhythms of the building below: they were curved in tentatively baroque style – and large enough to allow furniture, difficult to manoeuvre down the narrow inner staircases, to be taken in or out, or sacks of grain to be hauled up to the store under the roof.

Finally, a house in the main square of the Pied Piper's town of Hamelin in Brunswick, or, as it is now, Lower Saxony. Like a number of others in the region, it is built of mixed materials, stone below and wood on the upper storeys. But both parts are treated in the same way so that at first glance it is not clear whether the *Erker*, the bay window of the main drawing-room on the upper floor, is built of one or the other. The timber has lost its special character and in the brown and white decoration the materials are at odds with the inlaid design. The building has been most carefully planned and the composition of the façade has been meticulously worked out. But the basic weakness of using timber to compete against the increasing use of stone and brick in buildings still shows. In mixtures and compromises of this kind, the wooden house gradually lost the individual character that had distinguished it for centuries.

Eighteenth century house in the main square of Hamelin (Lower Saxony); an example of a composite building of wood and stone.

(Left) Detail of the lower part of a seventeenth century wooden house at Hildesheim (Lower Saxony), showing the richness and variety of the ornamentation. (Right) Detail of timber frame and brickwork of house at Schlitz near Cassel.

A large wooden house at Nuremberg on the River Pegnitz near the Herkersteg Bridge, an example of careful post-war restoration. Originally built in the sixteenth century, it was damaged during the Second World War and had to be largely rebuilt, when intrusive chimneys were removed. Today, though it is a reproduction, it bears a closer resemblance to the sixteenth century building than it did a generation ago; it lacks, unavoidably, the liveliness of ancient handworked materials, and the patina of age.

G. Opresco - P. Petresco

URBAN DEVELOPMENT IN SOUTH-EAST EUROPE

With the collapse of the Roman Empire and the disappearance of that unity which had held together – however feebly in some periods – so many disparate elements, the towns and cities of south-east Europe suffered the same vicissitudes as the rest of the empire. The settlements that had flourished along the banks of the Danube and in the provinces to the south of it: Viminiacum, Ratiaria, Naissus and Sardica; on the shores of the Black Sea: Tomi, Apollonia; and in Thrace, Macedonia and Illyria: Hadrianopolis, Thessalonica, Dyrrhachium, Salonae, and Pola – endured the invasions from beyond the old frontiers and the withdrawals that eventually dismembered the empire and its successor, the empire of Byzantium. In some instances, the ancient town plan survived. In others, it was radically altered under the influence of Byzantium. More often it was lost altogether as the new masters imposed their own political and architectural ideas. Byzantine tradition

held out most successfully along the coasts of the Adriatic and the Black Sea: as late as the twelfth century, the dukedom of Paristrion was imitating the social and political structures of Byzantium in the area that includes the present-day Dobruja.

Events from the eleventh to the sixteenth centuries largely determined the characteristics of towns in south-east Europe. By far the most important of these were the Ottoman invasions of the southern Slav states from the fourteenth century onwards. From the conquering Osmanlis derived those architectural characteristics most closely associated to this day with Balkan towns. Turkish architectural styles and details were, it should be remembered, imposed on or welded to a vigorous peasant culture and in any examination of Balkan buildings, the two must be considered together.

Nor did either Turkish or Balkan styles exist in a vacuum, for they were continually exposed to western influences. Turkish concepts of town planning, for example, owe a good deal to Byzantium. Groups of settlers from the west took up residence in the Balkans for various reasons, usually commercial. Notable among them were the Venetians, first on the Dalmatian coast and then further east, ever ready to turn as honest a penny as they might with anyone who would trade with them. Germans from the banks of the Rhine and the Moselle settled in Transylvania at the end of the twelfth century. Slovenia, Croatia and the regions between the Rivers Sava and Drava, and Voivodina enjoyed uninterrupted exchanges with the countries of central Europe and Germany. At the same time, the collapse of the Roman and Byzantine empires was accompanied largely by the collapse of urban society in south-east Europe and not until the eighteenth century and even later can the region boast of sizeable, well-organized towns.

Still, towns are mentioned in medieval documents. The Russian chronicle *The Story of Times Past* refers to '80 *goroduri*', that is, fortified towns in the Danube region at the end of the eleventh century. At about the same time, a Byzantine text that seems to be fairly reliable, the *Fragment of the Toparca*, mentions the existence of '10 *poleis*' or 10 towns. These may well have been towns of a very rudimentary type and only just recognizable as such, but they were enough to allow encouragement to the modest craftsmen within them.

Strong German influence on the ancient town of Sibiu in southern Transylvania is obvious in the main façade and, above all, in the high roof of the Haller house dating from the sixteenth century.

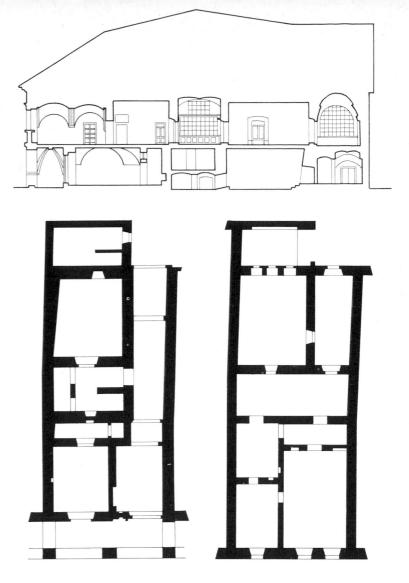

Longitudinal section and plans of the ground and first upper floors of the Peterman house at Bistritsa in Transylvania, a town with a large German colony. The length of this fifteenth century building is more than 103 feet.

By the thirteenth century, when the German emigrants had settled in Transylvania, we begin to hear more of towns, for example, Turnovo some 40 miles south of the Danube, the home of the brothers John and Peter Asen who led the revolt of Bulgars and Wallachians against Byzantium. Between the thirteenth and fourteenth centuries, it prospered remarkably. It had a number of terraced districts in one of which lived the town's craftsmen. Another was reserved for western residents and was known as the Frankish quarter.

To the same period belonged what was possibly the finest example of urban building in Bulgaria. These were buildings at Arbanasi near Turnovo but unfortunately they were destroyed in the earthquake of 1913. However, the towns of Cerven and Lovaci which date back to the fourteenth century still remain. Buildings of this period survive too in a number of Yugoslav cities such as Zadar, Dubrovnik, Split and Bitolj.

Considerable variations exist even within quite a limited area in styles of building and in materials used. Following an ancient local tradition, the builders of the fourteenth and fifteenth century houses of Suceava in the north of Rumania used wood as did those at Sibiu and Brasov in Transylvania. However, increasing use was made of stone in Transylvania in the fifteenth century.

Town plans varied too. In the largely autonomous towns of Moldavia and Wallachia houses were built surrounded by their own spacious gardens. But the towns of Transylvania resembled those of the west with narrow streets turning and twisting between buildings huddled together in groups. Moreover, from the fourteenth century onwards in Transylvania – at Sighisoara, for example – districts were defined within the town's fortifications in which the various craftsmen should live and work.

In the medieval houses of Sibiu and Brasov, as has already been noted, increasing use was made of stone. But the house plan was not altered. It still consisted of a single, long, rectangular room which was at once kitchen, dining-room, sitting-room, work-room, and bedroom. One of the shorter sides of the rectangle faced on to the street and was surmounted by the jutting eaves. A fenced courtyard with a wide entrance flanked one of the longer sides of the rectangle.

From this kind of house, common both to town and country, the town house of later centuries developed. The material used changed again, this time from stone to brick. Rooms were added, first to the courtyard side, later as an upper storey. By the second half of the fourteenth century houses were being built at Sibiu like the one illustrated, with crow-stepped gables, Gothic windows and vaulted rooms on the ground floor. In some cases, the gateway to the house is enlarged by the addition of a cellar and an attic, the latter being used as a storeroom connected with ground level by a pulley from the wide upper window or by a trapdoor.

A period of brisk economic development in the fifteenth century brought Transylvania into contact with Italy and Renaissance design. Italian influence is manifested in architectural decoration, not only of public buildings, but also of the houses of merchants and craftsmen. Shops, workshops and storerooms – often extensive as the premises were extended back from the street – took up the ground floor of the houses. On the street façade itself was a portico, often vaulted. On the upper floor lived the owner of the house and his family, and here we find growing elaboration of ornament. In a build-

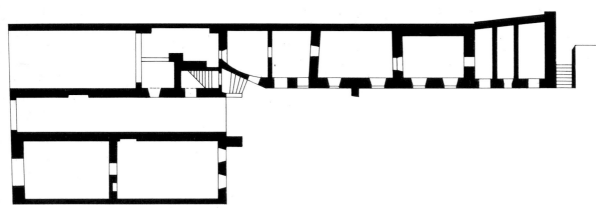

Section from front to back of the sixteenth century Hall house at Sibiu. Plan of the ground level of the same house. (The façade is shown on page 126.)

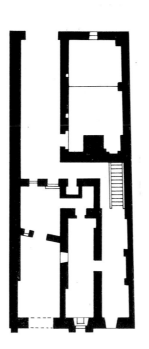

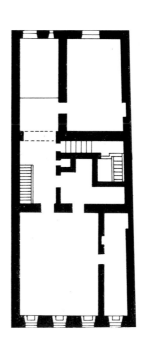

The city of Bistritsa was famous for its metal-workers. The sixteenth century building whose façade is shown here, along with plans of the ground level (left) and the upper floor (right) belonged to an argintarului (silversmith or jeweller). The façade is a little more than 33 feet wide. As in other parts of Europe, the larger door opens into the shop. Renaissance influence is evident in the design of the doors and windows.

ing in Bistritsa, dated 1480, the residential floor includes the drawing-room, sitting-room, two bedrooms, kitchen-dining room, and two other rooms.

In Moldavia and Wallachia, the great land-owners — boyars and the church — had for some time been taking up residence in the towns, large and small, and bringing with them from their estates numbers of servants and craftsmen. Their mansions, the centres of this particular society, were surround-

ed by shops and workshops. For the artisan who came in from the country, the only space left in which he might build was on the strip surrounding the ring of shops and workshops, and here, accordingly, he built his house with a garden round it, reminiscent of the house he had left behind in the countryside. This type of urban development with buildings scattered thinly through a maze of twisted streets remained typical of Rumania for centuries.

Wojciech Kalinowski

POLAND
LOOKS TO THE WEST

In the prehistoric period, a number of highly developed dwelling sites existed in the region that is now Poland. They lasted until the barbarian invasions of the fifth century A.D. Soon after, however, in the sixth century, wooden houses were being built and use was made too of brick and marl for walls. Towns arose that were to become centres of lay power and about the tenth century, having developed into flourishing markets, they began to expand into cities. The court and the church imported skilled craftsmen from the west – from Saxony, the Rhineland, Burgundy and Italy – but the resulting architecture was noticeably sober and undecorated.

At the beginning of the seventh century, the main type of house in the countryside and the villages was a wooden building in which the accommodation consisted of a single, more or less square room. By the thirteenth century and even more by the fourteenth, this basic type had divided into two; one in the large towns of the north, the other in the towns of the south. The first was related to northern European Gothic houses: the second was influenced by Mediterranean tradition. At the same time single-storey houses were built in most of the smaller towns as in the country, though brick and stone might be used as well as wood.

In the fifteenth century, middle class houses in the towns of central and southern Poland were still built with a fairly small plan area. They were two rooms deep with a large room at street level used by craftsmen or as a shop. The living-rooms were on the upper floor. The house façades overlooked the square or market place or main streets.

In the reign of Sigismund I (1506-1548), either because the king's wife, Bona Sforza, was a noble-woman from Lombardy or because of dynastic links with Hungary which was already permeated by Italian influences, the Renaissance arrived for the first time in Poland. Its effect was felt again soon after the middle of the sixteenth century in

Houses in Biecz, a small Carpathian town south-east of Cracow near the Polish border with Czechoslovakia (from a drawing made about 1850 by Jan Matejko). These houses, built between the fifteenth and seventeenth centuries, are typical of the provincial towns of central Europe. In general, they consisted of a ground and upper floor with an entrance below for carts; the upper part of the building was usually a store.

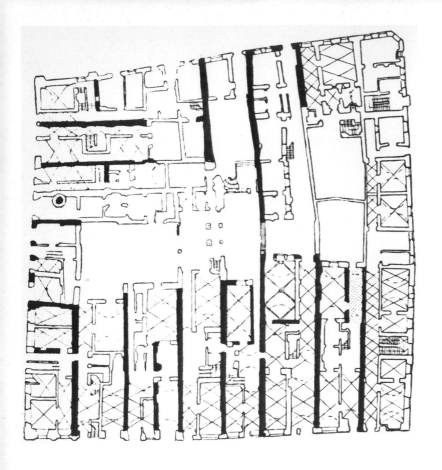

the reign of Sigismund Augustus; and again in the last quarter of the same century. The third wave of influence lasted for several decades of the seventeenth century. Architects from Tuscany, the Veneto and Lombardy came to Poland, among them Bartolomeo Berecci, Gianmaria Padovano, Giambattista Quadrio and Santi Gucci. A number of sculptors accompanied them. The taste for art moreover spread well beyond the circle of their immediate patrons. The desire developed, in particular, for larger and more elegant houses.

In central and southern Poland, the typical middle class house underwent certain changes. The ground floor room – used as a shop or workshop – was extended and the shop became a unit in itself. The number of residential rooms was increased so

Main façades (below) and plans (above) of fifteenth and sixteenth century houses in Warsaw (from Stare miasto Warszawie, Warsaw, 1956). *These buildings were built, in the fifteenth century, after a plan common in the Hanseatic cities in which considerations of space meant that the façade was comparatively narrow. (The early walls are shown on the plan in black). In the first half of the seventeenth century, most of these houses were enlarged; they were increased in depth to three rooms with the staircases set in the centre of each dwelling. The large reception rooms at ground level were divided to make shops and workshops. The façades were designed in the mannerist-baroque style fashionable during this period. Skylights were added to some of the houses in the seventeenth and eighteenth centuries.*

that the size of the building grew both in depth – with three rooms where before there had been two – and in height as other floors were added. Meanwhile, from Italy builders and their patrons had acquired new ideas about structure and decoration. The pitch of the steep Gothic roofs was lessened and they were hidden behind decorative parapets which surmounted the main façade. On houses planned after the medieval fashion, decoration of a strictly Renaissance style appeared. Middle class houses were enriched with courtyards, porticos and arcades as buildings took on a more imposing appearance. During the last Renaissance phase private houses of a north European type were popular and Dutch culture was highly regarded in Poland at this period.

Detail of an engraving by G. Braun and J. Hogenberg (from Civitates orbis terrarum, *Nuremberg, 1617) showing dwelling houses and the town hall in the market place at Lowicz on the River Bzara (Bsura on the print) south-west of Warsaw. The houses are the standardized single-storey European houses but upper floors with decorative parapets have been added to some of them.*

At Kazimierz, a small town west of Lublin on the Vistula, the brothers Przbyla built these houses in 1615. Their façades, which look on to the market square, are richly if rather heavily decorated; much of the ornament has a religious theme. The elaborate parapet is a curious and interesting mixture of traditional Russian or eastern European and mannerist-baroque elements. These houses provide a valuable indication of the taste at this period of prosperous craftsmen and merchants in central Europe.

RUSSIA:
THE HEATABLE HOUSE

From the founding of the state of Kiev during the eleventh century, until the end of the fourteenth century, two main types of house were found in Russian towns. In the north, there was a kind of of half-buried hut. In the south, it was a building constructed of tree-trunks entirely or almost entirely on the surface of the ground. It is significant that the term *izba* was already being used: it means a dwelling place with a stove, a heated house.

The so-called 'Artist's or Artisan's House' which was found in Kiev during excavations in 1938 tells us a great deal about the northern type. Buried to a depth of 3 to 4 feet, its walls were of wickerwork plastered with mud. The floor too was of mud with the addition of fired bricks. The wooden framework rose from a trench about 6 inches deep and the roof, probably of straw, may have been conical. The entrance, reached by steps cut into the ground, was sheltered by a lean-to type of roof. Inside, in the corner beside the door on a base about 8 inches high, stood the stove with a dome-shaped hood over it. It is not clear whether the smoke went out by the door, or whether a less uncomfortable way had been devised of expelling it through a wooden tube lined with clay and inserted into the hood. The owner's tools, whether he was a painter or a goldsmith, were kept beside the domestic pots and pans.

Similar huts still exist, especially in the north,

(Above) Constructional diagram of an old wooden house in Russia; the roof was also of wood, in curved sections like Roman tiles.
(Below) View of the interior plan of what is called 'The Artist's House' at Kiev which dates from the beginning of the thirteenth century. The shorter wall is less than 10 feet long.

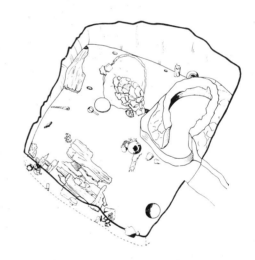

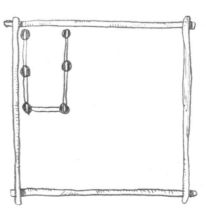

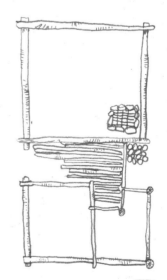

Plans of twelfth century wooden buildings at Novgorod on Lake Ilmen south of Leningrad. In the first (left) the longer side of the rectangular area is about 24 feet; in the second (centre) each side of the square is about 21 feet; in the third (right), the side of the upper square section is just under 10 feet.

at, for example, Suzdal and Ryazan. But in the south too there were houses mentioned in literary sources, constructed of boards or planks; and others of mud and presumably thatched with straw.

It was in the forest regions of the north, however, that wood predominated in building. Houses made entirely of tree trunks and dating back to the period from the tenth to the fifteenth centuries, have been discovered at Novgorod and the old part of Ladoga. The simplest, after the very modest semi-subterranean huts, consisted of a single habitable room, that is a single heated room. A further room was added, more lightly constructed and lacking a stove. It did contribute to the heating of the main room for it acted as a barrier between the heated room and the outside. Richer houses had a heated room for winter and another without a stove for summer. An intermediary room connected the two. In some cases, the building was on two floors and its plan can still be found today in the country. The hall opened into the main room from which a trapdoor led to another room below, used as a food and general store. The size of the house reflected its owner's economic position: the rooms may be as little as 8 feet across or as much as 43 feet. The diameter of the tree trunks, usually poplar or birch, is always between 9 or 10 inches. The gaps between them were stuffed with moss. The house's foundations consisted of sticks and stones. The floors were usually a double layer of bricks.

Heating was of paramount importance. Even when more elaborate forms of housing were developed, the stove stayed in a corner of the main room for a long time and when it was moved, it was to the middle of the room. At first, it was not so much a stove as we know it but a primitive hearth: this was protected by screens or, more rarely, by a brick wall. But enormous stoves soon developed which provided heat for cooking and on which people slept, wrapped in padded quilts. These furnished warmth, little of which was lost through the small vertical windows, set between contiguous tree trunks, and 'glazed' with mica or fish bladders (glass was first imported in the sixteenth century.)

A quotation from Guennady dating from 1076, sums up the situation: 'In winter, the rich sit in a warm room and are undressed without fear of the cold ('undressed' here probably means without outer furs). Think of the poor, however, round a wretched little fire, their eyes smarting with the smoke, hardly able to warm their hands while their backs and the rest of their bodies are frozen.'

From the sixteenth century onwards, the structure of the house grew more and more complicated. The porticos gradually acquired steps under the shelter of a roof that took on the appearance of a pyramid. Carved decorations with a great many ornamental motifs were already in use: a twelfth century colonnade of carved wood in which an assembly of monstrous beasts tumbled over one another was discovered at Novgorod.

The first town houses of brick were built in the fifteenth century. A courtyard surrounded by storerooms and the servants' quarters fronted the street, and within the containing wall of tree trunks there were usually an orchard and kitchen garden. Inside were pieces of furniture and brightly decorated ornaments: western influence had arrived.

This model of a group of thirteenth and fourteenth century wooden houses at Novgorod is based on the discoveries of plans similar to those on the opposite page.

ANO   1694

THE BAROQUE IMAGINATION

THE SEVENTEENTH CENTURY

Until comparatively recently, it was customary for art historians to end their examination of the Renaissance with a few observations on Elizabethan and Jacobean extravagances in England and then to proceed without pause to consideration of the baroque in the reign of Louis XIV of France. Thus unceremoniously the genius of Bernini and Rubens were overlooked and with them the first flowering of baroque art.

The seventeenth century saw a curious conflict of interests in art and architecture. Italy and the Low Countries led Europe until the middle of the century, not only in the major arts of painting and sculpture but in the craft or art of furniture-making. But the 'modern' house of the period was French for it was in France that the need was felt to furnish certain rooms of the house in different ways. For, during the Renaissance period, as we have seen, the house or home as we now understand it was unknown. Even well-to-do families lived in a single, large, all-purpose room. Where there were several rooms, one might be more private than the rest but even when he withdrew to it, the master of the household was accompanied by his family and servants. *Togetherness* was still an important ingredient of domestic life.

The division of the house into different rooms with different functions may have originated in part from the practical consideration that small rooms are more easily heated than large ones. It was probably also influenced, however, by a change in human relationships, by the appreciation of the pleasures of conversation – and in some instances the intoxication of gaming; the first of the famous Parisian salons appeared during this period.

In France as elsewhere, there was a considerable difference between the aristocratic and middle class interior although eventually the comforts of the latter persuaded the owners of splendid but uncomfortable palaces to reorganize, sacrificing first one reception room, then another, in the interests of ease. But before the nobles of France weakened in this way, ostentatious luxury distinguished the buildings they commissioned. It dictated the structure of the building, the splendours of the great public rooms and galleries, the deliberately overwhelming grandeur of the entrance. Comfort during these decades was for the middle classes among whom furniture retained a utilitarian function; among whom, indeed, the discovery was made that one's home could be a charming and delightful place in which to relax from business responsibilities.

he house in Lorca in Murcia known as the Casa de los Guevara *(now the seat of the Rocafull family) and a superb example of Spanish baroque. The splendid, almost overwhelming ntrance is flanked by heavily decorated twisted columns and surmounted by a splendid oat of arms with the date 'año 1694'. (For another example of this type of column, eminiscent of Bernini's in St. Peter's in Rome, see page 142.)*

On the Grand Canal in Venice, the Ca' Pesaro
is one of the finest palaces in the city as
well as being Longhena's masterpiece. Begun
in 1663, its construction was interrupted by the
architect's death in 1682 and it was not
completed until 1710. The façade with its faceted
bosses on the ground floor faces the Grand Canal;
in the middle is the majestic courtyard, surrounded,
according to contemporary accounts, by loggias
and wandering passages. The side facing
on to the rio was designed by Antonio Gaspari.

Agostino Tassi, Procession of the Prefect Taddeo Barberini (Rome, Banco di Santo Spiri-
to). The event commemorated took place in
Rome in 1631 and here we see the part of it
on the Corso near the Piazza Venezia. The
Corso ran along the line of the ancient Via
Flaminia in Rome and was used in the Middle
Ages for horse-racing: Pope Paul II straight-
ened it in part in the fifteenth century and
the process was completed in 1650. It also acquired pavements in the seventeenth century
and in 1736 the roadway itself was paved.
The houses on it vary from late Renaissance
to baroque. The building in the centre with
a tower seems to be shared among several
families.

Sergio Coradeschi · Michelangelo Muraro

THE URBAN SCENE
IN ITALY

After centuries of war, Italy in the seventeenth century was still a battlefield. Town planners took account, however, of new methods of warfare. The ancient city plan of square or rectangular pattern, often derived from the lay-out of Roman forts, was abandoned in favour of a more complex ground plan, polygonal or star-shaped. Towns and cities lay entrenched behind bastions that could withstand artillery fire. Land was as valuable as ever – indeed now even more valuable because of the increasing population. The new fortifications changed the course of streets. The broad squares and long gardens of the sixteenth century fell out of favour and there was a return to multi-storeyed houses and rows of buildings. In the nineteenth century the German poet, Heinrich Heine, wrote of Genoa: 'They had to use their space very economically, building very tall houses and making narrow streets; these streets are nearly always dark and only two of them can take a carriage. But the people, who are mostly in trade, use their houses merely as a

store and a place to sleep in at night while they spend the livelong day on the move or sitting in a doorway or rather under it, to avoid knocking their knees against people in the house opposite.' It was this shortage of building space that compelled even prosperous citizens to resign themselves to sharing the building that was their home – but in a fashion which respected the needs of the individual.

Structurally, the shared house differed from houses built for a single family only in the larger number of internal staircases. The aesthetic theories defined by Renaissance authors were still honoured though not much practised, and as new ideas were thrown up, in rapid succession, architects departed further and further from classical practice and builders, great or small, were free to construct as they wished and as the space available allowed them.

Building in seventeenth century Italy went ahead on a hitherto unparalleled scale. Whole sections of towns were built or restored. Working on this scale, architects were able to give an air of

unity to the entire section. At the same time, however, they were not averse to advertising their own expertise and ingenuity and the wealth of the 'building' owners. This they achieved by the use of extravagant, sometimes even bizarre detail, seen at its theatrical best in Venice.

The Serene Republic, too, prospered during this period from the enterprise of her merchants, her bankers and her land-owners. The government of the city and its ecclesiastical organizations, moreover, farsightedly looked to the well-being of the ordinary citizen and within certain residential districts commissioned the building of mass-produced houses, for people of modest means, of a standard of comfort and convenience so far unknown.

But the Venetians delighted in spectacle and even their essays in town planning are theatrical arrangements. The State completed the courtyard of the Doge's Palace with porticos and loggias and the religious authorities were no less demanding of the architects who built the church and monastery of San Giorgio Maggiore and the church

The fifteenth century Palazzo Falconieri stands on the Via Giulia in Rome beyond the church of Sant'Egidio and between the churches Santa Caterina da Siena and Ferdinando Fuga's Santa Maria dell'Orazione e Morte. It has two different faces and the one it presents to the Tiber (above) bears upon it the impress of the genius of Francesco Borromini. His is the severe logic of the plan of the three floors, the top one a loggia.

Where the Via Sistina meets the Via Gregoriana in Rome, close to the Spanish Steps, is the small house of the painter Federico Zuccari who died in 1609. On the Via Gregoriana side, not shown here, is the fantastic doorway in the likeness of a gaping mouth with eyes and nostrils as lintels.
Here (right) we see the Via Sistina side of the house with the loggia, of a later date and attributed to Filippo Juvarra; it was commissioned by the Polish queen, Maria Casimira in 1711.

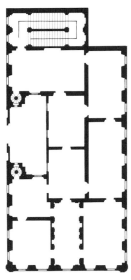

(Above) Palazzo d'Aste in Rome, designed by the architect Giovanni Antonio de' Rossi. As in the Palazzetto Zuccari, the irregularity of the site dictated the plan of the building (right). This differs in many respects from that of other houses of this baroque period and the arrangement of the small rooms foreshadows rococo taste.

of Santa Maria della Salute. It was an era of ceremony, both sacred and profane. As such the exaggerations of Longhena's Ca' Pesaro, barely restrained by a vague nod in the direction of ancient tradition, are entirely appropriate. Occasionally a certain linear sobriety still betrays the influence of Palladio but on the whole it is his contemporary, Jacopo Sansovino, Venice's chief architect during the sixteenth century, who prevails – and with him the baroque spirit.

Venetians of the early seventeenth century, accordingly, found Renaissance buildings stiff – as well as unfashionable. The large reception room lost its importance in the house. There was no need for neighbouring rooms to be so lofty, so mezzanine floors were introduced. More service staircases were inserted which made the various apartments independent. The house was much more comfortable than it had been. But the façade remained unashamedly ostentatious and grew more so as the years passed. In organizing their households, Venetians – though quite far north – were in the odd position of being compelled by the exigencies of their city's situation to adopt certain architectural features from other countries with which they happened to have political and economic connections. Lack of a reliable ground water supply meant that rain had to be collected, so their buildings incorporated wide roof terraces, like those in the drier parts of the Mediterranean. On the lower part of the building, however, dampness and danger of flooding reduced the number of doors and windows to an oriental minimum.

The Palazzo Moro-Lin on the Grand Canal in Venice, also called the 'palace of the thirteen windows', built by Pietro Liberi after a plan attributed to his colleague Sebastiano Mazzoni, both of whom were eminent painters in seventeenth century Venice (the plan has also been attributed to Liberi himself). This palace, which is very fine even by Venetian standards, was bought by the Lin family and then, in 1778, it passed to the Moro family who added a storey to it.

Interior of the Villa Aldobrandini, also known as the Belvedere, at Frascati, built by Giacomo della Porta between 1598 and 1603 for Cardinal Pietro Aldobrandini, nephew of Pope Clement VIII. This room is one of the private apartments of the house and affords an idea of the appearance of a drawing-room in a princely household. The decoration is austerely opulent. The gilding of the leather wall hangings is echoed in the door frames and panels. Such furniture as there is is set against the walls, leaving free the geometric decoration of the floor.

SPANISH SPLENDOUR AND SOBRIETY

When Philip II of Spain set about building the Escorial in the middle of the sixteenth century and so fixed Madrid as the capital of his empire, the city also became the home of the Spanish court and administration. The massive building programme subsequently carried out affected buildings in other parts of the peninsula.

Of the three architects who at this period worked on the Escorial – Juan Bautista de Toledo, Juan de Herrera and Francisco de Mora – we are here concerned with the last, who designed among other buildings the servants' quarters. De Mora's buildings were solid, four-square, with smooth-faced walls. The façades are austere demonstrations of the classical orders with large, rectangular windows, and the courtyards are colonnaded but they also include singular towers with steep slate roofs.

The entrance to the Colegio San Felipe in the Plaza della Justicia in Saragossa opens on to a patio dominated by this magnificent cornice. The building belonged to the counts of Arguillo and is an example of the survival in seventeenth century Aragonese buildings of sixteenth century features and the combination of these with baroque innovations.

The house in the Calle del Rastro in Valladolid where Miguel de Cervantes lived with his family about 1605. They occupied four rooms on the first floor. Though the house is now a museum, the original distribution of the rooms is unaltered so that it affords an accurate idea of domestic architecture at the beginning of the seventeenth century, unaffected by the baroque fashions that so profoundly changed the appearance of richer houses.

The patio of the Casa Dalmases in Barcelona. This late seventeenth century building contains not only obviously baroque ornament but traces of mannerist ornament as well. Its most remarkable feature is the massive and richly decorated staircase with ornate twisted columns, of the type used by Raphael in a tapestry for Pope Leo X, by Giulio Romano in some of his buildings, and by Bernini in his superb baldaquin in St. Peter's in Rome.

These towers were introduced by Philip II from Flanders and became so popular that they grew to be a typical feature of Castilian architecture in the seventeenth century.

At a less exalted level, dwelling houses were large brick buildings with heavy iron grilles on the lower windows; wrought ironwork decorated the balconies. In many cases, however, this was the only decoration. Inside the houses there was a large number of rooms, including public rooms, and in many there was even a chapel. But baths, part of Spain's Moorish heritage, had disappeared. The house in Madrid of the poet and dramatist, Lope de Vega, which he bought in 1610 and lived in until his death in 1635, was of this type. The house in which the creator of Don Quixote, Miguel de Cervantes, lived in Valladolid around 1605 has also survived.

In the north of Spain, distinctive architectural styles developed in the seventeenth century. One such was that of the Galician house – usually a country house – with its two wings spreading out from a rectangular nucleus to enclose the courtyard. Architects in the Asturias chose what they wanted from other styles and regions as did those of Castile.

Of the Spanish architecture of this period, the centre of Santander is one of the finest examples. The houses are, in general, rectangular with a pitched roof, a wide portico on the ground floor, a large balcony on the first floor, and a projecting cornice at the top of the building resting on a double or triple row of carved brackets. The first floor balcony has a parapet and either turned wooden balusters or an iron railing. Occupying a prominent position on the façade is a large heraldic shield in stone. In some cases, wings sweep out from the building to form a court of honour in front of the house. In others, a surviving medieval tower was enclosed in the new building and used as a decorative element. In the more splendid buildings there was a private chapel, often quite large. An impressive doorway dominated the wall which surrounded the whole building.

In the Basque provinces, there were, basically, two groups of houses. One was quadrangular without either courtyard or towers. Stables and storerooms occupied the ground floor as well as the hall and kitchen. The staircase from the hall led to the reception rooms and bedrooms of the upper floor. The other group shows clearly Castilian influence, with angular towers on the façade, ornately decorated doorways, and the inner rooms arranged round a central courtyard.

In the south of Spain, a distinction must be drawn between the buildings of upper Andalusia in which the new baroque ornament was applied to buildings still strictly Renaissance in style, and those of lower Andalusia. Here new ideas imported from Castile combined with the old *mudéjar* motifs and the craftsmanship in brick of builders who remembered Moorish techniques, to produce some magnificent baroque buildings. Rooms were arranged round two courtyards, one in the centre of the building, the other at the back of it and made into a garden. An ornate stone doorway enriched the façade, already decorated by windows with elaborate iron grilles and balconies of intricate brickwork.

Cadiz, the powerful terminus of traffic to and from the new colonies in America, reached the height of its splendour in the seventeenth century. Limited space on the narrow peninsula it occupies forced its residents to build up to three or four storeys and in some cases, to place towers and terraces above these. Rich geometric designs in brick, conspicuous against the dazzling white limestone, decorated the façades, as in the house built for Ignacio de Barrios from 1686 to 1693 by an Italian architect.

Aragon, which as we have seen had already developed its own style, was faithful to it – with variations. Courtyards, staircases and galleries were simplified but, as elsewhere, the doorway became more ornate and the carved decoration of the cornice along the top of the façade became exaggerated.

In Catalonia, the new ideas in architecture and ornament had little effect save in such a house as the Dalmases house in Barcelona with its magnificent staircase. In Valencia houses began to resemble more closely those of central Spain. In Murcia, the brief prosperity of the small town of Lorca produced some interesting buildings, among them the house of the Guevara family with its flamboyant doorway, twisted columns, splendid ironwork and attractive courtyard.

Other forms of regional building, which were to be brilliantly developed during the eighteenth century, began to appear during this period. An example is those houses in the Balearic Islands where corridors, courtyards and staircases are combined to create light, spacious and beautiful buildings.

143

(Opposite page) N. J. B. Raguenet, Pla
Dauphine et Pont Neuf (1777; Paris, M
sée Carnavalet). This is the oldest squa
in Paris, built about 1610 on a geometr
plan. The buildings shown are typical
the reigns of Henry IV and Louis XI
with their stone and brick walls and sla
roofs. The design of the façades, restrai
edly classical in style, was to remain po
ular for another two centuries; each co
sisted of four parts, the divisions mark
by strips of stone. The ground level w
its arcades projected slightly from the ma
body of the building. The two upper floc
were similar in lay-out save that the ma
floor rooms had higher ceilings and tal
windows as befitted the piano nobile. Hou
es of this kind tended to be let out;
the eighteenth century, more rooms we
added in the attics.

(Above) J. B. Martinez del Mazo, The Family of Velasquez (Vienna, Kunsthistorisches Museum).
(Below) Principal room of the house bought by Lope de Vega in Madrid in 1610:
there are similarities between it and the room in del Mazo's painting.

OPULENCE AND OSTENTATION
IN SEVENTEENTH CENTURY FRANCE

DANIEL ALCOUFFE

During the fifteenth century, official encouragement of trade and industry had two important effects on the development of architecture. It was accompanied by an increase in population and, in particular, by an increase in the numbers of the middle class. The middle class prospered and grew rich. They invested in property with which they wished to advertise their wealth and standing. At the same time, from every province in France people flooded into Paris, so that within the city walls houses grew taller. But these ancient walls were insufficient to accommodate the new population whose homes had thus to spread out into new working and middle class suburbs. The skilful handling of building stone also improved during this period, a circumstance most clearly displayed in the structure of staircases.

Towards the end of the sixteenth century, civil war halted building expansion. But with the return of greater stability during the reign of Henry IV, it was renewed with vigour. Architects of the late sixteenth and early seventeenth centuries inherited from their immediate predecessors an admiration

for Graeco-Roman and Italian models which suited the increasingly grandiose ambitions of the court and the church in the reign of Louis XIII. But in the field of domestic architecture it was possible to circumvent this monumental classicism. The treatises of Vignola and Palladio were widely read in translation and critically appraised: their readers perceived, sensibly, that the Italian lack of interest in, for example, fireplaces and windows was hardly relevant to French tastes. Under the influence of architects like Pierre Le Muet (who published a translation of Palladio) a type of house evolved which, while it accepted the Renaissance principles of regular order and symmetry, applied them with a lively sense of harmony and discipline.

The lofty roof was now dominated by tall chimneys. On the façades, regularly arranged windows and the carefully proportioned decoration of the stonework created a harmonious whole. Graeco-Roman features such as columns, pilasters and cornices with classical motifs were used and gave, as François Blondel, the seventeenth century French architect and writer on architecture, said, 'meas-

145

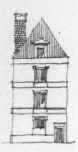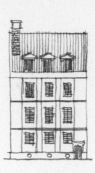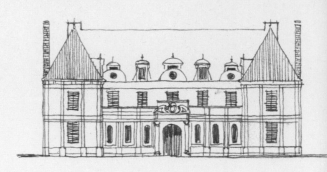

ure and order to all the rest'. Until the middle of the nineteenth century, indeed, the ornament used was for the most part antique in origin. In the seventeenth century it was applied with a rather heavy hand: at a later period, however, it was used with more skill and taste.

Admiration of effect conflicted with the demands of comfort and convenience. It did so most notably in the larger, more ambitious buildings of the period, which can on occasion look like pieces of theatrical scenery. And even in the middle class house, the overall plan tended to be sacrificed to the composition of the façade which looked as if it had been applied to the building without regard to what lay behind. In the dwelling of a 'nouveau-riche' family, the arrangement of the rooms was dominated by the desire for symmetry so that all the main rooms connected with one another and the doors were so placed as to ensure an abundance of draughts. The smaller, less important rooms and mezzanines were ill-placed and badly lit.

No expense was spared on doors and windows. A contract signed in Paris on 'the second day of the month of January in the afternoon in the year 1671' between Philippe Desnois, a painter of Rue de Figue, and Jean Delaistre, merchant glover and perfumer in the Rue St. Antoine shows this clearly. Desnois undertakes 'to paint in yellow, with two coats of oil, all the windows, the roofs, the banisters of the staircases, all the doors and the doors of the two shops and yet another,' providing 'the paint and the oil with all necessary tools and utensils.' He was prepared to do all this for 'the sum of 39 *livres*', which was a considerable sum. M. Delaistre was clearly anxious to put on a good show by using a bright and expensive colour, to be made all the brighter by the generous use of oil. Another Parisian document, the estimate given on 30th May 1643 by Jean Chrestien, master carpenter, for 'the work to be done in the two houses of Monsieur Victor de Chauray, esquire', affords an even

better idea of the kind of work done. With medieval exactness, the document specifies that 'first of all there are three carriage entrances to be made, each ten feet or so high, with small doors, each six and a half feet high, decorated with eleven panels and on the back covered with St. Andrew's crosses; one of these doors is eight feet two inches wide; the other two, seven feet eight inches: each one is divided into four leaves, two of them ten inches wide and the other two eight inches wide and four inches thick with equally wide transverse bars, and they must be decorated with cornices, friezes and architraves. The friezes will consist of a pattern of leaves or some other ornament in relief; and above the cornice, between the two leaves of the said doors, there will be the same decorations as on the leaves themselves, while at the top there will appear a scroll incorporating a monogram; and this scroll will cover the joins of the decoration which is to be placed above the cornice; the wood of the decoration in the frieze, cornice and architraves will be of a suitable quality; all according to the designs checked by Monsieur de Chauray, who will pay 110 *livres* for each of these doors, that is to say 330 for the three. Wooden doors are to be made an inch and a half thick by six to seven feet high and three feet eight inches wide, glued and faced and completed with lock and keys. These doors will have open or rather, glass, framed panels in them which Monsieur de Chauray will design, and these will have shutters on them: with regard to these doors, those with panels or glazed frames will be paid for at the rate of 10 *livres* each and the others at 9 *livres* each.' Nor was this all. 'Windows must be made with six panes,' it was further directed, 'six glazed frames and six shutters, which shutters are to be furnished with six panels each.' Again the dimensions and prices are stipulated. Finally, 'other windows, two-and-a-quarter feet wide, are to be set between two posts which, with their shutters, will be two feet seven inches wide: these will be paid for at the rate of 30 *sous* a foot,

The Grande-Rue in Richelieu (Indre-et-Loire). In 1625 when he was head of government, Cardinal Richelieu set about transforming his manor in Poitou. Six years later when his estates had achieved the status of a dukedom, he received royal permission to build a fortress-town near his castle, the inhabitants of which would enjoy special tax privileges. Twenty-eight identical building lots (each 255 × 64 feet) were in effect given to those willing to develop them along the lines dictated by the Cardinal on what was to be the Grande-Rue. His new town rose with remarkable speed and by 1635, the Grande-Rue had been built. The houses were very plain, of stone, plastered, with slate roofs and dormer windows with arched or triangular pediments. The ground floor consisted of a kitchen, storeroom, stable and paved passage; the upper floor of two rooms and a dressing room; the top floor of two more bedrooms. Behind the houses were courtyards, with wells and gardens. Similar but smaller houses were built in the side streets off the Grand-Rue. In 1642, the town was populated; in that year, however, the Cardinal died. Twenty years later, his town was dead too.

(Opposite page) Houses in the reign of Louis XIII. Gothic asymmetry yielded to classical symmetry, the focal point of which was the entrance in the façade of the house. Depending on the degree of ostentation desired and the resources available, the façade was more richly ornamented with pillars, pilasters, reliefs, sculptures and so on; it was surmounted — and here the effect was often very pleasing — by a dark slate roof into which dormer windows might be set. Side wings were added in some cases to enclose the entrance area in what was a convenient as well as a welcoming arrangement.

Small door in a house built in the last quarter of the seventeenth century in the Rue de Fouarre in Paris. During this period, the classical spirit penetrated even that stronghold of medieval tradition, the Latin Quarter, as we see from this charming doorway which is of a kind often found in buildings of the time. In the Place Dauphine (shown on page 145), householders had been still content with good, substantial materials; now they wanted decoration too: wrought iron, cornices, mouldings, rusticated stonework. Arches similar to this sometimes enclose not only the doorway but the window of a mezzanine floor; here, it includes a bull's eye window that lights the passage leading to the staircase.

Louis XIII armchair in walnut (35 inches high, 25 wide, 18 deep) (Paris, Musée des Arts Décoratifs). The sixteenth century chair was high-backed and hardly mobile; in the seventeenth century, this smaller chair was added to the furnishings of the house. The lines are still fairly rigid but the back is angled slightly. Chairs similar in design were produced in Spain and Flanders as well as in France from the late sixteenth century onwards: turned legs were a popular form of decoration.

bearing in mind that the said windows must be of the same quality as the others already mentioned.' In this estimate, the important items are size, price and decoration. The solidity of the windows is implied and the good workmanship taken, perhaps, for granted. And if we put these documents side by side, the painting to be done for the glover, Delaistre, and the carpentry to be carried out for Monsieur de Chauray, it is evident that money was no object when the client wished to make a good show.

While the classical rules were honoured, they were not always observed. The living conditions of the period, especially the overcrowding prevalent in the cities, would, indeed, have made it difficult for builders to observe them. Houses three and even five storeys high were much taller than their own width, often built of wood and not always soundly constructed. In these houses, often inhabited by craftsmen and their families, each floor was divided into four rooms. The house usually belonged to one of the families resident in it who rented out remaining rooms. As well as rent, the citizen had to contribute to street cleansing, lighting, fortifications and the lodging of soldiers.

Gillis van Tilborgh (c. 1625-c. 1678), Family Group *(Rotterdam, Boymans-van Beuningen Museum). In the average household in the seventeenth century, definite functions had yet to be ascribed to the various rooms, and the room in this painting probably ful-filled a number of functions. Though it is Flemish, it is similar to a French drawing-room of the same period with its silk-covered walls and wide fireplace surmounted by an imposing, ebony-framed picture. An oriental carpet covers the table; the chandelier is of the same type as that painted by Jan van Eyck in the* Arnolfini *portrait (see page 374). France imported furniture from Flanders though by about 1635 Parisian craftsmen were beginning to acquire the skill of their Flemish contemporaries in cabinet making. But such a cabinet as that on the left, made of ebony inlaid with tortoiseshell, ivory and bone reached Paris only about 1650, and in order to copy them Flemish workmen were employed.*

Louis XIV armchair in walnut (47 by 26 by 24 inches) (Paris, Musée Carnavalet), a statelier piece of furniture than that from the previous reign shown on the opposite page. Techniques for working wood improved during the seventeenth century and allowed craftsmen to produce the graceful curved arms, legs and stretchers. Such armchairs were sometimes gilded.

Opposite page) Gonzales Coques, Young Scholar and Girl at the Harpsichord *640; Kassel, Gemäldegalerie). Until about 1660 in France and Flanders, alls were brightly decorated; here, with gilded leather, which was ported from Spain and Flanders in large quantities to, among other untries, France. By the end of the century, however, such hangings were so being produced in Paris and official encouragement was also given the production of tapestries by Lyons and Tours. In more modest houses, alls were covered not with leather or tapestry but with Bergamo pestries obtained from weavers' rejects. Chairs were upholstered th cushions set on the wooden seats, but upholstery as we now know gained ground as strips of leather were nailed over horsehair and a covering fabric nailed to the framework (as in the Louis XIV chair, right).*

House of Jean Baptiste Lully in Paris. Appointed
director of the Royal Academy of Music in 1672, he invested
his considerable fortune in property. Daniel Gittard
built him two houses in the Rue des Petits Champs;
this one where he lived with his family, and one next
door which he let. Built in 1671, the year of the
establishment of the French Academy of Architecture
of which Gittard was a founder member, it exemplifies
the architectural ambitions of its age. In spite of its
modest size, it looks imposing with its rhythmic sequence
of pilasters, the alternation of ornament and severity.
The ground floor may have caused Lully particular pleasure
in its evocation of his native Florence. The interior was
decorated with frescoes by Bon de Boullongne
which have unfortunately disappeared completely.

The poorer classes moved house frequently in a search of lower rents; they found them in the suburbs.

In the territory that is now Belgium, there was the same divergence as in France between national taste and Italian innovations but the results were different. The brief independence of the western provinces of Flanders from 1585 to 1621 and subsequent pressures from both France and the United Provinces strengthened Flemish self-sufficiency and devotion to tradition.

Town life flourished during the fifteenth and first half of the sixteenth century when private building was profoundly influenced by the then-prevalent Gothic style. It was well suited to the country and retained its popularity, with its principal characteristics virtually unchanged, until the eighteenth century. Beneath the high pitched roof, the windows were placed one above the other in vertical bands, separated from one another only by a narrow strip of wall. Such a structure – in essence a glass cage – provided an admirable setting for the decorative flamboyance of Flemish artists. The new artistic language of Italy was discovered and artists and architects set about using it. The walls between the windows were widened to

(Below) Paris: house of Le Ménestrel who in
1670 was treasurer of the 'Conseil des Bâtiments
du Roi'; this attractive building is in the
Rue de Richelieu.

take pilasters. During the seventeenth century, builders realized that pilasters and columns need not be merely decorative elements; they could hold up an entablature or an archway. Attempts were made to reconcile the classical orders with local practice and predilection. Italian ideas of decoration became dominant but the structure of the house remained medieval.

The seventeenth century in France was a *grand siècle* for furniture craftsmen as well as architects, and French furniture of the baroque period has been collected since the middle of the nineteenth century; with such assiduity, indeed, that since the Second World War a flourishing trade has developed in fakes, restorations and adaptations. The quantity of authentic furniture is necessarily small for, compared with the number of present-day enthusiasts, the number of French and foreign buyers of it was limited in its own century. At the same time, a fondness for fine furniture gained so strong a hold on French householders that even middle class houses changed their appearance radically and often, as they did in later centuries. But the same householders would also prudently conserve furnishings not in immediate use, if only in the attic.

Just how much could be accumulated in each room of a middle class house in Paris at this time is indicated in the inventory of the possessions of Jeanne Elisabeth le Vau. It was drawn up on 20th April 1682 after the death of their owner, the daughter of the architect François Le Vau, and widow of Jean Rillart, receiver-general and paymaster to the clergy under Louis XIV. Her house, or rather apartment, was on the Ile Saint-Louis. The drawing-room 'beside the study of the above Monsieur Rillart' was furnished with 'a table and two small round tables in wood, Chinese style, the said table being furnished with a drawer.' Estimated prices follow. Then 'eight chairs and eight armchairs in walnut, upholstered in brocade with a green background, with the seats and backs in tapestry (English point), with silk fringes and braid in different colours; a large Venetian mirror 33 by 26 inches with a frame of dark wood covered with thin strips of gilt leather, and with a cord of silk and imitation silver; a large cabinet of walnut inlaid with strips of ebony; a harpsichord on a foot of dark wood, painted in the Chinese style; hangings of gilt leather in five pieces, surrounding the room; a door curtain of embroidered material, lined with green cloth; a large painting showing gladiators, on canvas, in a gilt frame; another picture, also on canvas, showing Diana and Endymion;

Antwerp house of the painter Jacob Jordaens. It is in the Rue Haute, one of the oldest streets in the town, near the port where Jordaens was born in 1593. In 1616 he moved to another house in the same street and in 1639 bought the house next door. Some years later, he demolished the two houses and built this small house to his own design. Of all the towns of the Low Countries, Antwerp adopted with the greatest enthusiasm the styles of the Italian Renaissance as Cornelis Floris's Hôtel de Ville indicated as early as 1565. In the first years of the seventeenth century, Peter Paul Rubens and the architect J. Franquart returned from Italy to champion the spread of baroque styles, particularly well suited to Flemish taste for drama in the arts. Jordaens made full use of baroque ornament in his façade — urns, pilasters, rustication, balustrades and reliefs — and added the individual touch of the broken pediment. He decorated the interior, naturally, with his paintings. In the eighteenth century most of these were removed in the course of radical alterations to the house; it has now been restored to its original appearance.

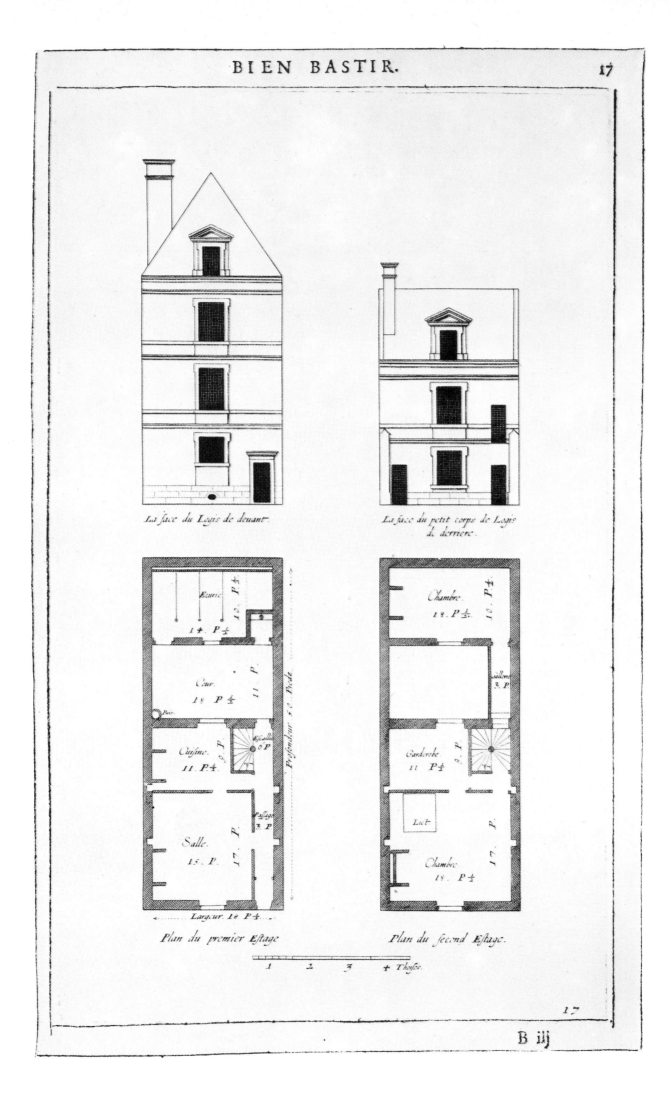

La face du Logis de deuant.

La face du petit corps de Logis de derriere.

Plan du premier Estage

Plan du second Estage.

Late seventeenth century house in the Rue Ste-Cathérine in Brussels. Here, Renaissance ideas did not oust traditional Gothic styles which were retained in the structures of buildings. But Italian influence made itself felt in a delicate application of the ideas of Sebastiano Serlio, the author of the famous and important Architettura *(first published in Italian in 1537). He suggested the strengthening of the design of a façade by the alternation of empty space and ornament. Here, restrained window decoration and the arched window on the third floor, give life to a formal façade. Flemish and Dutch writers on architecture took up Italian ideas and translated them into forms that could be turned to use by architects and builders in the Low Countries. This house probably shows the outcome of this international exchange, especially in the scrolls which complete the stepped gable; a later development was the abolition of the steps of the gable in the use of the swan-neck gable.*

(Opposite page) Plan for a dwelling house from Pierre Le Muet's Manière de bien bastir pour toutes sortes de personnes *published in Paris in 1623. The plate shows the front of the house (top, left), the back (top, right), the plan of the ground level (below, left) with a drawing-room, kitchen, courtyard and stables, and that of the upper floor (below, right) with a bedroom back and front, a dressing-room beside the staircase, and the connecting passage.*

another, showing a bull; and yet another, a landscape, in a gilt frame; eight vases of various sizes, and a figure in plaster imitating bronze.'

In Monsieur Rillart's study, the inventory takes account of 'a fire-grate and a pair of fire-dogs, a small shovel, tongs and pincers, all of iron; a desk in oak with two drawers, on it a green cover, and a small table in walnut; four chairs and four armchairs in polished walnut, two small stools of the same wood upholstered in red and yellow brocade, and two other stools covered in cotton brocade and green wool ; a large armchair in polished walnut, upholstered in material embroidered with red and black flowers on a white ground, and a cushion of the same material stuffed with feathers; a small bed with tall columns in polished walnut... the furnishings of this bed, hangings and curtains in silk brocade with red and yellow flowers, silk fringes and braid in various colours; a small walnut table with a drawer and legs in the form of twisted columns; a small casket of the same wood with four drawers that have a lock and key; a cupboard, also in walnut, with two doors, half covered in wire (it is not clear whether this formed a grill or was a rather obtrusive form of decoration) with lock and key; a cabinet in white wood with four shelves and another for keeping books in; a mirror of Venetian type in a walnut frame 19 inches by 13, with a

silk cord; four Flemish tapestries with vegetable motifs and a big cotton curtain at the window.'

Some of the objects in both rooms – such as the table with twisted column legs – may have survived from an earlier generation. But the cupboards, the mirrors, the Chinese style tables and many other items are almost certainly new and in the latest fashion.

The background to this abundance of furniture lies in the rigid etiquette which governed the court of Louis XIV. In every age there has been luxury furniture and ordinary furniture. At the court of *Le Roi Soleil*, the intricate order of precedence which developed was accompanied by a prolifer-ation of furniture styles suited to the standing at court of this or that courtier or official. This courtier might be permitted to enjoy the comfort of a chair with a back; that courtier might be confined to a stool. Each stool, chair, armchair, sofa and table played its part in this complex game.

In a remarkably short time, thanks to favourable conditions, court protocol conditioned the production of furniture for the entire kingdom. This explains why Madame Rillart's inventory is so long and why her house was so richly furnished, as were the houses of many of her contemporaries and her descendants. It also explains some, but not all, of the furniture of the period on the market.

Erasmus de Bie, Place de Meir at Antwerp (about 1650; Antwerp, Musée Royal des Beaux Arts). During the seventeenth century, Antwerp developed along lines that owed more to empiricism than a sense of architectural or aesthetic homogeneity. The Place de Meir, erected in a working class district, looked very elegant. The style of building is noticeably sixteenth century with its ranges of crow-stepped gables. The tower in the background is that of the cathedral.

The house known as Cromwell House in Highgate, London – it has no connection with Oliver Cromwell – built in 1637-38 and possibly the finest of Highgate's old houses though it was damaged during the Second World War. Inside is an elaborate oak staircase with the carved balustrades characteristic of the seventeenth century.

JOHN DRUMMOND

PALLADIO
IN ENGLAND

No century in English history saw such radical changes as the seventeenth. It began with Elizabeth I still on the throne, with the Tudor nobility the country's leaders. It ended with the country subject to a form of government that still exists, substantially, today. The years between 1600 and 1700 were occupied by the conflict of Crown and Parliament, the disasters of civil war, the execution of Charles I, the dictatorship of Oliver Cromwell, religious fanaticism and oppression in Scotland and Ireland, the restoration of the Stuarts in the person of Charles II, war with the Netherlands and, finally, the 'Glorious Revolution' of 1688, recognition of religious toleration, and parliamentary government.

In the architecture of this period we find a number of different styles which are difficult to chart as they appear to be unconnected either stylistically or chronologically.

The first 40 years of the century – that is, until the outbreak of the Civil War – are referred to, architecturally, as post-Elizabethan or Jacobean (James I reigned in England from 1603 to 1625). In the early part of the period we see evidence of the exuberance of the late sixteenth century and the influence of the writings of the Dutch Vredeman de

Vries and the German Wendel Dietterlin. But, what is much more important, it was also the period of Inigo Jones.

By the year 1600, Inigo Jones (1573-1652) had probably already visited Italy at least once and he was certainly there again in 1613 in the train of his patron, the great collector, Lord Arundel. He was an assiduous student and his copy of Palladio's *Four Books of Architecture* still exist, with his multitudinous marginal notes to show how carefully he had compared Palladio's drawings of ancient monuments with the originals, and how sedulously he studied the buildings Palladio designed in the Veneto. In his native England, as producer and director of court masques and plays, and designer of theatrical costumes, scenery and machinery, Jones was the most famous theatrical designer in the country. In 1615 he was appointed Surveyor of the King's Works and retained this position until the Civil War. His delicacy as a draughtsman, evident from a few surviving papers, his versatility, the success of the projects he undertook and the regard in which he was held, make his career comparable with that of Bernini.

Other Englishmen had visited Italy and had

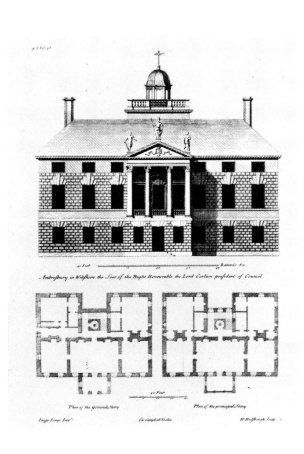

stood in admiration before the ruins of antiquity and the splendours of Renaissance architecture, including that of Palladio and his contemporaries. But Inigo Jones was the first to look at them critically and to understand them. He was the first to translate Mannerism into English in such a way that English architecture was revolutionized. A style was established that, even allowing for the inevitable changes and revivals of the eighteenth and nineteenth centuries, has survived until today.

The buildings that can definitely be attributed to Inigo Jones are few. They include the Queen's House at Greenwich (illustrated on p. 160). Even when it was completed in 1635, its classical and cubic forms must have seemed outrageously novel in a world still substantially Gothic, as England was at that time.

While the court was being educated in a Palladian taste in architecture, albeit interpreted by Inigo Jones, the merchants of London looked to Holland. In the reign of James I, there appeared for the first time the style that was actually called 'Dutch', the most characteristic element of which was the 'Holborn gable' which appeared for the first time in 1619. A drawing by John Smythson, one of a famous family of architects, shows what it looked like and it was used to good effect at Raynham Hall in Norfolk though this is rather an exception. The Dutch style was most often used in modest houses. Another form of it incorporated stepped or double-curved gables.

Another tendency, similar and almost contemporary, has been pointed out by James Lees-Milne, the architectural historian. It might be described as Flemish-classical although it was not derived from Flanders or from Rome but from Liguria, and its advocate was the Flemish artist whose restless genius exerted a profound influence on English artistic life, Peter Paul Rubens, author of *The Palaces of Genoa*. The approval awarded his architectural ideas owed something to the influence of Sir Balthazar Gerbier, Charles I's agent in the Netherlands, in the purchase of pictures. The distinctive elements of Flemish-classical were the hipped roof with overhanging eaves, dormer windows, magnificent ridge-tiles and – in the larger houses – a balustrade on the summit of the roof itself, round a central space and cupola with a lantern which illuminated the hall and staircase below. Examples of this style are Peter Mill's Thorpe Hall and Sir Roger Pratt's Coleshill.

The most famous English architect, Sir Christopher Wren, only got as far as Paris. The work for which he is best known is the rebuilding of St.

My Ladye cookes house in Houlborn at London 1619

John Smythson was one of a family of architects and master masons of the Elizabethan and Jacobean period: two of them were involved in the designs for Bolsover Castle in Derbyshire. When John Smythson went to London in 1618, he worked on this house 'belonging to my Lady Cooke' in the centre of the city, in Holborn, and reproduced it in this drawing (London, Sir Bannister Fletcher Library). Its distinguishing feature is the wide gable with its involuted scroll base, later to be known generally as the Holborn gable. It was an indication of the extent to which Dutch architecture influenced English. The older fashion of the bay window projecting on two floors was later abandoned as the Dutch style was developed.

Paul's Cathedral and fifty-two London churches damaged by the Great Fire of 1666. His authority was immense in a period of transition which corresponded to his busiest years, from the Restoration of 1660 to the death of Queen Anne in 1714, and in which one style was superimposed on another though the general trend was classical. If in fact there is such a thing as English baroque – which some deny – it can be identified with the work of Wren as well as that of Nicholas Hawksmoor (1661-1736) who also rebuilt a number of London churches; Sir John Vanbrugh (1664-1726) with his enormous country houses for the members of the Whig ascendancy; and Thomas Archer (1668-1743) who designed, for the most part, churches and mansions.

Middle class houses of the period rarely have anything of the baroque about them; still less can they be accurately described as Caroline, 'William and Mary' or 'Queen Anne'. Yet they have some individual features which for lack of a more definite

term are usually gathered together in the phrase 'Wren style'. These are houses planned for domestic comfort rather than display and in some measure they resemble those inspired by the Flemish-classical taste though they are – especially the smaller houses – more classical in design. In other words, they look back and blend the Palladianism of Inigo Jones with the simplicity of Dutch style of the same period: in some, recollections of the Jacobean period are evident in a few pedantic touches. But if we look carefully at them and think ahead, we can see that they anticipate the Georgian country house.

These houses were rectangular in plan and had a symmetrical front elevation. The builder, faithful to the precepts of Palladio and Inigo Jones, reduced the ground level to little more than a cellar and for residential purposes, it did not exist. Above, in the centre of the upper floor façade, was the entrance, often set off by columns and a small classical pediment. This central part of the façade, with the door

(Opposite page) View and ground floor plan of Raynham Hall in Norfolk (1619-1637). Its architect is unknown though, inevitably, the name of Inigo Jones has been associated with it and it is possible and indeed probable that his assistant, John Webb, had a hand in it. Dutch and classical elements are combined in it; here are the Holborn gables, on a splendid scale, mixed with a Palladian portico. During the eighteenth century William Kent made some modifications by introducing sash windows and the garden door, and by decorating two of the rooms.

The Stuart room in the Geffrye Museum in London. It has been furnished as the drawing-room of the Pewterers' Hall was in 1668 and exemplifies the taste of the age of Christopher Wren. Here are the plainly panelled walls and the rather over-powering plaster decorations of the ceiling of the period. The room contains, too, an excellent example of seventeenth century embroidery as well as solid Caroline furniture with leather or cane-seated chairs and a high-backed settle.

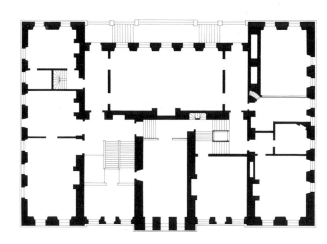

Of the experiment in town planning in London which covered the Covent Garden area and was executed by Inigo Jones in 1630-1631 nothing remains. Of the plans for the development of Great Queen Street and Lincoln's Inn Fields, carried out between 1637 and 1641, only this house survives (below), later named Lindsey House. It has been ascribed to Inigo Jones although now it is also attributed to Nicholas Stone (1586-1647) who did other work for the first owner of the building, Sir David Conyngham. It is the oldest surviving example in London of a terraced house conceived as an integral part of a comprehensive plan: the house was to form the centre of one side of a square. Since the seventeenth century, however, it has been drastically altered, in particular by division into two separate houses.

Front (above) and plan (below) of Eltham Lodge at Bromley in Kent, designed by Hugh May in 1663. When the exiled royalists returned home after the Restoration, they brought with them a taste for Dutch Palladianism of which May was one of the chief exponents. The style successfully combined stone and brick.

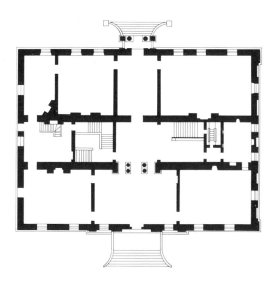

and windows on either side of it, projected in some cases, the whole being surmounted by a pediment which was either plain or decorated with a heraldic medallion. The material used was most often brick, with bands of stone between storeys and stone quoins on the corners of the building and the projecting entrance. The hipped roof ended at first with gutters and later, where possible, with a parapet and dormer windows inserted in the roof to light the attic floor. In the larger houses, the plan followed that already described of a central hall and staircase lit from a central cupola. Projecting wings were sometimes added with, as a rule, two windows on each floor. In the last quarter of the seventeenth century, the English or sash window came into use and was incorporated in most houses built at this period, superseding the casement window found in earlier buildings. Sash windows were, indeed, added to older buildings, among them the Queen's House at Greenwich and Hugh May's Eltham Lodge in Kent.

Fenton House in Hampstead, London, an interesting example of an English house in the Dutch style. Built of brick in 1693, its horizontal lines are emphasized by the bands of ashlar. The plan is rectangular though the central area of the façade, dominated by a pediment which is echoed by the smaller one over the main entrance, projects slightly from the body of the house. The pavilion roof slopes down to the eaves: the balustrade on the right anticipates the spread of the balustrade across the façade. There are the traditional seven openings on each floor of the façade, symmetrically arranged, and sash windows: dormer windows in the roof light the attic floor. The admirable simplicity of its lines is matched indoors by the arrangement of the rooms and their furniture, and the house as a whole indicates the successful conclusion of the search for comfort and convenience.

Among the few buildings that can definitely be attributed to Inigo Jones is the Queen's House at Greenwich, begun in 1618 for Anne of Denmark, consort of James VI and I. It is probably Jones's most characteristic work in the field of domestic architecture and when it was first built, the novelty of its simplified classical forms must have made a considerable impression on a world still steeped in Gothic ideas. Jones's combination of technical skill and understanding of the function of architectural styles directed English architecture along the path it was to follow for more than a century.

CHARLES F. MONTGOMERY JR.

THE PILGRIM FATHERS AND AFTER

H. Stoessel, View of New Amsterdam, *(1660; sold in 1968 by the Parke-Bernet Galleries). The original centre of modern New York 'based on Dutch records', according to the inscription, which shows Dutch buildings over the lower part of Manhattan.*

When the first British settlers set sail for the shores of North America in the early years of the seventeenth century, they took with them tools, weapons and other accoutrements which they considered – often wrongly – to be useful, and apparently irrational hopes of a new life and new fortunes to be made. Having left their native country to escape religious persecution and economic oppression, they set about re-creating in the new world replicas of the communities they had left behind, which they still regarded as home.

At first, however, in Jamestown, Virginia and Plymouth, Massachusetts, the houses they fashioned to withstand the rigours of those early winters were not much more than tents or trenches dug into the ground and roofed over, or low buildings of turf, branches, or tree trunks. The roofs were thatched with straw or reeds and any windows were sealed with oiled paper. In Massachusetts, these make-shift shelters preceded one-roomed houses with a wooden framework and mud (later board) walls.

By 1647, however, such progress had been made that one eye-witness could write: 'The Lord hath been pleased to transform all the tents, huts and hovels which the English lived in when they arrived into well-arranged and well-built houses, many of them furnished also.' In fact the richest and most enterprising residents of the coast towns now occupied houses of more than one storey, with a number of rooms and faced with wood. Wherever these were built, the basic principles in both the interior and exterior structure and the furnish-

ings were the same. Robert Beverley, describing the houses of Virginia towards the end of the seventeenth century, took pains to justify their obvious modesty. 'Private houses have recently improved a great deal,' he wrote, 'many gentlemen here having built themselves houses in brick with many rooms on each floor and several storeys high, and even a few houses of stone.' He continues, however: 'These gentlemen do not try to make them too tall, having enough land to build on; and as they have strong winds from time to time, buildings as tall as towers would be unsuitable. They always try to have large rooms which can be cool in summer. Lately, they have made their rooms much loftier than they used to and the windows much larger and closed with glass. Inside, they furnish their rooms with rich pieces of furniture. All the work of the kitchen, the laundry and the dairy is done in rooms separate from the main house which is thus kept cooler and cleaner.'

The style mainly followed combined medieval and Renaissance elements. The outline was simple and the two-dimensional appearance of the surfaces was enlivened by horizontal divisions. In French Canada, the eaves of the steep-roofed buildings were embellished in Gothic style and the outlines as a whole were relieved by the horizontal lines of porches. Heavy carvings and plain mouldings in the French style decorated much Canadian furniture.

The furniture of Massachusetts, however, provoked admiration. A visitor who arrived at Ipswich in 1686 declared: 'My lodging was so noble and

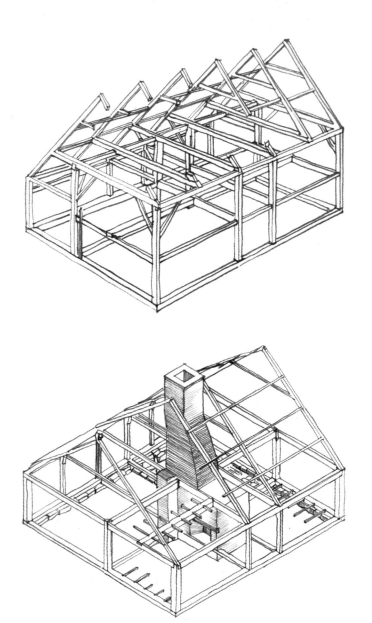

the furniture was so well arranged, that more than once I wondered whether even the king should accept any worse conditions than I.'

New York, or New Amsterdam, which belonged to Holland until 1664, reflected the influence of Dutch architecture, although we know from records of the period that by 1643 eighteen different languages were already spoken there. The façades of the houses were decorated with small enamelled bricks and with ordinary bricks set in geometrical patterns. The roofs were steep and under them the clean, white interiors resembled very closely the interiors of Vermeer, de Hooch and Avercamp. The houses of New England, New Spain and New Sweden also reflected the variations on medieval style of their inhabitants' countries of origin.

Furniture was not yet abundant or varied in function. Chairs were regarded as symbols of authority: many houses owned only one and that was the seat of the head of the family. The rest of the household had to be content with benches or stools. Heavy tables, generally of oak, with square or turned supports, beds high or low, sideboards that served both to contain and to display, and cots completed the furnishings of houses of the middle of the century. By about 1700, the richer houses possessed large and small tables, often inlaid, dressing-tables and reading desks. There were chairs with comb, or ladder backs, or backs of wooden panels, sometimes upholstered in cloth or leather. Chests and wardrobes were decorated with painted ornaments in red, white, black and brown, or with mouldings or inlays.

Structure of small wooden houses built in North America between the sixteenth and the nineteenth centuries. The techniques used were in many ways similar to those of shipbuilding and demanded considerable skill from the builders. The exterior was generally clad with shingles or planks of wood. The main parts of the inner walls were either painted or lined with planks planed smooth and set vertically, or, in the richer houses, lined with smoothly finished panels. The winters were hard so that windows were small and fireplaces large; chinks in the walls were stuffed with mud or straw. Houses expanded (below) along with the families that inhabited them. In his American Journey, 1793-1798, *Moreau de St. Méry describes the process: 'First, he (the settler) builds a second house faced with weather boarding at least twice as high as the first, which becomes its kitchen. Finally he builds a third house, even higher and larger, often of stone; then the second house becomes the kitchen and the first the hayshed.'*

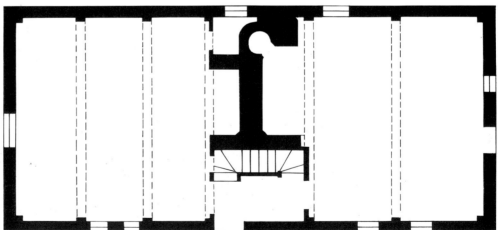

View of the front and plan of Parson Carpen's House at Topsfield in Massachusetts, built in 1683. The diary of the Reverend William Bentley (published between 1905 and 1914 at Salem, Massachusetts), describes in an entry for 1814 a clergyman called Carpen who 'had been a minister for more than 40 years' and gave his name to the house. 'Mr. Carpen's house is more or less in its original state,' he wrote. 'It has two floors, the second projecting over the first and the roof very high and steep. Inside the beams and joists are visible. The study and living-rooms of Mr. Emerson [Mr. Carpen's successor] on the left have now disappeared but what is left shows the original structure of the interior.' With its projecting upper floor, the small front door with its decorative bosses, and, inside, the attic beams (shown by dotted lines in the plan) and its pilastered fireplace, Parson Carpen's House — like many others scattered through the new colonies in the seventeenth century — reflects faithfully its medieval English heritage.

Potters and tinsmiths produced utensils that were still essentially medieval in form. Ironwork – used for locks and lamps – was sometimes still decorated with birds and hearts and other popular motifs. Towards the end of the century, more sophisticated designs were produced by the colonies' silversmiths, the first of America's artists. They made jugs, spoons, bowls, sugar-basins, cups, mugs, plates and candlesticks and decorated them with fine castings or engraved them. These silversmiths derived their inspiration from sources as varied as a book of Dutch fables or a piece of Chinese porcelain. And silver, it should be remembered here, was more than an ornament. In the absence of banks, colonists considered the wealth they had acquired to be safer, and certainly more easily identified, in the form of cups and candlesticks rather than coin.

The living-room of Hart House at Ipswich, Massachusetts, built in 1670, and rebuilt in the Henry Francis du Pont Museum at Winterthur in Delaware. It shows clearly the many uses to which a room in a small American house was put at this time, for it was at once sitting-room, bedroom, dining-room, kitchen and storeroom. Such rooms were well furnished as the inventory of the furniture in the living-room of another house in Ipswich in the year 1647 shows; it lists 'one table, three benches and one stool; one bed with a small bolster; one set of curtains and bedhangings; one mattress and a feather pillow; one straw sack and a woollen pillow; one white blanket; one pair of sheets; one green carpet; one other bed and mattress; one complete set of curtains and covers; one hemp mattress; one feather cushion; one pair of old sheets; two old blankets; one red carpet.'

Anne Berendsen

HOLLAND'S GOLDEN AGE

In the essentially middle class society of the Netherlands, the seventeenth century was a golden age of adventure and expansion at home and overseas, of growing wealth and good fortune. The Dutch achieved not only independence from Spain but founded an empire overseas, and when the occasion arose, drubbed the English at sea. In the buildings erected then, we see the reflection of this progress from comparative insignificance to prestige in the councils of Europe. Dutch architecture begins the century in homely, local style with an abundance of stepped gables and red brick, and ends it with a fine international flourish of classical ornament on façades that in any other country would have been described as palatial. The houses that Vingboons, van Campen and Dorsmann designed for their patrons — for the most part the merchant princes of Amsterdam — were in effect palaces: in Amsterdam, however, as in that other city of canals to the south, Venice, there has always been a marked reluctance to describe these princely mansions as such.

At the beginning of the century when an enormous amount of building was being carried out in Amsterdam, the *voorhuis* already incorporated the living-room while a small drawing-room, or a study, was often partitioned off from it. The spiral staircase had been placed at the end of a passage and the back room had become a kitchen.

On this basis Dutch architecture developed during the first half of the century. Every town created its own particular style. In Leiden and Haarlem, for example, we find the work of Lieven de Key, born at Ghent in 1560. His most famous building

(Above) Front of the Penninckshoek at Deventer in Gelderland, built about 1600. The steps of the gable are curved under the influence of Mannerism in its last phase.
(Below) Gateway in the town of Nijmegen, built about 1660. The vertical lines and solid stone surround of the gateway enhance its appearance of balance and solidity.

*Houses on the Herengracht in
Amsterdam. The second house from the
left with its splendid brickwork
and mouldings is the Bartolotti House
(see also page 167); its neighbour
on the right is the Theatre Museum.*

*The house at 168 Herengracht in Amsterdam, today the
Theatre Museum, dates from 1638 and was the first built
by the architect Philip Vingboons (1607-1675). Its façade
has been altered and the pediments that originally surmounted the windows have disappeared.*

*The House of the Heads — so called from the
human masks used as decoration on the
façade — on the Keizersgracht in Amsterdam.
It was built in 1622 and was probably designed
by Hendrick de Keyser (1565-1622).
A notable feature is the gradually
soaring line of the gable.*

is probably the Vleeschhal or meat market in
Haarlem, which in fact dates from 1603, but several
houses in the two cities demonstrate his plastic,
essentially craftsmanlike style and his very Flemish
talent for a lively realism. The public buildings of
Vredeman de Vries influenced, too, the design of
some middle class houses, in particular their façades.

In Amsterdam, the versatile Hendrick de Keyser, architect, sculptor and town planner, dominated
architecture. Born at Utrecht in 1565, the son of a
carpenter, he was a pupil of Cornelis Bloemaart,
like de Keyser a sculptor as well as an architect,
and an engineer. In 1594, he was appointed city
architect of Amsterdam and there, in buildings
like the Westerkerk, he did some of his greatest
work. By temperament he was a sculptor which
meant that he was above all concerned with three-
dimensional effects. These he created in his houses.

By about 1630, two changes were beginning to

affect Dutch architecture. One was a change in the status awarded to or claimed by architects, who more and more abandoned their former position as craftsmen and united into groups more like academies than guilds, characterized, perhaps, by a certain pretentiousness. The second change was the growing influence of classicism, which made itself felt in architecture before it touched painting. Jacob van Campen (1595-1657) was the first architect to work in the new style. The Royal Palace in Amsterdam, formerly the Town Hall, and the Mauritshuis in The Hague are two of the best known examples of his work.

A generation younger than Hendrick de Keyser, who died in 1622, was Philip Vingboons (1607-1675) whose influence on Dutch domestic architecture in Amsterdam makes him one of the country's most important architects. His clients were wealthy merchants and for them he designed houses that

(Above left) Bartolotti House on the Herengracht in Amsterdam (see also opposite page), a stately building by Hendrick de Keyser which is, however, less severely classical in style than the House of the Heads *(page 166). As the doorways indicate, it is now divided into two.*

(Above) The double house at 29 Kloveniersburgwal, Amsterdam, built by Justus Vingboons (1608-1675), brother of Philip Vingboons, for the brothers Louis and Hendrick Trip. The building was planned from the first for two families as the position of the entrances shows. The interior, too, is divided into two identical parts and the central windows of the façade are, indeed, divided down the middle by an interior wall. The chimneys in the shape of cannons refer to the Trip brothers' foundries. The building now houses the Royal Academy of Science.

(*Opposite page*) View of the Herengracht in Amsterdam by Gerrit Adriaensz. Berckheyde (1638-1698) (Amsterdam Six Collection). This artist faithfully recorded seventeenth century Dutch townscapes. Unlike the houses on pages 166 and 167, the buildings shown here are classical in style without elaborate gables but with a notable symmetry of design

Old photograph of houses in the Wijnstraat in Dordrecht, of which the second from the left is noteworthy. The fine façade is divided by pilasters with composite capitals; these pilasters are linked by heavy stone garlands as well as by a massive pediment dominated by the statue of a naked child. The house was built between 1650 and 1653 to the design of Pieter Post.

Reconstruction of the Ganzenmarkt in Utrecht, drawn by Victor de Stuers in 1874. The period in which the drawing is set is the middle of the seventeenth century and it shows wooden and brick buildings as they probably appeared at that time.

Huydekoper House at 548 Singel in Amsterdam, built in 1631 to designs by Philip Vingboons which were, however, only partially carried out. The print shows the front with its rusticated ashlar and the carefully planned fenestration.

were both elegant and comfortable, on the banks of the city's canals. By this period, the pitch of the roofs had been reduced and steps on the stepped gables were lower and fewer in number. The *neck* roof developed with the concave curves of the gable suggesting the line of the human neck and shoulders. In Vingboons's house-fronts, the narrow necks were flanked under the roof by corbels containing oval windows to light the attic. These corbels fulfilled an architectural function in shortening the sides of the façade which were otherwise too high. His application, too, of the architectural rules governing the use of pilasters was unorthodox. Since the fronts of his houses had little room for them, he sometimes used mere strips instead of vertical supports. It was also typical of his inventiveness that he used the central part of the façade to create an effective contrast between the various planes of the design, and at the same time made it easy to hoist goods up to the storeroom under the roof. (His clients were, as we have noted, merchants and their houses also possessed large basements and attics used as stores. On the main floor, there was a small office.)

The Rijnlandhuis in Leiden, built in 1612 by Lieven de Key. The façade with the stepped gable is characteristic of the styles of the previous century but the decoration of the windows is manneristic. The asymmetrical arrangement of door and windows on the ground level recalls again an earlier period.

Wardrobe with four doors (mid-seventeenth century; Utrecht, Brom Collection) faced with ebony, the high polish of which reflects the light so that, with the small copper plates inserted, there is a constant play of light and shade. The decorative motifs are borrowed from architecture; an example is the columnar ornament of the top section.

Vingboons also devoted a great deal of attention to the interiors of his houses and devised a number of new and convenient plans for them. Often he reverted to the principle of the *voorhuis* but he also used an arrangement with a central passage in which the old spiral staircase was replaced by a flight of steps rising straight up, with landings, often lit by a skylight. It was simple, with the simplicity of an interior by Pieter de Hooch, but it preserved much valued intimacy.

Contemporary with Vingboons was Adriaan Dorsmann who designed a house in 1666 for Rembrandt's friend, Jan Six. His example encouraged the construction of rows of buildings with majestic façades, faintly austere cornices crowned by balustrades and supported by pilasters. The entrance is the important feature and to enhance it, there are few windows, grandeur being given precedence over good lighting. The *voorhuis* became a hall. There were those architects in Amsterdam, however, who sneered at these 'walls with a few holes in them'. They were, for all that, imitated in the Dutch provinces.

From Friesland to Zeeland the Dutch provinces are, in fact, rich in seventeenth century architecture, for the large cities were not the only beneficiaries of the country's newly acquired wealth. In the province of Friesland, houses with modestly classical façades and decorated stucco interiors still stand, to recall the seventeenth century and later prosperity of the region, where the cupboards of the

Though this house was built in Haarlem in 1637, its plan is still Gothic and Gothic elements are retained in its façade. The steps of the gables are, however, smaller than in the previous century.

(Above, right) Dutch Interior by Pieter Janssen, known as Elinga (about 1670; Frankfurt, Städelsches Kunstinstitut) affords an excellent idea of an elegant Dutch interior with its geometrically patterned floor and the generously proportioned high windows. That it is a prosperous house is indicated by the paintings and the fine quality of the furniture shown.

The Little Street by Vermeer (about 1658; Amsterdam, Rijksmuseum) This may have been the view from Vermeer's house on the Voldersgracht in Delft. The house on the right was probably demolished in 1661 to make room for new headquarters for the Guild of St. Luke. It is a more modest house than that painted by Elinga or, for that matter, than those painted by Vermeer himself on other occasions and probably dates from the sixteenth century, though it may be earlier. The lower part of the building has been whitewashed. The painting shows how part of the windows was protected by shutters.

Another swan-neck façade (1671) dominated, however, by massive pilasters on this house at 's-Hertogenbosch. These are of brick. The brick often used at this period – and used here – was nine inches by two.

Houses on the Rapenburg, the most picturesque and elegant of Leiden's many canals. (The house in which Rembrandt was born is in a small street off it.) The two façades are of the swan-neck type which succeeded the Gothic stepped gable. In both the pediment is flanked by supports decorated in baroque fashion. These seventeenth century houses are probably the work of the same architect and there has clearly been a measure of co-operation in the planning of their appearance. Save for details of ornament, they closely resemble each other and one is virtually the negative of the other.

farmers were filled with gold and silver plate and their womenfolk wore golden helmets under their white bonnets.

Dutch interiors of the first half of the seventeenth century are, as we know from the paintings of the period, among the country's glories. De Hooch, Vermeer and many others show us those panelled and painted walls; the floors of marble or stone, plain or patterned; the ceilings with their wooden beams, unpainted or painted red or green; the whole bathed in light from the unshuttered parts of the windows. The furniture, in oak, is rarely as richly decorated as in the previous century but is probably more elegant, with a few ornamental motifs on corners and some sober inlay in ebony and bronze. There were pictures too, hung high above the panelling and catching the light. In no other period and in no other country are we so conscious of a pervading sense of calm and security.

Houses on the Spaarne at Haarlem, built at the beginning of the seventeenth century. They resemble houses built by Lieven de Key, the architect of the famous Meat Market in Haarlem; the liveliness of the façades suggests his style.

G. OPRESCO · P. PETRESCO

MERCHANTS' HOUSES IN THE BALKANS

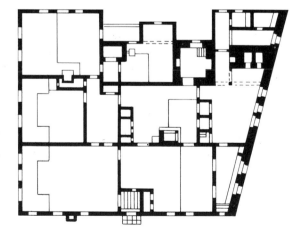

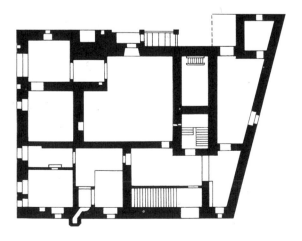

The house of the Constantsali family in Arbanassi, one of many houses of the kind built in this charming town near Turnovo in northern Bulgaria in the seventeenth century. The ground level windows (lower plan) are still obviously Gothic. (Upper plan is of the upper floor.)

Even in the unsettled conditions of the seventeenth century in south-east Europe – the Turkish army was turned back from Vienna only in 1683 – cities grew in number and size. The Florentine secretary of a Wallachian prince wrote of Bucharest and its 50,000 inhabitants and commented that the perimeter of the city was very large. The houses within it were, he added, widely scattered, whether their owners were merchants or craftsmen. Each householder had a kitchen garden full of fruit trees which made the house look very gay.

The process of city development gained impetus during the eighteenth century. Local building traditions were maintained in Rumanian towns like Tirgoviste, Sibiu, Brasov, Arges and Suceava as well as in Bucharest, and in some Bulgarian towns such as Samokov and Coproviste. Here, increasingly tall houses were built, mainly in wood. Such purely local products devoid of any oriental influence are not to be found south of the Danube during the next two centuries.

At Arbanassi near Turnovo in Bulgaria, the large houses closely resembled those of the boyars and rich Rumanian merchants. They were on two floors, the ground floor of stone, the upper one of wood. Below were the porter's lodge, the storerooms, stables and the secret store. The main staircase led directly up to the principal public room. The residential part of the house also included a sitting-room and dining-room, several bedrooms, large and small, and such service rooms as the kitchen and the bakehouse. As in the houses of Rumanian merchants, the comfortable interior contrasted with the forbidding exterior, with its massive, undecorated walls, its high-set windows and defensive entrance. These houses belonged to merchants who were frequently absent from home and who were keenly aware of the need for protection for their families: hence what has been called the 'ferocity' of Balkan seventeenth century houses.

It was not, however, universal. In the north of Rumania, the influence of the Renaissance penetrated, albeit gradually, and the shape of the Transylvanian house was enlivened by baroque elements.

BRICK
AND STONE
IN RUSSIA

Mihail Iljin

The house of A. Kirillov, Secretary of State, built in Moscow about 1657, shows a vigorous mixture of local and western European elements. The entrance to the private chapel is on the left.
(Below) Plan of a house built in Moscow about the middle of the seventeenth century by the painter Simon Ushakov; note the thickness of the walls.

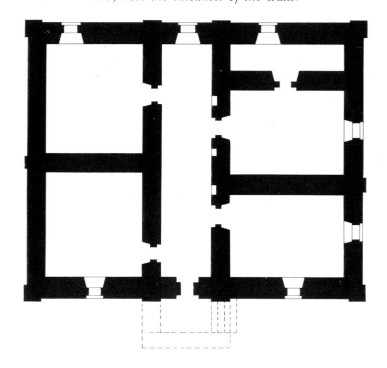

The establishment of a unified Russian state in the sixteenth century and the consequent increase in prosperity of the military aristocracy, the officials and the corporations of merchants and craftsmen, was reflected in urban building during the seventeenth century. The structure of society and the place within it of the householder, and his financial power, continued to be reflected in the house's size and decoration. In the diary of his travels the Patriarch Makarios, who visited Russia from the Levant in about the year 1650, describes the houses as 'new and made of stone and brick. . . We have admired,' he added, 'the beauty, the ornament, the solidity, the architecture, the many windows and the height of the floors which makes them seem like fortresses.'

At the beginning of the century most buildings were still made of wood on the traditional plan of two, three or four rooms within outer walls, the thickness of which varied from 12 to 14 inches. The stove, that fundamental part of the Russian house, showed obvious improvements, thanks to a more widespead and improved use of terracotta bricks, already in the sixteenth century the focus of decoration in domestic interiors.

The number of brick houses was, however, increasing. They were planned on the same lines as wooden buildings and were popular especially in those towns which were developing commercially – Moscow, Yaroslav, Pskov, Gorokhovetz – where it was desirable that rooms should be capable of being closed off securely, thus averting the danger of fire. To add to the sense of security, iron bars were set in the wall. But in the type of house most frequently encountered, with three rooms, we find a new design. In the house in Moscow, for example, of Simon Ushakov, the Russian seventeenth century painter, the hall is turned into a corridor and numerous rooms open from it on both sides; one of these must have been his studio. The homes of richer families were often two or three storeys high and sometimes contained a private chapel. On the upper floor was the dining-room and the 'best' parlour for receiving visitors. The windows, as the Patriarch Makarios noted, were numerous and had carved frames or architraves. A portico usually sheltered the main entrance.

Stone was used, too, often as the base of the house. In houses at Pskov, an upper storey with a wooden floor was built above this base and formed the residential part of the house. It seems to have been internally divided – half for men and half for women. Round this upper floor were sweeping circular galleries which formed an important part of the decoration of the building. The shape of the roofs varied. The rooms, with their low narrow doors, were probably warm and comfortable – and light, for the walls were thinly whitewashed.

During this period, the outer walls of houses

The house of the Pogankin family, merchants in Pskov, built between 1620 and 1630. This photograph shows a corner of the large courtyard with the covered entrance to the first floor of the house, as it appeared after many alterations. Originally (see drawing on page 177) this entrance consisted of a covered stone staircase set at right angles to the front of the house and leading from ground level straight to the first floor. Here, as the second plan on page 177 shows, were three ante-rooms with a storeroom on the right and an office on the left. In the adjoining wing after another office, were four reception rooms; there were other reception rooms on the top floor of the house.

were still so thick that the back staircases were carved within their thickness. After 1650, however, increasing use was made of stone by both the middle classes and nobles. By the end of the century, for technical and social reasons, the house was established as an arrangement of residential rooms, while 'public' occasions were held in the courtyard with its surrounding walls and elaborate doorway: pantries, storerooms, kitchens and similar rooms were confined to their own building, also made of stone. The courtyard varied considerably in size from 26 feet square to, perhaps, 130 by 80 feet.

Towards the end of the century, the exteriors of the principal domestic buildings in Moscow were being painted in bright colours; the observant Makarios took note of 'the abundant decoration, with paintings of many colours'. Of primary importance in the design was the main entrance, a strong dark section of the façade.

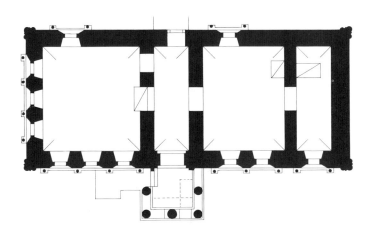

Plan (above) and view of the façade (right) of the house of the merchant Korobov, built about the end of the seventeenth century in Kaluga, south of Moscow. The front is 70 feet wide. The large room on the left is the room used for celebrations or feasts; that on the right, behind the two close-set windows is the bedroom.

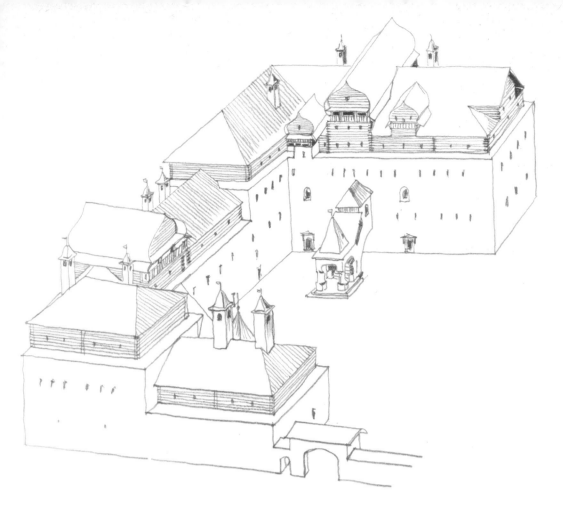

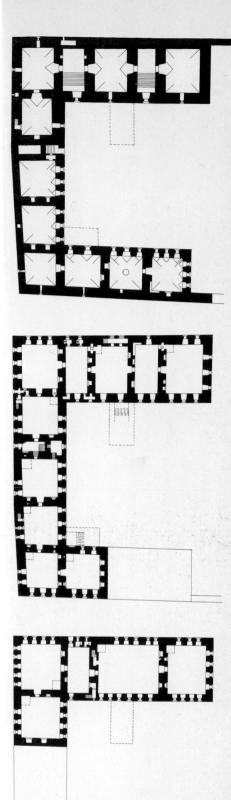

Reconstruction of the house belonging to the Pogankin merchants in Pskov
and (right) plans of the three floors of the original building (top,
the ground level; centre, the main floor; bottom, the second floor). The wall facing
the courtyard, in which the entrance staircase is set, is no less than 99 feet long and
gives an idea of the building's size. The part of the building facing the owner's
private wing accommodated the kitchen and servants' quarters. The row
of buildings which linked the two accommodated the employees and the less
important guests. These central buildings are of different shapes and sizes,
a characteristically Russian arrangement. The two topmost storeys
of the building were of wood. Note also the elaborate
onion-shaped roofs, reminiscent of Byzantine-influenced church domes.

Detail of the ikon of The Madonna of Jihvin *(1680) showing wooden Russian houses. This work of art in the Byzantine tradition depicts the method of construction of the houses with admirable accuracy; note the shingled roofs and the joining of the tree trunks at the corners.*

Detail of the ikon of The Annunciation *painted in 1659 by G. Kazanetz and G. Kondriatev (Moscow, Church of the Holy Virgin of Georgia). In addition to the three panels — one large, two small — which we see here, there are eight small panels. All show buildings of an idealized type in which recognizably oriental characteristics are combined with Renaissance elements.*

COLOUR
IN THE HOUSE

According to John Ruskin, coloured or polychromatic marbles appeared on the façades of Venetian houses when architects, feeling themselves at a disadvantage in an age increasingly devoted to pictorial decoration, attempted to introduce a form of ornament which they could themselves control. In the fifteenth century, there was no clearcut division between architects and sculptors — many craftsmen were both — just as there was none between builders and master-masons in medieval workshops. *Pace* Ruskin, however, coloured stone had been used to decorate Venetian houses — and houses elsewhere — even before frescoes.

Since building materials naturally have some colour or other, architecture might be described as an arrangement of coloured masses. Even a whitewashed wall is a coloured wall; sunlight changes it; shadows add other colours. A band of stone, however pale, inserted into a brick façade, creates a contrast that is obviously quite independent of light and shade. The effect may be created originally not for aesthetic but for practical and technical reasons; it may simply be convenient and practically desirable to combine thus two materials which happen to be available together as a result of local conditions.

But very often, of course, a band of stone or a stone facing is purely decorative. If an ornamental facing for a building is chosen at all, then it is chosen to produce a deliberate effect. If a colour is chosen, however simple it may be, it is chosen to create a particular impression.

Between a wall painted plain blue, yellow or green and the complexities of two and three dimensional patterns, there is an endless elaboration of forms. There is decoration subordinated to the plan of the building, as is a marble parapet or the pillars of a portico; there are carved ornaments, and ornaments designed to simulate more valuable materials; decoration designed to increase the sense

Schaffhausen, northern Switzerland; one of the old houses along the Vorder-Gasse. This, the Haus zum Ritter, *is decorated with figures taken from Roman history, painted by Tobias Stimmer in 1510; it was extensively restored in 1769.*

Stein-am-Rhein, also in northern Switzerland, is rich in houses with painted fronts. The buildings in the group shown here range in date from the seventeenth to the eighteenth centuries; their frescoes harmonize remarkably well; in some cases they are imposed on, rather than painted round, the structural elements of the building. The trompe-l'oeil of the house on the right pulls together the various elements of the façade, for example, the two square upper floor windows and the differently shaped row of windows on the floor above it.

Hausa house built of mud, in the Moslem quarter of Zinder in southern Niger. The ends of the poles or stakes that form the vertical framework of the building are put to decorative use as pinnacles. The walls of Hausa buildings are decorated with a wide variety of patterns. In this example, the central pattern is geometric; variations incorporate vegetable motifs. The patterns on either side of it are more common. In most cases, the colour of the mud is an integral element in the pattern and is here enhanced by the use of contrasting white and blue. The limited palette is handled with great assurance of touch and an instinctive sense of distribution of mass.

of space but still dependent on the structure of the building – such as niches or alcoves, whether empty or occupied. Interior decoration may be coloured fabric, such as curtains, or painted canvas, pictures that 'break through' the walls with an evocation of another scene which creates the illusion of a landscape, or even the illusion of other architectural forms.

The embellishment of buildings is a very ancient art, practised in the Far East from a very early period in Mesopotamia and Persia, in the palaces and villas of ancient Rome, decorated with marbles and mosaics, in Byzantium with its magnificent mosaics, and in the mosques and palaces of Islam with their superb tiles and calligraphic ornament. The painted exteriors of the Middle Ages in Europe are one variation on this tradition. Venice may have seen the first experiments in painting the outer walls of a house and it is probable that the practice spread out from there into the Veneto and thence to Padua, Treviso and north to Trento. From there it infiltrated the German states. Central Italy took

(Below) Painting on leather (32 inches by 68) by Federico Zuccari (Rome, Palazzo Venezia Museum), a section of which, shown here, depicts the painting of the outside of a house. Zuccari shows his brother Taddeo, then aged 18 (which dates the picture to 1547), painting black and white frescoes of incidents from the life of Furius Camillus on the walls of the Palazzo Mattei in Rome. According to Vasari, when his client, Jacopo Mattei, saw the first two frescoes he was 'not merely pleased but amazed'. In order the more eloquently to congratulate his brother, Federico Zuccari included Michelangelo on horseback in the picture, looking as astonished as everyone else. Unfortunately, since the paintings have disappeared, it is not possible to estimate how much of this admiration was justified. What is quite certain is that it is very unlikely that Taddeo Zuccari had a nude model on the scaffolding to pose for him.

(Opposite page) Incised decoration on the house of Bianca Capello in the Via Maggio in Florence. The house was restored by Bernardo Buontalenti (1536-1608) for the favourite, later the wife, of the Grand Duke Francis I. It is a fine example of a gentleman's house of the end of the sixteenth century. On the façade, the heavy stonework of the doorway contrasts with the comparatively delicate incised decoration: such decoration, also known as graffito *was known in Germany in the thirteenth century and was fashionable in Italy throughout the Renaissance period.*

(Below) Nude Woman (8 feet 4 inches by 4 feet 8 inches; Venice, Accademia Gallery), all that remains of the external decorations painted by Giorgione on the Fondaco dei Tedeschi in Venice; and the print that shows its condition two centuries ago. Many Venetian houses had painted façades, often the work of famous artists; the salt air has, unfortunately, destroyed nearly all of them.

to the fashion and some excellent Florentine examples were copied by other Tuscan cities. By the end of the century Rome, too, had adopted the practice and, as in Venice – where artists like Giorgione and Titian had been employed on this task – a school of specialists developed, led by Maturino and Polidoro da Caravaggio.

From paintings of this kind, it was a short step to monochrome frescoes which imitated marble or bronze reliefs or architectural features; and an even shorter one to *graffiti* which had the great advantage, as Vasari commented, that they 'stood up to water'. North of the Alps, however, it was above all polychrome decoration which developed, with the help of some of the greatest artists of the age, among them Hans Holbein the Younger, and which has remained in vogue until quite recently.

The Palazzo Dario on the Grand Canal in Venice, commissioned by Giovanni Dario who seems to have been secretary to the Venetian Republic in Constantinople about 1487, and designed either by Pietro Lombardo or by an architect in his circle. Venetian taste for drama is obvious in this marble-decorated façade with its roses and roundels which splendidly expresses the Venetian love of colour.

ELEGANCE
AND INFORMALITY

THE EIGHTEENTH CENTURY

When the prolonged ritual of the reign of Louis XIV came to an end, a longing manifested itself in France for bourgeois comfort and convenience. There and elsewhere, the formality of the palace was replaced by the informality of the *hôtel particulier* and the *maison de plaisance*. The drawing room yielded to the parlour and the boudoir. Small tables convenient for conversation superseded the larger pieces of an earlier period. The walls were clothed in fabric instead of wooden panelling. The front of the house might still be pretentious or bare, but inside there was genuine comfort and a sense of convenience that had never been known before. The new fashion came from England and was adopted with enthusiasm in France, in particular in the Paris of Louis XVI when things English were all the rage. From France and England it penetrated to every part of Europe and to the American colonies.

Grandeur gave way to elegance. The magniloquent classicism of the seventeenth century, it was realised, was not a genuine reflection of the world of Greece and Rome but an invention of the Renaissance. The realization brought a sense of relaxation. Furniture, fabrics, ceramics, silver, glass, released from the limitations of classical styles, became delicate, light, even frivolous. Workmanship was still of a very high quality. But building decoration and furniture design favoured the asymmetrical line, the irregular, decorated surface, the fantastic motif.

It was an age of small things, small pieces of furniture in small rooms, achieving a sense of harmony hitherto unknown, for often the furniture was treated as a unit with the rest of the house's décor and was designed by the architect. Cabinetmakers, workers in bronze, weavers of tapestries, painters and sculptors and plasterers worked together happily; the divorce of art and craftsmanship had not yet taken place. They coped with foreign influences such as the passion for *chinoiserie* in the middle of the century when Chinese furniture, fabrics, wallpapers or rather European interpretations of them were in demand.

Even kings, even the King of France, began to expect comfort. Versailles was divided into a series of charming apartments. The new proportions suited the less formal way of life with its gentler conversations, the soft music of the spinet, the clothes that were still very grand by modern standards, but easier to wear than the heavy, often padded garments necessary to withstand the chill of baroque drawing rooms. Ange-Jacques Gabriel, the architect of the Place de la Concorde in Paris, called the new rooms made out of large old ones 'mouseholes'. He also designed, nevertheless, the Petit Trianon at Versailles. Art and life were closely linked. The clothes of the lady of the house – her wide skirts, for example – and of her husband affected the design of furniture; this we can deduce not from paintings but from the furniture and from eighteenth century dress which has survived.

After the French attack on Brussels in 1695, part of the city was rebuilt in the original Gothic style. But when the upper or new town was laid out during the governorship of Charles of Lorraine (1744-1780), such conservatism was no longer fashionable and houses like this were built in the Place Ste-Catherine (1759). The influence of classicism is evident in the pediment, though it is modest in size, and in the organization of the windows. The placing of the dormer windows and the restrained decoration about them recall, however, the gables of an earlier period.

During the eighteenth century, the furniture produced by French cabinet makers was much more delicately fashioned than that of earlier periods. An example is this bureau à cylindre *(height: three feet; Paris, Musée Carnavalet). It makes use of an innovation by Jean-François Oeben, the great cabinet maker, whereby the opening of the desk drew out a small table; he specialized in locking devices in his furniture.*

Until the end of the age of Louis XIV, French provincial furniture retained the styles of earlier periods. By the eighteenth century, however, each region was making its own version of the models from Paris, adapting the new ideas to the materials available and the techniques practised in each district. In this wardrobe (eight feet eight inches high; Arles, Museon Arlaten), the doors are panelled, each panel being outlined by the serpentine lines of the rococo, typical of the craftsmen of Provence. Typical too of this kind of armoire *is the carving of the areas round the panels and the arched and moulded cornice.*

(Opposite page) The Honest Model *by Jean-Michel Moreau le Jeune (engraving, 1770). Though it has probably been tidied up, this studio is seen to share in the general improvement of living standards of the eighteenth century. In her* Mémoires *(Paris, 1865) Madame Roland, daughter of an eighteenth century engraver in Paris, recalls the room in which she studied as a child as being 'pleasant... charmingly furnished, with mirrors and a few paintings'. This studio, which belongs to the last years of the* ancien régime *is very elegant and the furniture is in the latest fashion.*

The death of Louis XIV has been correctly regarded as a liberation not only in politics but in the arts. No sovereign after him ever again dictated the taste of a kingdom as he had done. Reaction was decided and rapid and the century that followed may be looked upon, in large part, as a period in which individuality, sensibility and gaiety took revenge on academic rigidity and on what had become the solemn tastelessness of classicism.

Rocaille, the wayward curving line, the pretty rather than the beautiful perhaps, these are what later generations now associate with the reign of Louis XV, and they do indeed predominate in the decorative arts of the decades between 1730 and 1760. Yet, despite reaction against the styles of Louis XIV, respect for antiquity lingered on. Architects, the sons or pupils of those of the previous reign, made use of the classical orders in their buildings. Now and again, some rococo detail would sprout from the ornament of the building but, on the whole, building in the classical style continued to develop. If it lost in majesty, it gained in gracefulness and elegance of proportions clearly visible even in buildings compelled to be small for lack of space. Structure and decoration were in complete harmony.

But antiquity, it became clear, was merely biding its time. After 1755, it stirred again. 'Unquiet spirits cannot enjoy a long rest,' an unknown philosopher wrote some years later in *Country Pastimes*, published in The Hague in 1767. 'We tried to revive Greek architecture and an epidemic at once broke out. People build, eat and drink as if they were Greeks, we refer everything back to them.' This infatuation with the antique, at first no more than a fashionable craze, gradually took on a more serious and scholarly aspect. From 1778, the Académie Française confined its studies to ancient monuments and archaeology – admittedly of a fairly superficial nature – and decided how public buildings, including religious buildings, should be designed. Middle class houses escaped these excesses.

But if the exteriors of houses did not change greatly, the interiors did. The moving force was the fondness for comfort. The conventional and often arbitrary plans of the seventeenth century were abandoned. Householders wanted an easily managed house with the rooms arranged – service as well as living rooms – in a practical manner.

LE MODELE HONNÊTE.

A Monsieur le Comte De Stroganoff
Conseiller Privé, Chambellan Actuel de sa Majesté Impᵗᵉ de toutes les Russies
Chevalier des Ordres de l'Aigle Blanc, de St Stanislas & de Ste Anne

L.-L. Boilly, The Visit *(c. 1790; London, Wallace Collection). This shows a typical Louis XVI drawing-room with its intricately draped curtains, oval backed chair, and the desk with its straight legs. The graceful curves of the chair in the middle of the room belong, however, to the reign of Louis XV, while the rosette in relief on the door is a late eighteenth century version of a Louis XIV motif. The umbrella and cloaks indicate that it is winter; a few months later, these same pieces of furniture would be wearing their summer covers of flowered silk or printed linen, a fashion popular in the upper reaches of society and adopted, too, by the middle class.*

'Today it would seem ridiculous,' the unknown moralist continues, 'to build as people did a hundred years ago; what counts more than anything is the doors, the windows and the small apartment... Everything is sacrificed to the wish for fresh air and we would rather be scorched by the sun than wilt in darkness.' In his *Cours d'Architecture*, published in 1772, Jacques François Blondel, though himself the son and grandson of architects of the reign of Louis XIV, accepts these new demands and insists on 'the need to make the comfort of the interior go hand in hand with the harmony of the exteriors.' Rooms were no longer laid out in a row though a sense of length was still admired: it was obtained by the use of mirrors. Mezzanines, or *entresols*, which afforded extra space, were built above the rooms which, with their ceilings thus lowered, were more easily heated. More specialized uses were made of them. The typical dwelling now included a hall, a drawing-room, a bedroom, a dressing-room, and sometimes a bathroom. The larger reception room disappeared, to be converted into a dining-room, study, and library.

Because it succeeded in challenging the Italian baroque and because its exterior and interior satisfied the practical necessities of the time, French architecture became dominant on the continent in the eighteenth century. In the southern Low Countries which were Spanish at first and Austrian after 1730, the ascendancy of France was complete. Even at Tournai, which was French from 1678 until 1709, an occasional mansard roof and bull's eye window had been the only manifestations till then

In 1724 the Lazarists advertised their houses in the Rue du Faubourg-Saint-Denis in the following terms: 'Respectable Christian retreat. If any respectable persons, whether clerical or lay, wish to live a little apart from the great world, the religious of the mission of St. Lazarus can, for a modest sum, provide them with healthy and comfortable lodgings beside their own church... with all the necessities of life in health as in sickness.' Decorative corbels in the style of Louis XIV add individuality to these house-fronts and save them from anonymity.

of that epoch in the city. The eccentric lines of the rococo appealed to Flemish fondness for extravagant decoration and they began to use it on the façades of their houses. At the same time, French influence was further enhanced by the decision of the Hapsburg government of Flanders to undertake an urban restoration programme according to the best French principles of town planning. Flemish tradition, thus far tenaciously maintained, declined under the impact of French classicism, and the history of architecture in Flanders was fused with that of France.

Not everyone worried, however, about classicism or tradition. A large section of the population of France still wanted little more than a roof over their heads. One day in 1742, Jan Georges Wille, a young woodcarver, or rather, aspiring woodcarver, who had come to Paris six years before from his native Bieberthal, decided to change his lodgings. It was a decision attended by some mishaps which he describes in his *Memoirs*. 'I left my house and, after walking along street after street with my nose in the air, I saw "Furnished Room to Let" in large red letters on several doors. "This is what I want," I said, going into one of them, where a woman who had once been a fruitseller showed me a great many rooms, each dirtier and darker than the last and wretchedly furnished... I shrugged my shoulders and left. In the same street I went into another house that looked very fine and where the owner was a young lady. She received me very cordially and showed me a number of rooms that were unlet. But out of the corner of my eye, in more than one room, I caught glimpses through half-open doors of insolent-looking, bold-mannered youths with girls as experienced as they were free in their behaviour, since they were singing dirty songs with every appearance of enjoyment. This scarcely gave me a favourable idea of the house and I decided to leave. With a fib to its charming owner, I managed to escape; she believed me and we parted pleasantly. I then went into a house where I crashed into something while I was still in the hall, for it was full of rubbish; all the same, I carried on out of pure curiosity and found myself in a large, smoke-blackened room, every corner of which was filthy. In it lived a group of poor chimney-sweeps from Savoy, each of whom had the privilege of sleeping on a heap of filthy straw, at two *sous* a night, payment in advance. I beat a rapid retreat from that disgusting hovel, and to make up for it, I was shown some very fine apartments in other houses, more suited to a nobleman than to a young man determined to work as hard as possible at his job, even if he had to live poorly... I continued and chance led me to the Rue de l'Observance where at last I was lucky because,

In the last decade of the eighteenth century, the Rue des Colonnes was built in Paris, partly on the site of older buildings. Official building plans were drawn up and houses like this built. It shows how the Revolution, far from halting the classical revival, added fresh impetus to it, the only difference between the new and the old régime being that the Academy was no longer there to control excesses; this goes some way to explain the columns which are a Graeco-Egyptian hybrid. The Egyptian element foreshadows the popularity of such motifs after Napoleon's Egyptian campaign in the closing years of the century; Egyptian motifs had already been used during the reign of Louis XVI, in, for example, chairs by Georges Jacob, the cabinet maker.

191

During the eighteenth century, French provincial towns were largely replanned. An example is Bordeaux, until then a medieval city, altered at the will of the merchants and manufacturers who had grown rich from their trade with the West Indies. One of the new buildings was this in the Rue du Palais-Gallien, in which the windows with their pediments and the graceful mouldings interpret charmingly neo-classical influences. The relief over the door recalls the decoration applied to furniture at this period.

in an agreeable house where respectable people lived, I found an upper floor bedroom which I liked so much that I paid the customary rent in advance straight away.'

Jacques François Blondel, whom we have already encountered as a champion of interior comfort and exterior harmony, examines in some detail in his *Cours d'Architecture* the means whereby this may be achieved. In particular, he writes of the two engravings shown below. '*Figure I* shows the exterior decorations of a private house built after 1719 by the king's architect, M. Cartaud, in the Rue Saint-Martin almost opposite the Mabuée fountain. We have often mentioned this prospect in our course because of the harmony between all its parts, the excellence of its lines and the beauty of its walls... Visiting the house, one can see how the comfort of the interior at last corresponds to the harmony that has been achieved on the exterior.

In 1773, Louis XV bought the palace and gardens of the Prince de Condé in Paris to build the new district centred on the theatre of the Comédie-Française, with houses and apartments of a traditional and noble style (below). The mansard roof, already more than two centuries old, continues in use.

From the fifteenth century onwards, the parish of Saint-Gervais in Paris had a row of houses to let beside the church. In 1734 they were replaced by this row of buildings. The last house on the left, which is rather different from the others, was built in 1737 with an elegant stone façade and large windows. Fifty families were lodged in the buildings. (Opposite page, below, left) Present state of the house shown in the engraving next to it taken from Blondel's Cours d'Architecture *(see text). (Below, right) Front elevation of a shop by R. de la Lande (1788).*

'*Figure II* shows the front of a private house in Rue Saint Thomas-du-Louvre, built by an unknown architect. Its general arrangement, the way in which it is built and the style of the reliefs denote a person of taste and experience. It is very pleasing to find a proper cornice above the second floor: this separation of the attic from the rest of the house seems to produce a good result. The windows of the first floor are finely proportioned. They show that it is an important house although the lower part of it does not appear very high and the effect depends both on the use that is to be made of such a building and the district in which it is built. It should be admitted that the latter consideration must greatly influence any examination of a project of this type. For first of all we must be sure what kind of house we want: the house in which the owner himself lives, when he is well-to-do, must necessarily be quite different from the one intended for letting. If he proposes to let, shops or workshops are

needed. If the house is to be his home, the ground floor may have a portico before it, with a storeroom on one side and the kitchen on the other; or, instead of a portico, a false front door and a passage leading to the stairs, then the kitchen, the dining-room, and so on. Even as the owner's residence, it may include one or two shops, especially if the building covers a fairly wide area, and these shops, with a mezzanine floor perhaps, may be let to help cover building costs.

'Let there be no mistake. It takes more ingenuity and resourcefulness than we may think to vary the fronts of private houses. In towns there are a great many of them and they are put to a great many uses, so that we must not only love our art but also know a great deal about people and the way they earn their living. Otherwise all houses are likely to end up with the same character, whereas – like every other building – each house should have a character of its own.'

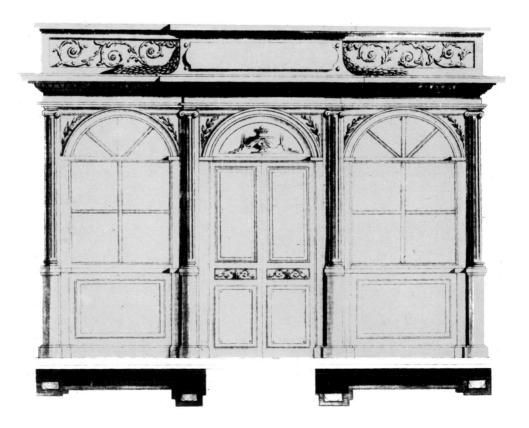

Signed furniture

When it was suggested that she should enter a convent, Louis XV's sophisticated daughter, Victoria, indicated the magnificent *bergère* on which she was sitting and said: 'I am too much tied to the comforts of this life: armchairs like this have been my ruin.' Even without her *bergère*, she might not have made a very good nun but the anecdote illustrates the French passion for fine furniture. The words *comfort* and *elegance* were never so exquisitely defined as they were in the France of Louis XV and Louis XVI. The great *ébénistes*, cabinet-makers like Roentgen, Oeben, Riesener, and Jacob, in their commodes, chairs, cupboards, desks and tables – with a multiplicity of styles, names and uses – came close to translating their craft into a major art. French furniture of this period is often considered the most beautiful ever produced. In today's salerooms it certainly continues to be the most expensive ever produced. And for collectors it has one great advantage in that some of it is signed.

The demand for furniture with panels of carved wood went back to the seventeenth century. It resulted in the formation of the guild of cabinet-makers, the members of which had to obey definite rules, one of which was that they must sign their own products. This they could do, however, only after arduous years of apprenticeship and after they had passed the guild's very stiff examinations. Very few cabinet-makers, accordingly, were privileged to sign their own works and most spent their lives working for others. Pieces signed by Riesener or Jacob or Oeben are rare. In the rest of Europe during this period, the authorship of pieces of furniture was seldom known.

The master cabinet-makers worked, necessarily, for a limited public. By contenting themselves with less fashionable craftsmen, the prosperous middle classes were able to buy a great deal of very fine, beautifully made furniture. The craftsmen themselves flourished and their financial security is evident from the inventories of the possessions of some of the painters, sculptors and craftsmen of the period. These inventories indicate too, as Pierre Verlet has noted in *Les Meubles du XVIII Siecle* (Paris, 1956), a constant movement of furniture. A. Loir, goldsmith to Louis XIV, who died a rich man in 1713, left a hall furnished with paintings and ceramics; six chairs, two armchairs upholstered with tapestry, a mirror, some more ceramics, a pier glass and a tapestry in another room; six chairs in walnut with cushions, a working table and an inlaid chess set from his study. The studio of the miniaturist Charles Boit contained in 1727 three rush-seated chairs, three oak tables, a reading desk, harpsichord and a backgammon set, all in walnut. The furniture in the house of the painter of religious and mythological pictures, Noel-Nicholas Coypel, included two small benches upholstered in brocade in his studio; an arras in the hall; a bed covered in silk, a stool, an *antique* inlaid desk, a dressing-table and bookcase in the bedroom; an armchair, an old sofa and two tables in another room. When François Lemoyne, official painter to Louis XV for the brief space of a year, took his own life in 1737, the following possessions belonging to him were listed: in the hall, a marble table with gilt feet, a large sideboard in walnut, a copper hand-basin and some tapestries; in the bedroom, a bed of cretonne and silk, nine armchairs, a bedside cupboard, a small bookcase and a tapestry. In 1780, the inventory of Jacques Soufflot, *architecte du Roi*, mentioned a drawing-room with paintings, statues, a sofa, twelve velvet armchairs, three small tables, a desk and a rosewood chest with gilded bronze mounts. The engraver, Jean Philippe Lebas, left in 1783 an even richer collection; in the study, a looking-glass over the fireplace, a pendulum clock, tables, small tables, curtains and candelabra; in a carpeted study, a buffet sideboard with four doors, and a divan; in the drawing-room, a dining-room table, basins, and so on; in another room, possibly the office, there was an old cupboard with china in it. And, an unsual refinement, in the bedroom there were a thermometer and barometer.

[T]wo engravings from the famous Encyclopédie *[of] Diderot and D'Alembert show the workshop [of] French furniture-makers in the eighteenth century. [T]he craft was very strictly organized; the ébénistes [(page 194), who included such masters as Oeben [an]d Riesener, worked with veneers and inlays; [th]e menuisiers were the joiners who worked in solid [w]ood. The pathway towards becoming a maitre-ébéniste [w]as long, arduous and uncertain. Signed pieces are [n]early always the work of the ébénistes though there [ex]ists in the Rijksmuseum in Amsterdam an armchair [th]at carries the mark of a menuisier, E. Meunier; [th]is is so exceptional that it has been suggested [th]at Meunier made the skeleton of the chair, [an]d that it was completed by a cabinet-maker [w]ho forgot to sign it.*

Bedford Square, London; one of the houses built to plans probably by Thomas Leverton in 1774. A later re-arrangement of the interior of the building produced the two entrances.

JOHN DRUMMOND

ENGLAND: THE AGE OF REASON

The period which followed the upheavals of the seventeenth century in England has been called the Age of Reason. It afforded an interval of serenity between the massive, even in some ways oppressive, baroque splendours of the reign of Queen Anne, and the raging romanticism of the end of a century that encompassed the beginnings of the Industrial Revolution at home, the French Revolution across the Channel and the arrival on the European scene of Napoleon Bonaparte. There were wars against France, but then there always were wars against France, always had been, and as far as the prosperous merchant or the placid landowner could see, there always would be. The prospect was pleasing but not as perfect as it seemed to Voltaire and Montesquieu, as the government of the country was for a large part of the century in the hands of an openly corrupt Whig oligarchy. Still, visitors gained a strong impression of comfort and stability epitomized in the robust red-brick houses of the period.

Early in the century, a taste for the works of Palladio was revived under the influence of Richard Boyle, third Earl of Burlington. At a time when the Grand Tour was beginning to be a necessary part of every well-born young man's education, he paid lengthy visits to Italy. An English edition of the works of Palladio appeared in 1715, and in 1725 there appeared an English edition of a building by Palladio in the shape of Lord Burlington's villa at Chiswick. During this period, moreover, manuals on building, architecture, cabinet-making and the like, proliferated. The new Palladianism was more bookish than it had been in the hands, say, of Inigo Jones. Architects and their clients had read the right books about it and seen the correct models. It would not, however, be fair to dismiss the Palladian buildings raised in England at this period as servile copies; they were, rather, accurate interpretations. Many of them were, moreover, designed to be set in English parks. Certain concessions had to be made to the English climate though there were

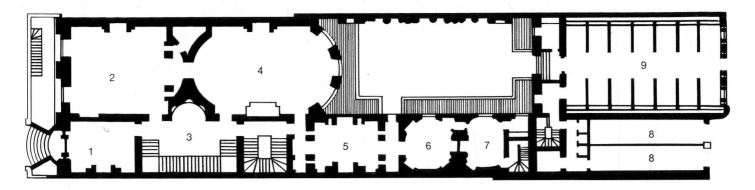

St James's Square, London. Plan of the ground level of one of Robert Adam's most interesting London houses, built in 1775 for his rich and cultivated friend, Sir Watkin Williams-Wynn, who gave him a free hand with both planning and decoration. The entrance (left) leads into an anteroom (1), then to the bottom of the main staircase (3) which leads up to the dining-room (2) and the music room (4); beyond are the library (5), a cloakroom (6), lavatory (7) and at the back the storerooms (8) and stables (9).

those, like Alexander Pope, who considered that not enough concessions were made. In the *Epistle to Lord Burlington* he refers pointedly to architects who

'...call the winds through long arcades to roar, Proud to catch cold at a Venetian door.'

The principal neo-Palladians were Colen Campbell who died in 1729, only four years after completion of the publication of what might be called the Palladian manifesto, the *Vitruvius Britannicus*; James Gibbs (1682-1754), another Scot and the architect of St. Martin-in-the-Fields; and William Kent (1685-1748), Lord Burlington's colleague in the designs for the villa at Chiswick. In addition, there was a legion of country architects, men of whom we are gradually learning more, who were responsible for many fine houses. In a period of good taste, the country architect or master-builder who trusted himself to tradition and local materials and had some acquaintance with the classical models, could hardly go wrong.

England's second attack of Palladianism was almost entirely confined to the large country houses. And at the same time, on a more modest scale perhaps, houses were still being built after the old Wren style with certain improvements of the period incorporated in them. Neither before nor since, has their elegance been equalled.

Building laws passed in 1707 and 1709 necessitated, admittedly, some modifications of the lines of the exteriors; their object was to reduce the danger of fire. The former prohibited projecting eaves and the latter required that window frames be set slightly back from the surface of the wall and be slightly arched at the top. The requirements were not always observed, but the roof with a small balustrade and windows with a curved pediment became typical of many London houses and from London became fashionable elsewhere.

If the Palladian vogue did not noticeably change the smaller country house, it influenced one kind of town house, the 'terrace' houses in which speculative builders were beginning to invest. London was never a city of palaces, like Rome, or of *hôtel particuliers* like Paris. In London, and in most English towns and cities, houses were constructed in rows aligned with the streets; each house in this row was an autonomous organism from cellar to roof-tree, each with its own entrance. Inigo Jones was, perhaps, the first to conceive of several houses as an organic whole when he planned the Piazza at Covent Garden (1630-1631), only a relic of which now remains.

The row of buildings designed and treated as a unified whole was a terrace. Where possible it faced some area not built upon, such as a park or a river. Squares, circuses, crescents, could be planned as architectural compositions. The sense of unity was enhanced by uniform decorations, usually incorporating classical motifs, and by the large pediment set over the central house in each group. The first and most famous of these groups of houses was built in Bath by John Wood (1704-1754) from 1727, and continued by his son, another John. Bath was a fashionable watering-place and buildings there were an excellent investment. The splendidly Palladian Queen Square, the Circus and Royal Crescent are early examples of speculative building. Other spas followed the example of Bath, and the owners of large, unoccupied tracts of land in the cities engaged in building projects which resulted in, among other achievements, the London squares and the New Town of Edinburgh. This system of development reached its height early in the following century with Nash's superb designs for the Regent's Park terraces in London.

The normal plan of the town house, especially in London, remained the same from the middle of the seventeenth century until the end of the nineteenth. In its usual form, it was part of a terrace or a square or an ordinary road. The entrance, set to one side, led into the hall with the staircase beyond. Beside the entrance was a room with two windows and there was another room behind this. The first, second and attic floors each had three windows. The reception rooms were on the first floor (a survival of the old *piano nobile*) and the bedrooms on the second floor. The kitchen and service area occupied the semi-basement; the servants slept in the attic. Coal was delivered through a hatch in the pavement before the house into a basement below.

Some of the splendid squares and terraces of the cities, including London, have been destroyed not so much by the bombs of the Second World War as by, ironically, the same spirit of speculation that brought them into being. Bedford Square in Bloomsbury, which survives from about 1774, is an exception. Others have been allowed to deteriorate into slums; others, again, are fortunately being rescued from the consequences of decades of neglect.

In a sense, the eighteenth century in Britain was over by 1750. The great writers of the Augustan age – Pope, Swift, Defoe, Addison – were dead and profound differences of thought and taste separate the second half of the century – admittedly the age

Elevation of the Right Honourable the Lord Herbert his House in Whitehall.

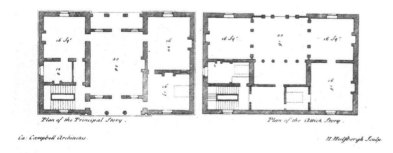

Plan of the Principal Story.   Plan of the Attick Story.

Ca: Campbell Architectus.   H. Hulsbergh Sculp.

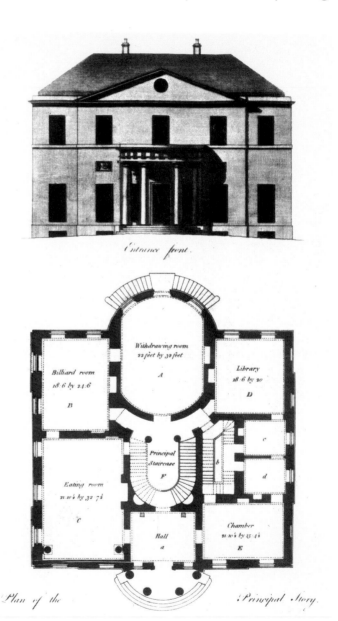

Plan of the   Principal Story.

(*Left*) *Façade and plans of the first and second floor of Lord Herbert's house in Whitehall (destroyed) built soon after 1717 to the design of Colen Campbell (from* Vitruvius Britannicus III, *1725). The most characteristic development of neo-Palladian architecture is to be seen in large country houses but there were smaller examples like this, suitable to urban surroundings. The moving spirits in the revival of Palladian designs were William Kent and his patron, Lord Burlington. Lord Herbert who owned this house was a friend of Lord Burlington and an enthusiastic Palladian. (*Right*) *Façade and plan of the ground level of Tendring Hall in Suffolk, designed by Sir John Soane (1753-1837) in 1784 and later published in his* Plans, elevations, etc. *(1788): the original designs are shown in the illustrations.*

of Dr. Johnson – from the first. These differences contained the seeds of Romanticism which was beginning to make itself known in the pictorial arts. The period saw, however, yet another classical revival but the difference between this revival and that of Lord Burlington and his contemporaries is summed up in the difference between the work of Sir William Chambers (1726-1796), a traditionalist despite his fostering of English taste for *chinoiserie*, and that of Robert Adam, his rival and contemporary. Adam had travelled in Italy (he was a friend of Piranesi) and in Dalmatia. In 1764 he published a magnificent folio of drawings of the Emperor Diocletian's palace at Split. Two years before, *The Antiquities of Athens* by James 'Athenian' Stuart (1713-1788) and Nicholas Revett (1720-1804) had been published. It was a massive labour of love for the two authors. The two publications stirred the fires of controversy as to whether Greek or Roman art was nearer perfection. (On the Continent, Piranesi and Winckelmann were embroiled in a similar dispute.)

But Adam's genius was too original to be doctrinaire. He used traditional Palladian elements in

Early Georgian room reconstructed in the Geffrye Museum in London. The panelling of painted pine came from a house in Chancery Lane and dates from the beginning of the eighteenth century, as the frame round each panel shows. The furniture is mostly mahogany and combines both elegance and solidity.

his designs but he took note of the discoveries that were being made in Greek and Roman art at, for example, the newly uncovered Pompeii and Hercullaneum, and of the work of his French contemporaries. His gift for 'movement' allowed him to breathe life into a static classical style whether it was intended for a great country house, a London terrace, or a more modest building. The fronts of his buildings were rarely merely two-dimensional. Often they were recessed in sweeping arches round doors and windows. He used a good deal of stucco decoration — wreaths, urns, *paterae* — inside and out. His handling of this ornamentation was light, elegant and restrained and avoided the frivolity of French rococo on the one hand and the heaviness of the Empire style on the other.

But exoticism and fantasy kept breaking through. In furniture, decoration and even in architectural design, the cabinet-makers and architects gave way every now and again to the taste for fantasy. Even an unregenerate classicist like Sir William Chambers published — and achieved a pop-

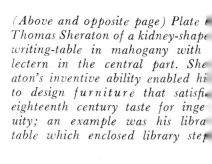

(Above and opposite page) Plate by Thomas Sheraton of a kidney-shaped writing-table in mahogany with lectern in the central part. Sheraton's inventive ability enabled him to design furniture that satisfied eighteenth century taste for ingenuity; an example was his library table which enclosed library steps

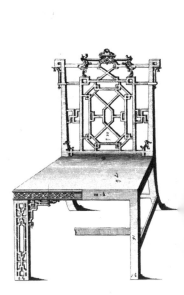

Even allowing for recent revaluation of Thomas Chippendale as a designer of furniture, his influence on the taste of his age was both far-reaching and enduring, and his first book of patterns, A Gentleman and Cabinet Maker's Director *published in 1754, is an invaluable guide to the furniture of the period. It contained many pieces of furniture of great originality.*

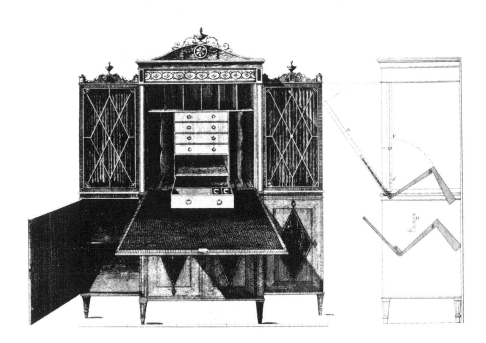

Between 1791 and 1794 Thomas Sheraton published – in parts – his first book on furniture, The Cabinet Maker and Upholsterer's Drawing Book and it is the furniture recorded in its 113 plates that we now describe as in the Sheraton style. His furniture was characterized by his predilection for straight lines in chair backs and legs; by his skill in the use of rare woods and veneers; and by the delicacy of his ornament. An example is this secretary-bookcase with its satinwood panels and its lightly decorated pediment.

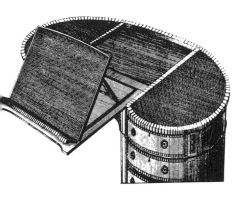

The third member of the triumvirate of English eighteenth century cabinet makers was George Hepplewhite. His Cabinet Maker and Upholsterer's Guide was published in 1788, two years after his death. It contained designs in which classical patterns were adapted to contemporary requirements with varying degrees of success, as the chairs below indicate.

ular success with – an album of *Designs of Chinese Buildings*, the outcome of a voyage to China as a young man. In Chinese vein, too, he designed the pagoda in Kew Gardens. The taste for *chinoiserie* was further nourished by Thomas Chippendale. In these same years, moreover, Horace Walpole was transforming his house, Strawberry Hill, into a 'small Gothic Castle' in an evocation of a fanciful Middle Ages very different from the passionate revivalism of the following century. (Chippendale published Gothic designs too.) Finally, the interiors of many English houses reflected an enormously increased and much more serious interest in antiquity. Robert Adam used Pompeian and Etruscan motifs. Enthusiasts began to bring home antiquities to grace their drawing-rooms. [Prominent among these was a distinguished member and correspondent of the Society of Dilettanti (the object of which was to encourage interest in classical art and taste), Sir William Hamilton, His Britannic Majesty's Ambassador to the court of Naples and, of course, husband of Emma.]

CHARLES F. MONTGOMERY JR.

ADAM
INFLUENCE IN AMERICA

By the year 1700, the eastern seaboard of North America had become in every sense a part of the civilized world. Dr. Alexander Hamilton, visiting New York in 1744, observed 'regular, closely built houses, generally rather tall, Dutch in style with pitched roofs. Some are built of stone; others, a great number, of wood, but mostly they are of brick faced with small glazed bricks, and the year in which they were built appears on many house fronts on iron plaques.'

In other words, towns were beginning to take on the appearance they would preserve until the middle of the following century and within them, the organization of commerce and labour and the construction of buildings was losing any residual medieval character. Less than seventy years after its foundation (1682), Philadelphia impressed a German traveller, Gottlieb Mittelberger, as a 'fairly large, fine city, built on a regular plan with wide main streets and many cross streets. All the houses, of stone or brick, are four storeys high and clad in cedarwood. To walk through the residential area takes almost a day and every year they put up nearly 300 new buildings. Obviously, and within quite a short time,' he predicted, 'Philadelphia will become one of the largest cities in the world. Already you can find in Pennsylvania anything that is found in Europe since every year a large number of ships come in from every country, including the West Indies.'

Pierce House at Salem, Massachusetts, now a museum, was built in 1782 for Jerathmeel Pierce, arms manufacturer and merchant. It is traditionally attributed to Samuel McIntire, the architect and wood carver who himself was born and died in Salem. The style obviously owes a great deal to the Palladian revival with its projecting, pedimented portico and its corner pilasters. A number of features, both interior and exterior of the house were taken, it is interesting to note, from the City and Country Builder's and Workman's Treasury of Design by Batty Langley, best known for his books on architecture and building which were extensively used by other architects. The inventory of McIntire's possessions in 1818 includes 'one vol. of Architecture *by Langley, one vol. of* Architecture *by Palladio', and a number of French and English works. In his later work, planned towards the end of the eighteenth century, he moved towards the more sober and elegant Federal style.*

What is usually known as colonial architecture, based on the English Palladian style, replaced the predominantly Gothic style of the previous, seventeenth century. Americans visiting London collected books of architectural patterns and, where possible, English architects who migrated to the New World spread a taste for Palladian symmetry and formality. Buildings in this style, allowing for modifications, were popular throughout the century. In them smooth or fluted columns flanked wide, panelled doors which, like the windows, were surmounted by pediments. The roofs sloped slightly and the projecting cornices emphasized the horizontal lines of the façade and the storeys piled one above another. During the century the number of pillars was in some cases multiplied to range along the whole façade of the house. After 1715, moreover, the entrance with its decoration often projected from the house.

Increasingly, each room acquired a definite function. The decoration, especially in the central hall, became more and more a matter of deliberate design. The finest interiors were usually lined with carved panelling and their ceilings were decorated with moulded plaster. After 1725, we find pillared fireplaces and, later still, inlaid or carved cornices were added to the fireplace opening or above the hood. It was customary to paint the wooden parts of the house in blue or green or in some bright colour. Towards the end of the century lighter colours were fashionable and even wallpapers, usually imported from France but sometimes shipped from China, gradually became more common.

It was clear that the colonists had acquired a taste for delicacy, though the gaiety of Dutch interiors – typical of these was the bright blue paint applied to wood – persisted. Dr Hamilton, whom we have already encountered, was an observant visitor and noted another Dutch practice in the use of 'cupboards and sideboards with china'. He tells us too that 'the kitchens [in New York in 1744] are very attractive' and usually have 'pottery plates and dishes on the walls, as if they were pictures, hung by a hole made at the edge of the plate or dish, through which a wire or a ribbon is passed.'

Signs of timid dabbling in the baroque are evident in some houses of the time, especially in the staircases with their polished, twisted banisters. More decisively, furniture and silver were influenced in three distinct phases during the eighteenth century. The first phase shows definite signs of mannerism with twists and twirls and strange proportions. The second, which may be regarded as the classic baroque phase lasting from about

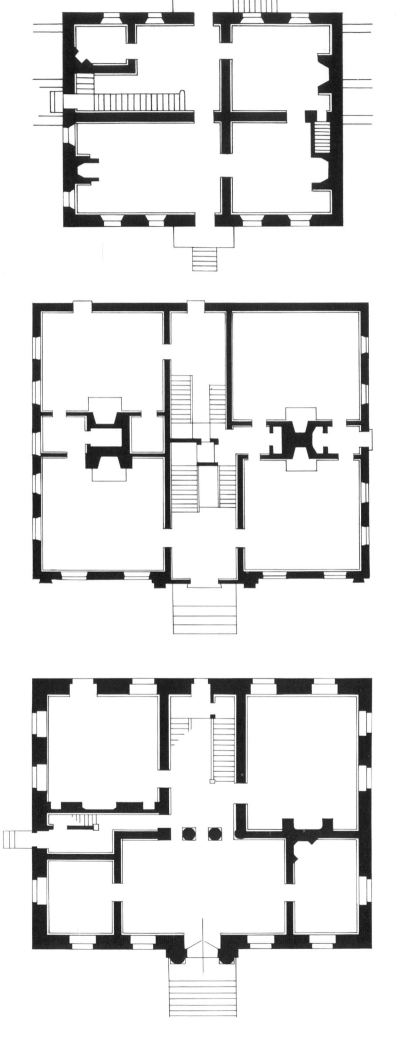

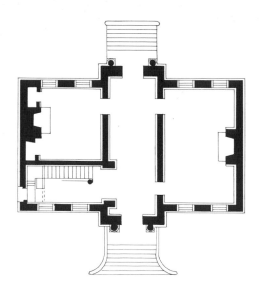

Plans of some of the finest eighteenth century houses in the older, eastern colonies. (Opposite page, top) Brice House at Annapolis; (centre) the John Vassall (later Longfellow) House at Cambridge, Massachusetts, 1759; and (bottom) Cliveden House at Germantown, a little before 1763.
(This page, left) House at Mount Pleasant (after 1761); (below) Chase House at Annapolis, built between 1769 and 1771; and the Van Rensselaer House in Albany, 1765.
They have in common a preference for symmetry in accordance with the taste of the period. This means that there are nearly always four rooms on each floor, that the entrance is exactly in the centre of the façade, and the arrangement of windows is dictated by the appearance of the exteriors rather than the requirements of the interior. The hall leading to the stairs is generally an extension of the entrance, or set at a right angle to it. But even within this apparently rigid framework, there is room – as the plans show – for a good deal of variety.

1730 to 1770, saw the use of a great many arched supports and the creation of three-dimensional effects. The third phase, which lasted until the end of the century, is characterized by the introduction and development of various regional forms and styles of ornament.

Thus, in Philadelphia the 'highboy', a tall chest, which in its smooth-fronted version copied English models, became – with the added feature of a swan-necked or scrolled pediment and an abundant use of rococo ornament – a new type of furniture. In Newport, Rhode Island, an unexpected way of treating cupboard fronts was developed with the use of raised and depressed panels, each panel surmounted by carvings of shells. A new form of looking-glass appeared in New York with lighter lines than earlier models and, instead of discreet inlay, an overall decoration. In the second half of the century, firedogs fell out of use in the British Isles where coal had replaced wood as fuel. In America, a firedog was designed in a completely new form, in the shape of a fluted column from which protruded a tongue of fire. And the Windsor chair, British in origin, provided the theme for apparently endless variations.

When he returned to England from his Italian tour in 1759, Robert Adam introduced to English architecture a whole new vocabulary of design, one derived from the discoveries at Pompeii and Herculaneum and expanded by the study of vases, urns, jewels and other antiquities. His interest – and that of his contemporaries – was quite different from that of Palladio: it was, perhaps, more academic, more impersonal. The buildings in which Adam gave shape and form to what he had learned influenced architects on the other side of the Atlantic, but after the Revolution, when they were the basis of what has been called Federal

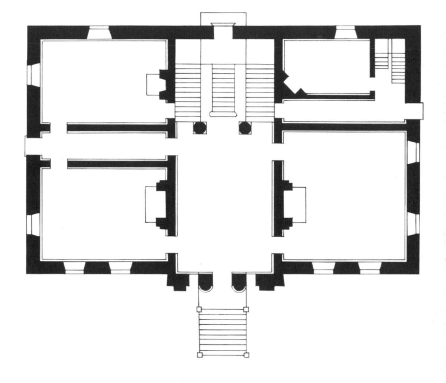

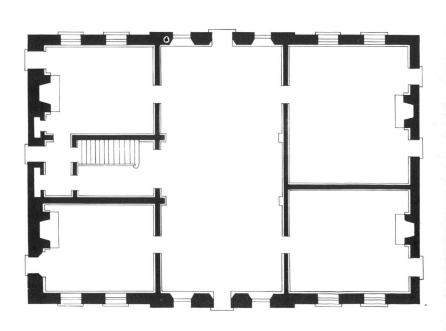

America's distinctive contribution to the
art or craft of furniture manufacture
was made during the eighteenth century
in pieces like this secrétaire
(Providence, Rhode Island, Historical
Society) of solid mahogany with its
vertical panels — carved usually
out of single blocks of wood, hence
the name of block-front furniture
applied to this kind of design — and
decorated with carved shells.
Block-front furniture was made
by John Townsend and John Goddard
at Newport, Rhode Island:
this particular piece was made
in Goddard's workshop for
Mr. Joseph Brown of Providence.
The workmanship is of very high
quality and the design is both lively
and dignified, baroque rather than
classical or rococo — but American
baroque with structure and ornament
harmoniously combined.

(Opposite page) The finest craftsm_
of the classical and Federal period in t_
United States is, it is usually claime_
Duncan Phyfe, who worked in New Yo_
from 1790 until nearly 1850. Every piece
furniture in this room is document_
as being one of his works or from
workshop (Winterthur, Du Pont Museum_
Up to about 1820 — when his desig_
grew heavier in style — he followed t_
styles of Sheraton and Hepplewh_
to produce his chairs and sofas with th_
backs decorated with garlands a_
acanthus leaves, his tables with th_
tripod legs and urn-shaped supports; th_
he varied with borrowings from Fren_
Directoire and Empire sty_

Adam. In private houses it was translated into fan-lights above and narrow side windows beside the main entrance; into façades decorated with shallower, more delicate reliefs; into round, oval and octagonal rooms with communicating arches between them; and into dignified staircases, either straight or curving. The style was launched in New England during the last decade of the eighteenth century when its principal exponents were Charles Bulfinch, one of America's first architects, and Samuel McIntire whose work was influenced by Adam, by the design books of Batty Langley, and by his contemporary, Bulfinch.

The Adam style affected furniture more than buildings. Curves were abandoned save on the backs of chairs, which were shaped like vases or urns. Legs of furniture were always straight and

fronts of cupboards, though occasionally allowed to curve, were not nearly as serpentine as the best baroque models. The straight line, light and graceful, triumphed. In furniture decoration, inlay took over from carving save in Massachusetts. But mahogany remained the basic material of the cabinet makers. The inlay, to which this furniture owes a great deal of its charm and elegance, was done either in very fine mahogany or in ebony and other valuable woods; the design of it was geometrical or used stylized forms of classical urns, leaves, scrolls and *paterae*.

In silver too, elegance replaced ostentation. The most common shape for tea and coffee pots was the urn and for the first time matching sugar basins and cream jugs were made. They were decorated in clearly outlined relief with crowns, garlands, rib-

bons and bows. Though less subject to the vagaries of fashion, however, craftsmen in pewter, china and glass were also impelled to make use of neo-classical designs. But it was only during the next century when large workshops took over from small shops, and when factories in turn replaced the workshops, that public taste played an important part in dictating the designs of such products. And only in the nineteenth century did the installation of more effective means of heating, lighting and cooking make a drastic change in domestic interiors unaltered for centuries.

But even in the eighteenth century, the desire for comfort at home encouraged the acquisiton of such possessions as ministered to that desire. The inventory of belongings left by a Boston merchant who died in 1800 shows a lifetime spent in the accumulation of furniture and objects, the present-day value of which it would be impossible to calculate. In a single room 'in the front' of his house, the following items were listed: a piano, a mahogany table, a card table, upholstered chairs, a large mirror (then valued at 20 dollars), two lacquered trays, a china tea service, an (incomplete) 'gilt china tray from Paris' and another 'in the form of a table in blue and white china', a case of '12 table knives, 12 forks, and 6 dessert forks with plated handles', a mahogany tray 'with several pieces in porcelain and glass', a set of fire irons, a carpet (valued at 10 dollars), a large family portrait (25 dollars), and two sets of the complete works of Shakespeare. There was also a bust of Shakespeare in the second

The house of William Bingham, built in Philadelphia about 1790 (contemporary print). It was said to be an enlarged version of the Duke of Manchester's London house. It seems, however, to be a fairly typical example of a Federal-style building. The English traveller, Henry Wansey (An Excursion to the United States, Salisbury, 1798) was invited to dinner by Mr. Bingham in the summer of 1794 and found the house and garden 'magnificent, in the best English taste, with elegant, even impressive furniture; the drawing-room chairs came from Seddon in London and were of the most modern type, with lyre backs and garlands in crimson and yellow silk (on the seats); the curtains were decorated with similar garlands; the carpet was one of Moore's most expensive; the walls were covered with a French paper in the style of the Vatican in Rome'. This final proof of splendour sounds rather odd.

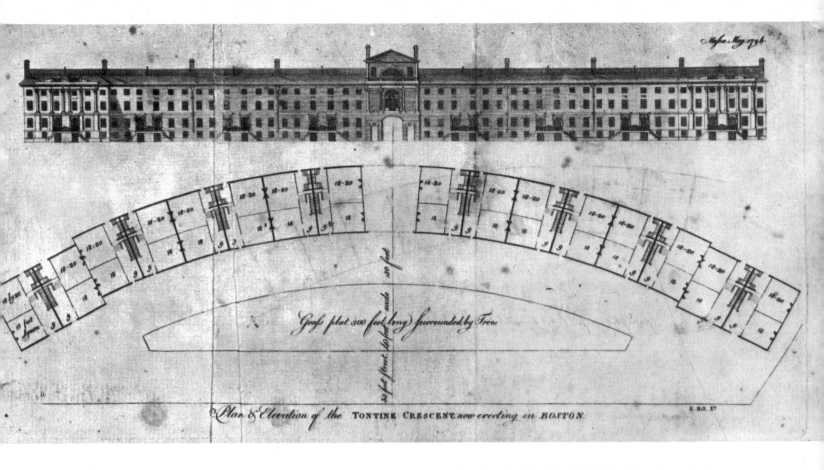

Front and plan of Tontine (now Franklin) Crescent in Boston from the drawing by Charles Bulfinch who planned
it in 1793 (Massachusetts Historical Society). It is the first American example of group planning of the kind common
in Britain in the middle of the eighteenth century. The inspiration of Robert Adam, which contributed so much to
the Federal style, is obvious. The crescent impressed visitors to Boston at the time and may even have impressed Bostonians.
In 1794 Mr. Wansey recorded of the city that its buildings 'had nothing special about them; many, including religious
buildings, were clad in wooden planks and the roofs too were of wood... The only exception was the western district
where the brick houses were beautiful and elegant with fine entrances and porches and steps up to the front.'

front room, one of the actor, David Garrick, two looking-glasses, three tables, large and small, a carpet, two trays, china, glass, lamps and chandeliers, six chairs and a gold clock.

In a house on the outskirts of Boston in 1791 the Reverend William Bentley encountered even greater domestic luxury. His description of it is interesting in that the paintings, books and, above all, scientific instruments show that the tastes of their owner were in perfect harmony with those of European intellectuals. 'I was courteously invited to lunch by Mr. Barrell and his family. He showed me his large and elegant instruments for recreation and philosophical (that is, scientific) experiments. There were birds fluttering in a globe inside another globe full of water, in which fishes were swimming. There was an excellent picture of Dr. Cooper, from an original belonging to the governor, and an original portrait of Clarke, together with various paintings, prints and Chinese ceramics. The owner of the house had taken part in the first expedition into the interior of the country and had brought back many extraordinary curiosities. His

instruments for experimental philosophy are really fine, especially those for electricity. His library was also good and the whole house seemed to be furnished with elegance, while the garden was better than anything I had ever seen. Behind the house was a small wood, in the middle of which there was a pond adorned with four ships at anchor and a marble statue in the centre. In the front of the summer house, the Chinese style was mixed with the European... in other words, no expense has been spared to make everything pleasant, instructive and comfortable.

The sovereigns of Europe who were prepared to barter a regiment of grenadiers for a Chinese dinner service were not alone in their passion. Across the Atlantic, it was shared by, for example, the widow of a very rich man whom Moreau de St. Mery met in Philadelphia during his stay in America from 1793 to 1798. A Frenchman lodged with her. 'This lady, who was very dignified and well thought of throughout the city, was 32 years old. But she gave her favours to the Frenchman who had discovered her weakness for china.'

SERGIO CORADESCHI · MICHELANGELO MURARO

PRACTICAL PLANNING IN ITALY

When the eighteenth century was well advanced, the appearance of a city like Rome could still disconcert Charles de Brosses, historian and encyclopaedist, who in 1739 or 1740 complained that because of the presence of some 'rather poor' private houses, and in spite of several fine monuments, 'the piazza del Populo [was] anything but a fine piazza'. He went on to point out that this kind of contrast 'is quite usual in these parts where there are nothing but palaces and hovels, and a splendid building is surrounded by a hundred mean huts: there are enormously broad and wonderfully straight roads that nearly always end in fine vistas – and yet lead to hovels, tortuous alleyways, and horrible, congested crossroads... I have a feeling that Rome is still suffering from the fact that it was burned by the barbarians and that when it was rebuilt, no attention was paid to order and design and every man built for himself wherever he found a vacant space.'

In the second half of the century, however, Italian building caught up with the times. Rooms were arranged to satisfy the demands of a way of life in which more time was spent indoors; instead of communicating with one another, they opened from a common corridor. The drawing-room, used for meals and for receiving visitors, was sub-divided into several rooms, each with its own function, dining room, sitting-room, study and so on. The kitchen was separated from the scullery, now reserved for the humblest tasks. The family bedrooms were on the floor over the reception rooms. Servants slept in the attics and ate on the mezzanine.

Furniture consisted mainly of light, attractive pieces decorated not with carvings in high relief but lacquered and painted. The fondness for interior theatre lingered on in the placing of the bed in an alcove or arched recess. For the rest, the fashion in furnishings followed that of Paris – a trifle breathlessly, perhaps, for the fashion changed with bewildering rapidity. In Italy, as in France, furniture was decorated with fine inlays, gilded bronze and ormolu mounts, painted china plaques, oriental lacquer, and – 'the poor man's art' – with coloured prints.

Outside, on the streets of the cities, a sober, reasonable and practical style of architecture evolved. Books of models – for houses, furniture, pavilions, palaces – helped spread it, moreover, beyond the cities into the provincial towns, where they were an important factor in influencing taste, not only during the eighteenth but well into the nineteenth century as well. To these models, it can be claimed, we owe much of the coherence that distinguishes Italian towns and cities.

Venice – characteristically, one might say –

(Opposite page, bottom) Sketch by Filippo Juvarra (1676-1736) for the barracks in the Piazza d'Armi in Turin (Turin Civic Museum). These buildings were designed about 1716 and, after interruptions, were completed twelve years later; part of them remains between the Via del Carmine and the Corso Valdocco. Though they themselves fall outside the scope of this book, they do demonstrate a break in style and a departure from the majestic austerity of the manner then fashionable in Italy.

(Opposite page and above) View and plan of the group of small houses planned by Filippo Raguzzini (1680-1771) in the Piazza Sant'Ignazio in Rome. The houses are grouped like a stage set and the architect took care that they should marry with the existing church of Sant'Ignazio by keeping their cornices at an appropriate level. The interiors are planned with equal ingenuity, as the plan of one of the side houses (above) shows.

Eighteenth century house in Lecce in the heel of Italy, close to the parish church of the same period. The extravagant ornament characteristic of so many of the buildings in this town is notably absent in this austerely handsome doorway.

was affected by the eighteenth century predilection for fantasy, and an elegantly Gothic style was there revived. The thrift of the merchants who created the city's prosperity was forgotten and a thirst for luxury took its place. Venetians desired above all to make a magnificent display and to accomplish this they chose the richest of furniture, fabrics, lacquers, carpets and porcelain. They added ornate loggias and staircases to their courtyards. The end of the Serene Republic was near and is perhaps foreshadowed in Guardi's *capriccios* of ruined monuments and wretched hovels. But Napoleon, determined to be an Attila to Venice, was still to come and meanwhile the republic's own artists added a final gloss to its history. Painters, architects, sculptors, potters, glassworkers, engravers, musicians and dramatists together created a splendid background to the city's penultimate scene.

Casa Torni in the Rio Santa Margherita in Venice. Like other eighteenth century buildings in the city, its façade is asymmetrical. An interesting feature is the arrangement of the top floor windows as a kind of ornamental frieze. The distribution of the upper floor windows largely conceals the narrowness of the site.

The Venetians had a passion for chinoiserie and their craftsmen were among the first in Europe to imitate the lacquered furniture of the Far East. Inexpensive methods of decorating pieces were devised, notably the application of engravings or small prints to furniture like this (Florence, private collection); a little paint and several layers of transparent varnish completed the operation. Such furniture was produced for those who could not afford the very expensive genuine lacquers; the skill of the workmanship was, however, sufficient to win it acceptance among collectors.

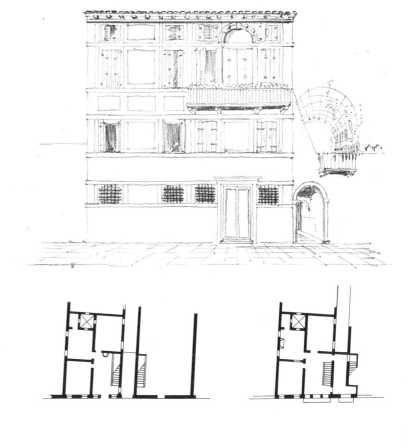

The splendour of the façade – as well as
of the hall, courtyards and staircases
of the Palazzo Labia in Venice
near the church of San Geremia –
demonstrates the depth of the family's
purse in the eighteenth century.
The drawing-room
contains frescoes by Tiepolo.

Small eighteenth century house in the
Fondamenta dell'Angelo Raffaele,
also in Venice. The Venetian fondness
at this period for horizontal division
of the façade is obvious here. The distribution
of the windows lends dignity to this quite
modest building, a dignity enhanced perhaps
by the coat of arms at upper floor level.

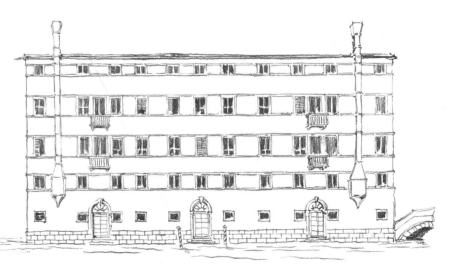

This building on the Rio del Vin
in Venice was built in the first half
of the eighteenth century as a lodging
house with shops below. Neo-classical
influences were beginning to make
themselves felt, though the designer of
this building, Antonio Visetti, has
suceeded in imbuing it with
a certain liveliness.
(Opposite page) House near the
church of San Vio, by the Academia
in Venice, in which the internal
structures both of the ground level
(plan, left) and of the mezzanine
(plan, right) have survived.

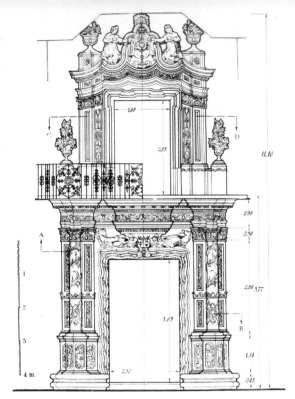

JOSÉ GUDIOL RICART - SANTIAGO ALCOLEA

NEO-CLASSICISM IN SPAIN AND PORTUGAL

Entrance of the Casa Bertemati at Jerez de la Frontera in Andalusia, built in 1785 for the Sopranis-Davila family, possibly to the design of an architect whose name is unknown but who designed other houses in the city. The elaborate doorway recalls the palace of San Telmo in Seville.

The progress of Spanish architecture in the eighteenth century from an austere form of the Baroque to an equally severe neo-classicism, has its origin largely in the influence on building of the royal residences, into which were poured the enormous financial resources of the previous century.

Royal models, indeed, set such a high standard in materials and workmanship that building was prohibitively expensive and few private houses were built in neo-classical style. Those that were consisted either of a single unit without a courtyard or of two courtyards with a spacious reception room in the centre. In both cases, the front was raised on a high, projecting base above which were large windows, an imposing pediment capping the façade and a pilastered top storey. It happened sometimes, however, that in the course of building, the house's owners revised their original grand and costly ideas and classical tradition was honoured only in the centre of the façade.

Northern Spain favoured the Baroque, which was handled with grace in Galicia, while the existing predilections in the Basque country were further influenced by French taste.

In Andalusia, Seville was still the centre of architectural activity. The internal arrangement of the house, established in the sixteenth century, began to be simplified. The main drawing-room now overlooked the street with a splendid balcony that surmounted the entrance. After 1750, a further modification introduced a passage direct from the entrance to the patio, where the staircase to the upper storey was set opposite the door itself. At the same time, a special entrance opening from the road was provided to the stables and storehouses.

The baroque grandeur of these houses can be enjoyed all over Andalusia. There are, however, interesting variations at Jerez de la Frontera, the home of sherry, where the prospering wine trade encouraged much building and many houses were built of brick, often adorned with neo-classical motifs.

Aragon clung to a fifteenth century type of private house but in Catalonia to the east, economic and architectural development progressed hand-in-hand and new building styles were adopted. Many merchants and industrialists built houses in Barcelona which were still predominantly baroque, but some turned to the neo-classical fashion. Typical of the new houses were the paintings on the walls, both indoors in the reception rooms and outdoors on the façade – though here they were short-lived because of the salt air. Houses in Tarragona and Reus show a similar taste in decoration. But in Valencia, a regional style with French overtones developed. Rococo façades were extensively decorated with plaster mouldings which framed paintings that have since disappeared. In Palma de Majorca and some of the smaller towns in the Balearic Islands similar decorations were also popular.

Portugal developed a style of its own in some superb buildings in which granite, limestone and glazed tiles or *azulejos* were combined, and achieved in the halls, staircases and gardens where they were used a delightful effect of gaiety. Indoors, the exquisite *azulejos* were used instead of tapestries; walls were lined with them and in many noble houses they were the most attractive feature, as for example in Malheiro Reimao's house at Viana do Castello. In Lisbon, too, they decorate the house of the Meninos de Palhava family.

P. M. BARDI

LATIN AMERICA: BUILDING FROM MEMORY

The haphazard siting of buildings in South American towns dictates the routes that the streets must follow. Lack of plan can also result in a situation such as this, where a nineteenth century building is being squeezed out by its neighbours and indeed faces demolition to make room for a new building. Note the effect on the appearance of buildings and streets of electric cables and television aerials.

Deep in the forests of Latin America, monuments of the continent's past are still being discovered, only to be swallowed up again by the ever-encroaching vegetation. In the forests of Brazil, *fazendas* have been found, abandoned when the slaves were freed and now completely overgrown. The monuments are, in some cases, those of civilizations that had perished before the advent of the conquistadors. Others recall the empires that crumbled before the European invaders. In the early days of their occupation, the conquistadors used whatever materials came to hand to raise modest, single-storeyed churches, stores, barracks and dwelling houses. Their models were their increasingly dim memories of their homes in Spain and Portugal. In the islands of the Caribbean, in Mexico, Peru, Venezuela, Colombia and even further south, in Chile and Argentina, the typical house was Spanish in style: in Brazil it was Portuguese, for the division of the continent dates back to the conquest.

These colonial towns were primarily fortresses in which the governor's palace with its grandiloquent coat of arms was the largest building. The small church was based on what could be remembered of the builder's home church, and convents and monasteries were built to accommodate missionaries. Last of all houses were built, though these were little more than barracks with communal rooms. Save, perhaps, for the governor's palace and the church, little attention was given to planning and the towns had about them an air of makeshift which was real enough, since a large proportion of their inhabitants hoped to go home one day quite soon with their pockets stuffed with the gold of the Indies. The native inhabitants, terrorized by the threat of the vengeance of distant kings in this life and oppressed by their new religion with fear of the next, were compelled by various means to do the building of the new towns, with indifferent results. In the end, conquerors and conquered lived under conditions of equal squalor and endured the

same deprivations – the only difference being that the Indians were slightly more accustomed to them. The honest Bartolomeo de las Casas told the Royal Council: 'The Indies were discovered through ill-luck.'

When Europeans took first Indian women and later Negro women, brought in as slaves, into their households, the dwelling house began to look more like a home and it was more jealously guarded as such with double locks on the doors. Individual houses began to be built and the Latin-American talent for individuality manifested itself. There was time and taste to cultivate flower gardens for decoration as against the vegetable gardens maintained for use. In some convent gardens medicinal plants were cultivated and medieval monastic tradition thus preserved.

Between the sixteenth and the eighteenth centuries, the continent settled down as a measure of stability was established. A population of several million people of mixed European and Indian heritage had, somehow, to be housed. How it was done is now difficult to say. In the general *Archive of the Indies*, now in Madrid, the buildings mentioned are almost exclusively ecclesiastical or hospitals. A petition of 1540, sent to the Office of Contracts for the Indies, indicates that not much regard was paid to housing. In it, the Bishop of Tierra Firma asks for 'skilled builders and masons' to teach the Negroes and Indians how to rebuild the cathedral, in the city of Panama, which had been destroyed; there is no mention of the rebuilding of houses. Earthquakes and fires were common disasters but the records of rebuilding refer to churches only. Houses were presumably rebuilt,

Houses of the Pueblo Indians in New Mexico.
These cubical buildings are, for the most part,
set in rows against a rock face to form terraces.
The houses themselves, built of sun-dried
mud brick, each consist of a single room, often
with an inner courtyard where the draught animals
are tethered. Their shape is probably derived
from the ancient dwellings of the
pre-Columbian inhabitants.

Huts with walls of small stones on a base of
larger stones, in the Tacora region
of Peru. In some cases, sun-dried brick
is used instead of stone and often, in both
cases, the walls are covered with rushes.
These houses are almost certainly
very ancient and their form is the classic
one of the building which must withstand
high winds at high altitudes.

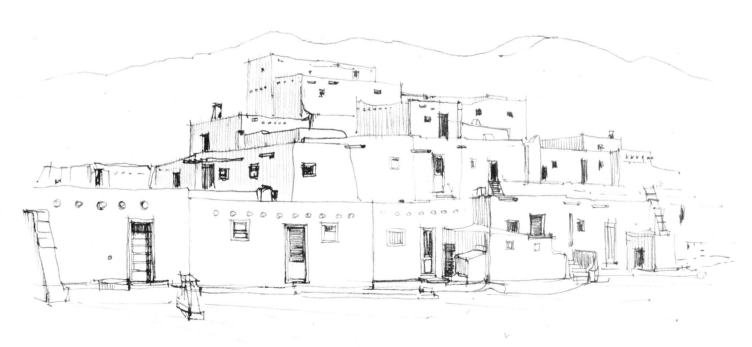

In his diary Christopher Columbus particularly mentions 'round houses that look like tents' in the Caribbean Islands. In some islands, he also noted, there were square houses, too, and this form has survived to influence the design of the typical rural Cuban house, the bohio. The walls are of horizontal planks, usually painted white; the doorposts and windows are gaily coloured green, red, orange and blue; the roof is of palm branches and sometimes these branches cover the whole building. Two units are joined here, one for resting, the other kitchen, dining-room and living-room.

The hut of the Chipaya in the basin of the Desaguadero River on the Argentinian plateau. The Chipaya are one of South America's most primitive tribes and have preserved their ancient way of life with people, livestock, weapons and tools gathered together inside their huts.

(Opposite page) Pueblo village of Taos in New Mexico, one of the most important settlements of its kind, where about 400 Indians still live. The roof terraces are used as a family meeting-place, kitchen, dining-room and, occasionally, stable. The windows, though few, are a comparatively recent innovation; the older houses have none.

too, though not necessarily by skilled builders and masons, so that their restoration was hardly worth recording.

For in the majority of cases, the man who built the house occupied it: he was at once architect, mason, water engineer, painter and furniture maker. He and his neighbours improvised and experimented and improved. With a few tools, some local labour and, later, carts to carry materials, house building was not too difficult. Even today, the working classes still build their own houses in the evening after a day's work and on holidays.

During the first pioneering century, however, the Spanish and Portuguese colonies in the New World were often in desperate straits. Planted in the midst of a strange continent, surrounded by hostile and barbaric Indians, commanded constantly to find more gold to send back to Spain to build the Escorial, the new colonists felt trapped. But the Americas offered compensations – the chance of a new life under, if necessary, a new name, the opportunity to start from nothing and acquire wealth, an intermittently flexible government, several thousand miles of sea between Spain and the colony, and, for the white man, a built-in sense of superiority. Automatically, in a sense, he was a member of the ruling class in a society in which the mass of the population were slaves – and he took full advantage of his position.

(Above) The fazenda of Engenho d'Agua at Ilhabela
in São Paulo. (Left) The Chemist's House in the
Largo do Boticario (which takes its name from the house)
in Rio de Janeiro, one of the few surviving examples
of an old middle class town house in Brazil.

The building known as the Sitio do Padre Ignacio
at Cotia near São Paulo. An example of a chapel house of
the second half of the seventeenth century comprising
a chapel and sacristy (plan, right) and an upper floor
(plan, left) used as a storehouse and sometimes
as a lodging. The length of the front is about 81 feet.

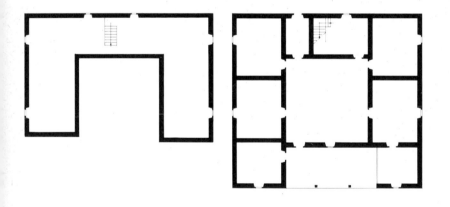

Brazil

The description of the background to the history of the house in Latin America is generally applicable throughout the continent. But there are variations from country to country and sometimes within the same country.

The Portuguese, who had already gained experience in colonizing in Africa and Asia, made use in Brazil of a type of dwelling that perfectly epitomized the completely new economy of the country which was incomparably richer and healthier than any other in Latin America. The house was a complete unit which catered for the material, occupational and even spiritual needs of its inhabitants. As such it had an air of permanence, stability and security and the owner lived in patriarchal fashion, an absolute ruler whose word could not be questioned. The main house was solid with the thick walls necessary in the tropics. Its sloping roofs and wide verandahs provided protection against the hot sun and heavy rain. Such decoration as existed was sober and practice of the arts was reserved mainly for the chapel which adjoined the house; the priest was treated as a member of the family. The building called the *senzala* housed the slaves who were well treated for they were valuable possessions. The house with its adjuncts of slaves' quarters, farm buildings, offices and workshops was the quintessential pioneer settlement.

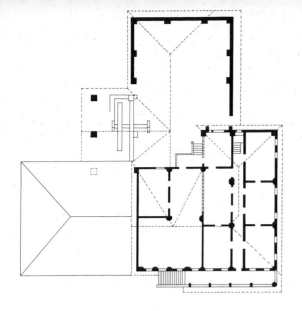

(Above, left) Plan of the whole of the fazenda *of Engenho d'Agua, built in the second half of the eighteenth century. The façade of the owner's house is shown on the opposite page; the* casa sede *is the house on two floors. Connected to it is the sugar-cane factory operated by the water power which gave its name to the estate. Buildings like this have been preserved by the* Diretoria do Patrimônio Histórico e Artístico Nacional del Brasile.

(Above, right) General view of the fazenda *of Pau d'Alho Barreiro, also in São Paulo. The central part of this eighteenth century complex was the master's house (on the right). The main front is shown below. The row of small houses in the background is the slaves' quarters. The plan (below, left) shows that the owner's house faced on to a formal Italian garden. Like Engenho d'Agua, it was also connected with the building in which the sugar-cane was processed. The house included a chapel on the upper floor at the end of the gallery (below).*

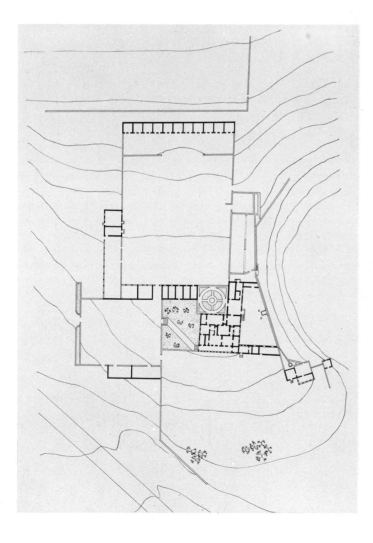

Spanish America

Environment, climate, the state of the economy and the influence of Spain dictated the forms of dwelling that evolved in the vast Spanish dominions. Most important was environment which included the materials obtainable, their suitability for building purposes and the degree of skill available to work them. Building manuals were plundered for designs of the family houses so desperately needed; the process continues and even today in small Latin American towns, plans for buildings taken from manuals, some of them new, some of them of respectable antiquity, are still sold. With their help, and with a good deal of ingenuity and common sense, people build their houses.

In Argentina, however, the early *ranchos* were fairly elementary in the architectural sense as were the later *viviendas*; practical necessity rather than taste determined their design, and the design of the furniture they contained. They improved as the middle class increased in numbers and influence and demanded more comfort at home. By 1638 we even find a bill of sale for a house in Buenos Aires which contains a billiard table: games were, however, popular among the colonists of the New World. With improvements in domestic interiors came considerations of town planning. By the eighteenth century, the city plan of Buenos Aires was completed in the *castrum* pattern which was very common in Latin America (the 'apple in a parallelogram' plan found in old Mexican towns by the Spanish invaders). The city included some round buildings that may have been the outcome of Jesuit ability and enterprise. The order was experienced in building as the early fortress chapels and splendid missions of Paraguay and Brazil indicate.

The two countries which had the closest and most constant administrative links with Spain were Mexico and Peru and there, beside the magnificently ornate churches, the privileged families who had won land concessions and the slaves necessary to cultivate them, displayed their recently acquired wealth in newly built houses that were as ostentatious as their resources allowed. The cities of Peru – Lima, founded by Francisco Pizarro in 1533, Cuzco, the ancient Inca capital and centre of a school of painting, Cajmarca and Arequipa – prospered but they were subject to earthquakes and

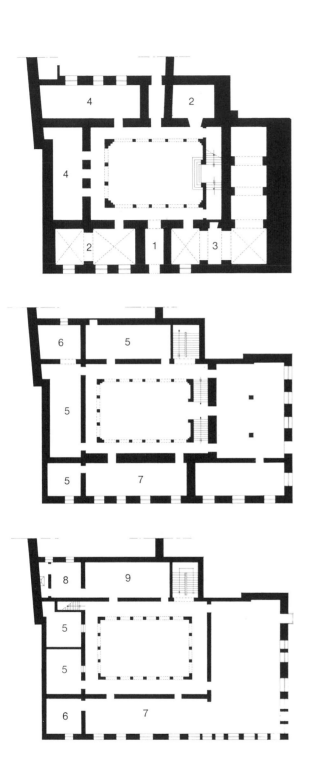

The House of the Counts of Arana at La Paz is one of the most representative buildings of the colonial period in the capital of Bolivia. The name of the architect is unknown, but it is known from the date inscribed in the scroll over the front door that the two lower storeys were built in 1775 and that the third was added in 1887. That the building was an important one is shown by the magnificence of the main entrance, the balcony much richer than that of the Cabildo at Potosi and made of stone, the decorative wrought ironwork, and the rusticated ashlar of the portico (based, perhaps, on Inca building stone). The original structure of the interior has, fortunately, survived and the functions of the various rooms can be identified. In the plans (top, the ground floor; centre, the first floor; bottom, the second floor), they are as follows: hall (1), service rooms (2), cellar (3), storerooms (4), bedrooms (5), dressing-room (6), drawing-room (7), kitchen (8), and dining-room (9).

Doorway in the patio of an elegant old house in La Paz, built probably about 1845. The plan of the patio, which is eight-sided, is unusual in South America, but the use of Ionic columns is, as we have seen with the Cabildo, widespread and not merely in Bolivia.

221

The House of Oquendo, one of the most famous of the many surviving buildings of the colonial period in Lima, Peru. In its complex structure, the choice and use of building materials, and the richness of its ornament, it resembles others of its period, the early years of the nineteenth century. It differs from many of its contemporaries, however, in its mingling of Spanish baroque with the styles of Louis XV and Louis XVI and the Ionic columns betray a neo-classical influence; the combination is remarkably successful. The central tower with its cupola seems to have been used by the first owner of the house, a Spanish banker called Osambella, as a look-out from which he could watch the movements of his galleons in the harbour.

Plan of an eighteenth century house in Coro, on the north-west coast of Venezuela, interesting for the dramatic placing of the two arcaded patios. (Opposite page, above) Plan of one of the oldest houses at Santo Domingo which dates from the sixteenth century; here the style is that which was common in northern Spain; the decoration was in the Gothic style. (Opposite page, below) Plan of a small house built in 1785 in the cathedral district of Buenos Aires.

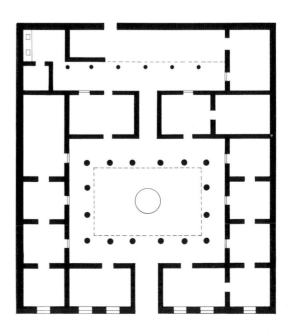

Calle Bolívar in Colón in the Canal Zone of Panama. The houses are fairly modern but they still have the Ionic columns that were so popular in Latin America during the eighteenth and nineteenth centuries. They demonstrate too the principal characteristics of houses built in the tropics before the advent of air-conditioning — colonnades and balconies with blinds to keep out the sun.

from time to time had to be rebuilt. The buildings that survived most successfully were the light, wood-framed houses of the working classes with their walls of reeds and mud. For the inhabitant of such a house an earthquake was alarming rather than dangerous. At the other end of the social scale, the great landowner defended himself against the earth's movements with massive walls of solid masonry, imitating the fortresses of the Incas and, indeed, plundering them in order to do so. Some of these houses still stand in Lima, among them the palace of the Torre-Tagle built in 1735, a fortress apparently defying fate as well as earthquakes.

Chile, like Paraguay and Colombia, was one of the poorer colonies and the houses reflected its poverty compared to the wealth of Mexico and Peru. Here too the householders had to take account of the possibility of earthquakes in deciding what materials should be used, and Chilean law relating to these natural disasters is technically very advanced. This charming country still has colonial houses which betray a very close link with the classic Spanish traditions of the sixteenth century.

Houses in Spanish Colonial style in Mexico City. In this large block of middle class flats, late rococo charm, slightly modified by neo-classical details, is attractively displayed in the coloured bricks laid so as to lighten a scheme that would otherwise be rather heavy.

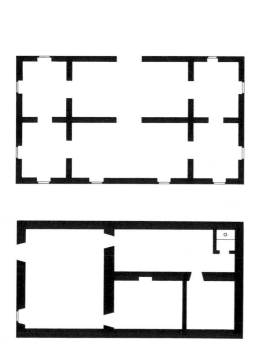

In the Cerro district of Havana which developed towards the end of last century, there are many houses like this. The importance of the patio on which the life of the house traditionally focused was being modified by the growing influence of the street as a part of everyday life. Classical details were popular in architecture in the early Republican period, from 1870 onwards. This is the house of a prosperous family, but working class houses survive which resemble it closely.

Their plan is simple, consisting of a patio under a roof of deep red Roman tiles. The main doorway advertized in carved stone the wealth of the owner in accepted baroque fashion and in accordance with practice throughout the Spanish dominions in Latin America.

In Venezuela too there is evidence of close architectural links with Spain. Recent research has shown that the early colonists were prepared to disregard the demands of the climate in order to build houses that were copies of Spanish houses, erected out of the same sense of nostalgia that compelled immigrants to North America to name their towns New Fribourg, New Amsterdam, and so on. More commonly, however, houses were built for shelter, comfort and for use and these necessarily functional dwellings are often aesthetically very satisfying. In Venezuela, for example, we find the type of building common to the Atlantic seaboard of South America: the two-storeyed house with the ground floor used as store, workshop or shop, and the upper floor used as a dwelling. The constant characteristic is the wide gallery screened by a trellis. (Today, even in those parts of Rio de Janeiro which are being torn down to provide room for more skyscrapers, whole districts of these house-stores survive, their façades covered in coloured tiles and their windows shaded by rolled shutters, two elements of their Moorish heritage which the Spanish colonists brought to the tropics.)

An important centre of Spanish colonial architecture is, of course, Cuba, and in towns like Remedios centuries have passed without making any apparent changes. In the older houses in Cuba, as on other islands in the Caribbean, the patio was the heart of the dwelling, the place to shelter from the sun and to relax. In more palatial buildings the patio was formed by an upper gallery under arcades with screens that provided shade and a degree of ventilation. Though such screens are now rendered unnecessary by modern air-conditioning, they are often retained as a decorative feature. The window is shaded by a horizontal *brise-soleil* which can be manoeuvred to allow light and air to enter and to shut out rain.

The architects of private houses in Spanish America can hardly ever be named. Some are known but identification of their work is a matter of guesswork rather than documentation. We know, for example, of an architect called Francisco Becerra who built churches and convents in Mexico and in Lima, Quito and Cuzco. But we know nothing of his work on private houses, though he has been credited with the invention of the corner balcony, a novelty that became amazingly popular in the eighteenth century.

It is possible that architects themselves were not called upon to build private houses. Presumably they were constantly occupied on buildings for the church and the religious orders and therefore passed their commissions for private houses to their master builders.

Wooden buildings from small towns
on the island of Cuba. These photographs
show houses at Jibara (left) and
Remedios (below), both in the northern
part of the island. The houses are
usually built in rows, linked by a gallery
that looks out on to the street, and
this is, in fact, what has been done with
these two fairly large buildings, each
of which seems to contain several houses
intercommunicating behind the
common verandah. Both show clearly
the influence of North American
architecture, perceptible from the
beginning of this century.

Ornamentation

Ornamental motifs introduced from Europe have often taken on new and exotic life in South America. At the same time, types of ornament peculiar to the continent have developed. An example seen here is the use of stained glass in Cuban houses where it was used to decorate doors and windows. The glass was nearly always in bright primary colours and the forms were often simple geometric ones (Opposite page, below). Sometimes, however, a more ambitious artist would depict flowers and foliage in an Art Nouveau *style (Above and opposite page, above). In this way, it was possible to add colour to the interior and to filter the strong light.*

So far no mention has been made of styles of ornamentation in Latin America and to discuss in detail its apparently endless variations would take a great deal more space than is available here. But the variations follow certain lines, more easily perceptible, obviously, in official buildings than in domestic architecture. The Manueline style of Portugal travelled, for example, to Brazil, where it was succeeded by the intricate inlays and heavy gilding of the Baroque. In Mexico we find the exuberant fantasy of the Churrigueresque and in Peru the rich delicacy of the Plateresque. Private houses were almost certainly influenced by these styles but Latin America transmuted them into something even richer and stranger: nor was neo-classicism, the least amenable of styles, immune during the period when the new republics were struggling into existence. Even liturgical symbols changed; the grape became a pineapple and the dove a heron.

The forms that decoration took in South American architecture during the centuries when the sailing ship was the only means of transport there, emphasize its distance from Europe. The Spanish or Portuguese heritage is perceptible, but what happened to that heritage is entirely of the place and of the people. And Europe's interest in the distant continent was not any greater than it was in President Monroe's doctrine. It was known to be large, overgrown with fantastic vegetation and infested with equally fantastic animals, and people tended to go or be taken there and disappear. It came as not too much of a shock to some Europeans to discover that as recently as the middle of this century the materials for the preliminary work on Brasilia were transported by air, for there were no roads.

Colonial furniture, what is left of it, is crude, strong, and to those who can set it in its place in history, a touching reminder of the Spartan spirit of

A small town in Honduras, the natural beauty
of which is enhanced by the frequent reminders
of the past encountered in such a street as this.
The high walls at the side of the street still shelter
the houses behind them, as they did during the period
of the Spanish Empire when the house was,
in fact, a fortress centred on the internal patio.

Interior of a house at Remedios in Cuba,
now a museum of colonial times. The furniture
dates from the first half of the nineteenth
century and betrays a liking for curved lines
that is typically Cuban and probably baroque in
origin. The Spanish heritage is, however,
also very evident in the richness of the effect
of curving, skilfully worked and polished wood.

House in Trinidad, built during the eighteenth and nineteenth centuries. The classical details were taken from public buildings. The iron bars represent, unfortunately, the superseding of the earlier wooden grills that took place during the nineteenth century in the interests, presumably, of security. The decorative cornice is achieved by an original use of single bricks.

the early pioneers. There are terracotta pots roughly decorated with geometric patterns; some native pottery has survived too. Nobles and landowners enjoyed greater luxury. Furniture was imported from Europe, and china from the east, bearing the arms of the new aristocracy and carried in ships of the East India Company. Spanish and Portuguese furniture found its way to the shops of the capital cities. Local craftsmanship did develop, if slowly: in Brazil in the eighteenth century, fine furniture in jacaranda wood was being made. But life was, on the whole, comfortless. The abbot of La Caille writes of a dinner given him by the Commandant-General in Rio de Janeiro. The dinner was not a success. 'The menu was based almost entirely on fish. They gave us very small, square, dirty napkins that even at best had already been used. And this was a very rich man.'

The house had no social function. It was closed to outsiders and formed one rigidly defined compartment in the life of its owner. Not till the first decade of the nineteenth century did it begin to open up to the outside world. Then, the Prince Regent of Brazil arrived from Portugal and for reasons of hygiene and convenience ordered that glass panes instead of grilles should be fitted in windows. Other changes followed. Furniture improved; curtains were used; houses were repainted. The English shopkeepers settled along the coasts of Latin America, did a roaring trade and sent orders home for –

as well as the usual dried salt cod, fabrics and cast iron – shiploads of furniture and knicknacks. Troops of craftsmen arrived with them, dedicated to the profitable refurbishing of the houses of the New World. Architects were summoned from Europe to help rebuild the cities after the best European patterns. Monuments were commissioned from European artists and laboriously imported. Houses were bedizened with marble façades. In Brazil, an architectural mission arrived in 1816 to preach an academic style that persists even today.

South America's position as an artistic and architectural tributary of Europe was enhanced by the flood of immigration in the second half of the nineteenth century. The immigrants nostalgically recalled the homes they had left behind in the houses they built in the New World, and towns like São Paulo show the results of this mixture of cultures in an incredible jumble of styles, Norman, Tudor, Florentine Renaissance, Moorish, pseudo-Gothic and even Chinese. If the householder could not rise to a distinctive national style of façade, a small bust of Garibaldi would betray that the family was Italian, or a white statuette in Portuguese pottery would show that the owner had come from Lisbon.

The house's achievement of social status coincided, fortunately, with improvements in such amenities as drainage and water supply. The development of town planning has been slower and it is in this direction that future progress lies.

Anne Berendsen

THE MERCHANT PRINCES
OF THE NETHERLANDS

In the Netherlands in the eighteenth century, the trade with the East Indies produced steady, very high profits for the merchants engaged in it. Having achieved even greater wealth than their predecessors of the seventeenth century, they used a substantial part of it on the enrichment of their houses.

Many of these houses still exist in Amsterdam, the heart of Holland's mercantile empire. At the Hague there are rather fewer but the quality of them is, perhaps, even finer. Characteristic of their façades is a horizontal cornice and long windows: the most prominent feature – as it was intended to be – was the entrance, centrally placed on the façade, surmounted by several rows of windows and crowned by the central crest or balustrades of the roof, the whole designed to form a unified frontispiece. Mansions in this baroque manner were designed by the French-born architect, Daniel Ma-

rot (1663-1752) chief architect to the Stadtholder who was also William III of England. To the Netherlands and England (where he worked on Hampton Court) Marot introduced a version of French seventeenth century baroque. It was during this period, moreover, at the end of the seventeenth century, that windows with transoms and mullions were replaced by sash windows (often called *English* though probably Dutch in origin); the windows with their distinctive glazing bars became a constant and essential part of Dutch and English façades. Another Frenchman who worked in the Netherlands, a little later than Marot, was Frederic Blancard who lived in Amsterdam from 1720 to 1740 and designed the little-known *Huize van Brienen* on the Herengracht.

The influence of France was maintained in the second half of the eighteenth century by

The Snouck van Loosen house in Enkhuizen, one of the 'dead' towns
of the Zuider Zee north of Amsterdam. This house, built in 1741 and later
enlarged by the addition of the pavilion and doorway on the right,
shows Dutch reluctance to abandon the Baroque though they have indulged
in a certain rococo extravagance in the interior (see page 232).
The treatment of the stone was peculiar to the builder
Jacob Vennekool and his circle.

Situated within a bend of the Rhine where it divides into two arms, and
with three canals – the Oudegracht, the Nieuwegracht, and the
Kromme Nieuwegracht – cutting through it, Utrecht owes much of its
wealth and most of its charm to water. The streets ride above the canals, and
the houses on the Oudegracht and Nieuwegracht have workshops
and shops below the pavements. This view, by an unknown draughtsman
in the eighteenth century, is of the Oudegracht and shows the
mixture of swan-neck and stepped gables, the characteristic shuttering
of the windows, and the height of the street above the canal.

(Opposite page) The blue drawing-room
in the house built in 1794 for Abraham van
der Hart at No. 17 Spaarne in Haarlem:
today this building houses the Royal
Academy of Science. French styles had
a considerable influence on Dutch eighteenth-
century architecture and decoration; but so
for political and historical reasons – the two
countries had, for a time, the same
monarch – did English fashions.

Corridor in the Snouck van Loosen house
in Enkhuizen (see page 231). The decoration
in marble and white stucco dates from about 1741.
The style is vigorously rococo with a number
of complex motifs repeated. The liveliness of
the exterior is seen here to be repeated indoors
as are the noble proportions
in, for example, the double doors.

Dutch cabinet of about 1720 (private collection)
with inlaid floral ornament. This piece probably
owes something to the influence of the great
French cabinet-makers though the style is known
in France as the style des Pays Bas; its maker
was probably also familiar with English
painted furniture of the late seventeenth
and early eighteenth centuries.
This is suggested by the treatment of the flowers
and their colouring which, allowing for the
exigencies of wood, indicate a not
too distant pictorial origin.

Pieter de Swart (1700-1793) who as a young man worked in France, and on returning to his native country designed in the style of Louis XVI. His houses were planned with the living-rooms opening off a corridor and, at the end of the corridor, the principal drawing-room. It was a style that continued in popularity for over a century. Its object was in part the theatrical one of creating an illusion of space, derived via classical revivals from Renaissance models: the decoration of the staircases, the garden pavilion and the walls of the courtyard, typically Dutch though they were, enhanced this sense of spaciousness.

This corridor or vestibule, whose floor usually consisted of stone slabs, accordingly gained in importance. In richer houses, a dado of marble panels was often surmounted by painted walls, or the upper parts of the wall were decorated in stucco. Very elaborate plasterwork in high relief was the speciality of Italian artists in Holland. A less expensive form of decoration in the vestibule was to paint the walls from top to bottom and to use slender pillars or pilasters instead of massive pillars to break the length. Doors, especially in the wealthier houses, were dramatically wide double doors: over them in many cases were paintings. The old *voorhuis* survived, but as a hall, brightly lit by a window above the door. The staircase, the embellishment of which had begun in the seventeenth century, also took on additional importance with finely wrought iron and stucco-decorated walls. The panelling of Dutch rooms was painted first in a clear greenish-blue and then in the pale green which had been a favourite in France since the 1720's. However, partly because of the nineteenth century predilection for covering these coloured walls with white paint, it is difficult now to obtain an accurate idea of the splendour of the Dutch rococo interiors.

A luxurious Dutch interior was probably heavy-looking in comparison with a French one but it suit-

These photographs (above and opposite page) were taken in Dordrecht during the nineteenth century. One of the most important commercial centres of the Netherlands in the Middle Ages, the city was separated from Brabant, to the south, by the floods of 1421. During the Dutch Wars of Independence it was one of the centres of resistance against the Spaniards.

Dordrecht is pre-eminently a city of water, as these photographs show, the canals being used principally for trade and transport though they could be utilized for defence. The backs of many of the houses open straight on to the waterways: jetties are comparatively few and far between.

Van Wyngaarden's bird's eye view of Dordrecht in the seventeenth century (Oxford, Bodleian Library). The ranks of houses with stepped gables are typical of Dutch towns of the period.

The lay-out of houses in the Herengracht — the Gentleman's Canal — in Amsterdam. In the middle of the row on the right is No. 475, shown opposite. The drawing is taken from the Grachtenboek (The Book of Canals) by Caspar Philips, a comprehensive account of Amsterdam, a city the beauty and fascination of which lies not merely in the quality of individual buildings — which, as we have seen, is very high — but also in their elegant grouping.

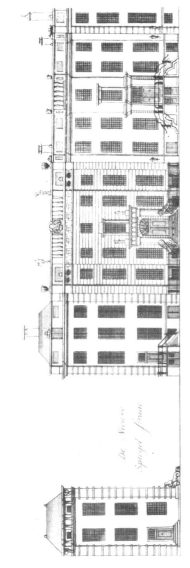

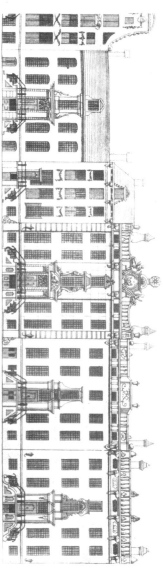

(Opposite page) The crest of the façade
of the Helmich House in Zwolle in Overijssel,
one of the eastern provinces of the
Netherlands. Now a museum, it is a fine
example of provincial rococo and, in its
exuberance and use of figures as ornamentation,
recalls similar buildings across the not
very distant German border.

ed the place and the people and provided the sense
of warmth and intimacy that was desired as much
as a sense of splendour. And the often extravagant
use of gilt decoration, the paintings in the centres of
the ornately decorated ceilings, the Utrecht velvet
that covered the upper part of the walls in some
houses – all these must have created at the very least
an impression of stateliness, warmed, however, by
the Dutch fondness for red, a colour that other
countries such as France handled with some reserve.

Furniture followed French and English models
but it is interesting to note that the Dutch never
capitulated to the curved fantasies of French rococo; their chair backs remained slender and straight.
High, solid wardrobes remained in use.

At the end of the seventeenth and beginning of
the eighteenth centuries, England and Holland were
closely allied. The Stadtholder of Holland shared
with his wife the throne of the United Kingdom
and his chief architect, Daniel Marot, worked in
both countries. And throughout the eighteenth century the tastes of, in particular, the prosperous
Dutch and English middle classes remained very
similar. They built the kind of houses that suited
them and the houses bore a noticeable resemblance
to one another.

(Below, left) Front of 475 Herengracht, Ansterdam (see drawing opposite). About 1730, French
taste, partly the outcome of the influence of exiled Huguenots, resulted in alterations to the house that
occupied this site to create the building we see now. The changes were made by Petronelle van Lennep.
(Below, right) Middelburg in Zeeland: house on the Lange Delft built in 1733 by Jan Pieter
van Baurscheit the Younger (1699-1768) for the de Brande family; the building is now the provincial library.

Gianni K. Koenig

GERMANY'S DOMESTIC REVOLUTION

From the Alps to Scandinavia, the idea of comfort or *Gemütlichkeit* spread quickly in the seventeenth century, especially in the Netherlands with their extensive bourgeoisie. The aristocracy retained their medieval and early Renaissance houses, uncomfortable and resistant to improvement. But the newly affluent built themselves town houses and created the townscapes we know today. The town has been called the formal structure of history, and it provides tangible evidence of the development of society. In this way, the emergence of a flourishing middle class as a link between aristocracy and working classes was immediately reflected in towns and cities. These consisted now, not of a palace or castle surrounded by the dwellings of the castellan's dependents, but of rows of houses, alike and yet individual, linked by the street before their doors.

Bernardo Bellotto's magnificent view of Dresden, with the Frauenkirche, gives some idea of the spread of this new type of building. The old wooden houses have disappeared; all the buildings in the painting are made of stone and grow higher with each decade. Those opposite the church still resemble wooden houses in form, and the rest of the row seems to consist mainly of rather narrow houses with only two windows on each floor and, in some cases, the *Erker* or bay window. Since this window projected, it was still made of wood which ensured that it was lightweight as well as strong.

Still in Bellotto's Dresden, the building in the

Bernardo Bellotto, View of Dresden with the Frauenkirche *(c. 1750; Dresden, Staatliche Gemäldegalerie). The detail of Bellotto's paintings has made them a valuable — and, as it has happened, necessary — record of the appearance of certain cities: his paintings of Warsaw, for example, were used as a check during the reconstruction necessary at the end of the Second World War. Similarly, this painting of Dresden affords useful information as to the wide variety of buildings in evidence in the city during the first half of the eighteenth century; seventeenth century buildings predominate.*

The practicality of steeply sloping roofs on buildings, in regions which suffer heavy rain and snow falls, is obvious. The varying of the pitch to form a mansard roof enabled the maximum use to be made of the space beneath, as in this house at Bonn where Beethoven was born in 1770. (Below) Germany is associated with wooden houses and this view of Freudenberg in the Rhineland gives some idea of their collective charm.

middle distance, on the corner of a street, looks like an apartment building, a form of dwelling that was soon to become very popular. The house with its *piano nobile*, in which the family lived on several floors, went out of existence and the grouping of the windows of this building — the arrangement being the same on the three floors above the ground floor — leads one to believe that the house was divided into flats, one on top of the other and each repeating the plan of the one below. The *Erker*, built of stone, is placed on the corner to become the bow window we know today. The attics too were expanded: they were no longer lit by tiny windows but were furnished with wide ones, thereby beginning the progress to the status of, in modern apartment buildings, the *piano nobile* in the guise of the penthouse apartment.

Changes took place inside the house, although the interior of the stone house preserved the memory of the wooden house. Walls were panelled up to a certain height in various forms of wood, from the simplest kind of wooden lining to intricately inlaid panels with geometric motifs. Furniture became more plentiful in quantity and more varied in design. Oak furniture was more widespread. Variations appeared on the basic chests and cabinets. Stools gave place to chairs though these were very often the simple type still found in churches with round, turned legs and rush or straw seats. But there were, too, small folding armchairs with their antique X-shaped frames, and then at last the large upholstered armchair with its broad, scroll-shaped arms, the ancestor of today's easy chair.

Pieces of furniture with special functions increased in number. Oak tables ranged in size from those fit for dinners and indeed banquets, with their typical bottle-shaped legs, to work-tables and card-tables with a small drawer under the top, and small toilet-tables that opened to produce a mirror. The

linen cupboard developed peaceably from the tall cupboard that had been used to stack firearms (powder being sensitive to damp). Last to appear on the scene was, perhaps, the most versatile piece of furniture, the chest of drawers.

Wooden floors were warm but the domestic revolution demanded more comfort. The Eastern custom of spreading carpets on the floor became popular as did the practice of covering furniture with fabrics, often valuable. Tapestries, no longer needed to keep out draughts, were taken down from the walls and cut and stitched into screens which possessed the advantage of being easily moveable.

The small furnishings of the house increased in quantity and quality too. China and plate, cups and cutlery, serving dishes and candelabra came into widespread use along with such special accessories as globes, and were often valued as much for their aesthetic qualities as for their usefulness.

Ever since it began to have a history at all, the dwelling house, with its inbuilt plan and accumulation of furniture and other objects, has been subject to the differing, often the conflicting claims of

the aesthetic and the functional. Development too far in one direction has usually been followed by reaction in the other. Rarely has perfect balance been achieved and that only when functional and aesthetic qualities have been exactly matched – when function has not been sacrificed to form, as happened at the end of the nineteenth century, or *vice versa* as has happened since. About the middle of the seventeenth century, however, the German house achieved something like a perfect state of equilibrium – as, indeed, did houses in other countries in northern Europe, their success being commemorated in the paintings of Vermeer and Pieter de Hooch. The light that streams in through the windows of Vermeer's paintings warms the simple, harmonious interiors and at the same time transfigures the objects and people within.

In the eighteenth century, this balance was in jeopardy and the swing had begun towards an excess of aestheticism. Superfluous ornament and bric-à-brac began to infiltrate the house; the grander buildings dedicated to a taste for balance and symmetry became cold and forbidding.

Perfectly preserved palaces of the seventeenth and eighteenth centuries survive and in them time seems miraculously to have stopped in order to let us reconstruct the life of their vanished inhabitants. But in middle class houses, which were never sufficiently committed to any single style to enable their owners to say 'Stop! This is how I want my house to look to posterity', it is difficult, indeed impossible, to find rooms, above all secondary rooms such as kitchens, in the condition they were in three centuries ago. Fortunately, however, the dolls' house, that expensive toy, a scale model of the house of a well-to-do family, was fairly common during this period. Houses were reproduced in miniature with great care and every tiniest detail was shown. The front of the dolls' house opens to reveal the interior, and as the structure of the walls and the arrangement of the furniture have been preserved, it is possible to catch from these exquisite models something of the atmosphere of seventeenth and eighteenth century houses and of the kind of life lived in them.

The dolls' house of the Stromer family in Nuremberg, dated 1639, shows an arrangement typical of wooden houses. The rooms of the ground floor and mezzanine were lower and narrower than those of the rest of the house; they were not strictly living-rooms but were used to accommodate children, servants and horses as well as the storerooms and laundry. On the first floor is the kitchen, crowded with pots and plates and dishes – probably more so than it was in reality – with most of the space apparently occupied by the enormous chimney and equally massive kitchen table. In the centre of the house, under the steep staircase that leads to the floor above, is the linen cupboard, and the pieces of armour on top are the clue to its original purpose as an armoury. Opposite the kitchen is the study-bedroom, a room in which two separate functions are intelligently united by setting the bed in a recess and closing it off with a curtain. This was a Renaissance arrangement – remember Dürer's *St. Jerome* – that was to persist throughout the nineteenth century. But the large green majolica stove tells how much heating had been improved since the days of Dürer. These stoves stored heat efficiently and even if they were not stoked up during the night, they kept the room warm until morning. There is another ceramic stove in the bedroom

The dolls' house is one of the most ancient of all toys though, in its remotest origins, its
may have been related not so much to children's play as to religious offerings: mo
offered to the gods of the underworld and to the spirits of the ancestors have been found as
apart as Etruria and China. Their present-day equivalents are modelled in plastic but as far
children are concerned, their use is the same for small Eskimos with their miniature te
sleighs and boats, as for the Ualata children of Mauritania with their tiny houses of delicat
painted baked clay. During the seventeenth and eighteenth centuries, dolls' hou
enjoyed a considerable vogue in Europe. A number of them have survived including t
splendid example which dates from 1637 (Nuremberg, Germanisches Nationalmuseu

241

above the study while the dining-room, which is above the kitchen, the warmest room in the house, is heated by that enormous chimney below.

Another of these models, also from Nuremberg, shows in detail the kitchen of a middle class eighteenth century house, furnished with perfect miniatures of the utensils of the period, from pots and pans to spits and grills. It is an extremely crowded kitchen with too many objects piled up into too small a space, and the balance discernible in a Ver-

meer interior is notably absent. The sense of overcrowding is, of course, bound to be exaggerated in these wonderful toys but it is possible that they reflect a tendency that did exist.

Yet even in the later dolls' houses, there is no sign of the hierarchy of rooms that was later to appear, epitomized by the institution of the 'best parlour'. Each room had an exact function whether as bedroom, study, drawing-room or dressing-room, and the whole house was lively and lived-in.

The dolls' house of the Kress family (Nuremberg, Germanisches Nationalmuseum) which affords some idea – possibly rather exaggerated, for this is a very crowded kitchen – of the appearance of an eighteenth century German kitchen with its splendid batterie de cuisine of pewter, copper, treen and blue and white earthenware. Miniature kitchens were popular toys and examples have survived from as early as the fifteenth century (Paris, Musée de Cluny.)

View of the front and one side of the eighteenth century Melik house in Bucharest in Rumania.
(Below) Façade of the Hagi-Prodan house at Ploeşti, also in Rumania (see also page 244).

G. OPRESCO - P. PETRESCO

COUNTRY BAROQUE IN THE BALKANS

The economic importance of the town in south-east Europe increased throughout the eighteenth century and from this intensive development arose the buildings that form the nucleus of so many Balkan towns today. In addition, the relationship between the residents of town and country was closer than ever before and this had important consequences for the plan both of the house and its setting. The richer townsmen maintained extensive interests in the countryside. Merchants found a market for their goods in the villages. In turn, the produce of the countryside went into the mills, stores and workshops of the towns. Craftsmen, and the merchants with whom they were closely allied, tended to group in two areas of the town. Some worked in the heart of the town or city, usually in shops on the line of the main street itself which formed the inner market. Others stayed on the outskirts, in the outer markets held on important holidays and used for goods which were difficult to transport. For obvious reasons, development was greatest in these outer areas, known by the Turkish name of *mahalale*. And apart from availability of space, considerations of fire and health affected their growth so that it is not by chance that tanneries, the shops of pork-butchers and bakers, and the workshops of soap-makers and candlemakers are removed from the centre of the town.

In spite of the danger of fire, merchants and boyars continued to build wooden houses. They were two-storeyed buildings with the lower floor a semi-basement. As a rule, this was vaulted and used for storage. The upper storey, which was in effect the ground floor, contained the residential part of the house made up of several rooms arranged round a drawing-room. The main entrance facing the street was fronted by an arched verandah, supported on small well-shaped columns; and reached by a wooden staircase from the street. In some houses there was a second verandah, generally a closed one, which projected over the back of the building.

Houses of this type exist in Argeş and Ploeşti in Rumania; a notable one belonged to a coppersmith who was famous in the district, others to the Dobrescu and Boiangine families. In some of them, the original ceilings and window frames of carved wood decorated with plaster still survive. But in spite of this concession to western fashion,

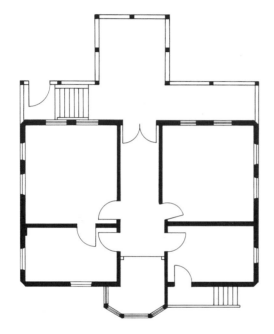

(Left) Back of the Hagi-Prodan house at Ploeşti. Here the building is slightly less than 35 feet wide. The plan (below left) of the house with its projecting, roofed entrance (upper part of plan) and the four main rooms is typical of a Rumanian middle class house of the eighteenth century.
(Below) View and plan of an eighteenth century house at Suceava in Moldavia (Rumania): the front of the house, with the steps to the entrance, is on the left.

(Opposite page) Bernardo Bellotto, View o Krakowskie Przedmiescie from the Cracov Gate in Warsaw (1770; Warsaw, Narodowe Museum) This Warsaw street scene shows the change tha had taken place in it during the eighteent century. In the background are modest suburba houses but the foreground is occupied by th mansions of the prosperous middle class who hav developed a taste for rococo

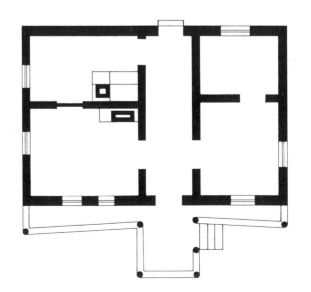

buildings in towns south of the Danube came to look more and more like those of Constantinople, especially in the course of the nineteenth century. And even north of the Danube in Bucharest, which during the eighteenth century flourished sufficiently to be able to support no fewer than 25 hotels by the year 1774, there was a hint of the oriental about the architecture of its buildings.

In general, however, architecture north of the Danube reflected western rather than eastern influences. Rumanian houses here were larger though they had the same raised verandah before the house. In Transylvania there was a good deal of Austrian baroque and ornamental plasterwork. The same is true of Croatian and Slovenian towns which were part of the Hapsburg empire, though it was Austrian baroque countrified compared with the Viennese originals. But the translation of these Viennese models to south-east Europe was not always to their detriment and often they acquired in the journey a solidity and an air of charming comfort unknown in the capital of the empire.

Wojciech Kalinowski

WARSAW:
A CITY IN DECLINE

In 1718, a certain M. Firatowicz was living and presumably earning some kind of a living in a house in Warsaw that had clearly seen better days. 'On the right of the hall,' an account of it runs, 'a shop with two doors, one of iron and one of wood; inside, with a single window opening on to the street, an intermediary room with a wooden floor and a green stove. Beyond the shop, a brandy distillery which had once been a large kitchen. In the ground floor room which has two windows, a white stove, the fireplace and a number of cupboards let into the walls. Then came a courtyard, more shops, rooms used for making beer and several cellars. A stair from one of these cellars led up into the residential part of the house which was on the first floor. Here there was one room with three windows on to Piwna Street, a white stove, the fireplace, a dark alcove (in which, however, there was a window); it was divided into lodgings for the workers. On the opposite side of the building was a similar room, again with an alcove. Between the two there were two kitchens, one large, one small. From the second bedroom, a passage led to a small room with its own green stove and window and this

in turn connected with a larger room with a single window and stove. On the second floor the arrangement was the same, there were the same rooms with their alcoves and stoves, small rooms carved out of larger ones and the kitchen divided.'

The impression is one of poverty and if the fate of this building was typical, it suggests a city in decline. Poland did undergo severe economic depression in the eighteenth century and this affected building. Except in the north-western provinces, the buildings raised were usually only of a single storey and made of wood. In town and city centres, houses were built in rows along streets and around squares; they had pitched roofs and were two or three rooms deep. (One of these rooms would be the *black* kitchen, that is, one without a means of escape for smoke.) Structure and ornamentation of buildings of this still basically medieval type were often strictly standardized according to the use made of them; the nobles to whom they belonged might, for example, use them to house craftsmen or their own employees. In favourable circumstances, blocks of these buildings were designed by architects but, on the whole, they were

Town hall and dwelling houses on the western side of the market-place at Rydzyna, a small Polish town south of Poznan on the borders of Silesia (Sketch from W. Trzebinski's monograph on eighteenth century brick buildings in the small towns of Western Poland, published in Warsaw in 1962; photograph by T. Barucki). The average width of the house-fronts was about 27 feet.

(Below) Plan for the western side of the market-place in the town of Biala Podlaska, west of Warsaw (Warsaw, print collection of the University Library), drawn up in 1777 by the architect Maciej Takimowicz. This is an example of the type of plan designed for middle-sized towns attached to important princely houses. The prince himself instructed his own architect to draw up the plan. The large buildings at either end were to be austcrya druga, that is, inns; the row of houses in the centre were to contain shops and dwellings for shopkeepers. In a plan rich in eighteenth century rococo detail, it is interesting to note that the counters of the shops were still, as they were in the Middle Ages, on the street.

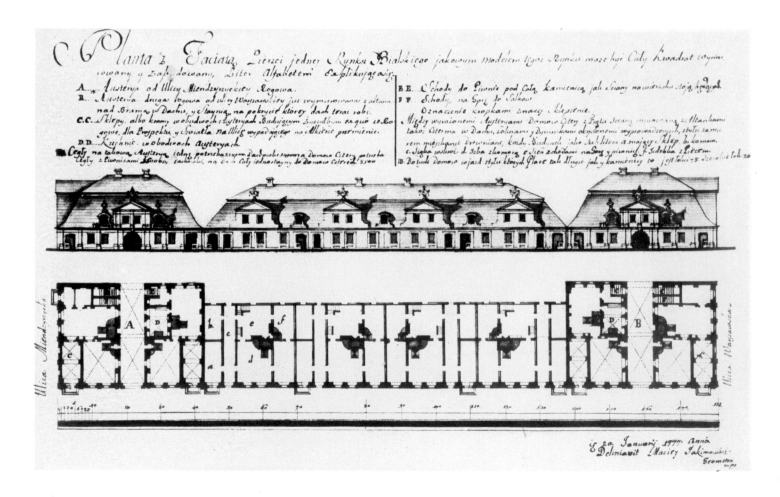

246

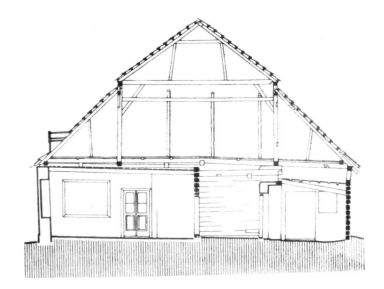

(Right, from the top) Frontal section, front, side section, and plan of a wooden house at Ciezkowice (by C. W. Krassowski and A. J. Milobedzki, Studia nad zabudowa miasteczka Ciezkowice, 1947). The house, which is typical of small towns in southern Poland in the eighteenth century, demonstrates the development of houses two rooms deep.

Above) Craftsmen's houses of the eighteenth ntury at Rakoniewice near Poznan. Here o they occupy one side of a market square nd while the plan seems more standardized than Rydzyna, it is not quite so rigidly defined at Biala Podlaska. Each house-front is about enty-seven feet wide (by W. Kalinowski, ity Development in Poland up to the Middle the Nineteenth Century, Warsaw, 1966).

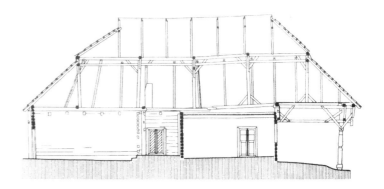

constructed by master builders and carpenters working without plans. This explains the absence of definite style, virtually complete save for a hint of baroque or rococo in the curve of a gable or a mansard roof, or the addition of pillars to the façade of a building overlooking the market place.

Only in a few towns were houses built on several storeys to house a single family. There was some private building in Warsaw in the reign of Stanislas Augustus when the city's population multiplied by four (in part because of reorganization of the city's boundaries and government). Speculative constructors put up buildings intended to accommodate many families; these were double-fronted but not usually very deep. The room lay-out was the same on each of the three floors used and the ground floor was used for shops. In plan and in the decoration of their façades, these buildings sought to imitate grander houses and they provided the models for the blocks of flats that were to appear in the nineteenth century. The fashions of western Europe, especially of France, were admired in Poland but in Warsaw as elsewhere, the use made of them was limited to façades and interiors.

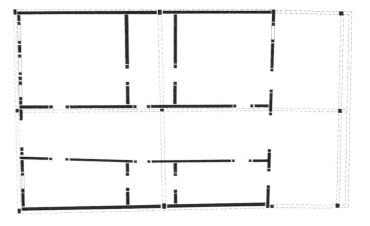

BUILDING TO ORDER IN RUSSIA

The upheavals in Russian society created by the reforms of Peter the Great influenced architecture as well, especially as one of the many tasks assigned to the police was that they 'should check that every building was put up in strict observance of the rules of His Imperial Majesty.' The structure of society changed, above all, in St. Petersburg which became the capital in 1714. An increase in trade and industry favoured the development of a working class. Minor officials began to appear. Merchants and craftsmen formed, as before, the nucleus of the urban population, in the new capital as much as in the old. But in the new capital they needed new houses and these conformed, perforce, to the dictates of the Czar.

In order that the new city should be furnished with buildings as quickly as possible, eminent architects were instructed to draw up plans for houses which should take into account the income and social position of the householders. Accordingly, plans were made out for modest houses – for 'soldiers, carpenters, and other workers of the lower class' – and for houses for the wealthy or the noblemen. Government plans which made building cheaper were popular and, the planners were confident, could not but improve the general standard of architecture. State plans for standard houses continued to be used, indeed, for about a century

and a half until the middle of the nineteenth century. During this period, many types of building were erected, some of them very simple, others much more complex. Their effect on Russian towns was often far-reaching.

The first plans of the kind were produced by the architect Domenico Trezzini, who left his native Lugano and went (via Copenhagen) to work in Peter the Great's new city. He gave special attention to wooden buildings but soon stone buildings were being built. Regulations for the prevention of fires obliged house owners to cover wooden ceilings with plaster and in stone houses to vault the ground floor service rooms. Tiles should be used, it was also ordained, instead of planks on roofs. After the middle of the century, when bricks came into widespread use, wooden houses were no longer built in the central districts of Moscow and St. Petersburg.

At the same time, changes in taste – from classicism to the Baroque – accompanied changes in house plans, in the distribution of rooms and the decoration of them. The new houses differed in a number of ways from those of the seventeenth century. The arrangement of the rooms, now lighter and more spacious, became simple and rational. Narrow, uncomfortable rooms and elongated halls disappeared. In some dwellings such as the priest's

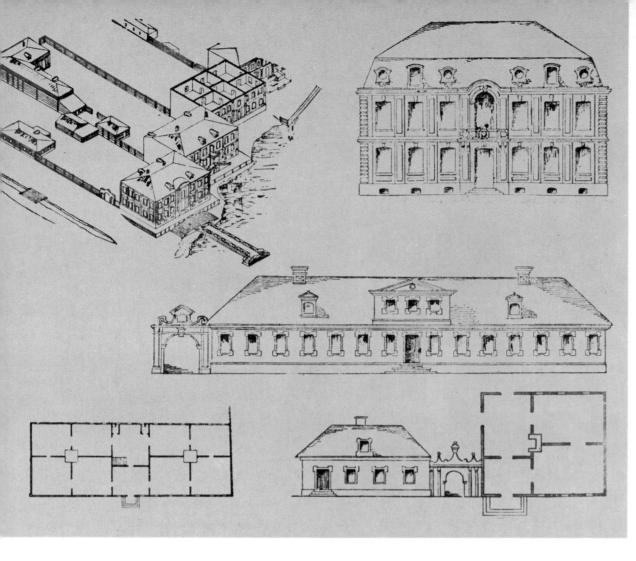

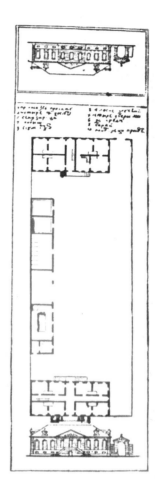

(Above) Domenico Trezzini's plan, drawn up in 1714, for standardized housing
in St. Petersburg. (Top) Dwellings for 'the nobles': these houses resemble
one another but are not identical: 'the nobles' were allowed some choice.
Each house-front is fifty-two feet wide and they are placed side by side
in order to save space. (Centre) Houses for the 'rich' (plan, below left); with their
porticos, these are over eighty-two feet wide.
(Below, right) House for 'the poor', forty-nine feet wide.
(Right) House attached to the Issakievsky Cathedral, St. Petersburg,
designed by Michael Zemtsov in 1739.

house for Issakievsky Cathedral, designed in 1739
by Michael Zemtsov, the skilfully planned interior
was organized to serve the needs of two families
or more. Western influence showed clearly in the
decoration of house exteriors; a small house in Ulia-
novskaia Street in Moscow is decorated with motifs
similar to those found in western Europe in the
same period, the middle of the eighteenth century,
whereas the asymmetry of the front suggests seventeenth century models. And the wealthier classes
got into the habit, according to Duke Shcherba-
khov, of decorating the interiors of their houses
with 'gilded plasterwork, silk tapestries in every
room, and very valuable furniture.'

As the population of the towns grew, town
houses with their 'French-style' gardens of flowerbeds and orderly paths used up more and more
land and government plans were produced for
houses more economical of ground, that is, terraced

*House from the second
half of the eighteenth
century in
Gorokhovsky Street
in Moscow.*

houses. Buildings of this kind began to appear in St. Petersburg between 1740 and 1750.

Skilled craftsmen were necessary for the decoration of houses in the styles that were fashionable in western Europe at this time. For this reason, such decoration was within the reach of comparatively few. Even in the baroque period, therefore, more sober forms of ornament appeared on Russian buildings. Pilasters and architraves were modestly proportioned and decorated and cornices were severe; classical styles which were popular during the second half of the eighteenth century were austerely imitated.

Certain minimum standards had, however, to

high architectural standard. Even the simplest possess this typical charm, as can be seen in a small private house in Gorkhovsky Street in Moscow.

In larger and richer buildings, the classical dignity of the façade is often embellished by bas-reliefs on mythological themes. Staircases and balconies with their exquisite ironwork delight the eye with their sweeping curves. At the back of these buildings, beyond the courtyard and the colonnade, small gardens were planted, often with a pool. Service rooms were accommodated along the flanks of the courtyard or in the wings of the main building. The plans reflected clearly those designs by Palladio for distant villas in the Veneto.

be observed. The *Short Manual of Architecture*, published in 1789, advises that 'in order to receive guests worthily, good houses are needed, with at least two rooms that communicate with each other.' Russian architects of the eighteenth century clearly operated on the same principle. The severe forms, balanced proportions, rare but elegant decoration and the decorum of their houses are admirably suited to the worthy reception of guests. The house of the merchant Dolgov in Moscow, designed by Bajenov, is a brilliant example. Although it resembles the standard buildings, it possesses individual features that appear in the perfect arrangement of the plan, the purity of its lines, and the delicacy of the structure. Typically, the original plan, which survives, contains sparse references to interior ornament and what there is is modest. In a number of Russian cities, buildings of the same period betray similar characteristics and reach a similarly

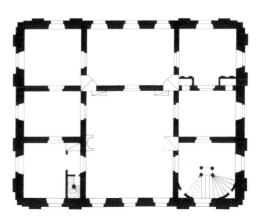

(Right) House of the Kologrivovykh family at Kaluga on the Oka River between Smolensk and Tula. The house was finished in 1805-06 but as this colonnade indicates, it seems to have been designed in the neo-classical taste fashionable in Russia during the second half of the eighteenth century. Only in the use of ironwork in the entrance (below) – which may, however, be an afterthought – do we see any hint of nineteenth century ornamentation.

(Opposite page) Façade, plans and section, with a photograph of the side view of a mid-eighteenth century house in Bolchaïa Ordynka Street in Moscow. The façade is sixty-six feet wide.

(Opposite page, below) Interior and plan of the upper floor in the house built in Moscow by W. Bajenov for the merchant, Dolgov, about 1765: the façade is sixty-nine feet wide.

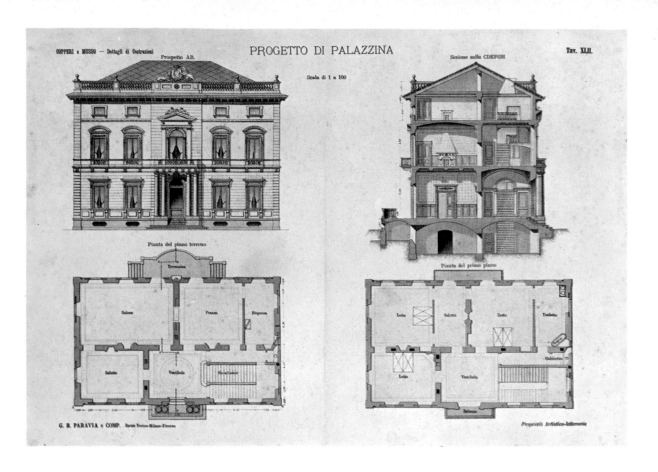

PROGETTO DI PALAZZINA

REVIVALS
AND FANTASIES

NINETEENTH CENTURY ECLECTICISM

By the year 1800, yet another revival of classical forms and ornament in architecture was under way. But for a year or two at the beginning of the century it was gently rivalled by the rococo, which lingered on even in Rome, where the papal court had succumbed to its delicate fantasies and had permitted some relaxation of traditionally austere academicism. This was not, however, the extravagant rococo of the eighteenth century but a more temperate and charming version of it, which created domestic interiors that were both comfortable and elegant.

It yielded, eventually, to neo-classicism, to the revival initiated by the excavations at Herculaneum and Pompeii, to which reference has already been made, by researches amidst the ruins of Ancient Rome, and, significantly, by Napoleon's expedition to Egypt which, despite some successes, proved a military failure but an outstanding victory for scholarship and the new science of archaeology.

It is the emphasis on scholarship which distinguishes this classical revival from its predecessors, though Robert Adam took cognizance of it. At its least inspired, in buildings and their furnishings, it deteriorated into pedantry. Occasionally, the revived Assyrian and Egyptian motifs used in Empire furniture look rather bombastic. But at its best, when ancient ornament was used in carefully controlled doses, there is great elegance and discipline of line in the furniture of the period and, in some

cases, an admirable appreciation of the qualities of the wood used.

Predictably, not everyone stuck to the rulebook. Equally predictably, the English led the way among those who did not. In England, of course, the picturesque had already been discovered in the eighteenth century and its pursuit was to continue in one form or another throughout the nineteenth century with a bland disregard of the elderly Goethe, who in 1827 condemned it as 'a mask which in the long run can do no good and in fact exercises a harmful influence on anyone who uses it.' Fashion dictated that one material should look exactly like another, that, for example, cast iron should be wrought to look like bamboo; that buildings should look as exotic as possible – Mogul or Moorish on the outside and Chinese on the inside; that functions should be disguised in, for instance, gas lamps got up as dragons. The more flights of fancy that could be packed into a single building the better: with Nash's Pavilion at Brighton, the Prince Regent, later George IV, scored an undisputed victory over all comers.

Critics of eclecticism did not, however, give in. It alarmed de Musset too. 'The apartments of the rich are show-rooms for curios,' he said. 'Our taste is eclectic; we take whatever we can find, one thing for its beauty, another for its comfort, another for its age, another for its actual ugliness; thus we are surrounded by scraps.'

(Opposite page, above) Model of a family house described in a popular Manual for Builders published at the end of the nineteenth century in Rome, Turin, Milan and Florence. It sets out to meet the demand for a small, self-contained house with a garden and contains, for all that, four reception rooms and three bedrooms on the two lower floors, as well as a wide staircase, a spacious hall and landing; but only one lavatory.

(Opposite page, left) Watercolour (Rome, Keats-Shelley Memorial House) of a drawing-room at Field Place, Shelley's home: a note on the back says that it was painted by Shelley's sister in 1816. Most of the furnishings, including the organ and the complicated draperies at the windows, are Regency in style and the English predilection for comfort triumphs, visibly, over their neo-classical environment.

DANIEL ALCOUFFE

THE FRENCH ARCHITECT'S DILEMMA

Questions of style, whether rococo or baroque, were not the only problems, nor even the most important, related to domestic architecture in the nineteenth century. The industrial revolution which was gathering momentum at the beginning of the century in France and Belgium, as in other countries in western Europe, was accompanied by vast movements of population as workers for the new factories concentrated in the towns. The process was so rapid that towns and cities could not provide sufficient accommodation for them, and attempts to house urban populations in comfort and at reasonable cost have absorbed an increasing amount of attention from architects from that day to this.

To begin with, however, the problem was hardly realized as architects coped with what was in a sense the dictatorship of neo-classicism. The more devout admirers of the style, strong in their faith in the matchless beauty of the antique, regardless – some of them – of the suitability of antique models to the purpose in hand, set themselves to re-create in the France of Napoleon and the restored Bourbons the architectural styles of Greece and Rome. They applied these even to tenement buildings until economy compelled them to relinquish such details as columns on the façade; but in the interiors, they inserted pilasters and half columns and splendidly arched doorways.

The result could be very elegant, as it was in the bedroom described by Barbey d'Aurevilly in *Les Diaboliques*: 'with an uncarpeted parquet floor and cherrywood furniture with bronze mounts everywhere – sphinxes' heads at the four corners of the bed, lions' feet on the legs, and lions' heads on the bedside chests and desks. The square table, of a redder cherrywood than the rest of the furniture,

(Opposite page, above) Giuseppe Canella (1788-1847) Rue Castiglione, Paris *(1829: Paris, Musée Carnavalet). During the First Empire, the face of Paris was changed; new roads, squares and bridges were built, land having been made available by the confiscations of the year of the Revolution, and by demolition. In the district bound by the Rue de Rivoli, the Rue de Castiglione, the R des Pyramides, and the Rue de la Paix, over 500 house and 40 ancient streets disappeared. A decree of 18 proclaimed that the future inhabitants of the new distr should not be employed at crafts where hamme or ovens were used; nor were they allowed to put out sh signs. Tax exemptions were also announced. It was attempt on the part of the planners to create an eleg residential district with straight through roads flanked more or less uniform houses. The architectural principles we still those of the ancien régime with classicism underlin perhaps, by the principal architects, Charles Perc and Pierre Fontaine. The use of ornament is discreet to t point of austerity. The shops behind the arcades we rather ill-lit but the total effect is one of confident dignt*

(Left) Percier (1764-1838) and Fontaine (1762-1853), like other architects of the period, also designed furniture. This fantasy, which is in fact a bed designed for a Madame M., is taken from their Recueil de décorations intérieures.

(Opposite page) Jean Baptiste van M (1819-1894), View of Brussels in 18 *(Brussels, Musées Royaux des Beaux Art*

with a grey marble top and brass rail, stood opposite the bed, against the wall between the window and the door of a large drawing-room; and in front of the fireplace was a big sofa of red morocco leather... In the four corners of the room, which was very high and spacious, were corner cupboards in fake Chinese lacquer and on one of them, mysterious in the half-light, stood an old bust of Niobe, supposedly antique... On the walls, which were panelled in wood painted a yellowish white, there were neither paintings nor prints.'

French houses of an older generation were, clearly, endangered by the emphasis on neo-classicism. Fortunately, however, the antiquarians or archaeologists who provided the materials for the classical revival also furnished arguments for the preservation of other houses less ancient. The value of classical architecture, it was noted, lay in its perfect adaptation to its environment and to the function of the building. Excellent results, it was also discovered, could be achieved by observing these principles. By about 1820, therefore, a few architects were declaring that architectural forms should express the demands of the building, that decoration should not be superimposed on it but should derive logically from the structure itself.

They did so at a time of important technical innovations. Concrete in the form we now know it began to be used about 1820: two decades later, the great Le Creusot ironworks were making massive iron girders for bridges. Cast iron in its apparently limitless nineteenth century variety took over many of the functions of wrought iron and even of stone.

Trapped between innovations and revivals, architects and builders had difficulty in deciding between 1830 and 1850 on the type of house best suited to modern life. Some reacted against neo-classicism, renounced decoration and produced sober, regular but stylistically arid results. Others remained faithful to classicism and to the belief that classical forms and decorations were in all situations and for all buildings the most appropriate.

Plans for the district round the church of the Madeleine were drawn up during the First Empire. They were finally executed during the Second, in the reign of Napoleon III. The houses of the square betray the taste for eclecticism of the period. This house (above) is No. 19 and it is distinguished by borrowings from a number of periods. The low archway of the entrance (shown in the photograph, left) is reminiscent of the sixteenth century; the orders of the façade are those fashionable during the First Empire; the decorations above the generously proportioned windows recall the styles of Louis XVI. The effect of the combination is, however, successful and the grandeur desired by the Emperor is achieved.

The Gothic, recently rediscovered by English scholars, seemed to romantics to be the true national style; it was, nevertheless, used mainly for public buildings. The Italian Renaissance style had its adherents. In Belgium, there was a return to Flemish baroque.

There was a glorious mish-mash of styles. Notre Dame co-existed with the Colosseum, the Renaissance palace of the Montefeltros in Urbino with a cast iron market building, the Taj Mahal, or anything else that the fertile wit of an architect could conjure up. We have a vivid picture of the apartment at No. 6 Place Royale (now the Place des Vosges) in Paris once occupied by Victor Hugo, from the pen of Eugène de Mirecourt: 'The enormous entrance hall faced on to the piazza, then led into the dining-room which was thickly carpeted and full of antique chests. A splendid panoply that seemed to have received the tribute of twenty centuries commanded the stairs; the arrow of the French warrior and the lance of the German were crossed with the sword of the Roman legionary; the *yatagan* of the Arab with our own arquebus, with the musket and the axe of the Paladin. From here, one passed to the drawing-room which was carpeted in red and had a marvellous tapestry inspired by the *Roman de la Rose*. In front of this was a broad dais on which the sofa stood and above it a kind of baldaquin; in the background, a standard with gold embroidery, taken from the Kasbah in Algeria in 1830, stood unfurled. Victor Hugo was the first to restore to us the taste for fine historical furnishings. The drawing-room of the Place Royale had an air of grandeur which made one regret the narrow cells to which the builders of Paris have confined us. There are two large full-length portraits of Madame Hugo and her husband, painted by Louis Boulanger, family friend and painter to the family, whose talent made their expressions seem so natural and lively that they look as if they are about to step down from their Gothic frames... At the end of a long passage,

By banishing the evil-smelling river Senne underground (1865-1868), Brussels acquired about two miles of new boulevards, including what is now the Boulevard du Nord, the Boulevard Hainaut and the Boulevard Ansbach. In the 1870's, houses were built along them and prizes were awarded for the best designs. Henri F. Beyaert (1823-1894) won first prize for this building which seems to show an enthusiasm for Italian Renaissance influences, especially in the balustrades, the use of faceted stone, and the urns and caryatids; but all this is set under a gable that carries most of the features of Flemish sixteenth and seventeenth century architecture. The result is, at best, uneasy.

the kind once found in monasteries, was the bedroom; then, in the study, there was a wonderful museum which the poet's imagination had filled with works of art of every kind. The sun shone in through an ogee window of painted glass, spreading a fantastic light on the armchairs of carved oak, the tapestries, the lacquer work, the china, the small statues and the old Sèvres.'

In the reign of Louis Philippe, the need for housing on a massive scale was pressing. Speculative builders worked quickly to fill the streets with lodging-houses and the solid, monotonous, depressing results of their labours, devoid of artistic merit, eventually gave rise to criticism. The Vicomte de Launay in the *Presse* of September 3rd, 1848, used the situation for his own purposes. 'Do you think, oh people,' he wrote, 'that the proud bourgeois you hate so much has more than you have? He owns neither castle nor palace, neither woods nor pastures, but lives in a small, gloomy apartment in what is called a lodging-house, that is, a beehive made of bricks and mortar. In this he enjoys not one of the pleasures of a life of ease; he lacks space and light, a fine view, and fresh air, rest and privacy and silence. He lives cheek by jowl with people he doesn't know; all he knows about them is their faults and he has no idea whether his neighbours are honest, charitable or humane. All he knows is that they are untidy and rowdy, that they slam doors, get home late and eat all sorts of weird food, polluting the passages with disgusting smells. But – you will say – this uncomfortable apartment is luxuriously furnished: even if he lacks a house, he has furniture. Oh, you are quite right and this is where the whole problem lies; the bourgeois in Paris has one real treasure, his furniture, and it is to defend this that he courageously risks death. And is it you, of all people, who want to attack him and carry off these precious possessions? Are we not right in saying that this fight is ridiculous and at the same time painful? To die for furniture – and what furniture! A worthless conglomeration of pieces without shape or form in which the bad taste of every age is brought together; furniture without value, style or art, ugly to look at and uncomfortable to use, furniture that would make painters and even daubers swoon with horror. But the bourgeois who admires it has given everything to buy it and having acquired it with patience and sacrifice, will defend it with his last breath. Demand his life – but not his appalling alabaster clock, flanked by two equally frightful alabaster vases with paper rosebuds in them; all this is what he calls a *garniture de cheminée* and God only knows how he struggled to acquire this frightful luxury... Oh people, if only you knew how ugly are the things you covet, you would let the bourgeois have his happiness... Do you really want to murder him for that wardrobe with its distorting mirror? For that ghastly mahogany canopy that hangs over his bed like a real stone of Sisyphus? For that awful *bonheur du jour* with its unsteady feet and that dreadful little cupboard where he keeps his drinks? For the vile-coloured china that would make you wince and the hideous lithographs bought in junk-shops? Is it for these things – so vulgar, ill-chosen and hideous – that you really want to kill him?'

In the reign of Napoleon III, whose ambition

French neo-classical furniture in mahogany (Paris, Mobilier National). (Opposite page, left to right and this page, above, left) Chair and armchair, front and side view, of the Revolutionary period, bearing the mark of Georges Jacob. (Above, centre and right) Armchair, front and side view, of the First Empire, marked Jacob D. for Jacob-Desmalter. (Below) The folding stool on the X-frame, a typical item of Roman furnishing, and the plain stool bear the same signature. Georges Jacob, the great maître-ébéniste of the reign of Louis XVI, was succeeded by his two very able sons who used the signature Jacob Frères: *when Georges Jacob the younger died in 1803, the firm became* Jacob-Desmalter et Cie *and, during the reign of Napoleon I, it enjoyed its greatest prosperity. Its workshops produced furniture in natural and inlaid wood, carved it, gilded the bronzes, and forged the metal fittings; employed in them were 800 workers whose deployment foreshadowed, in a sense, nineteenth century industrial processes. When the use of mahogany was forbidden as a result of the naval blockade of French ports, Jacob-Desmalter worked in native woods, maple, pear, cherry, and so on, the bright colours of which were admirably suited to the interiors of the time: these often retained the painted walls of the period of Louis XVI.*

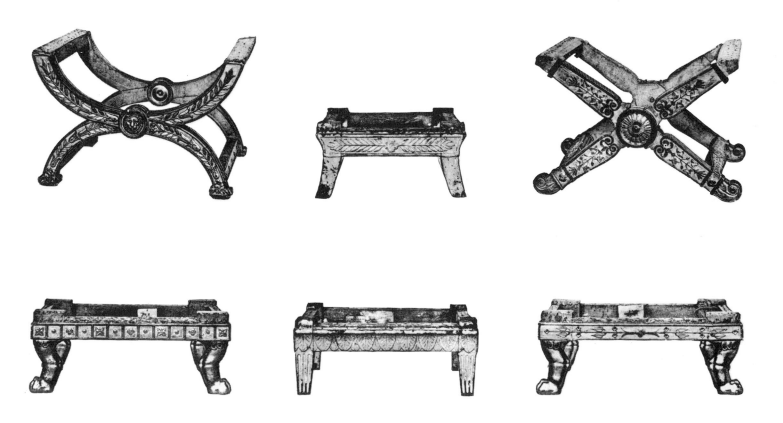

*From about 1830 onwards, revivalism took
a firm hold on furniture-makers who
reproduced every kind of style from the past.
In the early years of the reign of Louis Philippe
in France, Gothic style was popular as this chair
indicates (Paris, Musée des Arts Décoratifs);
but even as it was being completed,
reproductions were being fashioned of the
richly decorated, faintly monumental Boulle
pieces of the late eighteenth century.
By 1840, fashion demanded Henri II
dining-rooms and studies. Even Victor Hugo
invented furniture of this kind as the drawing
(below, right) shows. The style for bedrooms
and drawing-rooms was Louis XV.
(Below, left) a design for an alcove
in the style of Louis XV by D. Guilmard;
the curtains are puffed and draped in a
way that would have been unthinkable in the
rococo period; nor would the room have
been furnished with two such Gothic console
tables or a bed with panels à la Boucher.
During the Second Empire, the official style
was the* Louis XVI-Empress, *the
Empress being Eugénie, wife of Napoleon III.*

was to enhance the beauty and dignity of Paris, architecture became at the very least more interesting than it had been in the previous quarter of a century. Official approval was given to eclecticism; the architect was free to borrow whatever he wanted from any age. It was a freedom which required careful handling and this was often absent, as architects sought to outdo one another in the extravagance of their decorative efforts. At the same time, however, it was Charles Garnier (1825-1898), the architect of the Opéra, who designed what was to be for a considerable period the model dwelling in which reception and residential rooms were completely separated.

In furniture too, a similar effort was made to combine disparate elements. The industrial society was beginning to affect the livelihood of the craftsmen and to weaken the craftsman's credo that beauty and usefulness went hand in hand. But the machines were still too new for the realization to be general that new forms and new designs would have to be created for them; old designs were simply adapted to turn out mass-produced furniture and ornaments. It was an era of simulation; cheap cloth imitated expensive fabrics, wallpaper imitated wooden panels, and so on.

In Belgium, which had shared to the full in the decorative extravagance of the second half of the century, a new movement began which was to affect both interiors and exteriors in the last decade. It developed into Art Nouveau and the public, bored with eclecticism, accepted it with delight. Its success, which lasted well into the twentieth century, had an important effect, as we shall see, on European architecture.

One of the compensations of nineteenth century Romantic revivalism was the interest in and
preservation of antique furniture. Victor Hugo was one of the earliest collectors.
Another was Gérard de Nerval who bought a Renaissance bed, a Medici table,
and a Louis XIII armchair. The contents of this Intérior by an unknown French painter
of about 1880 (Paris, Musée des Arts Décoratifs) can be only partially assessed.
The chest on the right seems to belong to the sixteenth or seventeenth centuries, while the
gilt furniture is certainly in the style of Louis XVI which was extremely popular
during the Second Empire. The small console tables between the fake secrétaire and
the large table might be authentic examples of eighteenth century marquetry. The
paintings are arranged with a strict regard for neo-classical symmetry but the owner's
taste is remarkably restrained in its avoidance of quantities
of ornaments and in the plainness of the curtains.

Prosper Lafaye, (1806-1883), An Evening at
the Irisson's in Paris in 1839 (Paris, Musée
Carnavalet). The interior of a rich, middle
class house in the Rue d'Antin near the Bourse
in the reign of Louis Philippe. The owner
was an art lover and the walls of his drawing-room
are hung with his paintings, symmetrically
arranged. The floor is richly carpeted and the
room is lit by large oil lamps, soon to give
way to gas. Wing chairs stand round the room
and a sofa near the table; armchairs are grouped
around the fireplace and there are other chairs
upholstered in silk. A 'gondola' chair on
the right may belong to the period of the First
Empire and another, Louis XVI in period,
stands beside it. At the far end of the room, there
is a Louis XV armchair. We know that Irisson also
possessed a piano, presumably on the right of the
room, decorated with inlay in the style of Boulle.

JOHN DRUMMOND

ENGLISH REGENCY AND VICTORIANA

When Gothic became the English national style, one of the busiest architects in the country was John Loughborough Pearson (1817-1897). In this house, which he built in 1857 at Quar Wood in Gloucestershire, his handling of medieval detail looks oddly clumsy but convincing. The steeply pitched roof and the faintly ecclesiastical air were calculated to appeal to the taste for Christian *architecture.*

The arrival of the nineteenth century, which was to be an era of expansion and far-reaching changes in virtually every aspect of the nation's life, found Britain at war with France, George III on the throne he had occupied rather unsteadily for four decades, art and literature preparing for the full flood of the romantic revival. In architecture eighteenth century styles lingered on and, indeed, some seed sown in that previous century bore abundant fruit in the reign of George III's granddaughter. And in Britain, as in France and Belgium, the industrial revolution altered the face of the country and the nature of the society within which its inhabitants lived. The populations of towns and cities swelled; the population of the country as a whole rose from 7,000,000 to 12,000,000 between 1760 and 1821. Shrewdness and energy brought prosperity to the growing middle classes.

A number of decades passed before the appalling consequences of indiscriminate industrial enterprise became visible, and the first thirty years of the new era were in many ways a continuation of the grace and elegance of the eighteenth century rather than a preliminary to the vigour and audacity of the Victorian age.

The arbiter of fashion during this period was the Prince Regent and his favourite architect was John Nash (1752-1835) whose greatest work was his designs for the Regent's Park Terraces; his Regent Street has been re-designed within the present century. But in some respects, the most notable beneficiaries of Regency taste were the country's watering-places and spas. Here the gently sloping roofs, the attractively curving lines of the façades, the projecting eaves, the use of cast iron on the light, delicate railings of balconies and galleries, gave to these towns an atmosphere of gaiety and freshness, an air of perpetual holiday. In a number of houses, the impression is given not so much of a building in stone as of a pavilion erected for a magnificent picnic. The most splendid of these pavilions is, of course, Nash's Royal Pavilion at Brighton. The Regency custom of painting the exterior surfaces of houses, moreover, added gaiety to the townscapes; this was done not merely in small suburban villas and in seaside resorts but in the London terraces where the austere Doric or sombre Ionic of classical façades were softened by colour.

In contrast to this classically-based Regency, we have romanticism, the extension of Horace Walpole's Strawberry Hill Gothic, Chambers and Chippendale's *chinoiseries*, and other fantasies. Some enthusiasts, notably the wealthy William Beckford, explored time as well as space. The fruit of Beckford's exploration was the Gothic fantasy of Fonthill, built by James Wyatt (1747-1813) between 1796 and 1799; it quietly collapsed in 1825.

More moderate and less wealthy enthusiasts contented themselves with bits and pieces of Gothic borrowed from castles and cathedrals and applied to cottages or small suburban houses. The *cottages ornés* are among the most charming of these dwellings, in which we see too the influence of a variation on the 'back to nature' movement in the French windows opening to the garden.

An interesting development of this period is the self-conscious consideration of taste. In preceding centuries, a building might be well or badly planned but the question of taste did not arise. An architect or master builder of the eighteenth century would, indeed, have found the word meaningless in application to his work which was either 'correct' or 'mistaken'. But Regency architects, and others, examined this idea of *taste* and debated it – interminably. They discussed 'the sublime', 'the picturesque', 'the beautiful' and before the century was over, had embroiled themselves in the shattering 'battle of the styles.'

The period which takes its name from the long reign of Queen Victoria (1837-1901) defies definition save as *Victorian* and assumptions as to the meaning of even that have recently been called in question. It was an era of soaring imagination and imaginativeness, and astounding insensibility: of the loftiest of ethics and the most devout Christian morality, eloquently expounded in print and from the pulpit, and monstrous exploitation of human beings in the interest of profit. Money was poured into foreign missions in the expanding empire while fetid slums proliferated at home. It was the best of times and the worst of times, and in the arts it produced works of genius and works of extraordinary and positive ugliness.

In a sense the Victorians were always explorers, and nowhere is this more evident than in architecture, where they explored past centuries for styles which they might take to themselves and – perhaps this too was typical – exploit. The established taste for Gothic they took, however, and, so to speak, rationalized. It was believed widely not only that the Gothic style was peculiarly English, but that Christian architecture meant Gothic architecture. Architects who still adhered to classical styles were allowed to have their way in haunts of Mammon

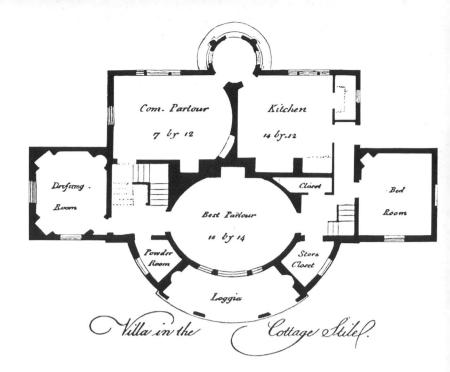

(Above, from the top) Plan and front of a cottage from a collection of designs published in 1795 by John Plaw. The beginnings of nineteenth century eclecticism are perceptible here in the neo-classical proportions of the façade and the Gothic windows: the portico, the special treatment of the chimneys and the gay imagination betrayed by the dormer windows recall the designs of the French architects, Claude Ledoux and Etienne Boullée.
(Below) Interior designed by R. W. Edis (Furniture and Decoration of Town Houses, 1881) with a classical frieze, a rampantly Gothic overmantel and sideboard, vaguely seventeenth century chairs, the whole being lit by an elaborate chandelier.

(Below and right) Reconstruction of a Victorian room in the Geffrye Museum in London in which, perhaps, there is a faint note of exaggeration in the four arrangements under glass domes on the piano. But the clash of patterned surfaces, the cheerful abundance of ornament, the air of comfort and substantial circumstances and the sense of security are accurate enough. We may not know much about art, the inhabitants of such a room might state confidently, but we know what we like; and what they liked was shining mahogany, red plush covers, rose-patterned wallpaper, knick-knacks in papier-mâché, china, glass and, of course, an aspidistra on the rather handsome chiffonier.

such as banks and railway stations, and Sir Robert Smirke used Gothic style in the British Museum. But Barry and Pugin's Houses of Parliament were indubitably Gothic to match 'our old Gothic constitution.' And where Parliament and the churches led, the people, especially the middle classes, followed and Gothic villas of varying degrees of elaboration were erected from one end of the island to the other. Augustus Pugin's villa at Ramsgate is thoroughly Gothic both inside and out as befitted the leading champion of 'Christian architecture.'

For all its eclecticism, however, several features recurred in the Victorian villa as the century progressed. Roofs remained steep and gables were garnished with carved woodwork or barge boarding. There was a preference for asymmetry which was more picturesque. Bay windows lost their Regency curves and acquired angles. Stained glass windows on staircases and occasionally elsewhere lent a dim, religious and, of course, Gothic light to the interior.

A prominent part in promoting the Gothic revival or rather, a particular aspect of it, was played by John Ruskin (1819-1900), whose passionate prose did much to influence the taste of those who read it. During the Battle of the Gothic and Palladian styles which ensued over the design of Government offices in Whitehall, he was regarded as one

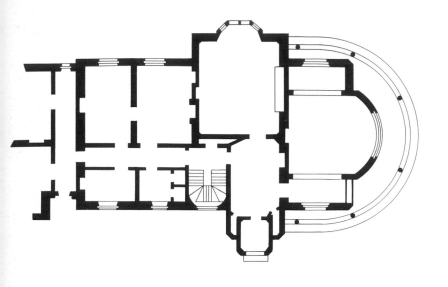

(Above, left) Plan of the ground level of a rustic cottage designed by Robert Lugar in 1828. Built on the Isle of Wight, by the sea, it is raised on pillars and has a heavy thatched roof. The four reception rooms and six bedrooms open off a central corridor; the drawing-room faces the sea beyond its wide rounded window. Only a few years before, in 1825, the Arundel pavilion (above, right) was built at Cheltenham in the classical and Palladian tradition, pillars, pediments and all. (Below) The house which Augustus Welby Pugin built for himself at Ramsgate in 1841. Pugin, a dedicated designer of Christian architecture, by which he meant Gothic revival architecture, made use of elements from medieval buildings, from castles, almshouses and churches. 'My writings', he wrote, 'have revolutionized the taste of England'.

of the leaders of the Gothic faction. He was, however, a champion in particular of Venetian Gothic and he espoused its cause so eloquently that houses in Venetian Gothic style became immensely popular. The possibility that the styles might not be entirely suitable to houses in the British Isles was hardly suggested.

A contemporary of Ruskin was, however, beginning to speculate on the nature of good design. He was William Morris (1834-1896) who, in reaction against the machines which were daily assuming more and more importance in human life and affairs, looked backwards in time to the Middle Ages, in search of an art in which beauty was not dissociated from use and suitability to the demands made on the object in question. Such art should not, he claimed, be the privilege of the few but should be available to all. Morris sought to revive the customs and mental attitudes of medieval craftsmen and from this sprang his Arts and Crafts movement. Materially, his ideas culminated in the establishment of a workshop to produce furniture, wallpapers and printed fabrics designed by Morris himself and sold through the London department store of Liberty's: consequently, what is here known as Art Nouveau is known in Italy, for example, as Liberty style — *il stilo Liberty*.

(Opposite page) At the end of the nineteenth century the pace of revivals seemed to be beginning to flag and there were signs of a renewal of English architecture. At Bedford Park, near Chiswick, Richard Norman Shaw planned in 1878 this row of cottage-villas in which traditional features were used and presented in a new and practical way. Later, with C.F.A. Voysey, he developed his ideas further and built this house (far right) at Colwall, near Malvern, in 1897, in which the heavy roofs, dominated by massive chimneys, surmount plain walls lightened by a continuous expanse of windows.

The Red House, designed by Philip Webb for William Morris at Bexley Heath in 1859. It was built in accordance with Morris's own pronounced taste for the medieval, though this did not prevent his architect from incorporating Queen Anne windows as companions to the Gothic arches and high-pitched roof. The arrangement of the interior is, however, remarkably modern in its distribution of space, as is the 'marrying' of the house to its environment.

Rounded balconies in Pittville Circus, Cheltenham, built about 1825. They are gay, light and faintly exotic in character. The confident handling of cast iron in this kind of construction is one of the notable features of English Regency architecture, often seen at its best in spas and watering-places such as Cheltenham and Brighton.

Morris was not himself an architect but he commissioned Philip Webb (1831-1915) to design a house in accordance with his own taste, the Red House at Bexley Heath in Kent (1859), which may be considered the point of departure for a new kind of domestic building. In plan the house derived from Morris's conception of traditional rural architecture, but the rare harmony and extraordinarily attractive arrangement of the house's interior make it a notable achievement in the history of British architecture, comparable in importance to Inigo Jones's Queen's House at Greenwich.

Contemporary with Webb was R. Norman Shaw (1831-1912) who, like Webb, enthusiastically plundered the styles of the past with attractive and individual results. Tudor, Dutch, William and Mary, Queen Anne, he made use of each period. One of his projects was the garden suburb of Bedford Park in London (from 1875), the earliest of its kind.

An architect who designed a house for Shaw's garden suburb was Charles F. A. Voysey (1857-1941). It was an early work and he went on from it to interpret English traditional styles with an assured taste that, with its emphasis on horizontal lines – especially in his arrangement of windows – and the merging of the house with its surroundings, has influenced modern architecture.

Wilcox-Cutts House at Orwell, Vermont, built in 1843 in the Greek revival style which had spread north from Virginia during the first four decades of the nineteenth century.

CHARLES F. MONTGOMERY JR.

NORTH AMERICAN NOSTALGIA

The Federal-Adam style, which was launched in America with Charles Bulfinch's buildings in Boston at the end of the eighteenth century, gained in popularity all along the eastern seaboard in the early decades of the following century. The use of styles of Rome was followed by a revival of those of Greece which spread north, south and west until about 1850, thereafter declining.

The nineteenth century passion for revivals and fantasies travelled successfully across the Atlantic from Europe. The Gothic Revival made the crossing in good order as did the taste for *chinoiserie*. Mrs. Basil Hall mentions in a letter of 1828 'a house in the Chinese style' on the outskirts of New Orleans. Henry Tudor, who visited the same city in 1832, put on record that 'as we went along the river, we saw very charming and pretty little houses, built right on the bank in the oriental style, entirely surrounded by verandahs.' French and Italian fashions also had their adherents. In 1813, the Reverend William Bentley registered the building of an 'Italian-style' house in the city of Salem and wrote too that in Massachusetts, 'we have seen the armchair of Mrs. Swan who says it was copied from a model she had admired in Paris.'

By the middle of the century, this pleasant eclecticism was beginning to give way before the influence of the picturesque style as championed by Andrew Jackson Downing. Variations of this, based on irregularity and asymmetry were the Italian and Venetian Gothic, the Swiss, and the 'bracketed' style. But whatever the style, Downing insisted on the principle that wood should be seen to be wood, and that stone should not pretend to be other than stone. His plans were suitable, essentially, for houses in the country or in suburbs but, under his influence, the streets of cities and large towns were lined with Italian Renaissance palaces appropriately furnished with cornices, arched windows and imposing staircases.

For certain types of building, the Italian or Tuscan style remained in fashion for several decades. Between 1870 and 1880, however, in the rapidly growing suburbs of the cities, building in wood, brought quickly from the forests of the west and north by the railways, returned to favour. The designs of Henry Hobson Richardson were influential in determining the forms of these new buildings, with their shingle roofs, low horizontal lines, and plain clapboard surfaces.

The fondness for historic styles which characterized architecture at this period also affected fur-

House built by James H. Calrow in 1857 but possessing characteristics that Basil Hall, a travelling Englishman, had noted as early as 1829 when he wrote of 'buildings with strange, high roofs and iron balconies instead of those miserable wooden projections that I so often found and for which I was unable to conceal my dislike. The portes cochères *are delightfully dark, and the patios in the Spanish style and the rooms lit by these balconies feel pleasantly cool in the summer.'*

(Below) Photograph of Broadway, New York, about 1860. The low pedimented building on the right dates from the eighteenth century; those on either side of it with their heavy cornices are in the Italian *style which had, by then, been popular for about a decade.*

niture. Large factories with improved production techniques put enormous quantities of cheap furniture on the market and if the workmanship was not as fine as that of the small workshops, the styles – Greek revival, Gothic revival, Jacobean or whatever the customer desired – were varied.

Everyone wanted domestic comfort. At the beginning of the century, new and improved kitchen stoves were fired by gas or electricity. There were similar developments in light, heating and sanitation. Inside the home and out, nineteenth century Americans took readily to the idea of change.

But if the United States had thrown off its allegiance to the British crown, it took much longer for it to free itself of its aesthetic allegiance to England and Europe. About 1840, the richest interiors were

still furnished with European pieces imported at considerable expense. Their arrival was considered worth recording, as Sidney George Fisher did when he wrote in his diary: 'Edward Biddle has had something quite new sent to him from Paris: an S-shaped armchair in which two people can sit side by side and at the same time look at each other.' A new house with the furniture entirely from Paris was worth a very detailed description. 'The furniture... is very expensive and in the best of taste. The front drawing-room is in *bois de rose* with hangings and upholstery in gorgeous and expensive fabrics, and with huge mirrors, shining chandeliers, hanging lamps, bronze ornaments and so on. The room at the back, that is, the dressing-room, is all in blue and white damask with gold motifs: heavy gilding covers even the wood of the chairs and all the rest: the chandeliers and lamps, etc., are graceful and exquisitely made... One thing above all struck me with its beauty – a firescreen made of a single piece of glass, very thick, and mounted in a rich, heavily gilt frame, which means that you can look at the fire and still be sheltered from its heat. The frame is identical with the one on the mirror over the fireplace so that the total effect – the fire glowing through the frame, the gilded fireplace, the large glittering mirror, the tiny flames of the chandeliers – is most attractive.'

Forty years later, the *Domestic Encyclopedia*, published in New York in 1877, made a list of pieces regarded as indispensable to a 'modest' household. It came to no less than 200 items, including the apple-corer and the 'bowl to keep water cool' without which no kitchen was adequately

(Right) View and plan of the 'cottage in bracketed style' designed by Andrew Jackson Downing in 1842: he was one of the first advocates of 'honesty' in buildings and opposed the practice of using one material to imitate another.

(Below) In the second quarter of the nineteenth century, the mechanical saw and mass production of nails meant that with their help, an unskilled man could build the kind of house that had previously required a team of workmen. New houses were designed which consisted of a light wooden frame covered with horizontal planks and a tiled or shingled roof; it was completed inside by the fitting of a floor and dividing walls. It appeared first in Chicago in the 1830's, spread to the frontier towns, and was later used throughout the United States.

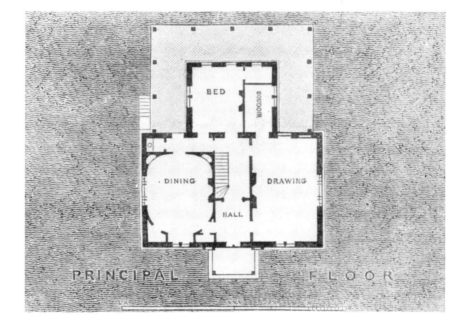

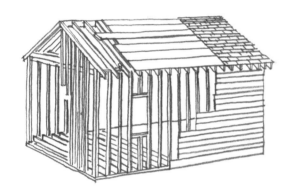

Isaac Bell house at Newport, Rhode Island, designed by the firm of McKim, Mead and White about 1882, is an example of the 'shingle style' with its low, comfortable lines, its timber cladding which has weathered to a warm brown, and its generous, well-balanced masses. Frank Lloyd Wright's early work was influenced by houses like this and by the houses of Henry Hobson Richardson (1838-1886) who reacted against the 'stick style' of Andrew Jackson Downing.

equipped. The sitting-room required a rocking-chair; at least two chairs, preferably folding, were also needed as well as many 'Brussels carpets of the American body type'. In the dining-room, the table should extend to twelve places: a coffee-pot of Britannia metal, a steel carving knife and a brass bell were also recommended. American factories were, clearly, hard at work, for variety of this kind in a 'modest' household would have been impossible if the householder had been dependent on imports.

manual the number of pages dedicated to the subject and the amount of good advice given on it make it difficult to explain why, in spite of everything, the servant problem goes from bad to worse until now it presents itself as an insurmountable obstacle in every household.' Here, one feels, the *Encyclopedia* failed those ladies who wanted something more than soft words and sympathy.

It is, moreover, surprisingly reactionary on that very American subject, hygiene and sanitation. 'Although there is no doubt that they are very useful,

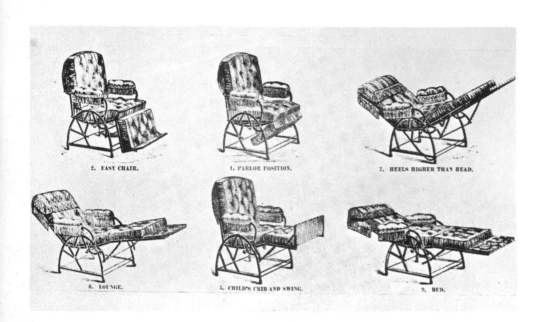

2. EASY CHAIR. 1. PARLOR POSITION. 7. HEELS HIGHER THAN HEAD.
6. LOUNGE. 5. CHILD'S CRIB AND SWING. 3. BED.

An adjustable chair from a catalogue of the Wilson Adjustable Manufacturing Company (New York, c. 1870). Furniture with more than one use is found in New England as early as the seventeenth century: it is often more ingenious than elegant but it was nearly always popular.

(Opposite page) Mid-nineteenth century (about 1860) drawing-room in the Museum of the City of New York. The furniture came from the workshops of John Henry Belter whose workmanship in rosewood at about this period is outstanding. In order to strengthen his furniture and avoid shrinkage, he used laminated — that is, layered — wood in which the grain ran in alternate directions in each layer, and from this he carved his chairbacks

Servants were, if possible, even more of a problem in the United States than they were in Britain. In 1827, Mrs Hall, whom we have already met in New Orleans, recorded her impression on visiting the director of the post office in a provincial town: 'First in a row was a Negro in white trousers; then came a girl with a black dress under a white apron with a number of holes in it, and finally a little girl of no more than ten or twelve. One of my correspondents remarks that the lady of the house in America must be a very poor housekeeper not to manage her household better than she does. But one must remember that the luxury of a good servant does not exist; only clumsy ones are available. They can find a good job or manage on their own easily if they are dismissed so that if you criticise the housemaid or the butler, they are likely to leave you immediately.' And to quote again from the *Domestic Encyclopedia*: 'Few things worry ladies as much as the problem of servants and there is probably no subject on which more has been written and said. In any domestic

water closets as they are built today are a discovery no one can be proud of,' the authors thunder. 'They seem to be clean but in fact they are filthy and a source of real danger. Wash basins in bedrooms too are a danger to life; the draintrap does not really keep out the gas in the drains and the drainpipe is the best possible entrance for every kind of infection, especially in bedrooms where the windows are closed and there is no chimney.'

Perhaps Thoreau was right when he retired to his famous cabin at Walden in the 1840's and wrote: 'If I consider how they are built and paid for, or not paid for, and how their economy is regulated, I am surprised that the floors of our houses do not fall in under the feet of the visitor who stands admiring the knick-knacks on the chimney piece, and drop them into the cellar, on to a floor that is at least solid and genuine, if not actually made of earth... Before we decorate our houses with fine pieces, we should strip the walls and our whole way of life, and put our elegant houses and easy existence on to a proper basis.'

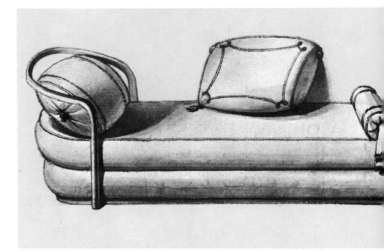

GIANNI K. KOENIG

THE WORLD
OF BIEDERMEIER

In Germany and Austria, neo-classicism had a profound influence on public architecture – on churches, theatres, banks, office blocks and so on – which continued until 1939. Its effect on domestic architecture was, however, much less. The first half of the nineteenth century was dominated by Karl Friedrich Schinkel (1781-1841) and to a lesser extent by Friedrich Gilly. The buildings themselves betrayed a taste for the classical or neo-Greek but this was never extended to the furniture and fittings. Schinkel's furniture was, on the contrary, anticlassical and bourgeois in spirit and form. He was influenced by French designs but the intellectual chill of France was dispersed in his sofas and armchairs with their generous proportions and air of warmth and good living. A characteristic piece of furniture was the large, curved corner sofa, built for comfort rather than elegance.

This was the world of Biedermeier, the immortal – and philistine – character featured in the *Fliegende Blätter* who gave his name not merely to a style but to an age. He was the jovial, middle class, respectable German intermittently exalted by romantic dreams, with a *stein* of beer at his hand

and a china pipe in his mouth. The decorative style named after him conjures up an impression of over-stuffed furniture, gleaming woodwork embellished by carvings or brass mounts, in general – *gemütlich* – an atmosphere of orderly, faintly claustrophobic comfort.

The fine flower of Biedermeier took, however, some time to appear. Schinkel's designs are, by contrast, so restrained that they seem almost functional and the rectangular divan he designed for the New Pavilion at Charlottenburg, with eight comfortable seats in a row, looks like the ancestors of the seats in the more comfortable modern waiting-rooms. His attitude towards the Gothic was always extremely cautious: not for him English extravagance. His fondness for homely comfort effectively overcame any weakness he might have entertained for medieval styles: the sofa did not exist, after all, in the Middle Ages and he disapproved of medieval pastiches. A number of middle class nineteenth century houses of this period survive, carefully preserved because of the fame of their owners, Goethe, Schiller, Hegel and Beethoven among them. (They were not averse to bourgeois comfort.

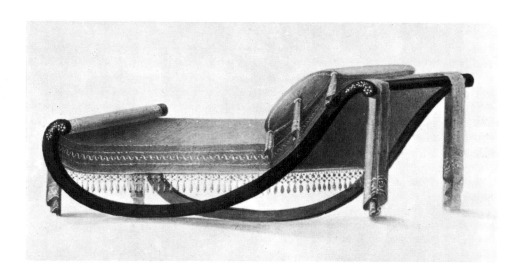

Joseph Dannhauser, the most fashionable cabinet-maker in Vienna at the beginning of the nineteenth century, began by employing French craftsmen among Napoleon's troops during the occupation of Vienna. Between 1815 and 1836, he interpreted Biedermeier with more elegance than was common and the designs shown here were produced in his workshops (Vienna, Museum of Applied Arts). They were distinguished by abundant draperies, generous curves and asymmetrical outlines which had their origin in a late flowering of the Baroque. The Biedermeier style in general also gave rise to a proliferation of small pieces of furniture 'for ladies', especially a variety of chairs.

Hegel found time to write long letters to the laundress complaining about the way she ironed his underclothes. *Sturm und Drang* co-existed with well-warmed slippers and a comfortable chair beside the fire.)

The style of Biedermeier, which dominated the nineteenth century in Germany, was quintessentially bourgeois. Unlike the various English and French styles which appeared and disappeared, it was a way of life as well. But as a style, it took elements from everywhere – from neo-classicism, especially of the French Empire variety, from German popular tradition, and even from the Baroque. Remarkable if misguided ingenuity went into the fashioning of furniture that was curved, carved and contorted into fantastic shapes, and excellent workmanship into the enormous upholstered armchairs which are still in use today.

This is typical of a great deal of Biedermeier furniture. It had no delicacy of form, made no attempt to achieve an effect of lightness or elegance, but, embellished with fittings as lasting as bronze or brass, it had a tremendous capacity for survival. And the very fact that it was not a genuine style with strict rules determined by a few designers, but a mixture of bits and pieces combined or thrown together from a variety of sources, prevented it from becoming quickly dated. If consistency of style is part of good taste, then good taste was, by and large, lacking in nineteenth century, respectable, middle class Germany. What took its place was, among other things, *Gemütlichkeit*, the essential ingredient of a quiet, friendly, pleasant, domestic life centred on the home. And this proved more durable than a style consistently pursued both outside and inside the house. When furniture and fittings were no longer of great aesthetic importance, they stood in less danger of falling out of fashion, since it was not a matter of great concern that this year's fashion was Venetian Gothic or Italian Renaissance or Greek Revival; it remained Biedermeier.

ANNE BERENDSEN

BUILDING FOR COMFORT IN HOLLAND

At the end of the eighteenth century and the beginning of the nineteenth, during the Napoleonic occupation, Holland's prosperity waned and the population of the towns and cities diminished. Few new houses were built, so few Empire-style buildings are to be found in Dutch towns. One or two people managed, however, to make some money and commission buildings; the more ostentatious of them compare poorly with their predecessors of the seventeenth and eighteenth centuries.

For obvious reasons, French taste was dominant. But English taste in ornament often permeated the interiors, and it suited the Dutch idea of family intimacy and *Gezelligheid*, the warm, happy security of the home. So dedicated, indeed, were the Dutch to the concept of the home as a comfortable refuge that during the nineteenth century, curtained, cushioned, and upholstered interiors were even more widespread than in Biedermeier Germany.

For those, however, who wished to indulge in the neo-classical tastes of the Napoleonic period but lacked the means to do so, inexpensive materials were treated in such a way as to give them the appearance of valuable ones: plaster was made to look like marble, wood was painted green and gilded to look like bronze in copies of the 'Pompeian' ornaments that were fashionable in France. Houses themselves were much less ostentatious than they were in the previous century. The typical house had an entrance hall lit by a fanlight above the door which was generally decorated in wood or metal. On one side of the passage, as before, were two rooms, a small courtyard, the kitchen, sometimes a small drawing-room at a slightly higher level and the staircase. At the end of the passage was the *saal*, the principal reception room which occupied the back of the building and opened into the garden. But the chiaroscuro decorations were gone from the corridor. Double houses, that is, semi-detached houses, were still built and in these the passage was placed in the centre. The plan of the first and second floors – and the semi-basement with the children's rooms and sometimes a study beside the storerooms – was the same as for the ground floor. The wooden panelling of the rooms was frequently painted grey and in the principal rooms, it might be enriched with a gilded cornice.

Innovations from France at this period transformed the traditional Dutch interior. They included the *porte brisée* or folding door, preferably with glass panels; and French windows which opened to terraces or gardens. A new motif in fireplace decoration was that of the shell. Floors were covered from wall to wall with leather mats in the more luxurious houses though woollen carpets made in Europe or the Levant were also used; and whatever the covering, rugs protected the areas most vulnerable to wear.

Where the householder had opted for the fashionable Empire style, its principles were strictly observed. Cheap editions of the works of Vignola and Palladio made it easy for any carpenter to find out about classical rules and satisfy the taste for classicism that followed the discoveries at Pompeii and Herculaneum. The object of neo-classical ar-

Music at Home, by an unknown Dutch artist (about 1830; private collection). The walls are hung with a paper which simulates an antique fabric draped between rows of garlands in folds as complex as those of the curtains at the window. The air of formality is challenged, however, by the small flowers on it. The chairs are 'after Sheraton': the table is recognizably Empire in style as is the fireplace with its miniature classical pilasters. Above it, on the mantelpiece, is a garniture of clock and ornaments, enshrined under glass domes, very fashionable at this period. The firescreen is 'after Boucher'. The best china is set out on the table. The enormous charm of the Dutch seventeenth century interior is absent but the sense of security remains.

chitecture in the Netherlands, as in France and Italy, was to create a fine effect.

But as the century advanced, Dutch preference for comfort defeated the advocates of the neoclassical interior. It developed, as in Germany, into a taste for the heavy, the solid and the enveloping. A typically Dutch piece of furniture was the table with leaves which could be raised and lowered, as on the English Pembroke table: it stood in front of the sofa, that is, the most important seat, but it could be easily moved about. For this, as for other pieces of furniture, dark, heavy mahogany was preferred and it matched well with the rich, heavy curtains with which windows were draped. These effectively protected the new wallpapers which clad the walls, first those parts above the dado; then, when the dado had been reduced to a mere skirting board, the entire wall. The first popular patterns were striped but, gradually, the bands between were decorated and the decoration took control of the paper. A minor innovation of the period about 1840 took place in the hanging of pictures. In the absence of panelling as a support for their often considerable weight, they began to be hung on cords. And since this was the Biedermeier century, the more of them that could be accommodated on a single wall, the better the comfort-loving, bourgeois householder liked it.

JOSÉ GUDIOL RICART · SANTIAGO ALCOLEA

SPANISH ROMANTICISM

Under the impact of political upheavals and civil wars and the loss of the colonies in the New World, the Spanish economy decayed. The flow of wealth from America that had financed so much splendid architecture dried up and there was little building in nineteenth century Spain. But some charming work was done and by the end of the century Spain, like other countries in western Europe, was already looking forward to a new type of architecture.

During the first half of the century, middle class houses in Madrid were built in the style created by Juan de Villanueva and carried on by his pupils: in these the materials were stone and brick, the predominant line was horizontal, and the decorative detail was neo-Greek. Neo-classical architecture of this type appeared in other cities too; in Vitoria, for example, in the houses of Silvestre Perez, in Barcelona in those of Xifré, and in Valencia in the house of the Vallier family.

During the reign of Isabel II (1833-1868), some middle class buildings were inspired by the delicate architecture of the Renaissance of the fifteenth century, what one might call pre-Bramante. Outstanding among them is the palace of the banker José de Salamanca, the most characteristic work of the architect Narciso Pascual Colomer. The ornament, in which stucco is moulded in Italian Renaissance forms, is exquisite. Inside, a generously proportioned staircase is decorated with a shell motif and in the splendid courtyard, Doric and Corinthian orders are combined, as they are on the façade. Later in the century, however, the influence of France became more marked; the results were often tasteful enough but uninspired.

Portugal remained faithful to its own Manueline style and its nineteenth century architecture was inspired by its more extravagant forms; oriental variations were added in some cases.

At the end of the century in the unsettled and sensitive atmosphere of Barcelona, Spain looked to *Art Nouveau* through the works of Antonio Gaudí. His designs for the Casa Güell, built in 1884, establish his status as an innovator. His extraordinarily individual form of *Art Nouveau*, developed subsequently, belong, however, to the twentieth century and to the history of modern architecture.

Detail of the façade of the house of the Marquis of Salamanca in Madrid. Narciso Pascual Colomer (1801-1870), who designed it, was the most important architect in Madrid during the reign of Isabel II, that is, in the middle decades of the nineteenth century. His preference was for Renaissance architecture of the early fifteenth century which he was able, as here, to interpret with a pleasing lack of pedantry despite the abundance of ornamentation.

SERGIO CORADESCHI

ITALIAN BRIC-A-BRAC

(Above) House at Rosà near Treviso planned by Giuseppe Japelli. Devoid of decoration or any pretensions to fashion, it has no more than a vaguely classical, perhaps Palladian air and its clean, uncluttered lines make it one of the first examples of functional architecture in Italy.

The industrial revolution reached the north of Italy in the first half of the nineteenth century. Cities, especially Milan and Turin, were transformed. In Florence, the temporary capital from 1865 to 1871, an ambitious building programme was initiated; after two centuries of inactivity, many new buildings were erected and many old ones torn down, often for no good reason. Then it was the turn of Rome, the capital of the newly united country, where residential districts were laid out for the expanding middle class and for, in particular, the expanding civil service. Many of these officials came from the north, from Piedmont in particular, and they brought to the capital some of the fashions of Turin in the shape of straight, tree-lined avenues, and multi-storeyed and uniform buildings. In his *Roma borghese* (1882) Giovanni Fadella writes that 'the new roads... stretch and spread themselves with the cheerfulness of Milan, the freshness of Genova, the directness of Turin and the luxury of Paris.' The walls of the houses, he adds, were 'like huge lumps of nougat with the red paint striped by chalky stone.'

The eclecticism of the period permitted any style – neo-Renaissance, neo-Greek, neo-Gothic – whatever the client and his architect wished. Some houses were built to simple designs making no attempt to imitate, and were almost functional in style; but on the whole, taste, both outside and inside, was poor. Knick-knacks and useless bric-à-brac cluttered interiors with their beaded fringes, intricate draperies, and unnecessary ornament. The glaring example of misguided taste – literally if one looks at his photographs – was that of d'Annunzio who opposed the advance of technology, the consequences of which he could not or would not face, with an appalling self-conscious cosiness. Taste having sunk so low, however, it was inevitable that an improvement should follow.

There were a few consolations. One, in the first

Though the Roman architect, Giuseppe Valadier (1762-1839), acknowledged his debt to classicism in other houses he designed, in this façade of the Casa Castellani in the Piazza San Lorenzo, he abandoned any decorative pretensiousness and set his upper floors on this solid-looking base.

half of the century, was the work of the Venetian architect, Giuseppe Japelli (1783-1852) who, in the full triumph of neo-classicism, inclined to romanticism and, indeed, betrayed some concern about the people who were to live in his houses. In the second half of the century, the Piedmontese Alessandro Antonelli (1798-1888) was an early example of the engineer-architect. His style was basically neo-classical but he succeeded in devising a form of it that was lively without being contrived. An example of his work is the house he built for himself in Turin, the 'slice of salami', as it was called because of the minuteness of the site (its depth varies from 13 feet to 6 feet); others are the Mole Antonelliana in Turin and the Cathedral in Novara.

Wojciech Kalinowski

HIGH LIVING
IN POLAND

The multi-family town house which had come into being in Poland at the end of the eighteenth century, spread widely in the nineteenth. Two or three storeys high, it contained shops on the ground floor and two, four, or six flats on the upper floors. Its longest side faced the street. In cities and large towns, compact rows of buildings of this kind lined the streets; in the smaller towns, they were built only in the central areas.

In the beginning of the century when colonies of craftsmen, especially textile workers, were established under state protection, the government recommended the use of a standardized house-workshop in the new industrial villages. In doing so, they were following the example set during the Prussian occupation of eastern Germany and western Poland in the reign of Frederick the Great; here single storey buildings were erected, two rooms deep, with a central entrance, on a fairly spacious site facing the street. Houses like this were widespread in the suburbs of towns and continued to be built until about 60 years ago.

The eclecticism popular in other European countries affected Poland, so that decoration might be classical in design or might be derived from any of the current historical revivals. New materials, such as cast iron, provoked new designs.

The second half of the century saw the building of the typical upper-middle class letting house, multi-storeyed, with a large number of flats of various sizes and a wide range of service rooms. At the same time there appeared workmen's lodging houses; these too were multi-storeyed with a large number of small rooms opening from a common passage.

(Above and below) Façade and plan of the ground level of the residential building at No. 3 Nowy Swist Street in Warsaw, designed by the architect Bogumil Zug about 1800. It is a characteristic example of the dwelling house in large and middle sized Polish towns during the first half of the nineteenth century and foreshadows the shared house of the present day. The design is, understandably at this period, strongly classical in feeling.
(Below, left) An apartment building at No. 17 Krakowskie Przedmiescie Street in Warsaw, designed by the architect Francesco Maria Lanci in 1847. The façade is still, clearly, based on classical models though an innovation is the use of cast iron.

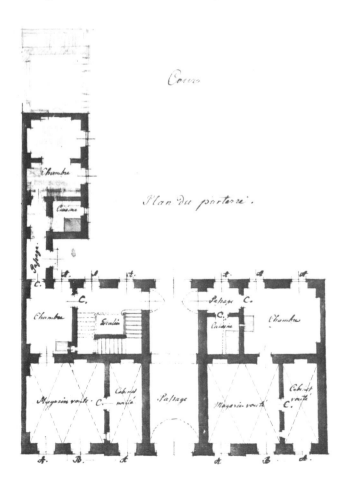

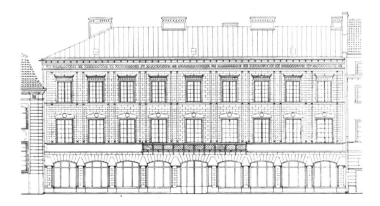

G. Opresco - P. Petresco

THE BALKANS MAKE PROGRESS

Complex economic, political and social developments brought about far-reaching changes in urban life in south-east Europe during the nineteenth century. Autonomous national states were formed out of the ruins of the European part of the Ottoman Empire. As commerce increased and industry advanced, some architectural styles, and with them some of the more antique buildings, vanished to be replaced by new buildings in new styles. The process was general in the new states but it happened with particular speed in Rumania and the northern provinces of Yugoslavia despite the strength of tradition. In the heart of the Balkans, change came more slowly.

In practical terms, the first victims were wooden houses which were extensively replaced by others in stone or brick. Controls on the development of towns became, meanwhile, more frequent; building regulations were drawn up; measures controlling the disposal of sewage and the provision of drinking water were adopted. Increased contacts with the world beyond the Balkans were made possible by the newly built railways.

The new styles of building were not, however, invariably contemporary styles. Rumania and Yugoslav towns, for instance, were rebuilt in a rather late baroque style modified by rococo additions; results of this may be seen in Transylvania, Croatia,

*(Below, left) Nineteenth century house at Elena, east of Turnovo in central Bulgaria. At the beginning of the nineteenth century, this small town was a flourishing centre for poets, writers and religious painters. In this house the influence of Turkish architecture is perceptible, as it is in many domestic buildings throughout the Balkans.
(Below) Similar features, but in a cruder form, are seen in this house of the Bobevscki family at Teteven, also in central Bulgaria. The difference is perceptible in the support of the wide roof.*

Sozopol, on the Bulgarian coast of the Black Sea, was once surrounded by woods which provided abundant building material for the old part of the town. Here, along the picturesque irregular streets are rows of wooden houses, the newest of which were built in the nineteenth century. They are built on a massive base of stone and their design shows clear Turkish influences.

Slovenia, Bosnia and Dalmatia. This style co-existed, however, with the neo-classical in the same regions and in others, in particular Moldavia.

Bulgaria, on the other hand, went its own way, ignored European fashions of the nineteenth century and adopted a so-called Renaissance style in which borrowings from Tuscany were mingled with local, oriental and western elements: some of the last dated back to the seventeenth century. To trace the various influences on Bulgarian architecture at this period would mean a study of relations, commercial, diplomatic and social, between Bulgaria and half of Europe and most of the Middle East for several centuries. Significantly, the most representative examples of this architecture are the houses of rich Levantine merchants at Plovdiv, Melnik and Bansko, and other buildings of the kind are scattered in small towns along the Black Sea coast from Sozopol in Bulgaria to Sulina and Constanta in Rumania.

Turkish influence is again perceptible in the arches at upper floor level in the building on the left, and in the Manuc inn (below): both were built in the first half of the nineteenth century in Bucharest. The capitals of the columns are, however, classical, in accordance with the fashion of the period.

283

(Left) Sarajevo, capital of Bosnia, was occupied
by the Austrians only in August 1878: until then it was
and had been for centuries under Turkish rule.
Evidence of this long occupation is visible in the
houses shown in this nineteenth century print
(from A Travers de Bosnie et l'Herzegovine
by Guillaume Capus); the projections at upper floor
level are typical of Ottoman architecture.

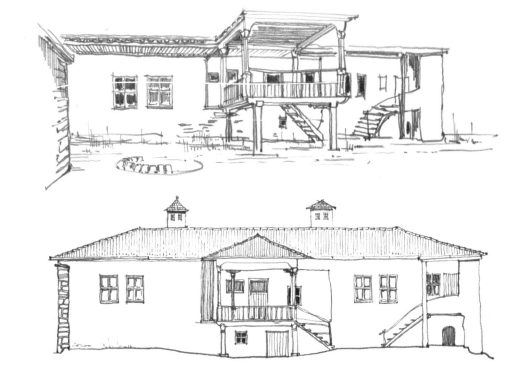

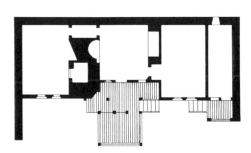

(Above) Views and plan of a nineteenth
century house in the Rumanian town
of Babadag in the Dobruja; here the effect
recalls Russian rather than Turkish buildings
and suggests a lingering Byzantine tradition.
(Left) View of a street in Belgrade (from
Serbien und die Serben by Spiridon Gopcevic,
Leipzig, 1888). The buildings here reflect
faithfully the varying influences to which
the city has been exposed. The bell tower is
Austrian rococo. The house in the foreground
on the right betrays a moderate classicism
of detail while its neighbour with its
rusticated ashlar and caryatids is baroque
in feeling: the mansard roof has wandered in,
apparently, from farther north.

During the centuries of Turkish occupation of the territory now occupied
by Greece, Albania and Yugoslavia, Byzantine architectural tradition continued
to be observed in civic as well as religious buildings. Gradually, however,
the influence of Turkish models spread out from Anatolia through
Constantinople to affect both exterior structures and interior organization.
These houses at Ohrid, the small town on Lake Ohrid in Macedonia
on the borders of Albania, Yugoslavia and Greece, lie on narrow,
winding streets at the foot of a hill dominated by a tenth century fortress,
and are typical of Balkan building well into the nineteenth century. The
wooden framework, the projecting storeys reminiscent of Turkish originals
in Constantinople, the absence of windows at ground level,
the decorative details that even at this distance in time suggest Byzantium,
the ornamental ironwork that by contrast looks to central Europe-
all combine to create buildings of enormous and enduring charm.

MIHAIL ILJIN

FUNCTIONAL CLASSICISM IN RUSSIA

The two periods of classicism in Russian architecture are divided by the burning of Moscow under Napoleon's army in 1812. After the fire the first necessity was to build houses, and wooden houses were permitted. The demands on builders were so great that one architect, Beauvais, was put in charge of a special building commission in which he himself dealt with façades. Under his direction a number of new forms were adopted and built, most of them good and some of them excellent. A similar service was performed by architects in St. Petersburg.

As before the fire, the models were classical but they were handled with restraint to produce sober and functional results. Nevertheless, the passion for

pillared porticos was such that special methods were devised to allow them to be built quickly, especially in wood. There was an abundance of models for decorative motifs in wood and plaster, for indoor and outdoor use, some of them taken from the designs of eminent architects and sculptors. It was not always possible to use the materials intended and the translation, for example of marble

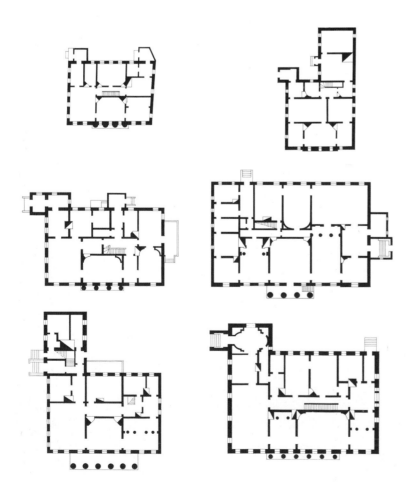

(Above) House in Taneev Street in Moscow, built in the 1820's. It is the reproduction in wood of a house of classical design. The decorative panel and the carved keystones over the windows, baroque in feeling, have translated surprisingly well, thanks, probably, to the skill of the woodcarver. (Left) Plans of early nineteenth century houses in Moscow: the bottom plan is that of the house in Taneev Street; the side shown in the photograph is that on the right of the plan and is more than sixty-six feet long.

(Opposite page, from the top) Details of wooden buildings of the first half of the nineteenth century. A portico with Tuscan columns (indicated by rows of dots) on a stone base. The phases in the construction of such columns: the inner framework of the columns applied to the poles which form the core and are square in section. To this inner framework is applied the outer casing. If plaster is to be applied it is preceded by trellis work which acts as a key. In the lower half of the page are details of flooring and of a trussed roof.

into wood, produced unexpected results. In some cases, it was necessary, moreover, to abandon plans for colonnaded porticos so that other forms of decoration, among them bas-reliefs, were restored to fashion. Exteriors were painted in two tones – either yellow and white or pink and grey.

Great care was given to interior decoration. The walls were painted blue or green or brown; moulded decorations were applied to the cornices. Drawing-room ceilings were painted with arabesques in *grisaille*. The formal furniture of the eighteenth century was replaced by mahogany pieces with bronze embellishments or by carved furniture in Karelian poplar or birch. Small portraits, water colours, and prints scattered about everywhere enhanced the pleasant air of intimacy of these rooms.

The function of each room was becoming more clearly defined. This led to a number of changes in the distribution of rooms even in fairly unsophisticated buildings. *A Short Manual of Architecture*, published in St. Petersburg in 1839, tell us that 'a house or apartment for a small family of modest condition may be called comfortable when it is composed of the following parts and when the following minimum dimensions have been provided, and reduced only when it is absolutely necessary: 1. The hall, which is indispensable in our climate in order to prevent the outer air from penetrating directly into the interior and to keep the internal temperature as high as possible. Its size may vary from 12 to 8 square yards. 2. The anteroom, which should measure 12 square yards. Although it separates the hall from the drawing-room and protects the inner room from draughts, it may also be used for hanging overcoats. 3. From the anteroom, a door leads into the drawing-room from which another door may lead to the kitchen, the study or some other room according to the arrangement of the house and its requirements. Those who are not very rich may use the drawing-room as a sitting-room, a dining-room, or for dancing. It should not measure less than 28 or 32 square yards. In order that it should look larger, most of the stoves should be in the next room and heat should be led in by suitable conductors. 4. The sitting-room should be beside the drawing-room: it is the most highly decorated room in the house and should measure at least 20 square yards. 5. The bedroom should be at least 16 square yards and at the same time should serve as a boudoir and workroom for the lady of the house. 6. The study should measure not less than 14 square yards and should communicate with the sitting-room or the anteroom; it

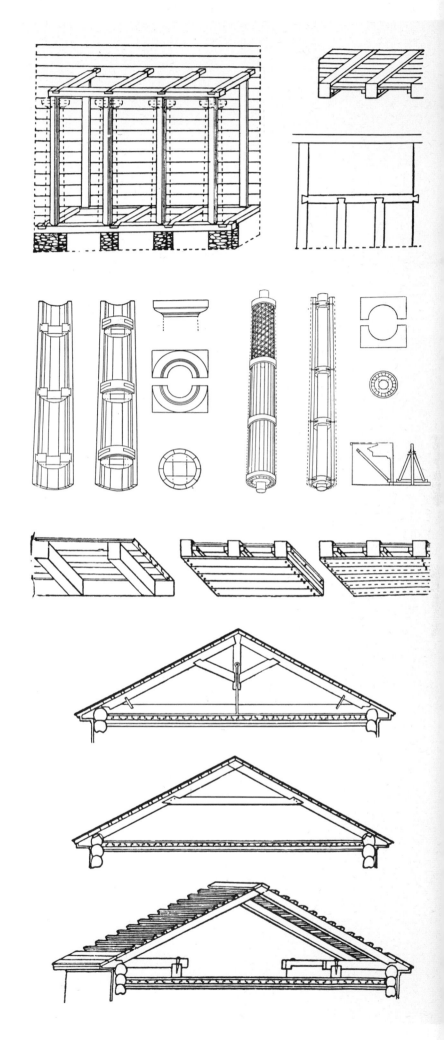

The Moscow town house of the family of Prince Volkonsky, built in the 1830's; its strict neo-classicism was inspired by French and Italian models.

serves the head of the family as a workroom or library; if necessary, it may be used as a children's room. 7. In the kitchen are the cooking stoves and the stoves *à la Russe*; the cook and maid live there and it should be not less than 20 square yards in size. If the height of the rooms, including the kitchen, is not less than 3½ yards, a mezzanine can be built.'

This mezzanine or *entresol* was very important. The reception rooms which faced to the street at the front of the house were used only on feast days and holidays and for family gatherings. The family itself lived at the back of the house, often in the mezzanine. The back and front rooms were separated by a passage.

About 1850, strictly observed classical taste had almost exhausted itself, leaving as a legacy a trail of buildings that sometimes demonstrated the academic pedantry substituted for comprehension of classical styles. Industrial development was increasing and, while for some time buildings were erected in the old style, decoration lost its way in amorphous outlines and fidgety neo-baroque details.

Multi-storeyed houses for letting were built from 1860 onwards. In appearance, distribution of rooms and interior decoration, there is nothing to distinguish them from the enormous buildings rising from every street corner in Europe. Attempts to imbue them with a distinctively Russian character failed.

Moscow: house of the Stanitsky family, built between 1817 and 1819 to the design of the architect Grigoriev; here too we see the influence of western classicism.

GIANNI K. KOENIG

MECHANIZED LIVING
IN THE TWENTIETH CENTURY

The industrial revolution which, to all intents and purposes, began in the eighteenth century, fundamentally transformed the way of life of civilized people. For centuries, the manner of living of most of the inhabitants of Europe had hardly changed. It was based on a largely agricultural economy and towns and cities had developed very often as markets for the produce of the countryside surrounding them. During the sixteenth and seventeenth centuries the towns and cities had increased their populations, partly by natural growth, partly by the attraction of craftsmen and labourers from the rural areas. Today, the majority of Europeans live in or close to towns. About 1870, only a quarter of the population of the United States lived in towns and cities: today, barely a quarter of it lives outside them. This reversal of a traditional situation was brought about by a revolution, a peaceful if often destructive one, involving the effects of water and fire on coal and iron.

The modern industrial town was born when factories moved from their sources of energy, for the most part close to a water supply, to the markets where their products were consumed. This happened fairly quickly and the failure to adapt living conditions with equal speed produced the slums and squalor that nineteenth century novelist and humanitarians described and attacked. The peasant who came to the town or city in search of work lost touch with his familiar surroundings and at the same time enjoyed none of the advantages – running water, light, heating – that made town life tolerable. In the middle of the nineteenth century, families cooked as they had done for centuries, on wood or charcoal-burning stoves; they drank or washed in water from wells and fountains that were nearly always outside the house; water closets and baths as we know them existed only in the houses of the well-to-do.

Housing reformers scored their first success with drainage, the safe organization of which was fundamental to health. The accompanying amenity of a piped water supply improved the convenience and cleanliness of kitchens and made possible, at least, the installation of bathrooms or water closets. Fuel too for cooking and heating, in the shape of gas produced from coal, was piped in with consequent improvement in cooking methods. The use of gas and oil for lighting prolonged the day so that it no longer coincided with the hours of daylight; to read or work at home by candlelight was difficult and a strain on the eyesight.

After gas came electricity and with it the entire battery of domestic appliances, washing machine, refrigerator, mixer, dish-washing machine, which have to some extent turned kitchens into small power houses and diminished the status of the fireplace as the centre of family life. The term

Detail of a building in the Piazzale Loreto in Milan, designed in 1959 by the architect Giulio Minoletti and the engineer Giuseppe Chiodi. The building reflected in it is not so very much older but seems to belong, as indeed it does, to a different and distant past; the contrast is not merely between stone and lime and glass and aluminium but between two ways of life. The designers of the newer building equipped it with a meteorological aerial as a means of regulating the internal temperature.

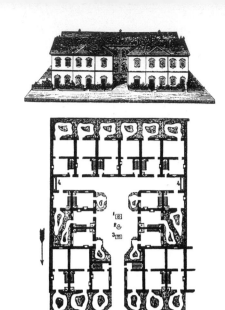

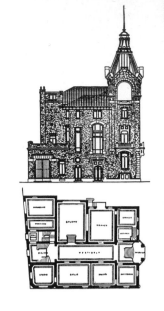

(Left) Façade and ground level plan of a block of flats designed by Eduardo Rossi for the Viale de Porta Venezia in Milan and built between 1880 and 1883. It was the kind of plan that remained substantially unchanged for several decades.
(Centre) Façade and ground level plan of working class houses, also in Milan (Fazzini archives, 1879-1882). The numbers on the plan indicate the well (1), pump (2), refuse heap (3) and wash-house (4).
(Right) Façade and plan of the Villa Marignoni in the Via Po in Rome (Giulio Magni Archives, 1887-1891).

'domestic hearth' is now largely a metaphor. Where once the kitchen and sitting-rooms, heated by open fires or stoves, were the only warm rooms in the house, central heating now heats the whole house and installations that were once the prerogative of a few private houses are now common in blocks of flats and may cover too, as they do in certain German and Dutch towns and cities, entire districts. And as buildings grew taller lifts became essential; electricity powered these too.

We live, then, surrounded by these machines, communicating with one another by another machine, the telephone, insulated from any direct contact with nature. Awareness of the loss involved in this divorce from natural surroundings has provoked attempts to compensate. The fallacy of the return to nature and the simple life – which was usually one of extraordinary complexity – is as great as the belief that the untroubled social relationships, a dubious premise, of medieval communities could be revived in this century. What we can do is recover something of what we have lost through carelessness. We can restore to towns and cities the green open spaces devoured by development and when new buildings are erected, light and air should be allowed to reach the streets beneath them. Already widespread car-ownership enables people to escape from the cities to the beaches and countryside but the tragic irony of the present situation ensures that they are merely escaping from one crowd to another; instead of solitude they find miles of parked cars. Those who stay

behind may enjoy the fume-free, peaceful charm of midsummer in an empty city.

During the last hundred years, social differences have been slowly disappearing. The gradual decrease in the number of hovels and slums has been accompanied by a corresponding reduction in the demand for mansions. The number of architects today who have received or are likely to receive a commission to build a new mansion in an old city is very small indeed, and the supply of buildings of this kind is more than adequate to meet the demand of those who can afford to live in them.

This means that the kind of building that once gave employment to architects no longer exists, that a chapter in the history of architecture has virtually ended. The age of Art Nouveau saw the last of the private commissions on this scale with such buildings as the Palais Stoclet in Brussels, designed in 1905 by Joseph Hoffmann, and the Palazzo Castiglioni in Milan designed two years earlier by Giuseppe Sommaruga.

Architects devoted themselves to other forms of design. The *villa*, that is, the detached, single family house set in a large garden, took the place of the mansion – for a time at least, for these, too, are becoming rarer – and its possibilities, both aesthetic and architectural, were discovered to be considerable. Any history of modern architecture shows that the best-known works in the field of domestic architecture of celebrated architects are almost always *villas*. By the standards of the nineteenth and, even more, of earlier centuries, they are small buildings far removed from the complex of buildings which comprised the Roman or even the Palladian *villa*. But small as the new *villas* were, their successors were further diminished to produce the sad rows of little houses that characterize so many suburbs.

The new buildings constructed during the first decade of the twentieth century accommodated every level of society. There were blocks of working class flats erected round a large, closed, rectangular courtyard; entrance to the individual flats was often from encircling internal balconies on to which the flats opened. From the point of view of the well-being of the residents, it is possible that the most successful of these buildings were those large enough to form a complete, self-contained little community.

Contrasting with these buildings, which at worst looked like enormous barracks, were the rows of small houses, usually two-storeyed, with a garden at the back and in some cases, another pocket-handkerchief patch at the front; these houses, often built by trade co-operatives, were typical in many ways of the 1920's.

Slightly higher in the social scale were two distinct types of house. One was the small, detached *villa*, more spacious and more expensive than the terrace houses we have just mentioned. The other was the flat or apartment building which generally contained between four and eight apartments, and the external appearance of which entertained pretensions to the grandeur of a Renaissance palace in Italy, for example, with its ground floor windows guarded by curving iron bars, its central entrance, its rusticated or fake stonework. Often the plan was U-shaped with a flat in each leg of the U on each floor; the flats themselves were usually arranged round a central passage with rooms on either side of it.

It was in reaction to this type of architecture, for example, that functionalists devised – with questionable results – new forms of building. They designed apartments in which wastage of space was reduced and the internal area was in some cases halved, but for all their good intentions, what they achieved in the end, with the help of speculative builders, was an increase in the density of the population of a given area. The object of the new designs was that more land should be freed for open spaces;

it was all too often forgotten and the space saved was used for the accommodation of more and more people until site densities of about 400 people per acre were reached.

Working class estates, generally planned and built by local authorities or the government, fared better. In France, Italy and Germany, statutes and regulations restricted the density of local authority and government housing to not more than 120 inhabitants per acre. On private housing estates, densities were nearly always of the order of 240 per acre, in other words, double those of working class areas.

On such estates, attempts are made to compensate for loss of space by improvements in appearance and function. Sometimes they are successful. More often they are not, and the tide of concrete that has washed over towns and cities is one of the sadder aspects of modern urban living; a case in point is Naples, altered by it almost beyond recognition.

Building regulations have been framed to safeguard the old parts of towns and these control, in general, such building as is carried out there. New buildings in these surroundings tend to be luxury objects, unrelated to their environment. The problem of relating the house to the town in which it is built is one to which modern architects have devoted a great deal of thought. One solution has been the creation of dwelling units on a larger and more comprehensive scale than before, as a means of avoiding the break between house and district or community. The first and most typical of these was le Corbusier's *Unité d'Habitation* at Marseilles which has been copied several times. There is also Adalberto Libera's horizontal unit in the Tusculano district of Rome. Many experiments in town planning in Britain, France, Germany, Italy and Sweden have utilized two types of building; tower blocks and rows of low, single-family houses. Such groupings may not be justifiable in terms of the mere provision of housing but they avoid the monotony of clusters of architectural megaliths.

A new district in Hanover where coal from the Ruhr is used to power the entire central heating system. The fuel is emptied from trucks into enormous burners which heat the water, which is then piped for domestic heating. The system makes the maximum use of coal while the householder incurs none of its disadvantages.

ART NOUVEAU
AND ECLECTICISM

(Top) Detail of the Stift house in Vienna designed by Joseph Maria Olbrich (1867-1908) in 1898.
(Above) A Gothic revival wallpaper (from A. W. Pugin, The True Principles of Pointed or Christian Architecture, 1841). These two illustrations demonstrate widely opposed viewpoints: the first suggests the uncluttered lines of twentieth century architecture and interiors, the second the heyday of Victoriana.

Architecture and, therefore, the design of the house we live in are always affected by the changes that take place in the other arts and in science. Such changes are, however, open to different interpretations. These differences are reflected, in modern architecture, in the contrast between the works of, on the one hand, Frank Lloyd Wright, an isolated genius, and those of what might be described as the champions of functionalism; Le Corbusier for one, and also the movement founded after the First World War, centred on and named after the *Bauhaus* at Weimar, later Dessau, of which the founding father was Walter Gropius and a later director was Mies van der Rohe. Their architecture is often referred to as functional, but the concept of functionalism is a very ancient one – all architecture must be in some degree functional – and in some ways it was, rather, a revivification of formal classicism. At the same time, Frank Lloyd Wright, bitterly opposed to the universally acclaimed European functionalism, designed buildings that were supremely fitted to their own particular function and, therefore, functional.

The eclecticism of the second half of the nineteenth century caused chaos in domestic interiors: the well-to-do middle class household, seemingly, like nature abhorred a vacuum and filled it with the maximum number of objects in what, until comparatively recently, seemed to be the worst possible taste (Victoriana is however, now being revalued). The centre of the house was the parlour in which all the family treasures were displayed – silver, china, pictures, trophies, miniatures, shells, souvenirs of journeys at home or abroad, diplomas, photographs of relations dead or alive, photographs of members of the royal family and leading politicians, dead or alive, small boxes in wood or papier mâché, stuffed birds, fish and animals of an appropriate size, embroideries, presentation volumes of literary works, the family Bible, brass trays from Birmingham via Benares, and mementos of sons bearing the white man's burden in the neighbourhood of India's coral strand.

The care and maintenance of the parlour can never have been simple, even allowing for the fact that the room was only used on special occasions. The demand for servants from the growing ranks

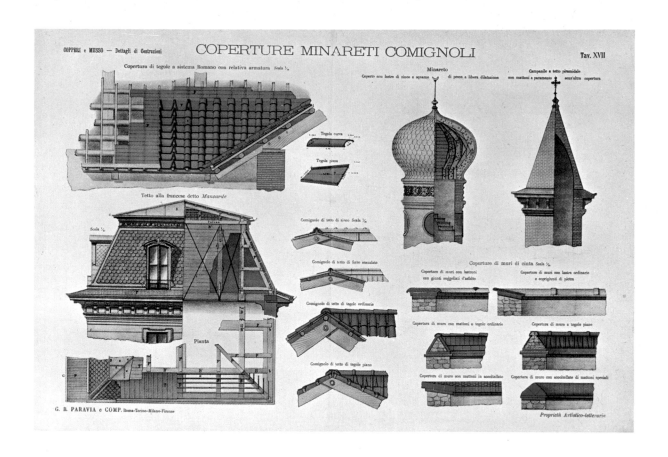

Plates from the Manual for Builders from which a small house has already been shown (on page 252). They demonstrate the fantasies to which late nineteenth century builders and their clients were mildly addicted, among them improbable onion-shaped spires and pinnacles, slightly more convincing in western surroundings; and the fretwork and barge-boarding — there are some monstrously intricate examples here without which, presumably, no nineteenth century bourgeois house could face the world. The mansard roof shown here was always, despite the bric-à-brac sometimes attached to it, a practical feature.

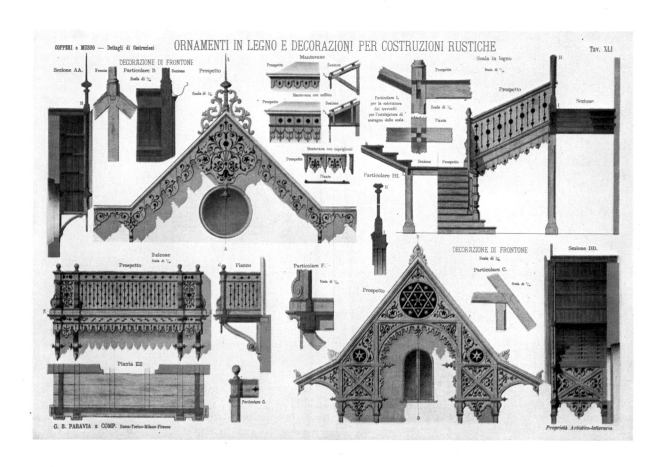

of the middle class unfortunately coincided with the departure of the potential labour force to other forms of work, mainly in factories. Dealing with the servant problem featured prominently in domestic manuals of the period.

The character of the dwelling was no longer determined by the architect but by the interior decoration. Rooms were reduced to featureless boxes which communicated with one another or were served by a common passage. What distinguished a bedroom from a drawing-room was its furnishing and the late nineteenth century architect, unlike some of his predecessors, was not concerned with this. His business was to design a suitable façade; internally, the plan of the house was more or less dictated beforehand, and the person responsible for its appearance was the owner. For him it was a setting for the furniture he had bought or inherited.

In the older peasant societies, changes took place slowly and were seldom made merely for the sake of change. They were undertaken carefully and cautiously. The kneading trough in the kitchen, for example, built and renewed from time to time over the centuries, remained always in the position discovered to be most suitable. A dresser might be added as it was needed, or a sink, if water were led into the farmhouse. The process was one of continuous but gradual growth in which one age fused with another, styles harmonized, and the results may still be seen in some of our older farmhouses.

But the increasing influence of the middle class and the enormously increased outlets for their spending power, in the shape of the products of the new factories at home and the cargoes of novelties shipped in from overseas, affected the quality of that elusive thing, 'good taste'. It could scarcely have been otherwise. The well-to-do nineteenth century householder was, in some respects, in the position of a child in a vast and beguiling toyshop

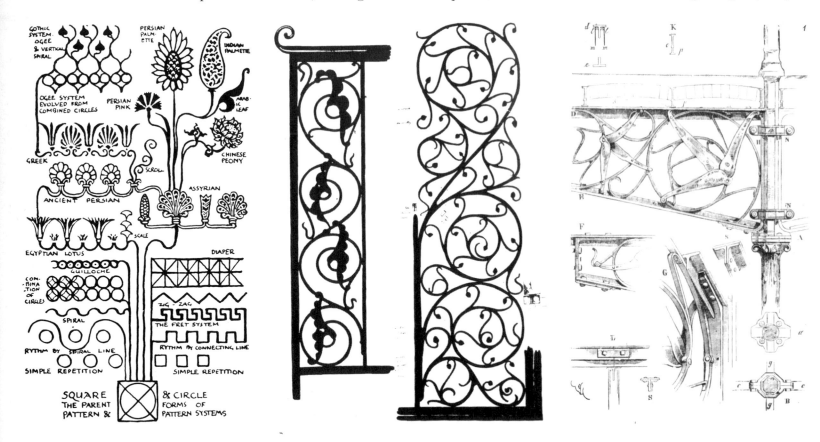

(Left) The interpretation of the development of motifs by Walter Crane, the English artist better known, perhaps, as a book illustrator (Line and Form, 1902); *ingeniously he has worked out the derivation of Indian, Arabian, Greek, Egyptian, Chinese, Gothic and Persian ornament. (Centre and right) The tireless Viollet-le-Duc, whose designs for ironwork in his* Compositions et dessins *and* Entretiens sur l'Architecture *(1872) show his inventiveness which was based, however, on a thorough knowledge, arguably misapplied, of historic styles.*

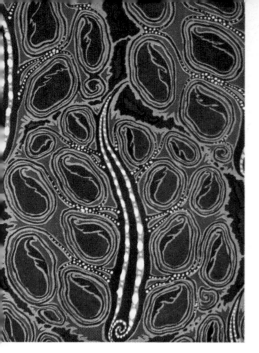

Designs for wallpaper from the little known collection, Samarkand, *by E. A. Seguy (Paris, about 1890). (From the left) The Persian palm or cone pattern, often used in carpets and familiar in Paisley shawls, here in* Art Nouveau *style: stylization has virtually excised any oriental influence from the middle pattern though a trace of it may linger in the detail of the background: a return to the palm or cone pattern, more elaborately detailed this time.*

in which all the goods were immediately available to him. It affected his judgment, hence the enthusiastic eclecticism of the parlour's furnishings; hence too the overcrowded junk shops of the 1930's when the children of the Victorians were setting up house and ridding themselves of their parents' treasures. In subsequent revaluation of Victoriana, it has been ruefully discovered that some valuable babies were thrown out with the bathwater so that today a Thonet bent-wood rocking chair, mass produced though it was, fetches an impressive price in the antique market.

In reaction to nineteenth century eclecticism came the movement known as *Art Nouveau* in Britain and France, *Jugendstil* in Germany, *Liberty* in Italy, and *Modernism* in Spain. By way of contrast to the prevailing eclecticism, it derived the inspiration for its style of decoration from plant life; a somewhat transfigured plant life, admittedly. The typical undulating, broken line of *Art Nouveau* was inspired by the growth of wistaria, magnolias and lilies, and by the wayward lines of vegetation that resisted limitation by ruler and compass.

It was never a popular style in its original form, though debased versions of it were used and circulated widely, and for several decades. Comparison of these with the designs of Charles Rennie Mackintosh, Victor Horta, the Belgian architect, and his compatriot, Henri van de Velde, betray their lack of delicacy and elegance and the lack of comprehension implicit in their production. The best of *Art Nouveau* may be seen in Britain, France, Belgium and Germany though, even here, the new language was often used in such a way as to give the impression that this was merely another style to be added to the eclectic sum of those which had preceded it. What might have been a revolution deteriorated into a reaction.

Art Nouveau as it derived from the work of William Morris was the first modern movement to care for the relationship between the work of the craftsmen and of industry; to care, indeed, about the total environment. It gave encouragement, accordingly, to furniture makers, glassworkers, silversmiths, textile designers and others who were prepared to design for mass production, thereby ensuring that though the goods produced were turned out in apparently limitess numbers, they retained the merits of the creator's originals.

(Opposite page) One of the most important and distinguished of Art Nouveau buildings in Brussels, No. 48 Rue Defacqz, built in 1897 for the painter, Albert Ciamberlani, to plans by Paul Hankar (1861-1901). Its distinctive feature is Hankar's treatment of the façade as a decorative whole. The number of elements combined is certainly impressive — the wide, almost horse-shoe-shaped windows, the polychrome sgraffito around and above them, and the delicate ironwork in which Art Nouveau influences are most readily perceptible. During this period of Hankar and Victor Horta, Belgian architecture flourished and affected the work of architects elsewhere.

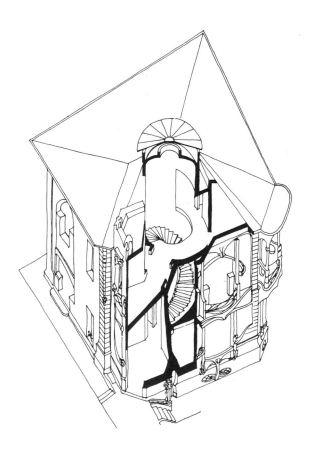

In Italy, examples of authentic Art Nouveau are rare. One of the few buildings in which the style is not merely applied to the outside but is an integral part of the structure is this small house by the Tuscan architect, Giovanni Michelazzi, who committed suicide during the First World War. It is in the Via Scipione Ammirato in Florence. The decoration of the façade and the wrought iron of the staircase shown in the two photographs is very delicate: the shape of the window resembles that of the Hankar house. The internal plan (above) of the house is interesting and significant with its spiral staircase at the heart of the house, and a separate function decisively allotted to each room.

Mackintosh and Art Nouveau

Charles Rennie Mackintosh, born in Glasgow in 1868, was Britain's greatest exponent of *Art Nouveau* and his place in architectural and artistic history is assured. His exceptionally disciplined line and the boldness of his use of colour gave to some of his work a perfection of style in which each single detail had significance and purpose. The glass door designed for the Room *de Luxe* in Kate Cranston's Willow Tearoom in Glasgow (with his wife, Margaret MacDonald, who designed the glass panel) is a masterpiece of elegance in probably the most famous of all Mackintosh's interiors. But the strength of Mackintosh's design lies not so much in his use of a curling line but in his own very individual, rigorous, mainly vertical linear rhythms, reminiscent not so much of the *Art Nouveau* movement as of the paintings of such artists as Mondrian. Essentially he was an architect and sought to create rooms in which the decoration was neither submerged by the structure nor obtrusive in it, but an integral and necessary part of a particular organization of space. This, as Frank Lloyd Wright was also to show, is the real business of the architect. One of his greatest and most fascinating works is the Library of the Glasgow School of Art with its gallery supported by wooden pillars.

Although, in some ways, it might have come from the *Bauhaus* — with its light fittings — it remains unmistakeably Mackintosh's creation.

He left Glasgow in 1914 and though he lived until 1928, Mackintosh designed virtually nothing more after 1917. He was, unhappily, a prophet without honour in his own country.

Other architects of the *Art Nouveau* movement are remembered as much for their furniture and furnishings as for their buildings. Richard Riemerschmid, born in Munich, also in 1868, designed furniture for mass production. His designs, as unaffected by fashionable foibles as those of working tools, could be produced again today and find acceptance. His qualities are best appreciated in his armchairs, designed in 1899.

The element of fantasy in *Art Nouveau* was developed by a French and a Belgian designer. In the staircase of his own house Hector Guimard, who designed many of the stations on the Paris *Métro*, gave to the line of the handrail a pure, almost calligraphic flourish; to his desk, designed in 1903, he added mouldings of gracefully elongated leg bones in order to soften the hardness of the corners. Detail triumphed here over design.

Detail was, equally, the preoccupation of his contemporary, Baron Victor Horta, who devoted a great deal of attention to handles, locks and handrails. He preferred metal, with its capacity for flowing lines, to the less malleable wood, and iron and brass were perfectly suited to his fondness for exposing the construction of his buildings, in which indeed, he made use of iron. Cast iron had already been accepted as a structural material. The idea of metal furniture was not yet accepted; that was still to come in Frank Lloyd Wright's Larkin Building in Buffalo in 1904.

(Left) Chairs with arms designed by Richard Riemerschm. in 1889. Chair and table designed by Charl Rennie Mackintosh for his own house in Glasgo in 1900 (Glasgow, University of Glasgow Collections (Opposite page) Door designed by Mackintosh f the Room de Luxe *in the Willow Tearoom of Miss Ka Cranston, in Sauchiehall Street, Glasgow (c. 1904*

Antoni Gaudí, poet-engineer

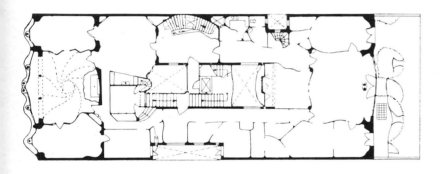

(Top) Small armchair designed by Gaudí for the Casa Calvet in Barcelona. Like his buildings, it has the air of an organic growth, as if arms and legs had sprouted from the framework.
(Above) Plan of the Casa Batlló in the Paseo de Gracia in Barcelona. Here Gaudí did not build a new house but adapted an existing one (1902-1907). But the plan shows how drastic his adaptation was; it altered the old structure beyond recognition and stamped it decisively with Gaudí's very personal imprint.

The work of Antoni Gaudí (1852-1926), the greatest exponent of *Modernism (Art Nouveau)* in Spain, was for long considered a curiosity, the fruit of a reckless, undisciplined imagination. But it is now appreciated that its wilfully contorted forms had a structural authority possible only from the drawing-board of a man who thoroughly understood the building techniques required and who was thus able to express himself in this way. Gaudí the artist worked hand in glove with Gaudí the expert engineer but even when one bears this in mind, the coherence of structure and decoration is remarkable. In the modern world, technical skill has become divorced from taste in art. Gustave Eiffel, the great French engineer, who built not only the tower that bears his name but also some magnificent bridges, lived in a house in Paris that was a monument to appalling taste. More recently, the attempts of even so great an engineer-architect as Pier Luigi Nervi, who can mould reinforced concrete into bold and perfect forms, to introduce decorative elements into one of his buildings (the Palazzo dello Sport, designed for the Olympic Games in Rome with his colleague Piacentini) can be most charitably described as unhappy.

Gaudí had an amazing capacity to conceive and carry through to perfection every detail of his design. He was not himself a craftsman but the decoration he used — pottery tiles, wrought iron, carved stone — is distinctively his. After his sudden death — he was run over by a tram — there was no one to continue the work he left unfinished such as the Church of the Holy Family in Barcelona.

He designed parks, villas, palaces and churches, but comparatively few ordinary dwelling houses. The few that exist are, however, exemplary in their use of space and arrangement of the rooms. They reflect the jealously enclosed Spanish way of life and open only on to interior courtyards, thus raising traditional defences against heat and cold, and inquisitive intruders. In the Casa Batlló, which belongs to the years 1905-1907, the façade is designed as a single, sculptural whole. Casa Milá, known as the 'Stone Quarry', and finished in 1907, is probably his best known dwelling house. Set at the intersection of two streets in Barcelona, the undulating horizontal lines of the façade combine

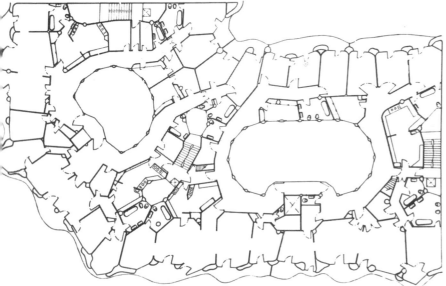

(Left) Elevation and plan of the
Casa Milá in Barcelona (1905-1907). It was
intended that the building should have
no inner dividing walls: the entrance was placed
in the basement, the roof of which is supported by
metal girders. Unparalleled in Spain and
largely elsewhere, are the flowing, exuberant
lines of the façade and the undulating stretch
of terrace on top of the building; it is
less a building than a piece of sculpture.
(See also page 304.)

(Below) Earlier is the Casa Güell
in the Calle de Conde del Asalto
in Barcelona, designed between 1885
and 1889, of which a section is shown here.
The site is small – only 72 by 60
feet – and its lines are notably severe
compared with the Casa Milá.

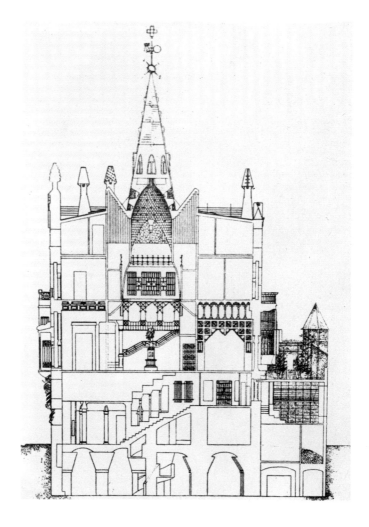

with the decorative detail of carving and wrought iron to create what is as much a piece of sculpture as a building. The roof, designed in parabolic sections, with fantastic chimneys, is a very strictly conceived folly in which imagination and logical construction cannot be divided.

Gaudí created a special style in furniture too. His anthropomorphic chairs with sculptured legs that look like human bones were not merely in the *Art Nouveau* idiom, but betrayed too the sense of death in life that is so important a part of Spanish character.

If certain aspects of *Art Nouveau* foreshadowed functionalism, it is not difficult to see how they are linked to modern architecture. Yet Gaudí seems to have no connection with it. His richly imaginative, stimulating designs move beholders to enthusiastic approval or equally profound disapproval, but he had no imitators and no disciples. Their absence means that Spanish *Modernism* ended with his death but it detracts not at all from his stature as a great original.

Gaudí's masterpiece in the field of domestic architecture is the Casa Milá in the Paseo de Gracia, Barcelona. It still excites amazement and, when it was built, it was so revolutionary that it provoked such satirical drawings as the one shown (right) in which it is depicted as a kind of dovecote for some very curious aeroplanes: this at least recognized the novelty of the building. Other caricatures were less kind, and the building's nickname in the city, La Pedrera (the Stone Quarry), is hardly admiring. In 1957, Le Corbusier observed that the gigantic chimneys directly anticipated abstract sculpture; for the rest, it was an early exercise in the use of the modulor in architecture.

Van de Velde and mass production

The Belgian architect, Henri van de Velde, one of the greatest exponents of *Art Nouveau*, linked it in his own life and work with the *Bauhaus*. Born in 1863, he died as recently as 1957. His place in architectural history is an important one though it has been overlooked by admirers of functionalism, but his main contribution to modern art has been in the field of furniture design, in particular the design of mass produced furniture, and graphic art. Among his finest achievements was the music room in the Folkwang Museum at Hagen in Germany (1901-1902) which develops *Art Nouveau* concepts to achieve a complete integration of architecture and furniture. This is evident in the 'architectural' piano and even more in the undulating line of the back of the sofa, continued in the wooden panelling of the walls and prolonged through the entrance. This free, fluent line dominates the purely deco-

Furniture by Henri van de Velde. (Above) Sideboard shown at the Düsseldorf exhibition in 1902. (Left) Desk and chair (Zürich, Kunstgewerbemuseum). (Below) Mass produced table and chairs for the same dining-room as the sideboard. The angularity of van de Velde's furniture is relieved by an undulating line as in the carved chair and sideboard, and his ability to reconcile good looks with the kind of design suitable for mass production was of the greatest importance to the history of interior design.

rative elements: the ornament is not superimposed on the structure but is part of it and cannot be appreciated apart from it; in this it is already functional or rational.

But van de Velde's most remarkable achievement was in the field of design for mass production. The demand was for cheap products in very large quantities. This meant that the designs must be simple in construction. Van de Velde's furniture possesses this pleasing simplicity and the additional advantage of freedom from the dictates of passing fashion. It was de Velde's understanding of this new type of craftsmanship which enabled him so to direct the School of Art at Weimar that it could be readily transformed into the *Bauhaus* under the direction of Walter Gropius.

THE BAUHAUS

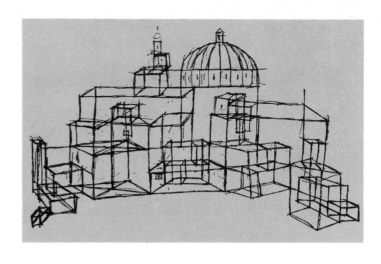

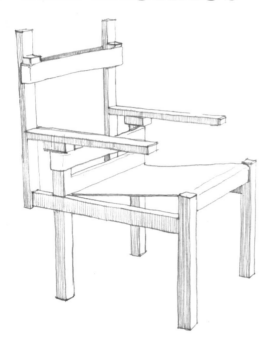

Chair designed by Walter Gropius in his years at the Bauhaus. By simplifying the concepts of Rietveld, one of the main movers of De Stijl, Gropius arrived at a design the perpendicular elements of which maintained the essential neutrality of mass produced pieces and ensured its appropriateness on a factory assembly line.

About 1914, the painter Piet Mondrian stimulated architects and town-planners of the Dutch De Stijl movement to cast aside naturalistic or conventional details in design and look at what was essential. Paul Klee provided the same kind of stimulus for the team of architects and designers gathered at the Bauhaus as this drawing, Santa A in B (1929), indicates.

(Opposite page) The armchair designed [by] Marcel Breuer in 1925 (29 inches high, 31 wide[)] the first model of which the artist Kandinsk[y] demanded for his own house at Dessau (henc[e] its name Wassily). This important product of th[e] Bauhaus was designed by Breuer for mass productio[n] though until 1928 it was put together, with i[ts] framework of steel tubing, by a single workma[n] Production was then taken over by the firm of Thon[et] and handed on to the firm of Gavina (Bologna[)]

The reaction to eclecticism which was *Art Nouveau* rebounded on those who wished to use it to undermine bourgeois taste. *Art Nouveau* was accepted, its symbolism neatly removed – or more often ignored – and it joined the bric-à-brac in the parlour where, as another new style, it sank without trace. The parlour was, however, threatened from another direction.

In 1919 the young Walter Gropius took over direction of the *Staatliches Bauhaus* at Weimar from Henri van de Velde. He was a Berliner, born in 1883, and a pupil and associate of Peter Behrens, an architect who began as an artist and developed into an industrial designer; he was design adviser to the AEG, the German electrical combine for whom he designed electric tea kettles as well as factories. Through him, Gropius acquired an understanding of the working of industry and, in 1919, there was launched the greatest teaching revolution of the century. Gropius converted the Art School at Weimar into something completely new, not an academy of the fine arts but a combination of laboratory, school and workshop which is now known simply as the *Bauhaus* – the house of building. Gropius had already worked out methods of standardization and mass production of small houses, and to these the artists, craftsmen and architects under his direction devoted a considerable part of their time.

In dealing with this problem, moreover, collaboration was encouraged with students in schools of engineering as well as with students in other schools of architecture. The results of the extensive research carried out culminated in the publication of the book *L'Habitation Minimum*, a collection of plans for houses, and the building of the modern district of Siemensstadt in Berlin. To this day, this plan has never been surpassed either as an exercise in town planning or as an example of what the lay-out of flats in a block of flats should be; thirty years later, at the end of the Second World War, the Siemensstadt plan was still the basis of building in new working class districts.

But the interest of Gropius and his *Bauhaus* colleagues was not merely in technology. He called in such *avant garde* painters as Paul Klee and Wassily Kandinsky to teach and ensure that aesthetics were not forgotten in their research. Much of the aesthetic impact of the house still depended, as it had done for centuries before, on its interior arrangement. The problem that Gropius faced was the high cost of the architect's contribution to this interior arrangement – Frank Lloyd Wright faced the same problem – and the difficulty of producing low-cost, standardized housing that was not a series

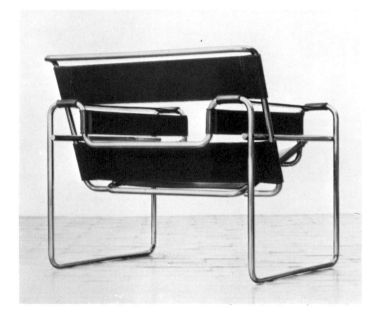

of anonymous, dreary containers of space divided into so many cubic feet per house. In the interests of cost, the containers had to be measured exactly and their design contrived to allow as much space as possible where it was needed, in living-rooms, and as little wastage as possible on passages, for, in the final analysis, Gropius had to take into account not merely an architectural problem but a planning and, therefore, a social and political one. Having provided standard interiors, therefore, the *Bauhaus* set out to influence society in favour of good design by supplying well-designed objects cheaply – objects in which, in Gropius's famous definition, 'the highest quality corresponded to the unlimited resources of mass production.'

Many of the small objects we use today were designed in the *Bauhaus*. The handle made of a tube of chromium-plated steel, which has been produced by the million, was designed by Gropius. The table lamp with its flexible arm and parabolic reflector, used everywhere in one form or another, originated in the *Bauhaus*. The most important invention in the field of furniture design in the first quarter of this century was the piece made from steel tubing, a material the use of which we owe in large part to the *Bauhaus's* most brilliant pupil, the Hungarian Marcel Breuer. It was not used, however, as Breuer intended. Since chromium-plated metal tubing, mass produced and used industrially for the handlebars of bicycles, was a 'finished' material (as wood is not for it needs to be polished as a final operation), it was fairly cheap. Its only disadvantage is that after a period of time – from 10 to 40 years – it deteriorates, whereas wood improves with age, acquiring a patina that enhances its appearance and often its value. Gropius and Breuer did not consider the deterioration of steel tubing to be a disadvantage and, indeed, the chair that could not become an antique object with secondary values unrelated to its function, was obviously what they wanted. It was designed, therefore, to be easily expendable, to be bought, used for a while and then discarded.

But European society was not ready for this kind of obsolescence and householders in general were not prepared to welcome tubular furniture into their homes. The German workman, like his contemporaries all over Europe, still made economic sacrifices to buy himself wooden furniture for his living-room and bedroom, designed, much of it, by industrial craftsmen in a mongrel mixture of styles which was sometimes called modern.

But Breuer's metal furniture was used in hospitals, offices, hotels, canteens and waiting-rooms of

Chairs designed and constructed in curved plywood by the Bauhaus in about 1924. Their purpose was the revival of the kitchen chair and the adaptation of its design to large-scale industrial production.

(Opposite page) Plan and north view of the house of the Bauhaus director at Dessau, designed by Walter Gropius in 1925. The ground level is arranged as follows: (1) terrace (2) bedroom area, (3) living-room, (4) dining-room, (5) office (6) dressing-room and bathroom, (7) kitchen. On the upper floors are another terrace, bedroom service rooms, laundry and servants' rooms

various descriptions. It was accepted as a symbol of the hygienic, the antiseptic, something which you used but which belonged to someone else, usually faceless, impersonal and vaguely in authority. Bus seats, bar stools and canteen chairs were made of metal tubing. The tube was often painted in bright colours. This *Bauhaus* furniture was accepted mainly for hygienic reasons even if it was not particularly liked. And the designer's original intention, that it should be an expendable, abstract work of art, was forgotten.

Like *Art Nouveau*, the *Bauhaus* expected too much of the society in which it was placed and the middle classes whom it both courted and fought defeated it. The Nazis were clever enough, moreover, to exploit German antipathy to this kind of revolution by a chauvinistic revival of national styles, of local traditions, of the idea of a little house in a little garden. The results were depressing and the only thing worse than Nazi architecture was Nazi art. It was not long before the *Bauhaus* was closed down by the Nazi regime.

Germany was not the only European country which was to react unfavourably to the ideas of the *Bauhaus*. In the early years of the revolution in Russia, enormous advances were made in the provision of housing. These ceased under Stalin's repressive regime in the 1930's. New social legislation coincided with a change of direction in both art and architecture and there occurred in Russia too a revival of popular traditions and regional styles. A similar reaction took place in Italy during the

Case for a five-valve radio receiver designed in 1946 by the architects Achille and Pier Giacomo Castiglioni and Luigi Caccia Dominioni, in Milan. In order to break with the tradition of the twentieth century object masquerading behind a nineteenth century, or earlier, casing, this radio was designed to use twentieth century materials — a synthetic resin was chosen — in a twentieth century style. It would be able, its designers planned, to stand on a table or hang on a wall. It was important that a receiver of such power could by this time be put into a case like this. The design was mass produced at the end of 1945 in two colours, red or white.

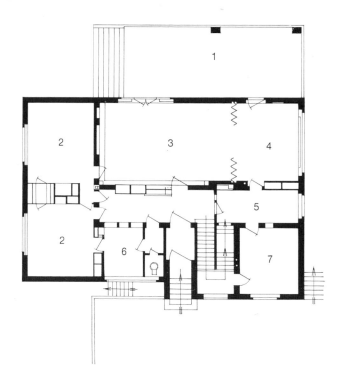

same period when there was a renewal of regional crafts from the Tyrol to Sicily.

There is, of course, a great deal of value in tradition and in traditional crafts. There is, perhaps, less in mass produced imitations of, say, traditional furniture designs and even less in the use of such imitation traditional furniture in inappropriate surroundings.

During this period, Italy pursued a characteristically individual path of its own in the battle of the styles. Italian Fascism, born a decade earlier than Nazism, countenanced *Futurism* (a political and artistic movement led by the artist and writer, Marinetti) and functionalism in architecture for a time at least; eventually imperial megalomania prevailed. But as late as 1935 Le Corbusier was still

being acclaimed in Italy, and Alban Berg's *Wozzeck*, banned in Nazi Germany, could still be performed in Rome.

More important, Franco Albini and Gio Ponti, via their journal *Domus*, could design and even influence public taste with a style that was a gentler but more acceptable version of the strict rationalism of the *Bauhaus*. Some of the designs of those years foreshadowed present-day industrial design. The brothers Castiglioni and Caccia Dominioni, for instance, who worked in Milan, suggested that the radio should not be considered as a piece of furniture but should evolve and appear as a new object like the telephone or the typewriter; that is, an object, the form of which was derived from its function, should replace the rather odd box.

Functionalism has produced some fairly odd effects. In São Paulo, Brazil, for example, this house was built as early as 1931 by Gregory Warchavich. The garden has been laid out on several levels, a feature which it would possibly be difficult to justify in functional terms.

MENDELSOHN AND EXPRESSIONISM

Erich Mendelsohn, who was born in Germany in 1887 and died in the United States in 1953, was probably the greatest exponent of Expressionist architecture. The most outstanding of his buildings in Germany is the Einstein Tower or astronomical observatory at Potsdam, built in 1921. The fact that it is still one of the most efficient observatories in Europe indicates that not all functionalism originated with Gropius or Le Corbusier. Examples of their work – Le Corbusier's Villa Savoye and the headquarters of the *Bauhaus* – have indeed proved difficult to maintain and, therefore, unfunctional, but this masterpiece of what was regarded as the more extravagant Expressionist movement remains in good working condition. It was functional and Mendelsohn designed the interior to work, that is, with fixed, very heavy hardwood fittings and equally solid furniture, the intention being to reduce vibrations, disturbing to sensitive instruments.

The house that Mendelsohn built for himself in Berlin in 1929-1930 and lived in briefly before racial persecution drove him out of Germany, is also perfectly preserved after 40 years. It stands on a gentle slope in the Rupenhorn park where its curved tip ends in the Wannsee, and its composition seems very simple. In the semi-basement afforded by the sloping site are the service rooms and servants' bedrooms. The house turns its back on the road and, on the south-facing front, the ground floor is entirely of glass. The large windows are electrically controlled in such a way that the vast single panes of glass can be lowered out of sight to turn the living-room into a loggia. In his furnishings, Mendelsohn typically rejected *Bauhaus* theories and with them Marcel Breuer's minimal furniture of tubes and canvas. He enjoyed comfort and loved music – he was himself a gifted cellist – and the interiors of his house compromise between the austerity of the Austrian architect, Adolf Loos, and the opulence of German and Austrian baroque tradition.

The feature, however, that was most widely copied was his continuation, in a line curving round corners, of the horizontal planes of the façade. The sweeping corner windows became a recognizable Mendelsohn motif in his later buildings, enormously popular in the years between the First and Second World Wars and copied in innumerable villas, office blocks and seaside pavilions. Mendelsohn did himself design such a seaside pavilion in England; the building – at Bexhill – indicates clearly, however, that his concern was not to devise a novel means of using window glass but the integration of interior and exterior.

The Berlin house is the least typical of his houses and the most uncommitted in its decoration, and for this reason it has dated very little. Thus it indicates not merely how the great German architect lived but also what an agreeable, comfortable house of the period could look like.

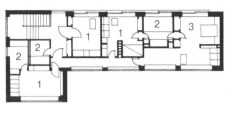

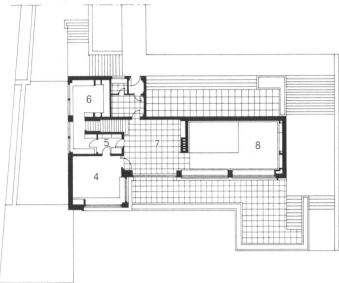

(Opposite page) View of the house built by Erich Mendelsohn for himself at Rupenhorn in Berlin in 1929.
(Above) Plan for the upper floor and ground floor and (below) the exterior of the large sitting-room projected, as it were, into the garden. The shorter side of the building, with its wide connecting terraces, cuts across the sloping site. The arrangement of the rooms is as follows: (1) bedrooms, (2) bathroom, (3) bed-sitting-room for guests, (4) dining-room, (5) office, (6) kitchen, (7) sitting-room with (8) an extension for music.

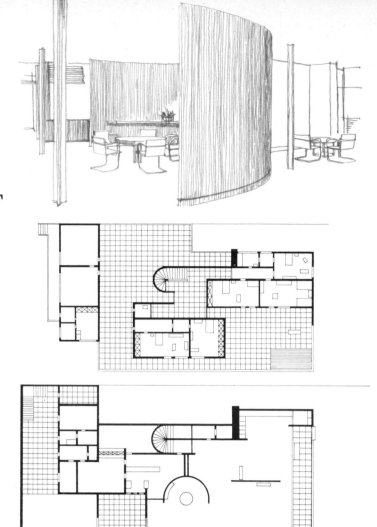

MIES VAN DER ROHE: THE QUIET ARCHITECT

Compared with the formidable output of Frank Lloyd Wright and the polemical passion of Le Corbusier, Mies van der Rohe produced comparatively little and produced it quietly. He has left very few buildings, but those that he built in the twenties and thirties are of such fundamental importance in the history of modern architecture that they require consideration in some detail.

Some of his earliest work has a neo-classical air. After the First World War, he developed a sympathy for Expressionism which gave rise to his fantastic plan for a skyscraper constructed of glass, even today an astonishing concept. Towards the end of the 1920's, however, his theories on internal spaces found expression in plans and architectural images in the German Pavilion of the International Exhibition at Barcelona in 1929, in the Tugendhat house at Brno in 1930 and in his experimental house shown at the Berlin Building Exhibition in 1931. The Barcelona and Berlin designs were exhibition pieces, purely theoretical; it was the Tugendhat house that put his theories to the test.

Important to understanding of the Tugendhat house is a knowledge of the site. The road on which it lies is several feet higher than the level of the house. The house was entered directly from the road, that is, at the level of the upper floor. Here the front door was screened by the semi-cylindrical casing of the stairs. Also on the same floor as the entrance hall were the bedrooms which were conventionally arranged.

What was revolutionary about the house was the living-room floor, as a glance at the plan indicates. The structure was carried on cruciform steel columns covered with shiny chromium plate; these were quite independent of the internal walls. The latter had become, in effect, free-standing screens, no more than a few inches thick, surfaced with such materials as ebony and other woods, marble and onyx. Thus the internal space is not divided into separate, adjoining rooms connected by doors and lit by windows but is a single unit, isolated

(Above, from the top) Dining area, plans of the upper and ground levels and (below) a view of the Tugendhat house at Brno, built in 1930. As in the pavilion at Barcelona (opposite page), Mies van der Rohe supports the ceiling on pillars, cruciform in section, of chromium-plated steel, placed inside the wide windows. He used free-standing screens of rich materials: macassar ebony in black and brown for the splendid screen round the dining area, and white onyx and gold in the living-room.

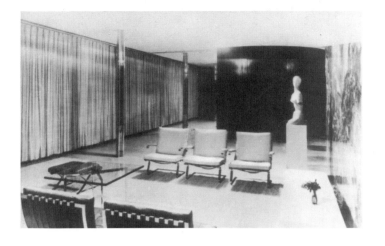

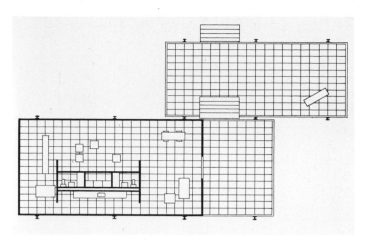

from the outside world by a single continuous wall of glass which can be lowered at will so that exterior and interior join.

Much has been said and written about Mies van der Rohe's chromium-plated columns and they have been criticized as an obstruction to the development of the inner life of the house. The designer himself, indeed, eliminated them from his American work and expelled his roof supports beyond the inner space to the outer edges of the building to leave the interior free. Yet, in the Tugendhat house, these columns are not merely supports but, like the columns in a Greek temple or in a church by Brunelleschi, they give rhythm, measure and order to the interior space which is thus defined, framed and seen to be properly proportioned to its human inhabitants.

This particular use of space and the integration of daily functions within a spatial continuum clearly derives from Expressionism, which reacted to the fragmentation of bourgeois society by abolishing walls to create large, shared spaces. In the dwelling house, this opening up of the interior could give rise to confusion unless it were strictly controlled, as it was by Mies van der Rohe, who disciplined space. The very contrast between the freedom of space and the strictness with which he controlled it gave strength to the architectural image.

The most famous room in the Tugendhat house is the dining-room or rather, the dining area, for it is formally defined only by a semi-circular panel faced in fine wood which echoes the shape of the table. Here too the disciplined imagination is at work and the smallest detail in the room is calculated to the last sixteenth of an inch. It was for this room that the architect designed his small Tugendhat armchairs which, like his Barcelona chairs (designed for the German Pavilion in the International Exhibition of 1929), were later successfully mass produced.

The Barcelona chair is probably the most wide-

(Above, left) Another view of the Tugendhat house at Brno. The chairs were specially designed for it by Mies van der Rohe.
(Above, right) Plan of the Farnsworth House at Plano, Illinois, designed by Mies van der Rohe in 1950.
(Above) Interior of the German government's pavilion at the International Exhibition in Barcelona in 1929.

In 1929, in the Bauhaus, Mies van der Rohe designed a chair with a frame of steel tubing which achieved great popularity in the United States in the 1930's. In his Barcelona chair (below) which is now a modern classic, he used cross steel supports and leather cushions.

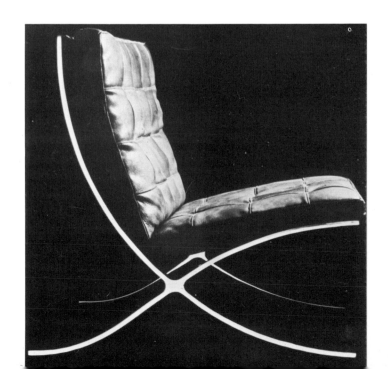

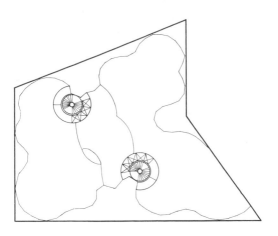

In 1920-1921, Mies van der Rohe drew up plans for this all-glass building thirty storeys high (left). Its lay-out (above) shows the use of free forms within a translucent skin. (Right) Apartment building at Lake Shore Drive in Chicago where Mies van der Rohe settled in 1937: it shows the development of reflections and transparency.

ly known piece of mass produced furniture and the one which has received most international acclaim. The elegance of its design depends on the contrast between the slender X-shaped steel supports, laminated and chromium-plated, and the solid cushions in quilted black leather. It has no arms and there is no way of altering it without redesigning it (the Tugendhat chairs have arms). But here one must bear in mind its original purpose. It was designed as a small chair to be used for short periods by spectators at exhibitions. After its success at Barcelona it was used in private houses; but without arm supports it is not an easy chair, merely a more modern and more comfortable version of the typical upright chair. Its comparatively high price has already given it the status of 'a modern antique' which was very far from the intention of the designer.

After he left Germany, Mies van der Rohe continued his study of the house in the United States. His large apartment buildings in Chicago are designed in the local manner; his Seagram building in New York is often described as the most beautiful modern building in America. The discoveries that the architect had made, however, in the organization of internal space in his European buildings is not so apparent in, say, the Chicago apartments. One box of steel, bronze and brick in a skyscraper is very much like another whether it be in Stockholm or Beirut, London or Tokyo. Mies van der Rohe's, however, achieved a precision of finish attained by few. They were perhaps too precise; chilly building bricks inveighed against by Frank Lloyd Wright during his long life.

It was in smaller, single houses that van der Rohe continued to experiment; for example, in the house he designed for the Farnsworth family at Fox River, Illinois, in 1951. The steel frame and glass walls create the impression of absolute spatial continuity. The house consists of a square, in the centre of which is the service area which contains kitchen and bathroom equipment. The rest of the house was free to accommodate the activities of eating, sleeping, talking, reading, dressing and so on. That disadvantages as great as those of the house of little boxes attend this kind of open-plan living has become apparent in recent years. There is a curious irony, moreover, in the fact that this twentieth century fashion is a reversion to a very ancient way of life indeed.

PHILIP JOHNSON: PERFECT DISCIPLINE

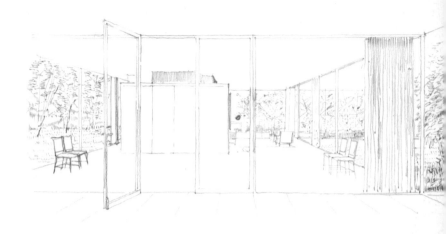

The most enthusiastic member of Mies van der Rohe's American following is Philip Johnson, architect and art critic, collector and essayist, born in Cleveland, Ohio, in 1906. The two men worked together on the Seagram Building with Johnson in charge of its decoration.

His own house in New Canaan, Connecticut was built in 1949, that is, two years before the Farnsworth House, and Mies van der Rohe may have drawn some of his inspiration from it. The differences between the two houses are interesting and greater than they seem at first sight, the principal one being the difference in structural method. In Mies van der Rohe's Farnsworth House, the supporting columns or girders are visible outside the walls; in Johnson's house, they are part of the framework as the supports are, say, in a piece of furniture where the various elements are fused together in the interests of a compact, efficient result, which is regarded as more important than the purely aesthetic pleasure of showing how the piece is put together.

Johnson's interior is even chillier than that of his colleague's. An elegant cylinder houses the building's services. It is balanced by the curves of a tall lamp which suggests a cylinder of light. Furniture and ornaments are precisely placed. The effect is one of perfect but forbidding good taste: if a chair were moved or another one brought in, the result might be like that of adding an extra figure to Leonardo da Vinci's *Last Supper*.

Not everyone, and indeed very few people, could live comfortably in such a house. But it is a most salutary and eloquent rejoinder to the phoney 'homeliness' pursued by the Hollywood house with its imitation fire, the television set disguised as an eighteenth century chest of drawers and plastic disguised as wrought iron. With immense authority and sureness of taste, Philip Johnson has taken up his position at the other extreme. It is not, however, on account of the strength with which it expresses a reaction against other styles that Johnson's house always retains its interest: its fascination is intrinsic.

Interior and exterior of the house built by Philip Johnson for himself at New Canaan, Connecticut, in 1949. The walls, supported by a slender metal framework, are of glass so that the apparent separation of inside from outside world is reduced to a minimum. Each detail is thought out with the utmost care, including the placing of the furniture.

NEUTRA
IN THE U.S.A.

No other architect, not even the great Frank Lloyd Wright, has as strongly influenced American architecture as Richard Neutra. The professional success of this Austrian born architect has been very great. He has built houses not by the dozen but by the hundred. Quantity of design is not of itself particularly meritorious but, in Neutra's case, the quality has remained consistently high. Admittedly his villas resemble one another; they bear a recognizable signature, the reproduction of which has been attempted in houses described as 'Neutra-style'.

This alone indicates the extent of his influence on American architecture. He has been reproached with giving his clients exactly what they want – hence his success – which may be interpreted to mean that he has been the servant of society. His antithesis is, of course, Le Corbusier. But it is worth remembering that while Le Corbusier's influence on the French way of life is debatable, Neutra's spatial concepts have become part of everyday life in the United States, especially in California. If the aim of architecture is education through art, then Neutra's patient infiltration of society through his clients has improved the average taste of Americans more than many a direct attack on their sensibilities.

Since he always works in the same way and has been doing so for about 30 years, Neutra has achieved an unusual refinement and rationalization of technique. Details have been studied, worked over, and repeated over the years; structural elements can be standardized and pre-fabricated. The result may be that a Neutra building costs less than the 'one-off' experiment of another less experienced architect.

In his concern that his buildings should seem to be an organic part of the landscape, his work would appear to resemble that of Frank Lloyd Wright. But even a superficial examination of his designs shows that it does not. In Wright's buildings, there is a central core while the rest is planned to merge with the surrounding natural scene. In Neutra's, each space has its own function and its own characteristic appearance; with regard to the latter, Neutra has never forgotten the dictum of his Viennese master Adolf Loos, that 'ornament is a crime'.

In the Kaufmann house which he designed for a site in the Colorado desert in 1946, the plan takes the form of four windmill sails. On the south are the garages, on the west, the service rooms, on the north, the guests' apartments – separated from the centre of the house by a patio – and on the east, the owner's apartment. In the centre, the fulcrum of this composition, is the large living-room which comunicates with the swimming-pool. On the first floor is a loggia, protected from the mountain wind and open on the opposite side. The ancestry of this type of design – the division of the interior into semi-independent areas with a central focal area – is obviously the Prairie Houses of Frank Lloyd Wright. It was a style indicative of the urban American's nostalgia for the open spaces of his own or his parents' childhood. But if the plan recalls Wright, the actual structure does not; it has flat roofs, wide windows, clean right angles and cuts neat squares and rectangles out of the surrounding countryside.

To hope that a building would survive in this desert, especially as water had to be transported from a distance in tanks, was expecting a great deal and it is now ruinous, buried in sand. Like Le Corbusier's Villa Savoye, its life was ephemeral.

The Tremaine house at Montecito in California was built in the following year. Its plan incorporating wings or sails resembles that of the desert house, but since it is built in a wood of oak trees, it is much more obviously linked with its environment. The roof still consists of a layer of reinforced

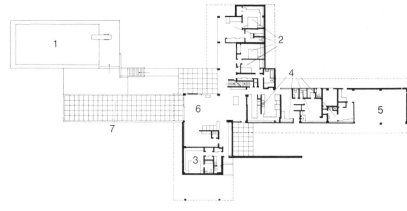

concrete but beams of cement reminiscent of the wooden beams of prairie houses add to it a certain sense of rhythm. The outside walls are of stone; the wide picture windows are without frames as such, although in the main bedroom, for example, the ceiling at the window and the dressing-table shelf form the horizontals of a large frame within which the picture is the landscape outside. In a sense this sums up the difference between Neutra and Frank Lloyd Wright; this house is not a part of nature for nature is something to be viewed from a distance, like a painting. At the touch of a switch, the curtains close and the show is over. The bedroom is again a closed box. The enjoyment of nature at a distance – a safe distance, one might argue – expresses a certain American way of life, the correct dress for the outdoor barbecue lunch, the loudspeakers in the trees to provide music for traditional square dancing. Europeans who have ruined and are still in the process of ruining their towns and countryside, who have abandoned their traditions, can only criticize it at the risk of being accused of hypocrisy.

(Opposite page and above) Tremaine House at Montecito, California, designed by Richard Neutra in 1947. (Opposite page) View from the swimming pool towards the house with its cantilevered roof. (Above, left) View of the garden from the wide window of the main bedroom. (Above) Plan of the single floor arranged as follows: (1) swimming-pool, (2) master bedroom, (3) bedroom and sitting-room for guests, (4) service rooms, (5) garage, (6) living-room, (7) terrace, or rather, an extension of the living-room.

(Right) Kaufmann House in the Colorado desert, California, designed by Neutra in 1946 and later abandoned. View of the patio, to the south, from which open the sitting-room and main bedroom; and plan of the rooms which are: (1) swimming-pool, (2) living-room, (3) main bedroom, (4) apartment for guests, (5) service rooms, (6) garage, (7) patio.

ALVAR AALTO: PRACTICAL SIMPLICITY

Alvar Aalto's contribution to modern house design is a very special one. He was born in 1898 in Finland, a country that geographically, economically and spiritually seemed, and in some ways still seems, remote from the bustling highways of the world. The Finnish way of life, of which the *sauna* is probably the most familiar symbol, is simpler than that of most other European countries. The long distances between towns and cities, often crossed by water, and the slow progress of the year from long winter night to long summer day mean that life moves at a more leisurely pace than elsewhere. We often make the mistake of classing the Finns with the Swedes and Danes as Nordic but they have more in common with the people of central Europe and their language is, of course, related to Hungarian or Magyar.

Between the wars, Aalto worked in his own country and since the end of the Second World War he has worked in the United States, France and Germany. Of the houses he has designed, the Carré house at Bazoches near Paris, built between

1956 and 1958, seems to sum up all his previous experience in the field of housing design. It is also one of the few houses built in recent years that has said something new about modern living.

The main entrance opens on to the centre of the house, the hall. The bedrooms with their respective bathrooms – the main bedroom has a *sauna* – open on to it. To the right of it are the living-rooms and library. To the left of the main door, and still opening from the hall, is the dining-room with the kitchen beyond. So large a central area could easily become a huge, useless room like an ancient railway station but Aalto invests it with life and light by his variation of level and his ingenious use of lighting. Large cupboards are so placed as to afford privacy to the bedrooms. The overall result is aesthetically satisfying and functionally efficient. This large house has no passages and no wasted space. One feature is indicative of the architect's attention to detail. One of the major inconveniences of a library is the fact that some shelves are too high up. Aalto has taken ad-

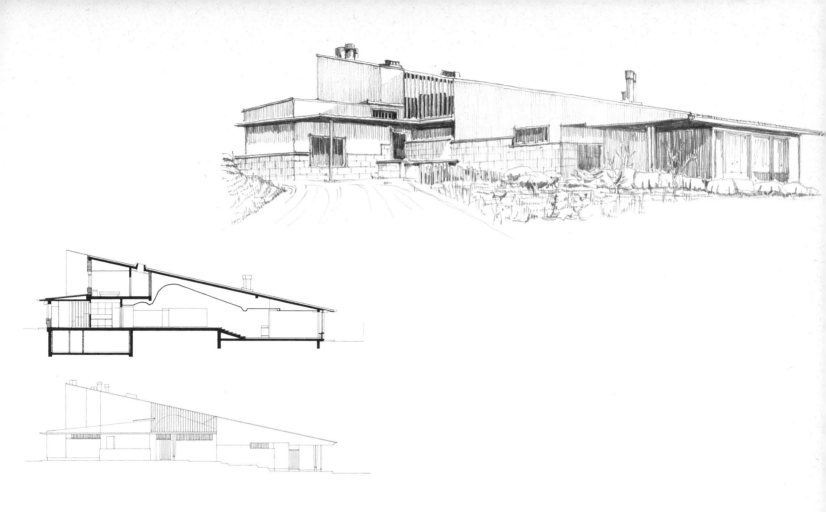

vantage of the unevenness of the site of the house to raise part of his library by as much as 3 feet so that he has been able to make provision for two sets of shelves, both of them accessible. Other details betray the same kind of resourcefulness, itself the result of an innate simplicity, good sense and never-failing sense of humour which allow him to address himself afresh to each new problem.

Aalto's concern for the wider problems of town planning means that his designs for dwelling houses are rather rare. He was one of the architects invited to contribute a design to the Berlin Interbau or International Building Exhibition of 1957, as a result of which the Hansa quarter of the city was constructed. To this imaginative experiment he brought his own approach to the problem of group housing. His Berlin house turned out to be deceptively simple in appearance. Like the Carré house, it had no passages and the rooms centred on a large open living-room which commanded an equally spacious terrace. But after several years of use, the Aalto house has been found to work.

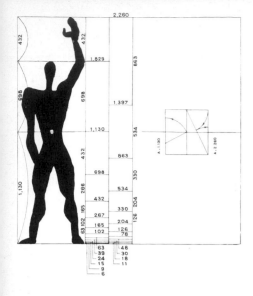

LE CORBUSIER:
PROPHET AND POLEMICIST

No modern architect wrote and talked so much about the architecture of his own age as Charles-Édouard Jeanneret, better known as Le Corbusier. The best known of his dicta, *La maison n'est qu'une machine à habiter*, he later claimed never to have written or said. There is no doubt, however, that as an architectural polemicist he fought, often alone, for nearly half a century against what he regarded as the reactionary, bourgeois and academically sterile, and against war and speculation. Ordinary doubts that architecture could in any way alleviate, let alone abolish, such evils were not shared by Le Corbusier. For him the social revolution started by setting man in a different habitat, a better one than that gradually evolved from the extension of the medieval city.

Instead of sprawling, depressing working class districts, Le Corbusier proposed the *Unité d'Habitation*, in other words, a horizontal skyscraper surrounded by greenery, an even larger architectural entity than those with which we are familiar. The aim is by careful and concentrated planning to obviate the fragmentation that is so obvious a part of modern living. The space occupied by each dwelling is rigidly controlled and organized and the open or garden space which each householder, in a more conventional type of house, might claim is merged to create one continuous green space, uninterrupted even by the buildings themselves, for they are raised above the ground on Le Corbusier's characteristic *pilotis* or stilts. Roof gardens provide even more open space.

Le Corbusier built his *unités* in several cities. The prototype was built at Marseilles in 1952; it was repeated at Nantes three years later and in Berlin as part of the 1957 Interbau. The plan is by now fairly well-known. A series of 'streets' lead to the apartments which are arranged in twos, each occupying a floor and a half. The living-room is the height of both floors, each of which is seven

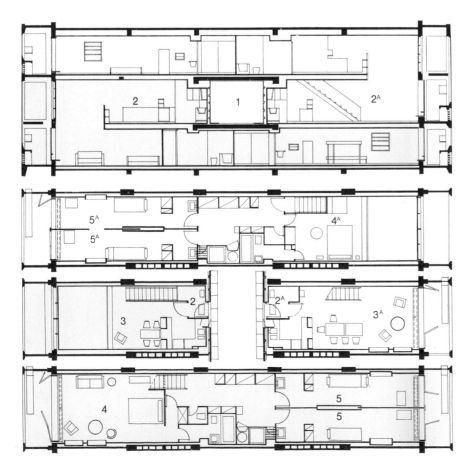

(Above) Le Corbusier's modulor *consists of a system of correlated proportions based on the golden section and the human figure. The human figure is divided into two at waist level, making two measurements which, Le Corbusier maintained, govern every other bodily proportion. From this beginning, he evolved a scale which he could apply to any plan or design whether for the cover of a book or the lay-out of a town. (Left) Plans of the* Unités d'Habitation *at Marseilles. On to the inner road (1) there open the entrances of the upper apartment (2A) as well as the lower one (2). The plans show the similarities between the apartments both in the sitting-rooms (3 and 3A) and in the bedrooms for adults (4A) and children (5 and 5A).*

Le Corbusier's Unité d'Habitation *at Marseilles (1946-1952). Each apartment is on two floors and the balconies are also on two floors; the partitions between the balconies are painted in pastel colours.*

feet six inches high, the *modulor* measurement invented by Le Corbusier. The whole apartment is 15 feet wide – two *modulors* – and about 50 feet long. The centrally placed service rooms are well lit and ventilated artificially. Each unit houses about 350 families which means approximately 1600 people, that is, as many as a sizeable residential district. This means that shops for essential goods and communal services – laundry, hairdresser, newsagents and so on – are necessary in the centre.

Concentration of so large a volume of people within so constricted a space raised the question as to whether the experiment was socially viable. How, in effect, have those who live in a *unité* reacted to the experience? In Marseilles, there were, to begin with, enormous difficulties, and local residents stoutly resisted the suggestion that they should take part in an experiment, the outcome of which was very doubtful. The arrival of large numbers of Algerians solved the tenancy problem and they proved excellent tenants for this colossal ant-hill.

By way of contrast, the Berlin *Unité* was an immediate and unexpected success. Built on a splendid site overlooking the former Olympic stadium, it is inhabited by prosperous middle-class Berliners. There, the German sense of discipline, the tolerance of large quantities of people in comparatively small areas, and the regard for a neatly landscaped environment won acceptance for Le Corbusier's ideas more quickly and more painlessly than was the case among the notoriously individualistic residents of Marseilles. The architect himself, it used to be rumoured, was infuriated by the willing acceptance of his ideas by Berliners whom he found uncongenial. Perhaps, however, he misread the situation. His own Swiss precision – he obtained part of his training at an art school founded for the training of engravers (for the watch industry) – predicates a level of taste, a love of order and a concern for the common good that

(Left) Terrace of a unité *with a children's playground, swimming-pool, and ventilation tower (partly visible on the right).*
(Above) The pilotis of the Marseilles unité *between which is the artificial ground reserved for the services of the building: above are the sun-balconies.*

The Villa Savoye at Poissy, near Paris (1929-1931)
one of Le Corbusier's most important works
in the field of domestic architecture; sited in the
midst of green fields, it dominates
but does not quarrel with its setting.

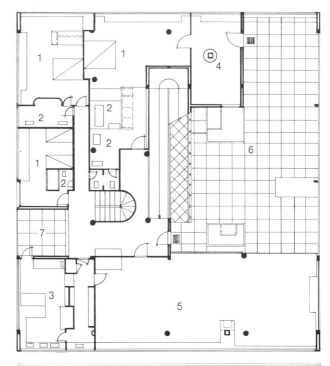

(Right) Plan of the residential floor of the
villa: (1) bedrooms, (2) adjoining bathrooms,
(3) kitchen, (4) drawing-room, (5) living-room,
(6) terrace garden, (7) small terrace.
According to Le Corbusier's modular rule,
the constant measurement which repeats itself
throughout the house is the distance
between the pilotis, fifteen feet. The plan of the
terrace-solarium is especially interesting in the
arrangement of the open spaces (squared zones)
whereby both the hanging garden and the natural
setting of the house may be seen.

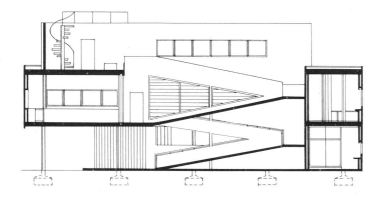

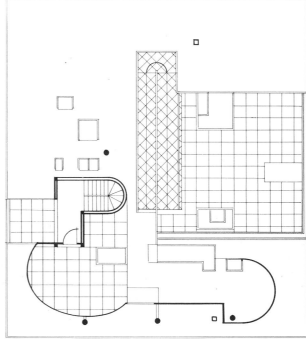

(Above) Cross section of the Villa Savoye.
The house stands on pilotis, between
which there is room for several cars;
ramps connect the
various levels of the house.

Roof-solarium of the villa. Le Corbusier
considered the roof garden as the
real garden of the house inasmuch as,
in a rainy climate, it would more quickly
dry out under the sun.

are far from characteristic of the average Frenchman to whom his ideas are addressed. Those to whom they do appeal are either the highly sophisticated or the first generation peasant from a still fairly primitive background.

Solutions to the problem of collective living absorbed much of Le Corbusier's attention but he also worked on commissions for individual houses. His most famous are the villa at Garches near Paris and the Villa Savoye at Poissy, also near Paris. The Villa Savoye is, with Mies van der Rohe's Tugendhat house and Frank Lloyd Wright's Falling Water, one of the most important and influential examples of twentieth century architecture; it is also one of Le Corbusier's finest achievements.

It was built between 1929 and 1931. The house, massively square, is raised above the ground on the *pilotis* that the architect was to use so effectively in his *unités*. The internal volumes of the house have been patiently organized to achieve and maintain a wonderful sense of spatial freedom. A terrace joined to the approach ramp – the *promenade architecturale* – unites the various levels on which the life of the house is conducted. The large rectangular living-room and dining-room face on to the terrace and are indeed a part of it. The character of this area is defined by the decoration designed by the architect. Where Le Corbusier differs from Mies van der Rohe is in his idea how the house functions at night. The principal bedroom is actually a sequence of gradually narrowing spaces, each with its own particular function – bedroom, with a solarium, and, screened off, bathroom and lavatory. The house was obviously designed with

the strong personality of Madame Savoye in mind; it is, moreover, something much more poetic than the 'machine for living in' which he may or may not have described in *Vers Une Architecture* several years before. The house proved difficult to maintain and, after it was damaged in the Second World War, it lay derelict for years and is only now being restored to its original splendour. For anyone who visited it during those years of neglect and found it used for storing straw and manure, with pigs rooting on the ramps and hens pecking on the terrace, the sensation was a curious one, as if an archaeologist were to excavate the remains of a flying saucer or the rusting fragments of an as yet uninvented space ship. The phenomenon of genuinely modern or, perhaps more accurately, *avant garde* architecture which appears long before popular taste has caught up with it is always an unexpected one.

After the Second World War, Le Corbusier turned for a period to comparatively informal work such as the famous Notre-Dame du Haut pilgrim chapel at Ronchamp which belongs to the years 1950-1953. But his attention was quickly diverted to the large-scale problem of designing a new capital for the Punjab, divided between India and Pakistan by the independence of the two countries. The result was the massive achievement of Chandigarh. The late 1950's saw too the two *unités* at Nantes and Berlin and the modest Jaoul houses at Neuilly-sur-Seine. The only houses comparable with the Villa Savoye are the Villa Shodan and the Villa Sarabhai in Ahmedabad in India. The favourable climate and the sophistication of his

Entrance hall of the Villa Savoye. Even in a building that allowed so much light in the interior, Le Corbusier still sought to create 'real architectural movement which would show constantly changing, unexpected, and sometimes amazing aspects.'

The Villa Shodan in Ahmedabad in the state of Gujarat, India, planned in 1952 by Le Corbusier, who kept natural factors such as the strength of the sun and the prevailing winds very much in mind. The remarkable ingenuity of the plan is underlined by the boldness of the contrast between light and dark on the façade, created by the arrangement of the rooms and enhanced by the projecting floor. (Right) The complex plans of the villa. (From the top) North-west-south-east section: (1) roof solarium, (2) galleries, (3) terrace, (4) waiting-room, (5) bedroom, (6) dining-room, (7) sitting-room. North-south section. North-west-south-east section: (8) library. East-west section, (9) guests' bedrooms, (10) bathroom, (11) hall with a ramp, (12) service rooms. North-east-south-west section showing the ramps leading as far as the first terrace (3): the highest terrace (3A) and the cellars (13) are reached by staircases.

Indian clients allowed him to integrate interior and exterior volumes in a way at which he had hinted in the Villa Savoye. The Villa Shodan is remarkable not only for its horizontal but for its vertical continuity and for the series of dramatically stepped windows which afford the exciting perspectives of a Piranesi drawing.

In the Villa Sarabhai, as in the Jaoul houses, Le Corbusier made use of vaulted roofs, thereby introducing the element of the arch which had been so thoroughly repudiated by the fathers of functionalism and their followers. Despite the rout of academic classicism, Le Corbusier as well as others realized that the error within it lay not in the architectural elements of classicism themselves but in the way they were used. Used intelligently and without prejudice, they could enrich a building. The language of architecture is like the language of any other art and like the language we speak it is always changing. Phrases become clichés; then the clichés are revived and given new life.

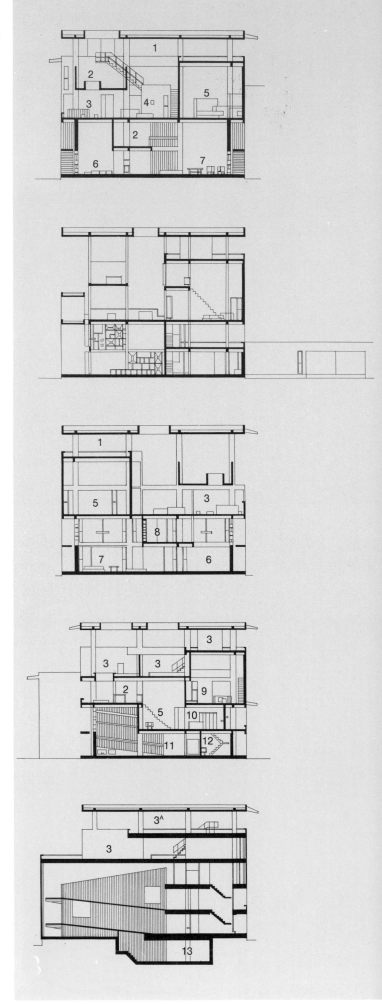

(Above) South-west façade of the Villa Shodan from the swimming-pool. (Right, above) Hall with one of the windows which are, on the inside, display cases for ornaments, portraits and so on. (Right) Staircase between the first and second terrace. Externally, the building has the rough surface created by pouring concrete into wooden shuttering, but for the areas under the roof and for the ceilings, concrete was poured into metal moulds, and the surfaces so formed have been painted in very bright colours which contrast admirably with the other surfaces.

The Villa Sarabhai, also at Ahmedabad, was designed by Le Corbusier in 1955, again with the sun and the prevailing winds well in mind. The structure of the interior allows cool air to penetrate and circulate while the wide verandahs keep the sun at bay. These cover about a quarter of the surface of the building. The interior is lit by a large number of windows carefully aligned in an asymmetrical arrangement. Many of the rooms have barrel-vaulted ceilings which strengthen the structure of the house and enable it to support the garden that Le Corbusier planned for it, and for which he demanded not rare or exotic blooms but the plants of the countryside.

Interior of the Villa Sarabhai. (Above, from the top) The library: the dining-room which also serves as a living-room.
(Left) The ground-floor verandah seen from the courtyard facing the park. Detail of the dining-room: note the barrel ceiling also visible in the library.
(Below) Rooms on the first floor: as in the other rooms, the many windows also serve as shelves.

HANS SCHAROUN: ORGANIC LIVING

Hans Scharoun: ideas for a Volkshaus, *drawn between 1939 and 1945 in Berlin; one of his most futuristic ideas.*

The concept of organic living, suggested by the German architect Hans Scharoun, occupies a special position in the history of European architecture. Like Scharoun's own career, it is difficult to fit into any account of the modern movement. After the First World War, the exponents of Expressionism turned either to functionalism – like Gropius and Mies van der Rohe – or like Erich Mendelsohn, tried to reconcile functionalism with creative ardour and mitigate some of its more extreme rigours. The Expressionists brought a Utopian vision to bear on the agonies of those first terrible years of defeat. They in turn were defeated, however, by the economic miracle of the Weimar Republic. With the triumph of Nazism, the best of German architects went into exile and found employment and inspiration in the New World. But one stayed behind, with his master, Hugo Haering; he was Hans Scharoun who, having resisted the blandishments of the *Bauhaus*, also declined to yield to those of the Nazis or of the Americans, but continued to pursue his own way in Berlin, trustfully hoping for better times. They were 20 years in coming and only then could he get on with building what he had been contemplating since 1919. Among the most important of his buildings was the Philharmonia, the large concert hall erected in Berlin for the Berlin Philharmonic Orchestra. Few artists have been so obstinately and tenaciously attached to their vocation, their principles and their city; the Russian architects who suffered under Stalinist repression may be so described but their tenacity was never rewarded; rehabilitation came too late for them.

In order to understand Scharoun's contribution to a solution of the problem of living in a house, we should consider not so much the famous Siemensstadt project, in which Gropius was also involved, as the small house on the Wannsee which he built for a lawyer called Baensch. It is remarkable because it was built – in Berlin – in 1936, that is, at the very height of Nazi success. To find in that time and place the most original building of its period is astonishing. In order to build it Scharoun drew up a false plan and then built what he wanted. The results from one point of view were unhappy. The owner was expelled from the Nazi party and died in poverty while Scharoun lived in seclusion until the end of the war.

Why was this small house so remarkable as to arouse the wrath of the Nazi leaders? Its form was revolutionary for, by Nazi and indeed by popular German standards, it lacked order and formality. But the apparent informality concealed a very precise plan in which the interior volumes are organized according to the principles of 'organic building'. This principle both Haering and Scharoun had championed on two fronts – against the Nazis and against the *Bauhaus*.

The ground floor of the Baensch house, intended for daytime living, is planned as a single space as in the houses of Mies van der Rohe. But the model for the plan is not the crystal but the leaf, the shell or the flower. If we compare the dining-room of Mies van der Rohe's Tugendhat house with that of the Baensch house, we find that the dining area of the first is defined by a semicircle, as it were a kind of backcloth of fine wood, the

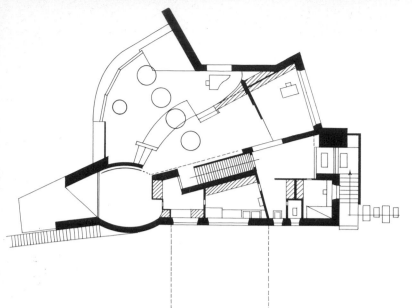

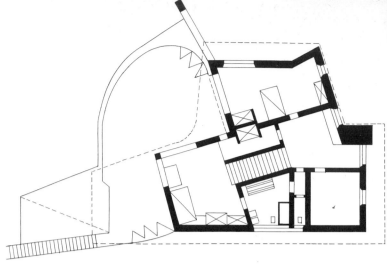

curve of which repeats that of the table; in the Scharoun house, it is the wall itself that curves to repeat the circular movement of the table. The movement is continued, moreover, beyond the table by a curtain which can be used whenever necessary to divide this space from the living-room. But – and this is something that Mies van der Rohe would not have done – the elliptical interior space of the dining-room is further defined by the large window that opens on to the garden. On plan, this may look irritating but in reality, the effect is surprisingly successful because of the sense of space beyond the glass and of continuity between interior and exterior; and when the window is open, the continuity is actual.

The crescent shape of the living-room is a consequence of the house's position facing the Wannsee. From within, therefore, one has a panoramic view of the lake. And since the site is a sloping one, the room is on two levels which again enhance the sense of spectacle from the interior. One side of the living-room encloses a conservatory

Plans by Hans Scharoun for the ground level (left) and the upper floor of the Baensch House in Berlin (1935-36). The dining-room, which can be recognized by its elliptical shape, is the centre of the composition; radiating from it are rooms of different levels; the variations allow even the most distant of them to enjoy the view over the Wannsee.

(Below) The methods of design of Hugo Haering are most clearly demonstrated in this plan of the ground level of a dwelling house: Haering's influence on Scharoun and the concept of organic architecture was very great. Note how in the drawing, the four living-room chairs (left of the patio) are deliberately different from one another (and rather Biedermeier in style). Unlike Mies van der Rohe, Charles Eames and other modern designers, Haering dismissed furniture as unimportant and argued that the character of the interior of the house was determined entirely by the structure of the walls and the spaces they enclosed. (Opposite page, below) Haering's plans defining the 'habitable body' (1945-1948).

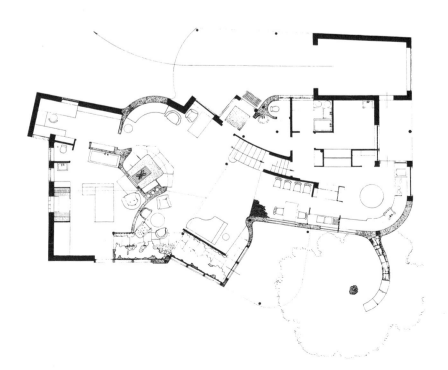

and at one point the curved windows are doubled so that greenery can be brought into the house in winter. The room narrows towards an alcove intended for a grand piano, lit by a round window. The upper part of the room widens into a study. According to its owner, who is deeply attached to it, it is 'fully occupied when there are two people in it and equally pleasant when there are twenty.' This versatility is a tribute to Scharoun's plan.

The upper floor is also rich in ideas. Scharoun conceived the bedroom in the same organic way as the living-room. The windows are so contrived that objects set in them stand out against the sky or the waters of the lake. The curved terrace occupies the roof of the living-room. Doors lead to it from the bedrooms and a flight of steps connects it with the garden.

Scharoun admits that he owes many of his principles to Hugo Haering whom he considered his master. Unfortunately, only a few plans by Haering, who was born in 1882, have survived. After the Second World War he died, exhausted and almost forgotten, in his native town of Biberach. But what does remain shows clearly how great his contribution might have been to German architecture. And while Scharoun's forms are so personal that they cannot be confused with those of any other architect, the inspiration for them is comparable to that of one other architect, Frank Lloyd Wright.

Exterior, facing the lake, and interior of the Baensch House. The furniture shown is not that originally planned by Scharoun but the structure of the house is virtually unaltered.

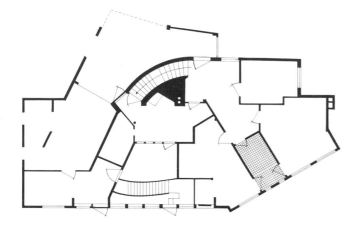

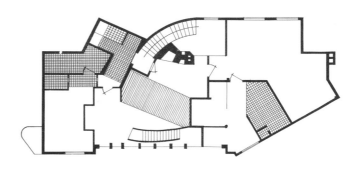

FRANK LLOYD WRIGHT: LIVING IN TOMORROW

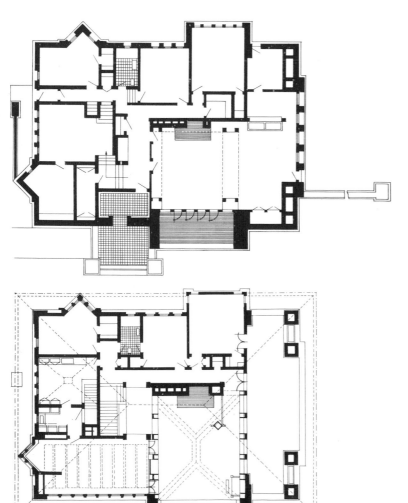

(Above, right) Sketch by Frank Lloyd Wright of the house for E. H. Cheeney at Oak Park, Illinois (1904). Here too, Wright built the Heurtley House (above, view of the front). (Below, from the top) Plans of the ground and upper levels. Here the lines of the building are predominantly horizontal, a feature emphasized by the lines of the roof.

The history of architecture in the first half of the twentieth century is dominated by the brilliant, isolated genius of Frank Lloyd Wright. With Horta and van de Velde, he exerted a powerful influence over the architectural scene in the early years of the century, and the house that is probably his masterpiece, Falling Water at Bear Run, near Pittsburgh, Pennsylvania, set the seal on that golden age of functionalism in the 1930's. His prophetic later work, especially the Guggenheim Museum in New York, has probably still to be accurately appraised. Such intellectual vigour, so great a capacity for hard work, and such good fortune as he enjoyed are rare in the history of art. He made his mark while a young man and as an old or at least elderly one of over 80 was still designing brilliantly.

His principal preoccupation — not shared by all of his contemporaries in architecture — was the house for living in, for the most part, the individual dwelling. On this he focussed his theories on the organization of space. The series of Prairie Houses, which he began in the 1890's and most of which he designed in the years before the First World War, is an uninterrupted sequence of images; each one has something new and urgent to say.

In the Heurtley house of 1905, the form is still compactly rectangular with a large hipped roof. But a radical revolution had taken place in the interior. The ground level was no longer the main floor but was designed for guests and included the children's playroom — a room that opened on to the loggia which created an area of strongly shadowed contrast on the house's façade. The living area of the house was on the upper floor where the rooms centred on a spacious living-room. The

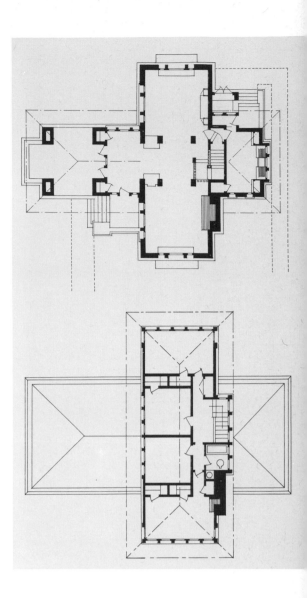

(*Right, from the top*)
*Plans of ground and upper
levels of Martin House,
built by Frank Lloyd
Wright at Buffalo in the
state of New York, in
1906. The horizontal lines
and bold projections fore-
shadow the later prairie
houses. (Left and below)
Wright's sketch and plan
for the Obeler House in
Los Angeles (1941).
Wright used squared pa-
per in an effort to control
his restless imagination.*

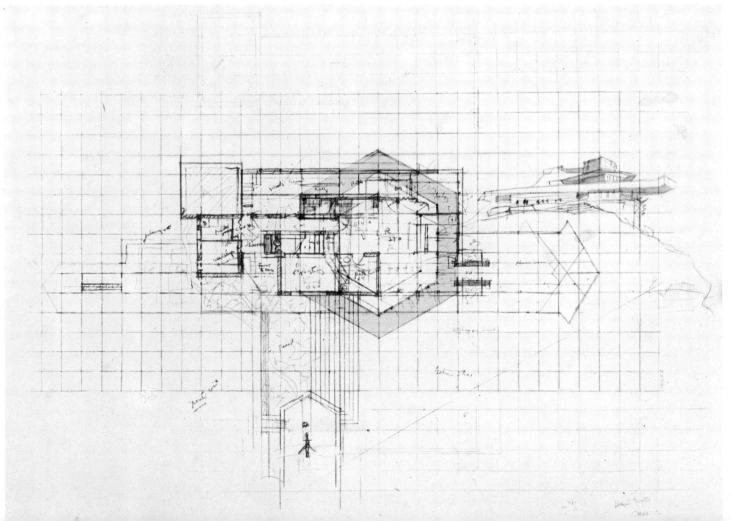

effect was one of a spiral of kitchen-dining-room - living-room - terrace. The hub of this spiral was the staircase which led to the other rooms. As a house it was perfectly functional – and revolutionary. No more walls with holes in them for windows but a solid, clearly visible stone base, above it the virtually continuous line of the windows, and above them the prominently projecting roof. The traditional grammar of the house seemed to have been re-written. Instead of two storeys, arranged traditionally one on top of the other, the walls are concentrated on a single, massive base or on large columns. The windows, and behind them the rooms, are perfectly ordered, each one contributing to the composition as a whole. The house is no longer a box sub-divided into smaller, isolated boxes, each one with a door and window. Wright's interior is broken up and re-composed into a sequence of autonomous volumes each differing from the rest in size, height, lighting and function, the whole united by the wide roof.

In the Roberts House of 1908, Wright extended the small amount of interior space available by the introduction of an element that was later to become typical of his work – as it was of that of Le Corbusier – the 'double volume', that is, the doubling of the height of part of the living-room by its extension into the upper floor. It is hard to believe now that the house was built as long ago as 1908, for its simple, bold lines appeal so strongly to present day taste; only details of its decoration betray that it belongs to the period of *Art Nouveau*.

What is often regarded as the finest of the Prairie Houses was also built in 1908. This was a villa built for Mr Avery Coonley at Riverside, Illinois, with garages, stables, a gardener's cottage, an Italian garden, a swimming pool, courtyards and loggias; it formed part, that is, of a large and impressive complex of buildings. As in a Renaissance palace, the residential part of the house is on the upper floor, the *piano nobile*. Only the large living-room for the children and some secondary service rooms opened on to the terrace and swimming-pool. Bedrooms, dining-room, kitchen, and the enormous living-room were all on the first floor. Two symmetrical staircases, facing each other and lit from above by lamps the shape of which reflected that of the roof, led to the living-room which projected over the swimming-pool. The lamps focussed attention on the glowing colour of the ceiling. After half a century, this living-room has not dated; it is still perfectly preserved and used, and remains delightful. The wide fireplace, the wall surfaces of visible brick and fabric-covered panels, the very low ceiling (only six feet high) which gains height in the centre of the room, the beams of this ceiling, the simple furniture of benches and wide sofas – all these help to make this house incomparably beautiful and comfortable; it was

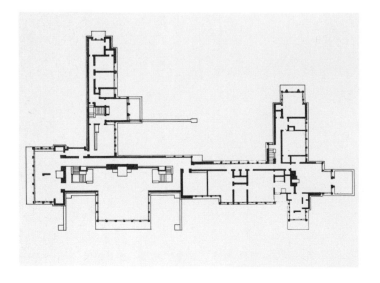

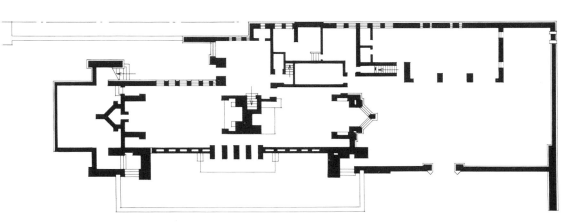

Of his Prairie Houses, the Robie house is probably Wright's greatest stylistic achievement. After a brief flirtation with functionalism, Wright designed this 'informal' organism in which an essential part of his plan is the change in level of the ground and upper floors (left and below).

In the Robie House, Wright achieved absolute spatial continuity and in his plans for it he reached out to integrate with and conquer the house's setting. The uninterrupted spread of the windows, the predominantly horizontal lines, the use of unadorned brick, all these help to relate the house to its surroundings.

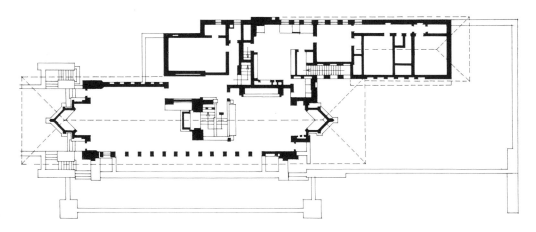

matched, and possibly surpassed, only many years later in the house known as Falling Water.

The Robie house in Chicago is better known than that built for Mr. Coonley but its elongated interior does not show Wright at his best. The exterior is, nevertheless, remarkable. The long stretches of brick, the projections that overshadow the continuous row of windows, the treatment of the bricks themselves – all this adds up to a house of unusual sophistication which requires study in the same way as any other of the key works in modern art as, for example, Picasso's *Demoiselles d'Avignon* which was painted at roughly the same time. When, for a number of reasons, it became

uninhabited, it was decided to restore and preserve it; the decision was implemented, however, only after a fierce battle with speculative builders who planned to demolish it and built a modern multi-storeyed building on the site.

From Wright's second period, the best known and perhaps the most beautiful house is Falling Water, built from 1935 to 1939 for a Mr. Kaufmann of Pittsburgh. The audacity of its structural concept – a series of terraces superimposed one on the other, projecting over a waterfall – is not, as it might have been in less gifted hands, pointless exhibitionism but is part of a carefully and subtly composed whole. In the interior, Wright aimed not merely

An important landmark in the history of American architecture is Falling Water, the house built at Bear Run in Pennsylvania in 1937 for Mr. Kaufmann, owner of a Pittsburgh department store. In the field of domestic architecture, it is probably Wright's most vigorously imaginative work. As one admirer acutely observed, he takes advantage of atavistic traits in American character to present a temple dedicated to nature, evoked by the wood, the spur of rock on which the building stands, the waterfall beneath it, the rocks that are part of the sitting-room floor, the central fireplace and the massive supports that recall the bridge of a ship.

In the context of Wright's work, the Kaufmann house is a remarkably simple one. The plan (left), which takes advantage of the changes in the level of the site, incorporates a few vertical features (walls and the stove) opposed by three horizontal elements (see section above), the galleries that appear to balance on the water flowing beneath them. The house is no longer a box: its walls are dissolved in glass and the external world, once held outside the walls, becomes a part of the house.

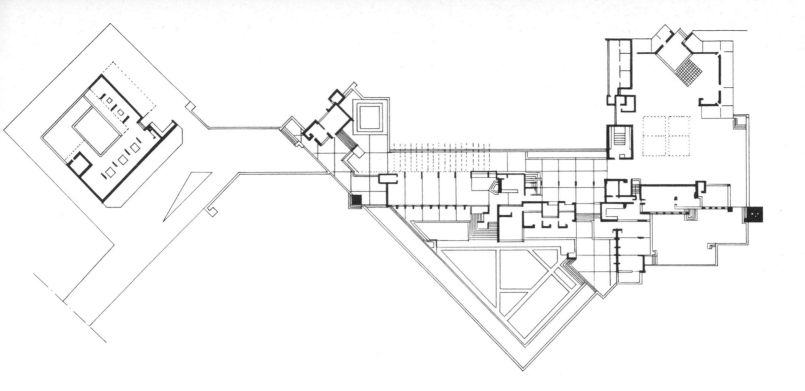

at complete fluidity but at complete continuity between it and the environment of the house, at a blending of indoors and out. The rooms are arranged after the conventional fashion of most ordinary European or American villas; kitchen, dining-room and living-room on ground floor level, service rooms at the back, bedrooms on the first floor, a separate guest wing. It is a mistake to imagine that masterpieces are inevitably composed of entirely novel concepts. In architecture they may be created by the imaginative use of conventional spaces and volumes. In a house like Falling Water, Wright brought such imagination to bear on the relationship between the house and its surroundings and on their integration in the 'organic architecture' he championed, as a contrast to the classical concept of a building independent of and indeed opposed to nature.

For obvious reasons, it was on the rare occasions when he built for himself that Wright enjoyed the greatest degree of freedom. Taliesin West, his winter home in the Arizona desert, is probably the building in which his treatment of the ordinary elements of a house – floors, walls, doors, windows, roof and furniture – is most revolutionary. Built in 1938, the great stone walls are continuous without a break. The house is lit by the translucent ceiling spaces between the beams of the roof; seen from the outside, each beam appears as a rib with a thin surface covering. The floor in the living area may be raised or lowered according to the function of each part of it. One of the architect's happiest inspirations is the large, studio-music room. A house on a desert site such as this is difficult to maintain and each year, when it is re-occupied, it has to be dug out of the sand again, beams renewed, lights replaced and parasitic vegetation destroyed. But there is compensation in the pleasure of living in a house so appropriate to its surroundings.

Taliesin West in Paradise Valley near Phoenix, Arizona. Plan (above) and view from the pool. This was the winter headquarters of the foundation Wright directed. He began building it in 1938 and, when he died twenty years later, it was still incomplete. The complex consists of sloping terraces, rocky parapets, concrete ramparts, the whole being finished by a roof composed of baulks of timber and canvas through which light filters. Desert rocks are embedded in the concrete of the ramps. Natural and primitive elements are exploited to the full to give the impression of an oasis, a shelter 'on the edge of the world'.

Wright's absorption in the problem of the individual dwelling was part of his concern for town planning and the problems of accommodating people in an urban society. His own ideal was his Utopian Broadacre City which was neither town nor country and allowed two and a half acres of land to each resident. But he examined too the vertical city and tried to introduce to skyscrapers something of the volumetric freedom he had achieved in individual houses. The St. Mark's Towers project that he designed for New York in 1929 revolutionized what was then the basic concept of the skyscraper. The load of the building was to be carried by a central cruciform structure which would support the four apartment blocks that radiated from it. Each apartment was a duplex, that is, on two floors. The upper storey, it was intended, should be narrower than the lower so that the rest area could look down on the living area. This meant an alternation of projecting storeys. Wright designed a variation of this building in which he connected the wings to create what looks like a vast faceted stone, with the contrasts and combinations of inner and outer space typical of his work.

Because of the Depression, these fascinating plans failed to materialize but Wright, who was attached to them, put them forward again, in modified form, in what is now considered the masterpiece of his mature years, the Price Tower at Bartlesville in Oklahoma. The cruciform structure is there but the wings or arms are divided not into four duplex apartments but into six offices and one duplex apartment. Only one of the four arms is occupied by apartments. Part of the upper storey is recessed from the lower storey so that, as usual, there is a room with a view. But part projects beyond it, thus creating a surprising plastic effect. The new tower is better than the earlier plan since, unrestricted by the double symmetry of the 1929 project, each facet of it enjoys a variety of perspectives that from every point of view is new and extraordinarily pleasing both to the man in it and the man in the street below. Wright rejected the functional theory of skyscrapers which permitted a certain modular element to be repeated an infinite number of times. He recognized the logic of the idea but he changed the proportions. His tower on its wide base develops regularly with a clearly defined and well understood rhythm, and culminates not in a cleanly chopped top but in a gradual reduction of the storeys and a final inventive flourish which finishes off the building as conclusively as does the lantern on Brunelleschi's dome in Florence.

Other works by Wright are more dramatic.

Wright planned a new type of skyscraper in 1929 in his St. Mark's Towers project for New York. It was never built but when he was eighty he succeeded in building the splendid eighteen-storey tower block of offices and apartments (above) in the small town of Bartlesville, Oklahoma, for the B.C. Price company. Each group of offices and apartments (see plan below) is on two storeys, thus proving that it is possible to build a skyscraper without inhibition, that is, without sacrificing the freedom associated with the single-family dwelling.

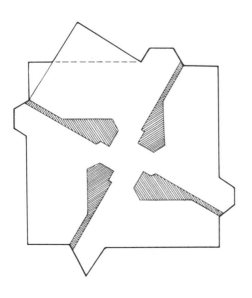

more poetic, more organically integrated into the landscape but the Price Tower is, with the Guggenheim museum (completed after his death in 1959), his most demanding and difficult work and the one in which he most eloquently preached technical and structural revolution. It recalls the last work of a great artist, for nothing seems more miraculous than that a man of genius should continue, in his old age, still to produce work so brilliant that it astounds his admirers and even his critics. Wright's architecture has its roots in that – by now – almost legendary age in America when only one American in eleven lived in a city. At the same time, however, he looked not backwards but forwards to the society of the future for which he designed buildings that would be comprehensible in tomorrow's world. His opposition to functionalism as he understood it and to the cities of the machine age in which millions were compelled to live, and his constant fight to recover in architecture what had been lost in the mushroom growth of the cities, were not the outcome of nostalgia for the past but a realization of the necessity for the integration of men and women with their environment, and of the growing dangers inherent in their alienation from it.

Design for the Cooke House in Norfolk, Virginia, about 1948. During the Second World War, Wright affirmed that the circle rather than the square or the polygon is the most natural form with which to achieve harmony with the landscape. As a result, the fulcrum of the composition of the Cooke House plan is not the large internal fireplace, but the swimming-pool, from the centre of which radiate the lines that define the spaces occupied by the living-room and dining-room. The night area, on the right, is set at an angle but all its angles are within the range of 120 deg. to 60 deg. and eschew the right angles and intersections that Wright considered unnatural.

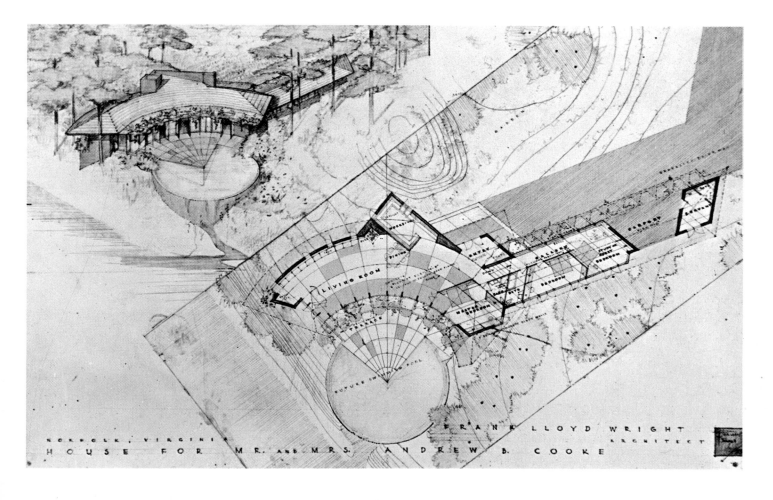

POST-WAR DESIGN
IN THE HOME

The American troops who arrived in Europe at the end of the Second World War brought with them no white telephones, swimming-pools and twelve-cylinder Packards. Instead, they brought field telephones, rubber dinghies, jeeps and folding aluminium chairs, strictly practical objects, well-made, simply designed, durable, with their form dictated by their function. Designed by whom? Mostly Germans: designers influenced by the tenets of the *Bauhaus*, by, in particular, Gropius and Breuer. These two, with a number of other German architects, left the Fatherland in the 1930's for, in the first place, England, where they worked for a number of years. Then they moved on to the United States. The objects they had helped to design returned to Europe before them.

These commodities, common enough in the United States, were not a great success there. They were associated with war and in the post-war years in America there was an understandable urge to forget about war. Design went through a period of doldrums. But in Europe it improved.

In the years of recovery from war, functionalism became not a matter of choice but a necessity and one turned to good advantage. Industrial design, foreshadowed in the work of Peter Behrens and the Bauhaus, made a lasting impact on the home. The architect no longer designed furniture himself but chose the best pieces available on the market and composed his rooms with them – and pieces of this quality were now available. Furniture and furnishings influenced by such artists as Saarinen, Wirkkala or Jacobsen came on to the market to be purchased eventually by those who did not always appreciate their distinguished ancestry.

Mass produced furniture has survived to become respectable and, indeed, certain pieces have been established as classics. The influence of motor car design may have contributed to this acceptance. The man with several thousand pounds to spare for a motor car is more likely to spend it on a prestigious Jaguar or Maserati than on a custom-built car that would become unfashionable in a comparatively short time. Much the same happens with mass produced furniture. The range of excellent designs available includes relatively cheap versions of Scandinavian and other designs and, at the upper end of the price scale, the armchairs of Mies van der Rohe, Charles Eames and Le Corbusier which are the Rolls-Royces of the furniture world.

The furniture designed by Marcel Breuer in 1925 is still being mass produced with no change of form and for this it has been bitterly criticized. Its misuse, to which reference has already been made, is now compounded by its acquisition of almost antique status. Present-day versions of it are bought as examples of the furniture of a previous generation but, at the same time, the Breuer chairs being made today are absolutely identical to the prototypes and are not replicas; they are the same chairs but they are being made 30 and more years after their design first appeared. If they are regarded as fake antiques, the fault lies not in them but in those who so regard them. If the Piazza dell'Annunziata in Florence is now a car-park, we can hardly blame Brunelleschi; and if the Delft plate which was made to hold a joint of beef is hung on the wall as an ornament, this means that its beauty has got the better of its function.

In his house at Santa Monica, California, Charles Eames demonstrated that the living area can be acceptably furnished with mass produced objects. For the exterior of the house, he used pre-fabricated units of the kind usually used in industrial building. The interiors he equipped with well-designed, factory-made products. The operation was entirely successful; whether it would have been equally successful for a less talented householder is doubtful.

CHARLES EAMES: BLUE-PRINT FOR COMFORT

Charles Eames, born in St. Louis, Missouri, in 1907, is remarkable among the post-war generation of American architects in that his career has been given to industrial and furniture design. In an age of specialization he has declined to specialize although his fame is popularly derived from his designs in a particular field. In his curiosity and wide range of interests, he resembles such artists as the Italian graphic artist Bruno Munari or the Swiss Hans Erni. He has worked on typographical design, on animated cartoons about architecture and its use of space, and on new games and books for children. These projects compete with furniture design for his attention. He has somehow managed to escape the often intolerable pressures placed on many of his contemporaries by the voracious demand of the American market for new designs, new models. Eames has worked and continues to work at his own pace and on his own. From this independent approach have come some of the twentieth century's finest designs. His armchair of wood and leather, with its accompanying footstool, versatile adaptation of the chaise-longue, is now more than 15 years old. It has attracted the compliment of dozens of imitations which lack, however, its elegance and its comfort. Its curving outlines place it unmistakeably in the fifties when cars, radios, refrigerators, electric razors, all the impedimenta of mod-

Charles Eames' armchair, designed in 1956. The easy chair is now a classic which, despite its still high price, has sold in thousands. In it, the technique of the aircraft manufacturer is combined with that of the constructor of the dentist's chair, in the curving of the wooden (in this case rosewood) backing and the use of articulated joints. It is a perfectly functional design; the whole body is enabled to relax with the help of the headrest, sloping back, padded seat and stool.

The technique whereby Charles Eames' metal chairs, designed in 1951, are made is an advanced one and the electrically soldered steel wires and rods of the skeleton are strong as well as elastic. The seat and back, in whatever material used, are easy to insert. The structure, seen here from the side, has proved versatile within the two basic types possible (they differ in distance from the ground, the one being eleven inches, the other sixteen).

ern living curved. And yet it remains dateless, as only an example of brilliant design can; as are, for instance, the Olivetti Lettera 22 typewriter, regarded as one of the ten best pieces of industrial design in the last quarter of a century, and the Volkswagen 1200. These, like an Eames chair, have a completeness of form in which every detail is in harmony with the whole and is derived from a precise functional requirement. A sense of surprise, even shock, that any object perfectly designed for its purpose can give when its absolute rightness is revealed, attaches to the Eames chair. In the same way, the Barcelona chair designed by Mies van der Rohe was perfectly suited to the demands made of it, which were that it should provide a brief resting place during the rigours of an international exhibition; to criticize it for not being an easy chair is to misread its function.

In his 1948 design for a curved plywood chair (later made in plastic) with supports made not of tubing but of iron rods, Eames reverted to *Bauhaus* principles of a reduction to essentials. The chair was seen merely as a support which would raise the user above the level of the floor, but by minimal means. In his armchair, Eames reversed the process. He began with the image before him of a position of complete relaxation — feet off the ground, arms supported at a comfortable level, back supported and support, and to some extent shelter, for the head; hence the padded seat and adaptable back, the curving head-piece, and the stool. His armchair settled round the sitter, adapted itself to him. It looks, as has on occasion been pointed out

with a tinge of apprehension, like a dentist's chair; which is fair enough since the articulated joints which link the parts of the chair have been taken from barbers' and dentists' chairs with their adjustable headrests. What Eames has done is simplify them to his own elegant style.

One of Eames' rare buildings is his own home at Santa Monica, California, built in 1949. For it he used cheap, pre-fabricated elements of the kind used for factory building. The details are different but the overall result is much the same as that achieved by Philip Johnson or Mies van der Rohe in their houses — at considerably less cost. The austerity of the interior spaces is modified by the furniture, and by lamps, flowers, statues and rugs. The interior does not possess, indeed, the grandeur or the splendid perspectives of the Johnson or Mies houses but it does demonstrate very clearly a talent for living.

What Eames seems to say through the medium of his house is that American society cannot afford the custom-built house (and if American society cannot afford it, what society can?). If people are to be housed at reasonable cost and in houses that achieve at least a minimum aesthetic standard, then the help must be enlisted of industrial designers who can, at a reasonable price, provide the artistic excellence which it is often hard to find in architecture. In our *admass* civilization, moreover, we have probably lost the capacity to look at art purely as art or architecture as architecture; our appreciation is often filtered through design, good design, that is, of the type that Charles Eames has given us.

WRIGHT
VERSUS
MASS-PRODUCTION

Under the influence of the *Bauhaus* and its architects, there was a move, in the years after the First World War on the part of architects, to plan interiors which could exist as designs independent of the furniture placed in them, most of which was mass produced. Throughout the whole of his long life, Wright fought this idea. In his organic architecture, the form of the house's interior spaces grew out of the uses made of them and, within these spaces, furniture played an important part and was inseparable from them. His benches and beds and tables are often carved out of the building itself or fitted into its structure. The result is, of course, that moveable furniture is reduced to a minimum.

In Wright's best work, this integration works splendidly but the principle is too individual to be universally applicable. It demands a close contact between client and architect that is not always possible; which brings us back, indeed, to the problems of the expensive custom-built house. Mass production, which calls for economic conformity, militates against the integration advocated by Wright and his followers in organic architecture.

Attempts have been made, admittedly, to reconcile mass production with Wright's ideas. In 1964, the Italian architect, Leonardo Ricci, held an exhibition in Florence in which he showed furniture that was a logical extension of Wright's concepts in, however, a very personal way. The extraordinarily shaped furniture was alleged to be capable of being produced in quantity but the likelihood of sufficient people being found willing to buy it at any price seemed small. Fantasies involving a mixture of science fiction and a reversion to cave dwelling are, on the whole, unpopular.

Relations are tenuous between the architect and the majority of the public who are, in the last analysis, their clients. Architects continue to build single, 'one-off' houses for individual clients but the place of these in architectural history has diminished greatly in importance since the period of the Palladian mansion or even the Victorian folly. Whether it is always realized or not, architecture is now the business of everyone.

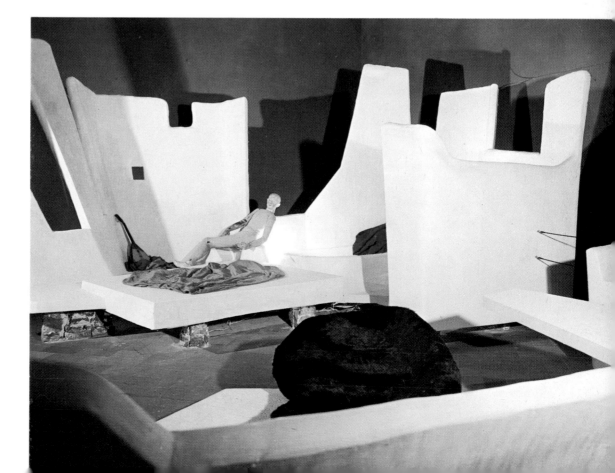

Proposal for a living area for two people by Leonardo Ricci (1965). Its object was to abolish separation of function among the rooms of the house and the designer carried his theory to the point of abolishing the special area reserved for kitchen and bathroom. This reaction against bourgeois standard — and return to primitive architecture — was shown at Expo '67 in Montreal where, unfortunately, it was interpreted as an example of low living standards in the south of Italy.

ITALY REVIVES ART NOUVEAU

Art Nouveau, as mentioned before in this volume, flourished in Britain, Belgium, France, to some extent in Germany, and, if we include Gaudí, Spain, but not to any noticeable degree in Italy. During the late 1950's, however, a new *Art Nouveau* style appeared in Italy which drew down upon itself the disapproval of critics in England and America. It developed first in Turin among architects who were pupils of Carlo Mollino, and these were followed by architects in Milan centred around Ernesto Rogers and the review *Casabella* which, fully realizing the irony of the situation, took up *Art Nouveau* at the point where it had disappeared from fashion.

There were a number of reasons for this new movement. The middle classes had taken at last to functionalism but functionalism of a debased type. The name *Swedish* was attached to the style in which craftsmen accustomed to local styles and ornate forms of decoration turned out a vaguely Scandinavian type of furniture. For the rest, the designs of Franco Albini and Paul Nelson were imitated, poorly, by the score. At the same time, designers seemed to be temporarily defeated by the problem of improving popular taste. Further up the social scale, the clients of the designers, the pace-setters, feeling that popular taste was overtaking them, demanded not only something different but something exclusive to them as well. And *New Art Nouveau* came along at the right time. Objects planned almost as a joke by a group of intelligent young men, under the influence of nostalgia for a past in the advantages of which they had a touching faith, be-

came fashionable, especially in the industrial north of Italy. This nostalgia for *Art Nouveau* aroused the hostility of critics outside Italy who saw in it not a cultural revival but a wilful anachronism. But the critics overlooked the fact that, unlike the people of France, Germany, Belgium and England, Italians had been able to enjoy the age of Aubrey Beardsley and the *Yellow Book* at one remove. Given the means to do so, they were determined to enjoy some of the pleasures that the rest of Europe had savoured and discarded – admittedly, half a century late.

Like all revivals, *New Art Nouveau* was short-lived. Within five years it was all over. But only elderly architects who had been innoculated against *Art Nouveau* when they were boys resisted its fascination. One of these was the architect Giovanni Michelucci who, while the younger men were wallowing in *Art Nouveau,* was turning traditional forms to use in his furniture designs. A craftsman at heart, one of his finest designs is for a sideboard that is a twentieth century version of the peasant kneading trough. The top lifts up; below is, in theory, the space for the bread dough while it is rising. Functionally it is an anachronism but aesthetically it is pleasing.

A more recent trend in interior decoration, and one to which Le Corbusier gave his approval, is the introduction of antiques or, at least, old furniture into a modern, functional environment. This has two obvious advantages. Older furniture modifies the often daunting austerity of the modern house.

343

At the same time, it gives it a place in the modern home without compelling the owner to indulge in period pastiche. Houses totally in period, whether the period be modern or historic, can easily resemble museums. But the addition of an antique chest or chair or mirror can warm a composition of glass, steel, and concrete.

There is also, of course, the taste that combines functionalism with surrealism, as flat-irons are turned into lamps, boots into umbrella stands, pistols into cigarette lighters, corner-cupboards into radiograms and, the worst indignity of all, antique chests and book-cases into the housings of television sets. But the eighteenth century armchair which is comfortable and useful in itself can safely be introduced to the company of one by Charles Eames. Good designs are tolerant of one another whatever their respective ages and conditions. Bad design shows up badly in their company.

Given sure and confident taste, it is possible to furnish a modern house with the furniture of other periods without creating either a pastiche, a museum or a superior antique shop. This drawing by the architect, Mongardino (about 1950), shows how easy it would be, however, to teeter over into a decorative joke: he has designed here an eighteenth century hôtel particulier in a small top-storey flat (with terrace) in a modern block.

(Opposite page) Living-room-study on two levels designed by the architect Pierluigi Spadolini at the Florence exhibition of antiques in the modern house (1962). The antique pieces shown are seen to advantage in uncluttered surroundings and against mainly plain walls: the exception is the wall on the right which consists of a photographic reproduction of a fifteenth century plaster wall in the Villa Tornabuoni in Florence.

In the ultra-modern environment of this flat in the Morumbi Gardens at São Paulo (opposite page) designed by Lina Bo for an art-historian in 1950, things ancient and modern have been mixed with a steady and confident hand. One group (right) contains this fifteenth century chest, and the antique sculpture and box on top of it, set against the wide, metal-framed window.

Detail of The Annunciation *by Carlo Crivelli (1486: London, National Gallery).
It demonstrates vividly how far paintings can help the architectural
historian in their record of structural features, decoration, furnishing and
social customs involving, for example, the keeping of
animals or birds in the house and the fondness for flowers and plants.*

ETTORE CAMESASCA

ANATOMY OF THE HOUSE

So far, we have tried to give an idea of the history of the ordinary house. We have dealt with its design, its structure, its surroundings, its furniture and furnishings, its importance in society, and the changes that have marked its development from the rough shelter of branches to Frank Lloyd Wright's Taliesin West. We have touched too, inevitably, on the lives of the people who have lived in all these houses.

But since our principal concern has been the house as a building, some aspects of its importance to the way of life of its inhabitants have been sketchily treated and, in this final part of the book, we shall make good some of these omissions. In particular we shall examine the ways in which people have used the house, how they have made it serve them, what they have demanded as a means of display or as a refuge. Then we shall look at particular features of the house and their changing history – the kitchen and its equipment, the bedrooms and their appurtenances, bathrooms, the accommodation within the house for works of art, ornaments and other such possessions, the lodging of servants, and certain other aspects of living in a home.

As is the case with the history of the house as a building, some of these subjects are far from fully recorded. But even within such limitations, a number of the contributions have something new to say about the history of the house.

'Furniture is too closely connected with the decoration of the interior for the architect not to be involved in it. If the spirit of the house's decoration is divorced from the building and out of harmony with it, all sorts of nonsense will come of it; it will not just pervert the essential forms of the building but make them disappear altogether'. Thus wrote

Pierre Fontaine and Charles Percier, the theorists of the neo-classical house of the early nineteenth century. 'Mirrors hung up for no reason, tapestries chosen haphazardly', they went on, 'will create clutter where there ought to be space and leave space where something ought to fill it. In buildings, the construction is like the skeleton of the human form; it should be beautified but not completely hidden. The building establishes the kind of decoration that should be used, allowing for place and climate and type. If the decoration is not planned at the same time as the building, if the building's form is not related to its ornament, in others words, if two conflicting interests are involved in the erection of the building, then whatever its size and importance, it will have no spiritual value.' Messieurs Fontaine and Percier are still worth listening to. But do their theories still hold good? Are there other possibilities?

Our earliest ancestors do not contribute much to the argument. In the earliest houses, the interior was dictated by the form of the exterior. The dwellings of hunters and nomads tell us very little more than that mats and skins were used as carpets and that they possessed curtains and hangings. The houses of primitive peoples in Africa and Asia have simple exteriors and, sometimes, interior partitions. More advanced cultures in, say, South and Central America may build in stone and brick but the interiors are still of little importance.

A great deal has been said and written about primitive sensitivity to colour, and it has usually been concluded that primitive cultures were and are interested in intensity rather than quality and that refinement of this taste took place gradually. Much of what we know is based on the famous palaeolithic cave paintings of France and Spain.

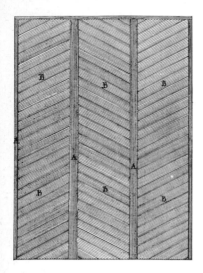
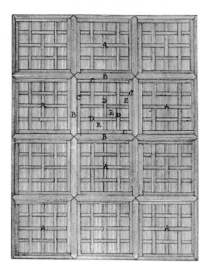

These lead us to suppose that red and black must have been the dominant colours, where colour was used, in the earliest huts, to be followed later by yellow, brown and white. In much later but still fairly primitive cultures such as that of the Haida in British Columbia, red continues to preponderate in the often stylized motifs used; and if in some of these cultures the range of colours available is narrow, they are used often with a delightful, self-confident elegance.

In ancient Iraq, painting was an important part of interior decoration and was used to imitate architectural features such as colonnades as well as to depict animals – very lively lions, bulls and goats –and floral motifs. Other means of decoration were used too. Buildings had coffered ceilings of carved cedarwood, inlaid with other woods or with ivory, with bosses of bronze or rosewood with lotus-flower motifs. Wide porticos enclosed the entrances. It may be that in the Hittite houses of Hattusas (modern Boghazköy) skins, mats and fabrics were already used to divide the interior of the house.

It is not clear whether these refinements were developed in this part of Asia or whether they were introduced from elsewhere, possibly from further east. Certainly, the rich Persian dwellings of antiquity had coffered ceilings, deeply carved and inlaid, often with Indian ivory, painted, and with bronze rosettes. Painted walls were probably rare but fabrics there were, ablaze with colour and rich in fantastic designs, hanging before the doors and the portico and spread on the floors to serve – with padding – as beds. The brilliant light and air and the clear, translucent skies fostered in this corner of the Eastern Mediterranean world a love of colour. One result was exquisitely enamelled bricks and tiles; at Khorsabad they were mostly yellow or blue; in Nimrud too they were yellow and

blue of an extraordinarily deep hue, and red, black and white. In Persian enamels blue and turquoise were combined and white and orange used in contrast; tiles of these colours were particularly used on the lower parts of walls; above them, bands of linear or geometric decoration mingled with processions of men and beasts.

The results of ancient interior decoration may have been, in many cases, more impressive than attractive. Certain periods in the history of ancient Egypt – the reign of the heretic Akhenaton is one – may have produced more pleasing effects indoors, albeit within a restricted society. In the Old Kingdom, however, the rich houses along the Nile had ceilings of valuable woods, both local and imported, and murals with abstract and later floral designs. Sometimes enamelled bricks or tiles were used on the walls but more often they were hung with fabrics; curtains too hung between the pillars of the porticos facing the garden. Other materials, heavily trimmed and either embroidered or printed, served as door curtains or as upholsteries. The colours used were for the most part red, yellow, black and white. The interiors of Cretan houses of antiquity, not so far from the mouth of the Nile, were similar.

The houses of Mycenae were organized differently. Their interior divisions gave furniture, hangings and the decoration of walls and floors a new importance. Four columns were set about the fireplace thereby focussing attention on the hearth as the real centre of the house, a concept that was to have a very long life.

The cities submerged by the lava of Vesuvius tell us something of Hellenistic Greece. In Herculaneum the pattern of the Mycenean house was retained while moveable screens and partitions created secondary rooms. Linear and geometric designs, especially in mosaic, decorated the floors. Such fur-

(Opposite page, from left)
Details of a plate in the
Encyclopédie (1771-1777)
by Diderot and
D'Alembert, dedicated
to the menuisier
en bâtimens: wooden floor
in point d'Hongrie
which is still quite
common in Europe, and
parquet carré,
a more elaborate design.

Detail of a wall-painting
from the vault of a tomb
at Deir el-Medinah,
west of Thebes (Turin,
Egyptian Museum).
The decoration, which
belongs to the period
of the eighteenth dynasty
(that is, about 1500
B.C.) may be an imitation
of the tapestries that
were fashionable during
the New Empire in Egypt.

niture as there was stood against the walls which were decorated with scenes from everyday life and landscapes.

Greek architecture and sculpture as we see them today are often a wan reflection of ancient Greek taste which loved colour and used it boldly, often to differentiate between various architectural elements. The Romans were no less enthusiastic about their bright reds and yellows and blues; they also used a reddish purple of which the secret has since been lost. The expansion of the empire into the east and increasing contact with the countries of the eastern Mediterranean greatly influenced not only their use of colour but other aspects of the in-

House of the family of Prince Gagarin in Moscow, designed by J. Beauvais, known as Bova, in 1817: detail of the drawing-room ceiling.

(Left) Haarlem, No. 106 Spaarne: drawing of eighteenth century decoration in the corridor.

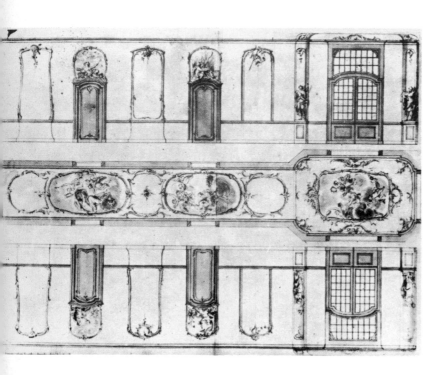

terior of the house. They adopted mosaics – via Greece from Egypt – and used them with a skill which by the period of the Byzantine Empire amounted to brilliance. And from the Levant they imported hangings and carpets the cost of which seriously affected the Roman balance of payments. Furniture increased in quantity and improved in quality; rooms, now furnished, began to look smaller.

The eastern Roman Empire with its capital at Byzantium, later Constantinople, maintained the flow of luxury goods from the east; the trade in silks and damasks, carried along the ancient silk road from China, grew in importance. The effect on the domestic interior of this trade with the east can for the most part only be surmised – though with a fair degree of certainty. The riches of Byzantium were, however, one of the formative influences on the art of the Middle Ages.

Of the most ancient Chinese dwellings we know no more than we do of the most ancient European dwellings. If later records and examples are any guide, it is probable that astrology and geomancy played some part in their siting and construction. But in historical times the houses of the Far East, like those of the west, consisted of a number of rooms each with a well-defined function; as in the west, these functions probably developed gradually as the needs of the house's inhabitants changed over the centuries. The house was divided, basically, into two parts – public or reception rooms, and the rooms reserved for the family – and the division is maintained today in the Moslem world where the *harem* is divided from the *selamlik*. In the houses of the wealthy, there was and still is a servants' quarter.

In the traditional Chinese house, the principal room was the *ta-t'ing*, or reception room, dominated by the four pillars which supported the roof. Furnishings and decorations were simple and unobtrusive. On the end wall a scroll might be hung on which might be painted a landscape; before it stood two tables, one large, one small, 'the table of the eight ancestors'. Other tables and chairs stood against the other walls. The large *ta-t'ing* might be divided by light wooden screens or trellises supported by slender pillars and connected by elegantly arched doorways. The same kind of arrangement was applied to the library (the *shu-chai*) and the most important room in the house, the ancestors' room (the *t'ang-fu*). The decorative quality of the screens and trellises which divided the rooms, the imaginative use of ornament within these smaller spaces, and the simple but adaptable furniture, must have created very pleasing interiors; the pleasure was doubtless enhanced by the silken glow of the carpets.

As in China, the traditional house in Japan altered little for about two thousand years. The houses shown in paintings of the fifth century A. D. could be mistaken for modern houses of a traditional type. Their character, simple, strong, delicate, is the same; so too is their respect for nature, their harmony with their environment, their aim, indeed, to reduce to a minimum the barriers between inside and outside. And so we have, basically, a large single room divided not by permanent walls but by a series of translucent screens. The inside world is divided from the outside by another set of such screens. A verandah surrounds three sides of the house with its undecorated beams and supports. The appearance of the houses changes then, with the changes in the natural world outside it, and with the wishes of the owner. The colours used are the natural ones of nut brown, olive grey, a greyish grass green and a pale clay colour. The visible structure creates part of the total aesthetic effect and the rectangular shapes are reflected in the floor mats (*tatami*). The light that filters in is more than a means of illumination – a positive ingredient in the house's construction. Despite the appearance of timelessness, it was not until the Ashikaga period (1392-1568) that the Japanese house acquired its definitive form; then a section of the outside walls was taken up by the asymmetrical arrangement of shelves on which valuable objects were displayed. Earlier, from the Heian period onwards (794-1188), paintings had been hung in the empty spaces between the beams or painted there; the most popular subjects were landscapes, flowers and birds.

In India and in the Moslem world, climate and a partly nomadic way of life strengthened the links between interior and exterior. In permanent settlements, in towns and cities, there was a tendency to stay indoors in winter and in the height of the summer's heat. But courtyard and garden were still an integral part of the house into which furniture was carried as it was needed. The amount of light admitted to the house was strictly controlled, for light meant heat in the long summer. Windows and balconies, whether large or small, were screened by intricately carved screens of wood or stone; pierced bricks were also used. Panes of glass were used, especially in the windows of the public rooms, but these too were screened by wooden panels. The colonnades that separated the interior from the outside effectively filtered the sun's rays. The light that was permitted to enter struck upon interiors decorated with colourful tiles, mosaics, or inlays of coloured stones, sometimes semi-precious stones and at a certain period, mirror glass. When, during the eighteenth century it became possible to make mirror glass in large sections, it was used to cover entire walls. To break the lines of rooms, niches were often constructed in the walls, creating there a contrast between the light of the central part of the room and the shade of the alcoves. The ceilings of the principal rooms in the house were often domed, which was useful in a practical sense as a means of circulating air, and aesthetically pleasing. Internal galleries, with screens, allowed the inhabitants of the *harem* to watch the feasts and celebrations held in the room below. Furniture was minimal. Carpets or tiles covered the floors. Curtains usually

(Left) Amsterdam, No. 475 Herengracht: detail of the elaborate plaster ornament, eighteenth century in date.
(Above) The Hague, No. 15 Prinsengracht: plasterwork, slightly earlier in date (1740) but no less elaborate.

screened doorways: as a rule only the front entrance was fitted with a strong door. The house, it will be detected, was highly functional in that it was entirely appropriate to the demands made of it.

The rich Moslem houses of the east were celebrated for centuries in the west for the taste, skill and beauty of their decoration. Since, however, exactly defined religious rules forbade the artists of Islam to portray any living creature, their art was one of abstract design, of highly stylized paintings and carvings of plants, trees and calligraphy. When Mehmet II, conqueror of Constantinople, wished for paintings to decorate his palace, in particular paintings of historical episodes incorporating human figures, he invited the Venetian, Gentile Bellini, to his recently acquired capital in 1479. Bellini's stay there was not particularly comfortable but from it we have his splendid portait of Mehmet. Moslem artists meanwhile were restricted, save, on occasion, in paintings for the baths and the *harem*, to variations on the endlessly flowing, convoluted line which they handled with such skill, to stylized treatments of flowers and fruits, and to intricate calli-

Detail from Lady at the Spinet *by Jan Vermeer (c. 1670: London, National Gallery); here we have a glimpse of the marble floor with its chequerboard pattern, and the skirting of blue and white Delft tiles, each with a different design (ship, hunter, etc.).*

graphic motifs into which they wove verses from the Koran. They worked with tiles – the factories at Iznik, the ancient Nicea, reached their apogee in the sixteenth century – in mosaic, and then on plaster, white until the eighteenth century, later coloured and gilt. In the west, from the early Middle Ages onwards, the blind arches, the fantastic arabesques, the floral and calligraphic ornament, the domes, screens and alcoves of the Moslem artists and architect passed into Europe via Spain and the Moorish occupation; from Spain, it crossed the Atlantic to the New World.

Indian houses of the period of the Moslem conquests were probably not greatly different in structure from those of the Islamic west. Their builders did not suffer, however, from the prohibitions which restricted their contemporaries in the west and, as far as one can tell from literary references, houses were decorated with carvings and paintings of musicians, dancers, the deeds of the gods and erotica.

When the Roman Empire finally collapsed and the barbarian tribes – Goths, Vandals, Visigoths, Burgundians, Franks and Huns – swept south to their new homes, some of them across the Mediterranean into North Africa, Roman law and government were, for a time at least, set aside. The period that ensued used to be described as the Dark Ages though, as we now know, it was very far from being dark in many senses; the tendency, moreover, to extend the Middle Ages backwards is also making inroads upon it. Art and artists certainly did not disappear or cease to exist during this period, as we know from the magnificent illuminated manuscripts and ivories they produced. Domestic architecture

Antonello da Messina, St. Jerome in his Study *(c. 1474: London, National Gallery). An excellent record of the structure and furnishings of a medieval study: here it is open to inspection; very often they were closed.*

may have stood still until the styles of the invaders were assimilated as they probably were by about the ninth century. During the reign of the emperor Charlemagne and his successors (from the eighth to the tenth centuries) we know that wall painting probably attained remarkable heights of skill and elaboration and was executed in palaces as well as churches. At a lower level of society, such decoration was unlikely and the house with its single, all-purpose room probably had few adornments.

The creation of comfort is, as we have seen, an important factor in the organization of the house and an early aid in this direction was the wall-hanging or tapestry with which, at its finest, comfort could be combined with beauty. One of the centres of production was Arras in northern France, hence the name by which tapestries are sometimes known. We have fragments of tapestry from the fourteenth century but the great epoch of these, especially of the Gothic tapestry, was the fifteenth and early sixteenth centuries when they were being woven not only in France and Flanders but in Germany, Switzerland and Italy. To this period we owe the splendid pastoral and hunting scenes, the episodes from the lives of saints and heroes, and the curious symbolic tapestries – for example, the hunting of the unicorn – from the factories in Paris, Tournai, Arras and elsewhere. They were woven in wool and silk; in the richest hangings of all gold and silver thread was added. It was very slow work; even in a medieval working day a good workman might finish no more than a few square inches. Tapestries are still produced today – – by slightly improved methods – and Tournai alone still fulfils orders from all over Europe.

The tapestry was, however, a luxury. A painted wall cost less and an order for a mural was more quickly filled than one for a tapestry; it cost less too than a hanging made of the fabrics brought home by merchants from the Levant, having risked tempest, pirates and tax-gatherers to do so. Painted walls had, moreover, a considerable start on tapestries in the Middle Ages. The interior of an early medieval house where the householder was able to use paint or employ a painter was probably very gay. The tranquil beauty of Romanesque sculpture as we know it today makes it easy to forget that originally it was brightly painted. The householder of the same period brightened his house to the very beams of the ceiling. Floors resisted treatment to some extent. For centuries, they were made of hard-packed earth which was difficult to keep clean. This was succeeded by cobbles or brick paving, or by stone slabs, and their subdued colouring must have thrown into relief the vivid colours of walls and ceilings.

Furniture was scanty and remained so in Gothic buildings where the architectural style was to some extent reflected in the lines of the furniture. But as Rome had been influenced and, according to some of her historians, corrupted by the luxuries of Asia – the Levant in particular – so medieval Europe fell a victim to the same temptations. The Crusades increased trade with the eastern Mediterranean and the home-coming Crusaders brought such luxuries as silks and spices with them, or discovered that they had grown accustomed to these amenities. The

Detail of a mosaic floor of the Alexandrine period in Greece (Rome, Lateran Museum): it was probably designed for a banqueting hall.

Saracenic designs of eastern fabrics were imitated in the west while the import of the originals continued. That they were extremely fashionable is apparent from the work of miniature painters of the period; they show, in fact, men and women dressed in clothes which match the tapestries, but this may be merely a medieval miniature licence.

Southern Europe too yielded to the wave of colour. Interior decoration in some Italian houses took the form of intricate geometric motifs. In others, the upper part of the wall was decorated with a narrative painting or with paintings of figures executed above stylized ornament incorporating geometric shapes and formalized flowers. The murals painted in bedchambers often illustrated medieval allegories of love, biblical incidents and stories of chivalry and marital fidelity. A more sophisticated taste was that for paintings of grotesques by such artists as Perin del Vaga.

Earthenware floors were replaced by floors of polished or glazed brick, especially in the private family rooms. In the public rooms, there were marble floors. The stone was used first in the shape of smooth, polished slabs, then later, in the fifteenth century, it was inlaid either with marble of another

Detail of the elegant staircase with its balusters decorated with acanthus leaves, from the Palazzo Gondi, one of the finest of fifteenth century houses in Florence: it was built between 1494 and 1501 to designs by Giuliano da Sangallo.

colour or with a hard, black plaster. Mosaic floors were rare. Ceiling beams were left in their natural colour, but in coffered ceilings the centre of each square was often painted. Wood was used to good practical and aesthetic effect. A dado, up to two feet high, served as a backrest for chests and benches. Intricately carved and painted mouldings enriched it and linked it with the scheme of the wall above. Later again, as prosperity increased, floors too took on colour in the form of oriental carpets. Reserved at first for churches, they later became more common in private houses.

The carpet is a very ancient item of household furnishing. At the beginning of the second millennium B.C., an Egyptian artist depicted in the wall paintings of Beni Hasan the sacred bull lying on what was presumably a carpet from what is now Iraq. Carpets were probably made there during the period of the Roman Empire and were certainly condemned as corrupting luxuries by Roman moralists. In one of his more edifying passages Plutarch describes how Cato refused to have in his house a carpet he had inherited; it was oriental and connoisseurs considered it worthy of the finest drawing-rooms, whether hung on the wall or laid on the floor. Carpets had been used in the west as floor coverings from the time of Alexander the Great. Their use in this way is probably Persian in origin and the ancient term for a carpet in Persia is 'a thing to tread on'. A fabric created by knotting (which is what distinguishes the carpet from the tapestry) is, indeed, generally described in the east as Persian and, whatever the confused early history of the carpet, the most beautiful examples from the sixth century A.D. onwards have been Persian. They reached medieval Europe in the ninth century. The Byzantine Empire kept trade routes open so that the Carolingian court at Pavia was able to buy carpets from the east. But six centuries passed

before the carpet made a visible appearance in artistic history, in paintings. It appears quite often, especially in Tuscany, so that one may surmise that the Venetian monopoly of the Levantine trade had been broken and that Florentine or, more precisely, Pisan merchants were engaged in distributing the riches of the east in western Europe.

The fact that certain designs and colours tend to be associated with certain towns, districts or weavers makes classification of oriental carpets comparatively easy. Each group of carpet weavers, indeed each family, used its own designs, guarding them for generations. The colours they used they made from vegetable sources which gave distinctive, long-lasting dyes. Over the centuries, an enormous store accumulated of animal and plant motifs, some of them stylized beyond recognition save by an informed eye. Weavers used the designs traditional to their own culture but were not averse to borrowing from their neighbours so that, in spite of the strength of tradition in the craft, it was constantly revivified by new ideas. To this, and to their beauty

Palazzo Contarini dal Bovolo in Venice: the name of this building in Lombard style is taken from its famous spiral staircase described in Venetian dialect as snail-like. It was probably designed by Giovanni Candi about 1499: staircases like it, though usually less splendid, were fairly common in Venice.

as well as to the precision of their craftsmanship, may be attributed the admiration that Persian carpets have enjoyed.

By the early Renaissance period, houses were more sophisticated in structure. And however rich, for example, the Italian house of the time was, however varied the decoration, the structure itself determined the organization of the interior which also seemed to reflect the austerity of its environment. Perspective and effect were important and were pursued indoors as well as out by architectural devices and by the use of *trompe l'oeil*. But while they pursued their public lives in this stately ambience, people made provision for privacy in the shape of the small study, a room within a room. A similar manifestation of the desire for seclusion was the addition of the small, private staircase.

But the emphasis in Italian houses of this period was on a self-conscious formalism in which interior ornament was carefully planned with walls and ceilings regarded as an artistic entity. In the grandest houses, celebrated artists were appointed to execute or at least supervise this decoration; exterior decoration might be related to interior or, if not, it was at least in harmony with it. This search for artistic unity is perhaps most perceptible in the work of the mannerist painters, in, for example, Giulio Romano's paintings for the Palazzo del Te in Mantua and the decorations of the Farnesina that Baldassare Peruzzi designed for Agostino Chigi, the Sienese banker, in Rome.

Close ties between France and Italy helped to spread Italian fashions in living. But once outside

Italy, they were adapted to French requirements, for in France it was realized that the rooms of a house could in fact be arranged in such a way as to contribute to the comfort of the inhabitants. The convention of the carefully organized sequence of rooms planned to create an impression of opulence rather than of ease lost ground. Specific functions were assigned to specific rooms. The process was aided by improvements in the means of heating, that is, in stoves.

North of the Alps, where the climate necessitated spending much of the year indoors, the art of domestic living was much better understood than in the warm south. Here the balance of power between interior and exterior was reversed and the interior penetrated the outside world by way of balconies, bay windows, and covered porches in which, however, the inhabitants of the house were protected from the elements. These projections affected the appearance of towns and cities – not always in the interests of sound town planning.

Behind them, the long campaign was fought out to retain warmth and keep out the cold: psycholog-

(Right, above) Detail from Jan Vermeer, Sleeping Woman *(1655-60: New York, Metropolitan Museum). On the table lies a carpet with a scorpion motif, typical of Turkoman and Caucasian carpets.*
Detail of the carpet given by Cesare Borgia to Machiavelli (San Gimignano, Civic Museum); probably woven in central Persia towards the end of the fifteenth century.

Garnerey, Queen Hortense in the Boudoir
of the Palace in the Rue Ceruti in Paris
(c. 1810: Paris, Lefuel Collection).
Note in particular the draping of fabrics
to reproduce the interior of a pavilion
or tent, and the elaborate pelmets:
this evidence of Romanticism is slightly at
odds with the Louis XVI furniture.

(Below, from the left) Miniature from the
Heures Boucicaut *(Geneva, Public Library):*
again a heavily draped room, this time a bedroom,
in fabric with a pattern of fleur-de-lis.
The rococo interior in the Portrait of Jan van
Vollenhoven *by H. Pothoven (1771: Amsterdam,*
Rijksmuseum), showing the predominance
of the curving line.
The bedchamber of the Count de Mornay,
painted by Delacroix (1832: Paris,
Louvre), again fabric-lined to give the
impression of a tent.

ical as well a practical weapons were used, that is, the appearance of comfort and warmth was stressed in, for example, the kind of fabrics used. The Elizabethan house owed much of its charm to the fabrics used as wall hangings, to the richness of damask, brocade and velvet. These reduced draughts and cut the chill of stone walls but, more important, they created an atmosphere of ease and intimacy. Sometimes fabrics were replaced by hangings of Spanish leather which were conducive to an atmosphere of padded, peaceful seclusion.

An important part of the Renaissance house was the staircase. In Italy the balusters were often of pale marble, pink or grey; the handrail too might be of marble or bronze covered with velvet. Improvements in their construction often added to their size, so that they swept in the grandest manner possible from one floor to the next and artists carried their frescoes from floor to floor along the wall of the staircase. In some cases, however, the staircase was kept outside the building and some splendidly fantastic effects were achieved, as in the *Bovolo*, the spiral staircase shaped, allegedly, like a snail, which is attached to the Palazzo Contarini in Venice.

The alterations in the structure and plan of the house, consequent on the search for comfort in the seventeenth and eighteenth centuries in the Low Countries, England and France, have already been mentioned. During the same period, Italian architects remained, on the whole, faithful to their belief that the shape of the interior was or should be dictated by the architectural skeleton of the building. The formality of their designs was enhanced by their use of stucco ornament. The effect created is quite alien to those of us who are accustomed to informality and it is possible that our lack of enthusiasm would have been shared by a merchant of

the time from London, Amsterdam or Bordeaux. Italian prestige in the arts ensured, however, that Italian fashions were watched and imitated, with certain modifications, and architects elsewhere turned to advantage Italian insistence on artistic and architectural unity.

From the seventeenth century onwards, in most of Europe, social and technological changes wrought important alterations in domestic interiors. Socially, the gulf between the stately home and the middle class dwelling house narrowed not so much in terms of size and ostentation as in the fact that the hedonism of the middle classes began, apparently, to affect their social superiors so that they too began to demand comfort at home.

A significant technical innovation was the use, in quantity, of wallpaper, machine-made, strong and less expensive than other wall coverings. It had been used in China for centuries and from the middle of the sixteenth century it was imported to the west. Its transport from the other side of the world made it at that time an expensive luxury. A century and a half later, nevertheless, it was still being commissioned in Canton from Chinese artists. Patterns were supplied from Europe which the Chinese reproduced in their own way with charming – and remarkably durable – results. But its manufacture had begun in England, France and Italy so that the days of this delightful and for once authentic *chinoiserie* were numbered.

Let us now turn from walls to floors. During the end of the sixteenth and beginning of the seventeenth centuries, mosaic was commonly used in Italy; the finest designs were those in which the

tesserae were arranged in geometric patterns using a limited range of colours. Such floors offered a suitably sober background to the display of carpets. Their glowing, jewel-like colours – they can be appreciated from paintings of the period – showed to great advantage against the restrained mosaics. Within these rooms, furniture, always improving in quality and variety, was carefully arranged. Walls, ceiling, floor, furnishings and furniture combined, therefore, to achieve a delightful harmony.

This sense of apparently uncontrived, gentle harmony was the great achievement of eighteenth century interiors and, indeed, this air of informality and reasonableness was not confined to that branch of the arts that is concerned with decoration, but was also extended to fashion in dress and manners. It was perhaps an entirely artificial informality but, as one may detect from the paintings of Watteau and his contemporaries, it was none the less charming.

Such paintings convey an impression of ephemeral delight but this informal harmony was short-lived. In France, the rigours of the Republic and afterwards the neo-classical splendours of the Empire, together with the classical revivals elsewhere (merely the latest, as we have seen, in a long series) undermined this harmony even if it did not entirely destroy it. At the beginning of 1797, an article in the *Magazzino di mobili*, published in Florence, suggested 'decoration for a drawing-room'. The authors took a fairly austere view of their subject. 'Our first thought', they wrote, 'has been to obey a most necessary law which seeks the unity and uniformity of the whole, something that (leaving aside the merits of the harmony and matching of colours) should always be the main object of the composition... On these sound principles we have based our efforts.' Dissymmetry they refused to tolerate, having given their approval to strict purity of design. The approach was very Italian. Dedicated to the pursuit of classical ideals, architects condemned their clients to surroundings in which the formidable Cato might have felt at home, save that he would have disapproved of the splendour of the decorations and the sequence of rooms continuing apparently to infinity, an impression strengthened by the use of mirrors. Those parts of the house which had been formalized lost their air of intimacy. Wall decorations were inspired by ancient reliefs of episodes from ancient – preferably Repub-

Corner of the marriage chamber on the first floor of the Palazzo Davanzati in Florence (see page 79), so called from the wall decoration, probably painted to commemorate a marriage between the Davizzi and Alberti families whose arms are carved under the brackets that support the hood of the fireplace. The lower part of the wall paintings simulates a tapestry hanging from the cornice and the top imitates coloured marble: the narrative painting tells the ribald story of the châtelaine of Verzi, the incidents of which take place in a loggia. The richness of the colours is typical of the late Middle Ages.

German design for the decoration of a drawing-room 'in the modern style' published at the end of the nineteenth century; motifs like these were popular for several decades though they were not always handled as lightly as this.

lican – history. Persian carpets were clearly out of place in such rooms and were replaced by new ones in keeping with the rest of the decoration and furnishings. The France of Napoleon's empire suffered too from this *furor classicus*, though less seriously. The classical revival, as we have already seen, also affected England and English architecture and furnishings; but there the most famous cabinet-makers and designers of furniture took care that their neo-classical designs should be attractive and useful as well as reasonably authentic; their talent for compromise ensured them widespread success.

Yet, all this ostentatious classicism was about to be challenged by so dizzy a succession of styles and fashions that in the midst of the worst excesses of nineteenth century Gothic, Romanesque or Renaissance revivals, one almost regrets the former's dignity and sobriety. The principles of Percier and Fontaine with which we began this chapter were forgotten in a welter of romantic eclecticism. The new 'fashionable' room bore no relation at all to any other room in the building let alone the appearance of the building from the outside. A really enterprising householder could accommodate under his roof rooms of all ages and all nations; here a medieval room, there an Indian; here a Chinese pavilion, there a small archaeological museum. The Chinese room might be more Chinese than anything in the Forbidden City (and might have been furnished, or alleged to be furnished, with part of the booty of the Summer Palace in Peking); the Gothic study might have left Peter Abelard quite breathless. To avoid the horrors of empty space, every corner was filled with ornaments and bric-à-brac, many of them of dubious quality.

In the age of the antimacassar, mass production helped to satisfy the demand for ornaments, furniture and furnishings. Mechanical weaving and Jacquard looms brought carpets to the mass market. The cotton spinners and weavers of Lancashire together with their fellow-workers in France, Germany and Italy shrouded the world with their fabrics. Curtains were draped over doors as well as windows and every piece of furniture that could be garnished with upholstery or cloth in some way was so adorned. Even the decorative cover spread over, say, a table was itself decorated with fringes, tassels, bobbles, braids, ribbons and lace. Decoration of windows was elevated to the status of a minor art and was as subject to fashion as the contents of a lady's wardrobe. Muslins, velvets and brocades, separately and in combination, were flounced and fringed, looped and twirled, folded and gathered into astounding arrangements. Wallpaper, machine-produced in enormous quantity and freed from the limitations on its design imposed by the woodcut, soared to greater heights of extravagance and decorated the walls of modest villas with roses of a magnitude and hue that no gardener ever imagined, with experiments in the Japanese style that would have bewildered Kyoto, and imitations of Spanish leatherwork that would have appalled a Cordovan craftsman. There was a 'feeling' for nature, and flowers and trees ran riot over furniture, whether carved, inlaid, painted, printed, embroidered, or woven.

An interesting sidelight on this use of ornament was the symbolism attached to it by certain authors. When Nathaniel Hawthorne, for example, was set-

Edouard Vuillard, Woman Reading *(1896: Paris, Petit Palais). Interiors like this with its plethora of patterns, mainly floral, reached the height of their popularity about 1900. Certain wallpapers were very popular and the patterns turn up in more than one interior.*

ting the scene for some sinister action, he referred to the rich, heavy folds of sumptuous curtains. And elsewhere in literature of the period rich, dark velvet curtains, braided perhaps, usually signified a room inhabited by someone about whose moral character we were expected to entertain grave doubts; white muslin was, by contrast, synonymous with sweetness and innocence.

If this tendency had been confined to literature, it would not have mattered so much. However, even houses of bricks and mortar were caught up in it: red was used in bedrooms to signify passions and repressions, yellow and gold in dining-rooms to show opulence, blue in drawing-rooms to suggest depth of feeling and so on, through every colour of the rainbow.

Art in the home

Discussion as to when the first work of art appeared as part of the furnishings of a home begs the question of what is a work of art and at what point were certain objects so regarded. It is probable that the first objects to be treated as works of art, that is, as additions to the house which were not by our reckoning strictly necessary to its running and maintenance, were images of the gods.

It may have been the Greeks, and possibly those Greeks who lived and worked outside their homeland, who extended the admiration of painted walls to paintings on wood. How they mounted them is uncertain; they may have been set in frames that were part of the wall. Vitruvius mentions a painter who emigrated from Sparta about 30 A.D. but the method of framing he refers to seems to be a simple, temporary affair.

The oldest surviving frames are those which surround Byzantine icons and they are made of filigree or enamelled metal. Frame-makers were a late development and appear about the early seventeenth century. In 1620 we find Giulio Mancini, the Sienese physician and art lover, expressing his dislike of 'ornaments', as he called them, which

'hold the painting out and expose it to harm'. Apparently he preferred those of which the projecting structure 'gave the paintings protection and majesty, especially if they were black, in the case of small modern pictures, or gilt for work the colours of which had been dimmed by the years.'

By the period of the Roman Republic works of art, in the sense in which we know them, were already collected. Not all Romans approved. Cicero, who might have been accused by some of taking a warped view of art connoisseurs, commented ironically in his *Paradoxa*: 'When I see you contemplating a picture by Echion or a statue by Polycletus and giving squeals of admiration, I say that you are a slave to folly'. Fortunes were spent in Rome on works of art, mainly Greek, although we do not know how they were arranged other than that sculptures were placed in the dining-room.

Not until the end of the Middle Ages do we have any information as to the distribution of paintings on the walls of houses. Framed paintings begin to appear in works of the Italian Renaissance but they leave a great many questions unanswered. Where, for example, would such paintings as Raphael's portraits of Angelo and Maddalena Doni (now in the Pitti Palace in Florence) be placed? What was the practical use of the so-called 'covers' on such a painting as Lorenzo Lotto's superb *Allegory* (now in New York): they were presumably designed to protect the picture below but in what way?

About other aspects of the place of the work of art in the house we can be more precise. For a long time there was a close link between the profession of the householder and the decoration of the house. The soldier, the general rather, tended to collect or commission portraits of ancient warriors and battle scenes; the scholar usually betrayed a predilection for reminders of writers of the past and episodes from their greatest works. In the study of the Montefeltro Duke Federigo of Urbino, scholarship was acknowledged by the mingling of allegory with likenesses of classical sages. The fashion persisted into the eighteenth century when the nobleman Raimondo Buonaccorsi decorated the drawing-room of his palace at Macerata with paintings, large and small, inspired by Virgil's *Aeneid*; but, whereas in the Renaissance all the paintings would probably have come from a single hand, Buonaccorsi's paintings came from Naples, Bologna and Venice, and a painter of murals whom Buonaccorsi came across by chance painted further episodes from the epic on the ceiling.

The busts of poets, philosophers and musicians – Homer, Dante, Shakespeare, Plato, Goethe, Milton – were a few of the members of this select pantheon, who presided from the highest shelves over nineteenth century libraries; they were the last examples of this kind of occupational or professional homage.

Paintings with religious subjects – often in contemporary dress – were also executed in private houses, usually, of course, in the chapel, and one of the finest of these, as well as one the most appealing, must be Benozzo Gozzoli's *Procession of the Magi* in the chapel of the Palazzo Medici-Riccardi in Florence, with the Medici and their household riding through a spring landscape. Religious paintings were later collected for themselves, as works of art, rather than for use in the family chapel. Raphael and some of his contemporaries appealed, in particular, to the devout nineteenth century householder who, if he could not obtain or afford an original, was prepared to settle for a copy. Frame makers flourished in the attempt to keep pace with the demand for the ornate gilt frames deemed suitable to the Old Masters, most of the Old Masters – the genuine examples, that is – having lost any frames they might once have possessed. Most of these nineteenth century frames have since been relegated to attics or destroyed for the sake of the gold leaf used in their manfacture, but by themselves they form an interesting commentary on the taste of the age. They were not always chosen in the best of taste and when, in particular, Italian primitives came back into fashion, the fussiness of their frames often conflicted – and still does in picture galleries – with the painting they contain.

Decoration of nineteenth century interiors with works of art is associated in one's mind with walls covered from chair-rail to ceiling with paintings in a variety of media. There were those interiors where collections of water-colours or pastels or miniatures were skilfully arranged but for the most part they jostled one another on overcrowded walls. Edgar Allan Poe was one of the critics of this practice of using pictures like rather large postage stamps and the walls as an album – but his contemporaries continued serenely in their customary wholesale manner, forgetful often of the difficulty of discerning the finer points of a watercolour when it is hung just below ceiling level or of the overwelming effect of a large, tastefully varnished and darkened oil painting on a neighbouring group of pastels.

There were one or two exceptions to this general practice of crowding rooms with bric-à-brac. They were the self-confident interiors of the richest of American apartments, the most princely of German houses and palaces in Portugal, the owners of which either felt no need to compete or had submitted to the exceptional authority of interior decorators.

An odd sidelight on the arrangement of pictures in a house concerns the late Renaissance and baroque fashion for what have been described as *pitture lascive*, which might be erotica or ordinary nudes. The vogue for them was greatest in Italy and Germany where it was recommended that they should not be shown to 'old maids' or 'scrupulous people' but should be relegated to private rooms for the delectation of the head of the family and, presumably, the enlightenment of his sons, for they were also described as being useful in the education of 'fine healthy boys'. The fashion did not outlast the seventeenth century for the powerful academies of the arts of later centuries banned the study of the nude. In 1781, Casanova, of all people, thought it his duty to inform the

J. H. Schonfeldt, Chamber Music *(Dresden, Gemäldegalerie). This painting provides an interesting insight to the treatment and arrangement of paintings by collectors; here the emphasis is, very noticeably, on symmetry.*

authorities of the Venetian Republic that 'undressed' models were being copied in certain Venetian studios. In the following century, academic prohibition was reinforced by a social veto on the appearance of the unclothed or undraped human body; exceptions were occasionally made for cherubs either carefully posed or sheltering behind a convenient trail of ivy.

Possession of original paintings has always been limited. In the fifteenth and sixteenth centuries when most towns supported at least a handful of painters, ownership of a painting was a prerogative of the rich. Even the successful craftsman had to be content with a cheaper woodcut if he wanted a picture, usually with a devotional subject, in the house. As far as is known, such woodcuts began to be produced in Germany at about the end of the fourteenth century when they were part of the stock-in-trade of friars. They were always popular whether as aids to devotion or as decoration, even after the advent of the more delicate copper engraving at the beginning of the fifteenth century. Woodcuts were, indeed, so much a part of the decoration of a house, nailed to the wall and not carefully cherished within covers, that like other much-used items of household plenishing, early examples of them are very rare.

Erotic woodcuts were also circulated during this period and were doubtless as popular though it is hardly likely that they were nailed to the wall. The

(Above, top) In one of the many elegant eighteenth century houses in the Lange Voorhout in The Hague, the pictures are arranged in rigidly symmetrical fashion. (Above) Johann Zoffany, Sir Lawrence Dundas with his Grand-daughter (c. 1770, Richmond, collection of the Marquis of Zetland). This is the house, clearly, of a genuine art lover, who has left his paintings in their original frames rather than force – or cut – them into frames conceived as more appropriate to the room's décor. There are a number of Dutch paintings, invariably seascapes enlivened by ships (Englishmen seem uninterested in them otherwise) and two parts of a predella from an Italian Renaissance altar frontal, as well as a number of bronze figures.

Edouard Vuillard, Portrait of Madame Bénard (1930: Paris, Musée Nationale d'Art Moderne). There is a telephone on the patterned table cloth but otherwise, the arrangement of the room is nineteenth century with the pictures hung symmetrically; they are probably for the most part family portraits in a variety of media.

introduction of other subjects took place slowly and these were for the most part mythological or allegorical, designed for customers of a slightly higher social level. Early subjects for reproduction may have been the paintings of Raphael or Mantegna. Peter Paul Rubens astutely established a school of engravers to copy his paintings. During the eighteenth century, famous paintings were translated into prints on a large scale. Paintings of interiors at the beginning of the nineteenth century show, however, no more than a few prints hanging on the wall for, until then, prints were not regarded as ornaments but were preserved in albums to be examined closely at leisure. But, by the middle of the century, they were being framed and added to the wall decorations in villas and palaces alike. Improvements in the technical processes of reproduction multiplied the types of print available and reduced their cost. Impressively framed, large sepia prints took their place in drawing-rooms and small, brightly coloured oleographs performed the same function as the peasant's woodcut.

Sculpture, in the common sense of the word, that is, individual pieces unrelated to the structure of the house — as distinct from those works of art for which a place, a niche or a pedestal, was designed by the architect in the house's plan — entered the middle class home rather late in the day. Exceptions were, of course, statues of the Virgin Mary or the saints, which fulfilled a different function. It was not so much an interest in art as the passion for archaeology, inspired by Goethe and his fellow-enthusiasts, that brought sculpture indoors during the eighteenth and nineteenth centuries. Genuine antiquities, whether from home or abroad, led the way and it was not long before the Victorian manfacturer's talent for imitation was able to supply the demand for reproductions in bronze, brass and plaster. And so to the ranks of water colours, sepia prints, aquatints and the rest there were added models of the *Discobolus*, *Laocoon*, the *Apollo Belvedere* and other suitable examples of Graeco-Roman art.

Bric-a-brac

Originally, a trinket or a knick-knack could be anything at all – a toy, a weapon, a tool, a box or pot, a fragment of rock. A trinket now has a certain overtone of value and in some cases may be synonymous with an *objet de vertu*. It is nowadays quite often the nucleus of a collection whether informal or properly pursued. But in many households, both past and present, it has been and remains the kind of object which it is pleasant to have in the room, that is attractive to look at and handle, and if it can satisfy the craving for antiquity from which many suffer, so much the better. Such objects lend themselves, moreover, to arrangement in cases or on tables for the admiration of their owners and acquaintances. It was William Hale White, better known as Mark Rutherford, who issued the warning that 'men should not too carefully analyze and condemn the various ways thought up by nature to save them from themselves, whether this be through coins, old books, curiosities, butterflies or fossils.'

The passion for collecting is, as we know, an ancient one and has proved, over the centuries, an abundance of ammunition for disapproving moralists. Seneca abominated the passion for 'objects, dead things to which a pure soul that remembered whence it came could never become attached.'

The collections of objects found in Egyptian and Mesopotamian tombs are, of course, of a special kind and were designed for burial with the dead. In Greek territory, the states themselves and the temples housed collections. The love of works of art for their intrinsic merit was a later development, evident in the later centuries of Greek history and, as we have seen, in Rome.

Paintings of medieval interiors do not betray much in the way of superfluous ornaments or tell us much about them. Probably there were not many, partly because few householders possessed the resources to buy utensils and plenishings over and above what they needed, partly because some centuries were to pass before such ornaments were available in quantity, and partly – in certain periods – because of legal prohibitions in the shape of sumptuary laws on conspicuous consumption. The attitude of the church, too, was hostile to unnecessary wordly possessions. 'How many eye-catching folderols lead men by every art to clothes, shoes, vessels, and all sorts of man-made trifles?'

Shortly After Marriage, one of the scenes from Hogarth's Marriage à la Mode *series of paintings (1745: London, National Gallery). The furnishings are predominantly those of the early eighteenth century; very much of the period are the chairs with their carved cabriole legs, the tripod table, and the paired Ionic columns. In the room beyond, a curtain is partly drawn over a picture presumably not of the type to be shown to elderly spinsters. On the mantelpiece are some dubiously oriental knick-knacks and an even more dubious antique bust.*

Picture of the Museum of Ferrante Imperato, *probably engraved by G. M. Mitelli in the second half of the seventeenth century, shows a remarkably heterogeneous collection of marvels and monsters of a kind not too uncommon in noble houses of the period.*

St. Augustine wrote. 'In all this,' he added sombrely, 'they go far beyond what is necessary and moderate.' The churches were themselves, of course, owners of many magnificent art collections and patrons of artists. But the books, hourglasses, bells, inkwells and astrolabes that we have seen in the studies, whether ascetic or moderately cosy, of St. Jerome, had a functional use for all the charm of their presentation by Dürer.

Towards the end of the Middle Ages, we find the mania for collecting manifesting itself in the home of, for instance, Duke Albert V of Bavaria. The inventory of the 3407 items in his collection covers a bizarre assembly of objects, among them 'the egg an abbot found inside another egg, a small piece of manna that fell from heaven during Lent, an embalmed elephant, a hydra and a basilisk.' He and his fellow collectors rejoiced in whatever was curious and exotic, from junk to precious stones, exquisitely illuminated books and whale's teeth, oriental handwarmers and unicorn horns, and the pride of one collection was the skull of John the Baptist as a child. The collections of the Italian princes, the cabinets of the Medici and the galleries of the Gonzagas and the Montrefeltros, may have been a little better organized. That collections of varying degrees of pretension existed is evident from Galileo's explanation of the difference, to his mind, between Tasso's *Gerusalemme Liberata*, a poem he disliked, and Ariosto's *Orlando Furioso* which he admired. The first he compared to the 'den of some curious little man who has enjoyed adorning it with things that are exotic or old or rare but that are no more than trifles, such as a petrified crab, a dried chameleon, a fly or a spider caught in a piece of amber, or some of those clay mannikins said to be found in the tombs of the ancient Egyptians.' Ariosto's epic he saw as resembling 'a gallery decorated with a hundred ancient statues by the most famous sculptors, or the finest works of celebrated painters, with a great number besides of vases, agates, lapis lazuli and other treasures.'

In neither case do we detect the kind of pleasure afforded by the bibelot. The first kind of collection described by Galileo sounds too much like a natural history museum and the second too dauntingly formal. Both require that the objects described should be most particularly arranged and should not be placed here and there in haphazard fashion. And yet if the ornaments that people display today on their mantelpieces or on sideboards, tables or shelves have to be matched during earlier centuries, it must be in these clusters of curiosities. It is probable that amateurs without the means or the inclination to form homogeneous collections of objects picked up things as the fancy took them or as opportunity offered – as did Lorenzo Lotto's prelate, seated comfortably amidst his possessions.

In the late sixteenth century, cupboards or cabinets in which curiosities were kept became fash-

Lorenzo Lotto, Churchman in his Study *(London, British Museum). This drawing may depict the younger son of a noble family who, like other men in the same position, went into the church while still young. The jumble of books and ornaments seems to be carefully arranged.*

ionable in western Europe. And these were often ornaments in themselves, rich in inlay and carvings. At the end of the century, Madame de Rambouillet carried the taste to its logical conclusion and used large bibelots in the shape of enamelled *buffets* to house small ones in the form of Chinese porcelain, glass, gilt boxes, and mirrors in ebony frames, which she put on show, naturally, in the reception rooms of her house.

As house interiors diminished in stateliness and formality, as more and more houses of a comfortable size were built and as the rooms of old and new houses acquired more and more furniture, the bibelot multiplied – for the most part during the eighteenth century. France to some extent led the fashion and there collectors indulged in the bagatelles which were typical of the period, in Chinese and soon afterwards in European porcelain, and in exquisite trifles in glass and china and precious metals. Antiquities or imitation antiquities were the desiderata of the neo-classical period, but when that passion waned under the influence of the Romantic revival the bibelot-hunter came into his own.

Neo-classicism was still dominant, however, when Maria Edgeworth visited the home of Thomas Hope (1769-1831), the collector whom Lord Byron contemptuously dismissed as 'a house furnisher', at Deepdene in Surrey. 'This house is furnished splendidly', she wrote, 'but I feel it is overdone for a country house. Even without considering the question of comfort, there are too many Egyptian ornaments, gilt or bronze, and all of them horrible . ... In every passage, in every drawing-room, crowds of terrifying bronze, stone and plaster monsters.' From the drawings that have survived, we know that each monster had its appointed place.

Miss Edgeworth might have been more sympathetic to the setting described by Tennyson in 1847. 'That morning Walter showed me the house... On the tables, every age and region were jumbled together, great double-edged swords and snow shoes, ornaments made of lava, sandalwood fans, amber, old rosaries, concentric spheres of ivory intricately carved, the terrible Malayan *kris*, fighting clubs from the South Sea Islands; and hung on the wall, among the monstrous horns of elk and deer, the arms and armour of his ancestors.' It was the ancient urge to accumulate, the magpie hunger for curiosities: Duke Albert V would have loved it.

Collections of curiosities could be and were arranged formally but, during the ninethenth century, the tendency was to disperse them throughout at least the public rooms of the house. Oscar Wilde threw up his hands in horror at the 'wax flowers,

Detail from the Dressing of a Young Bride, *a wall-painting from Herculaneum or Stabia (Naples, National Museum). This harmoniously disposed still-life indicates the kind of objects in use at the time – the large glass jug, the finely carved table – and the artist's pleasure in their arrangement.*

atrocities perpetrated in woollen cross-stitch, and the antimacassars without end.' Edmond de Goncourt, typically, analyzed the situation. 'On this wall, in careful disorder and with the picturesqueness of a studio, was every kind of showy, striking object, gilt pots, Japanese embroideries, shining branches, and even stranger objects astounding the beholder with their originality and exoticism.'

The passion for bric-à-brac, described by Tennyson, did not infect all countries equally and at the same pace; indeed, as late as the middle of the nineteenth century, the Dutch had still to catch up with it. By the late nineteenth century, however, at the high tide of the Victorian era, the preoccupation with knick-knacks was at its height and had given rise, too, to a new type of furniture designed solely for display, the *étagère*.

But even with these, it was difficult to keep pace with the exotica brought home from the ends of the earth by empire-builders and explorers. After 1853, for instance, when Commodore Perry delivered President Millard Fillmore's message to the Japanese government – packed in a special gold-hinged, rosewood box – the fashion for things Japanese scattered throughout Europe an extraordinary assembly of *samurai* swords, *netsuke*, lacquer boxes, fans, lamps and jade. Then the founders of the folklore movement encouraged an interest in country pottery, fabrics, furniture, wood carvings and wrought iron. The ethnographers joined in and extended their scope to Asia, Africa and the Americas so that to the swords and the *satsuma* porcelain were added African *assegais*, strange musical instruments, and, doubtless occupying the same place of honour as the skull of John the Baptist as a baby, the occasional alleged shrunken head. The glass-fronted cabinets, the vitrines, the what-nots filled to overflowing and the corners of the room acquired a detritus of spinning-wheels and plant-holders, for this was the great age of the aspidistra and the maidenhair fern. Weapons bristled from the walls between the watercolours executed during holidays at home and abroad. And apart from the loot of five continents, western craftsmen themselves turned out brass ornaments, caskets and containers of all kinds – some of which they foresightedly exported first overseas. Industrious fingers at home decorated silk cushions and table covers and embroidered those covers of which Wilde complained.

D'Annunzio's villa above Lake Garda at Gardone, the *Vittoriale*, shows the lengths to which the passion for curios and bibelots could be carried as late as the 1920's, when this depressing monument was built. It is a mixture of an alchemical and a diocesan museum, a temple of the goddess Kali and a flea-market, a welter of the medieval, the Byzantine, the Renaissance, the barbaric, and the erotic.

It has, however, a fairly respectable ancestry in the studios of painters and sculptors. The room described by de Goncourt was in fact the house – though not the studio – of an artist. And it is in the house of an artist, James McNeill Whistler, in the Rue du Bac in Paris at a slightly later period, that we find hints of a change in taste in interior decoration. The drawing-room, we are told, was furnished simply and though there were pieces of antique silver and blue and white china well in evidence, there was plenty of room to admire them; and though the symmetry of Victorian arrangements was avoided, they were set out harmoniously. In this as in other respects, Whistler's taste contradicted that of his period and even now the passion for bric-à-brac has a tendency to flare up again, in general in reaction to a preceding fashion, in particular in accordance with the advice of magazines concerned with interior decoration. Ornaments of all sorts are spread around living-room, bedroom, kitchen and even bathroom, although their arrangement is often influenced by a predilection for asymmetry which can be ascribed to Whistler.

Towards the end of the sixteenth century, cabinets made in Flanders and Germany were exported to other European countries. They were highly decorated with carved ebony or bronze mounts or inlays of coloured marbles and ivory. Such cabinets were often used to hold medals, cameos, coins and other small antiquities.

Biedermeier *plantstand or* jardinière, *one of the designs of Joseph Dannhauser (see also pages 274-5)*.

Floral decoration

Vases of flowers as well as valuable objects, it has been suggested, were displayed on shelves in the houses of Ancient Egypt. It is possible, but all that we can claim with any certainty is that flowers were used to decorate public or private altars on the occasion of a solemn sacrifice, a marriage, a funeral, a civic, national or personal feast. Flowers were an essential part of the decoration for feasts, and presumably orgies as well, in Nineveh and Babylon. In Rome, dining-rooms were adorned with them, columns were wreathed in them, rose petals were added to the winecups and streets, circuses and forums were carpeted with flowers on feast days. In the first century B.C., Varro mentions that flowers were grown for the house and some of the paintings at Pompeii seem to confirm that they were used much as they are today.

That the love of flowers survived the collapse of Rome and the barbarian invasions is evident from the Latin poetry of these centuries and of the early Middle Ages. In the sixth century, for example, we find Venantius Fortunatus offering a bunch of flowers – and a poem – to his patron, the lady Radegunde. Later, in the age of chivalry, wreaths of flowers were used to crown the victor of the tournament and supplied some of the symbols of the courts of love. They became an important part of

heraldry. The lilies of France adorned standards, armour, horse trappings, and coins – and were used to brand criminals. And there is no lack of pathetic accounts of medieval prisoners-of-war who cultivated tiny gardens during their imprisonment.

But bunches of flowers in a vase – unless they had some religious, heraldic or allegorical significance – are not found in western paintings until the end of the sixteenth century. An exception are those blooms on the windowsill of the sumptuous bedroom depicted in a miniature in the Boucicaut *Book of Hours* (page 356). They appear more prominently in several paintings by the Venetian Carpaccio but again this was exceptional. Portrait painters often painted their subjects holding a flower but, for the most part, flowers as part of the décor of a room were usually overlooked.

Yet, as Guicciardini notes, domestic plants were cultivated in the early sixteenth century, above all by the people of Flanders. At Antwerp they had acclimatized some exotic plants which painters and miniaturists copied for scientific purposes. In 1560, the arrival of the first tulips from the Levant launched that 'tulipomania' which raged in the Netherlands for more than a century and which has, indeed, never quite vanished. In 1635, a good example of one called the *Semper Augustus* with

G. F. Kersting, The Embroideress *(c. 1815: Weimar, Schlossmuseum). The fondness for flowers and plants which was to grow to such dimensions in the nineteenth century is shown at an early stage in this simple interior, with the vase on the windowsill and the picture, on the left-hand wall, crowned by a branch.*

(Opposite page, above) Eugène Delacroix, Vase of Flowers on a Console-table *(1848: Montauban, Musée Ingres), a composition rich in glowing colour with which, however, Delacroix himself was dissatisfied. (Below) Studio of the painter Hans Makart, who has been credited with the invention of arrangements of dried flowers which achieved a widespread vogue at the end of the nineteenth century (From a painting by R. von Alt in 1885: Vienna, Kunsthistorisches Museum).*

a red and white flower and a blue tinted base, fetched more than 10,000 florins. Tulips also appeared on the tiles manufactured in the famous Delft factories.

The Dutch were fond of flowers indoors and to the seventeenth century belong those paintings of imposing flower arrangements with every petal defined and every dewdrop glistening. But whether these early exercises in flower arrangement were in fact used to decorate rooms and how they were used, is uncertain.

By the end of the eighteenth century, the flower seller had appeared on the streets of towns and cities and vases of flowers began to be seen on windowsills. Neo-classical taste took a sober view of such decorations and their use was carefully controlled; containers were in general vaguely Greek or Egyptian in character.

Romanticism and early nineteenth century sensibility with regard to Nature brought flowers indoors. About 1820, small vases of often wild flowers were arranged in the drawing-rooms and boudoirs of central Europe. Small plants in clay pots were often found on windowsills – even on the imperial windowsill of the Emperor Francis I of Austria, as can be seen from the painting by J. S. Decker.

Romanticism and Biedermeier combined later

in the century to festoon Europe with blossoms and branches. Glass and porcelain and pottery were tortured into weird shapes meant to hold flowers and plants; sometimes they were shaped like plants as well and complicated arrangements of glass vases formed centrepieces on dining tables. Climbing plants spread themselves over façades: 'Houses which had been of bare stone were stifled by greenery', Virginia Woolf noted in *Orlando*. Real or, on wallpaper, reproduction ivy climbed up the drawing-room walls too, wherever there was space. Statues were garnished with plants. The large, round ottoman, still found in theatre foyers, had in the centre a vase of flowers or a plant. Jardinières in wrought iron accommodated more plants and even the most modest of villas usually contrived to have a conservatory or at least a glass porch in which Nature – within reason – could be given her head. A painter, Hans Makart, is given the credit for inventing, more or less, the use of dried grasses, reeds and bullrushes, a collection of them being known as a *Makart-Bukett*. And where Nature failed, industrious man and woman could contrive flowers in silk, wax and paper. But Nature aided by more efficient heating indoors did not often fail, and nineteenth century householders conducted successful experiments in raising in the temperate north the plants of sub-tropical zones, while a house-holder with green fingers could produce the won-drous effect of a bazaar overrun by a jungle.

It is a northern taste and understandable in a region where the flowering season is short, and where the dim light of winter is prolonged. Southern light and colour hardly require such compensations though Moslem houses do make special provision for flowers in the niches of reception rooms. In Japan the art of flower arrangement has been developed to a very high level. Flower arrangements are part of the furnishing of the alcove of honour, the *tokonoma*, along with scrolls and other works of art. And from Japan we acquired – along with the lacquer boxes and the lamps – the chrysanthemum for which the initial vogue proved remarkably long-lasting. Japan's distinctive style of flower arrangement, now fairly familiar in the west, arrived in Europe rather earlier than we tend to think. Whistler's house in Paris, to which reference has already been made, included a Japanese bird-cage and with it 'charming flower arrangements in blue and white dishes.'

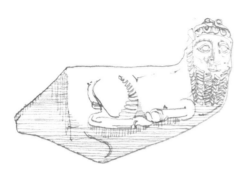

Lighting

Traces of soot in prehistoric caves show that the problem of artificial lighting is almost as old as man. In the *Iliad* reference is made to torches, which were probably one of the oldest means of producing light. A branch of resinous wood is not too difficult to find and evidence of them has been found in the Hallstatt culture of the Iron Age. The primary source of artificial light must have been, however, the hearth. In the fifth century A.D., heaps of straw and canes provided illumination for the Goths. But the torch, including the storm torch, was the most important means of lighting into and throughout the Middle Ages as one may see from the iron torch holders attached to medieval houses and still used in the seventeenth century. Another method involved, however, the filling of braziers with pieces of pitch or chips of resinous wood which were lit to afford a strong if smoky light. In the well-wooded areas of northern Europe, this form of lighting continued in use until very recently. The evolution of the candle represented a considerable advance: the Etruscans used them and passed them on to the Romans.

It is quite probable that even older than the torch is the lamp fuelled by some combustible liquid. Rudimentary stone lamps, with a hollow to hold melted fat and a wick, have been found in Magdalenian caves and the same basic shape continued in use for many thousands of years. From about the third millennium B.C. they were made of clay in Egypt and the regions of the Tigris and Euphrates. Lamps burning oil are mentioned in the *Odyssey* and bronze ones have been found amid the ruins of Crete; these are, on occasion, elaborate affairs on tall stands with two wide lips. They appeared too in the Phoenician colonies from Carthage to Sardinia. From about the fifth century B.C. the Greeks used oil lamps and the Romans followed their example. By this time, there were two variations on the same basic theme; the older was open, the other was closed to keep, as far as possible, impurities out of the oil. Subsequent changes affected the closed lamp and many variations were contrived.

Roman craftsmen were, indeed, remarkably ingenious in the matter of lighting. A long list might be compiled of the varieties of oil lamp and the forms of candelabra, to which references are made in literature and of which examples have been found in excavations. The commonest type of oil lamp was always the clay lamp but others were of bronze or precious metals. They might be disc-shaped or moulded into the form of a head or series of animal heads, and one lamp might contain a number of nozzles for the wicks. Christianity brought changed forms of decoration and many lamps carried the Chi-Ro monogram.

In Coptic Egypt, the form of the lamp was often simplified into a chalice shape. In the Moslem world, lamps were larger, sometimes of glass; these, usually semi-circular in shape, were used until the

fifteenth century. A little after the year 1000 A.D., a type of lamp shaped like a vase with a small base and a wide lip was in use in Europe, and remained so for several centuries until the portable lamp was introduced; this was a slender shaft on a wide base with covered fuel holder and one or more wicks, carried by a ring on the top. This remained the commonest type of lamp until the seventeenth century.

In Imperial Rome there were lampholders, the forerunners of chandeliers, of a number of different kinds, suited to candles and oil lamps. They were, as a rule, of bronze and often took the form of columns or trees with a number of branches which might be fixed or moveable. In subsequent centuries few changes and few improvements were made. In paintings we begin to see lamps hung from the ceiling; in Van Eyck's portrait of *Jan Arnolfini and His Wife*, an elaborate chandelier with a single candle burning hangs over the head of the happy pair. Elaborate lamps appear in the Italy of the Renaissance; sometimes they consist of a single light, sometimes of several lights, contained in cups of glass or metal hung on chains. At the end of the sixteenth century there was a fashion for glass lamps, produced at Murano and in Bohemia, but during the Renaissance the brass oil lamp appeared.

In the sixteenth, seventeenth and eighteenth centuries anyone who could afford them preferred candles. Making them was a household chore and the candlesticks and candleholders devised for them were often very beautiful. To put out the flame, extinguishers shaped usually like a dunce's

(Above, left) Bronze nightlight, probably Venetian of the seventeenth century (Florence, National Museum): this was a version of the veilleuse of the sixteenth century and later, in which a subdued light shone from the traceries of the lamp's sides.
(Above) Tapestry symbolizing the month of January from the series mistakenly thought to have been designed by Lucas van Leyden (print by G. Goutzwiller): this set of tapestries was woven several times by the Gobelins factory in the seventeenth century.
(Below) Bronze lamp in the shape of a satyr's head, from the school of Riccio da Padova (Washington, National Gallery, Kress Collection): one of the many patterns of lamp fashionable during the Renaissance and inspired by classical mythology.

cap were made and, in the case of chamber candlesticks, often attached to the candlestick itself; and to trim the wick or the snuff from it, there were candle-snuffers shaped like a pair of scissors, with a small box for the snuff attached to one blade.

The oil lamp was not neglected during this period. In the middle of the sixteenth century Girolamo Cardano, the mathematician, invented, among other things, a lamp with a fuel tank on small columns from which the fuel flowed into the container only when it was needed. By the eighteenth century, lamps of many varieties were on the market. In 1776, a certain Léger used a plaited wick and found that it produced less smoke and smell. In 1780, one Argand fitted a plaited wick into a lamp in cylindrical form and improved the draught and thereby the light. Finally, the lamp on the inspiration of a M. Lange acquired a glass shade, which improved the light again. In Lange's lamp, however, the fuel was paraffin and not oil, and paraffin lamps have survived until the present day. Nineteenth century ingenuity devised endless variations on the basic oil or rather paraffin lamp, and many were patented.

Changes in methods of lighting have frequently provoked criticism on the grounds that the new light damaged the eyes. Madame de Genlis complained of Argand's lamp that it compelled young people to wear spectacles. The advent of gas lighting inspired Charles Nodier, the contemporary and friend of Hugo and de Musset, to damn it as a source of withered trees, blackened rooms, widespread slaughter by slow asphyxiation and the destruction of cities by explosion.

After gas, electricity. The essayist, Maxime du Champ, said it dazzled but did not illumine and the journalist Edmond Texier made the ill-starred prediction that Paris would never succumb to its graveyard glow. But Paris did and so did the rest of the world, and then indeed there was light. Designers and decorators were, however, caught unprepared by its arrival and could do no more at first than adapt existing gas lamps to it. The gas lamps were in turn, adaptations of oil lamps and candle-holders. It was a long time before design caught up with electricity and shapes were devised that were suitable for it. Designers are, indeed, still catching up.

(Opposite page) Detail from the Portrait of the Arnolfinis by Jan van Eyck (1434: London, National Gallery). This splendid chandelier, with its presumably symbolic single burning candle, was probably made in Dinant, south of Namur, from which copper and brass ware (dinanderie) was exported all over Europe. The workmanship is Gothic; the branches, each of which hold a single light, are supported by a straight central trunk and are decorated with stylized leaves.

(Below) G.F. Kersting, Reading (1814: Winterthur, Reinhart Picture Gallery). Kersting painted many interiors like this, with a single figure reading, writing or working (see also page 370). Since the source of light is important to his subject, he informs us not only on the nature of early nineteenth century interiors but on the types of lamp and lighting used. This painting shows the lamp with three candles which was fairly common during the Empire period.

H. Birger, Interior of the Furstenberg House (1885: Gothenburg, Kunstmuseum). This must be one of the first paintings of an electric chandelier. It was made first to reflect the soft glow of candlelight in its cut crystal drops, then adapted to gas lighting and finally to electricity.

Lamps designed by Trouvé between 1880 and 1885: it is unlikely that they gave a very powerful light.

375

Hot and cold

The house was developed as a shelter from the weather. It was intended to protect man, especially at night, and his fire. Different climates presented, as we have seen, different problems for which each culture devised its own solution. In Greece, Aristotle wrote: 'For well-being and good health, the house should be well ventilated in summer and sunny in winter; to achieve this it should be protected from northerly winds and be longer than it is wide.' Xenophon, seeing the problem differently, suggested

instead: 'The southern half should be higher to enjoy the winter sun, and the northern half lower to keep out cold winds.' To the east, in Damascus, the wind blows most harshly from the south so that the houses have their winter rooms on the north side and their summer rooms on the south side.

The stove was slow to develop. The focus of the Greek and Roman house was the primitive hearth, often in the middle of the room with a hole overhead in the roof to allow the smoke to escape. It was used for cooking as well as heating, and was, as we have seen, a source of light. For heating, the Greeks also used earthenware containers of embers; these probably originated in the East where the *kangri*, the pot of embers covered with a heavy cloth and set beneath a table, is still a widespread form of heating from Turkey to India. But the Romans discovered the advantages of central heating by means of the hypocaust, that is, the leading in of heating from a furnace through clay pipes.

So sophisticated a form of heating was, obviously, only for those who could afford it and the central hearth continued in use for the majority of the population as well as for the incoming barbarians who swept over southern Europe. Before the fireplace could be re-positioned against the wall, it was necessary that house construction should have progressed to the point where chimneys could be built, and that materials that were sufficiently fireproof could be used. Still, by early in the thirteenth century, such a fireplace is recorded in Venice and by the end of the same century, there were others at Pisa. Soon they were so popular that according to one chronicler, where there had not been a single fireplace of this kind at Piacenza in 1320, by 1388 there was hardly a house without one. The same story could be told of the rest of Europe. First, possibly, the fireplace was set against the wall; later, influenced perhaps by models in the Near East, it was built into the thickness of the wall itself. And from this has developed the enormous variety

(Opposite page) The fireplace designed by Giuliano da Sangallo for the upper floor drawing-room in the Palazzo Gondi in Florence, built between 1490 and 1501. This photograph from the Brogi archives illustrates the decline of such impressive fireplaces with the insertion of a utilitarian and inelegant coal-burning stove.

(Right) Rococo fireplace and chimney piece in an eighteenth century Dutch house in the Wijnstraat in Dordrecht; it is of a piece with the rest of the drawing-room's décor. (Below) Stove of the kind invented by Benjamin Franklin in 1742 and popular in the United States for over a century. The two sketches (below) are taken from the American Family Encyclopedia (New York, 1845) in which they are accompanied by a lengthy explanation of their efficiency in creating currents of warm air to heat not only the room in which the stove is set, but also the room above.

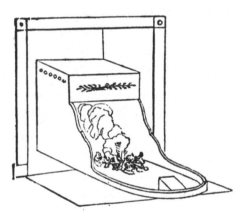

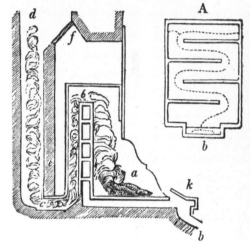

(Opposite page) Some of the fireplaces illustrated by Sebastiano Serlio in his famous treatise on architecture (1537). They are markedly classical in inspiration though Serlio was concerned with their efficiency and appropriateness to their setting. The second, he advised, should be used only in small rooms. The fire, he also argued, should be lower than a man's face so that the flames, which are harmful to the eyes, may warm all of the rest of the body, especially if the person is standing, without harming the sight.

of fireplaces that we know today. In his *Dictionnaire du Mobilier*, Viollet-le-Duc describes the fireplace, for example, of the Counts of Poitiers: it was thirty feet broad, six feet deep, and divided into three hearths. In order to reach the level of the fire, it was necessary to climb a dozen steps. This gargantuan fireplace occupied the end wall of the main hall and served a number of adjoining rooms.

Decoration of the fireplace often reflected the decoration of the building. Throughout the eleventh century, it was squat, square and solid, built of stone. But by the sixteenth century, decorative interest had already begun to concentrate on the mantelpiece or the setting of the hearth. By the end of the eighteenth century, we find the fireplace faced with marble and trimmed with bronze ornaments to match the *garniture* of clock and candlesticks on the chimney-piece. It was during the nineteenth century that the decline began in the splendour of the fireplace and its setting; since then it has gradually degenerated into the small frame of smooth

Victorian stove from an English catalogue of the year of the Great Exhibition, 1851. Carefully designed, its workmanship is excellent. Manufacturers employed painters and sculptors to design new models for them and also, on occasion, organized competitions for the best designs: their enterprise constituted an early link between art and industry.

Joseph Heintz the Younger, Bullfight in the Campo San Polo in Venice *(Venice, Museo Correr). This detail shows the Venetian chimneys admired as early as the fourteenth century by the Florentine chronicler Villani. As well as these bell or lotus-shaped chimneys there were others shaped like dice (appropriately in Venice), like urns and cones, and others again embellished with arches. (Below) A stove designed in fine, flowing* Art Nouveau *style by Victor Horta for his own house in Brussels in 1893.*

tiles which today is seen universally.

In the 1740's, Benjamin Franklin had evolved a method of heating more than one room from a single fireplace but the enclosed stove as we know it now is largely a nineteenth century development. Early examples were decorated in neo-classical fashion and in the bedroom designed by Percier and Fontaine for 'citizen C.I.', that is, the portrait painter Jean Baptiste Isabey, the stove 'placed inside a pedestal of terracotta, covered in marble and bronze', was passed off as the base of a bust of Minerva. Very beautiful stoves of majolica, coloured at first, were designed on classical lines (the firm of Feilner in Berlin produced many of them); later the stoves were white, relieved at most by some geometrical motifs or very restrained decoration in bronze.

In some houses, stoves and fireplaces conflicted. Stoves were placed in fireplaces and the pipes led up the chimney; the British Isles, however, resisted the introduction of stoves as, indeed, they were to resist the advent of central heating. About 1840, a stove was devised that would circulate hot air through a series of pipes; it was, in fact, the same kind of system as had been adopted by certain me-

Further suggestions from the treatise on architecture
by Sebastiano Serlio (see page 376) on the subject
of fireplaces. The first six are in the French style; the rest
are 'according to the custom in Italy', though not,
apparently, to the custom in Ferrara 'where they
weigh too heavily on the walls' or in Venice 'where they
reach a fearful height because of the winds'.
(Right) Two central heating radiators made by the
firm of Koerting in Hanover about 1890: the one
on the right (from Meadow House in Mansfield, 1897)
has vaguely bamboo-shaped columns which
were thought to increase the radiant surface.

dieval monks in Greenland who used the waters of a thermal spring in this way to heat their monastery. Central heating in all its guises has meant the end not merely to a complex household routine but to an attitude of mind, and has thrust into obsolescence the accumulated proverbs and metaphors of centuries, save, perhaps, in Britain where capitulation to it has taken longer.

The other aspect of shelter from the weather is, of course, that of keeping cool or rather, of keeping heat out of the house. Paintings on Egyptian tombs show buildings with, on the roof, what look like the wind vanes still common in the Near East. In the Nile valley, the large jars of water drawn from the river and set on wooden tripods in the sheltered shadows of the room were cooled by servants with fans. In jars of porous clay, water evaporated through the walls of the jar and cooled what remained. A more expensive method of cooling the atmosphere has always been by fountains, the effect of which may be as much psychological as practical.

Keeping food cool and, indeed, preserving it is an ancient problem. It was solved early by the ice-box or, on a larger scale, the ice house, dug out of the ground in a suitably sheltered spot and, once filled with snow or ice gathered during the winter, covered with earth again; the ice was used to cool water or wine, to make frozen puddings, and preserve meat and fish. Machines to freeze food, as well as to blend them, were suggested as early as the beginning of the seventeenth century and again in the eighteenth, but it takes time for technology to catch up with inspiration so that the refrigerator is a comparatively modern invention.

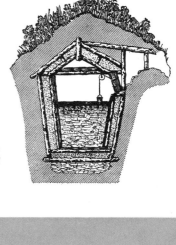

(Right) An ice-house of American
pattern, from about the middle
of the nineteenth century.
(Below) Wind vanes on buildings in
Hyderabad in West Pakistan; they help
to create currents of
air and cool the interiors.

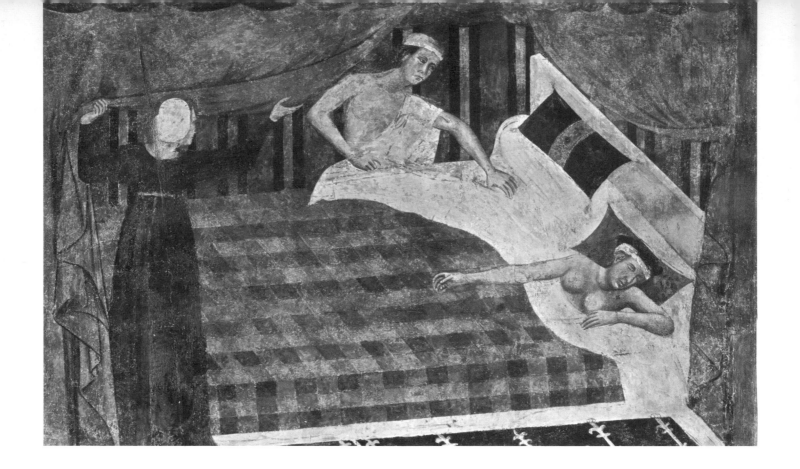

The bedroom

For all its importance in the household, the fireplace gave rise to a great many complaints. In 1520, at the height of his career and, indeed, just before he died, Raphael was consulted by the Duke of Este – the husband of Lucrezia Borgia – about some fireplaces that were to be built in his castle at Ferrara. What worried the duke was not their decoration but their efficiency; he wanted a fireplace that would not give off too much smoke. And so the letters passed back and forth with requests for details, explanations, designs and models. The Kings of France too, one gathers from contemporary accounts, suffered abominably from cold in their palaces of the Louvre, Fontainebleau, Marly, and Versailles. The mother of the Regent of France recalled later how in 1695 the wine and water froze on the king's table. Letters from Madame de Pompadour to her brother mention ice at Marly in the middle of April. Malherbe counted the number of pairs of breeches he wore one on top of the other by the letters of the alphabet; one day he told Racine he had reached the letter L. Madame de Maintenon's complaints about the bedroom of Louis XIV in winter are well-known: 'No door or window shuts properly and we have draughts that are like nothing so much as American hurricanes.' The royal doctor, Delorme, discovered that it was comfortable to sit beside the stove in a sedan chair and

several ladies copied him. Madame de Maintenon improved on this by inventing a kind of moveable recess, rather like a confessional; it increased in size until it contained not only an armchair but a bed. Gossip alleged that it betrayed her longing for the throne but, when Louis XIV died, the princesses took over the invention with enthusiasm.

Fireplaces, it must be conceded, failed miserably to heat vast spaces of baroque drawing-rooms, and doors and windows failed to keep out the cold. And fireplaces were fewer, even in rich houses, than one supposes. The massive fireplaces that did exist

Jean-Michel Moreau le Jeune, Le Coucher de la Ma-
riée *(c. 1770). There is a frivolous grandeur about
this bedchamber with the* putti *on the ceiling, heavily
draped bed with its crown of ostrich feathers, and the
otherwise rococo décor of the room.*

*(Opposite page, above) Fourteenth century fresco in the Palazzo del
Populo in San Gimignano, recently attributed to Memmo
di Filippuccio. The subject is not clear — it may have been an
erotic fable — but it does illustrate the medieval habit
of sleeping naked and the hanging of curtains round
the bed, not merely to create a room within a room but to
ward off the worst of the draughts.*
*(Below) The curtained bed is illustrated again in this
print by Bosse (1602-1676), taken from one of his paintings.
An important function of the bed was, indeed, to provide
warmth as well as a resting place. The receiving of
visitors while in bed was quite common, though paintings of
the kind are often justified by such
a title as* Λ Visit to a Newly-Delivered Mother.

*In some circumstances,
the problem was that
of finding room, as
unobtrusively as possible,
for a spare bed. American
furniture-makers
devoted considerable
thought and ingenuity
to it, as this illustration
from a catalogue to
the 1876 Philadelphia
Exhibition indicates.*

contributed to headaches and chronic colds and ca-
tarrh. That they scarcely even worked is plain from
the correspondence between the Duke of Este and
Raphael and it is quite clear why a whole volume
of Philibert de l'Orme's *Architecture* is devoted to
the proper functioning of a chimney. Houses were
abandoned because their fireplaces failed to work
properly. All sorts of contrivances were invented to
improve them — small windmills, wheels and so on
— by architects and others, but in the middle of
the seventeenth century another architectural theo-
rist, Savot, could think of nothing better than the
time-honoured expedient of opening a window to
let the smoke out and a draught in, in order to
revive the flames.

From all this, it is clear why it was socially acceptable to receive one's guests in bed — acceptable
for the host or hostess, that is; the guests were probably none too warm. And even in bed, supplement-
ary heating was necessary in the shape of bed-
warmers to which comic and libellous names like
monk or priest were given. Bedrooms were heated
with braziers, usually portable. But it was warmer
in bed.

So it has been, probably, for several thousand
years. Homer mentions soft couches on which the
hero takes his ease with his favourite handmaiden,
but not much else. (This has not, however, prevented scholars from estimating that the bed shared by
Paris and Helen measured six feet by fourteen).
The placing of beds in Greek and Roman houses
indicates a consciousness of draughts. No longer a
heap of skins or pillows and coverings, the bed was
often set in a recess which afforded the occupant
some protection from cold and draughts. Shelves
and cupboards seem to have made up the rest of
Graeco-Roman bedroom furniture.

In the Middle Ages, the campaign against cold
heralded the advent of wooden panelling, often
splendidly carved. The floors were strewn with straw,
rushes or sweet-smelling dried grasses as indeed
they continued to be until the seventeenth century.
We know little of the bed as a piece of furniture in
the early Middle Ages. Between 1000 and 1200 A.D.,
it was presumably a purely utilitarian piece of furniture, albeit one of the most important pieces in
the house, placed as it was in the main room which
served as living-room, dining-room and bedroom for
the owner of the house and dormitory for his dependents. In the romance of Tristan, we read how
the hero reached Iseult in the royal bed without
having to set foot on the floor. Quilted, padded
and embroidered covers, or fur coverings, solved
part of the heating problem. In the fourteenth cen-

tury, it is probable that curtains were hung round the bed in order to afford more shelter and warmth, possibly also to give some privacy, though the importance of privacy to the medieval mind is difficult to estimate.

By the fifteenth century fixed beds, as opposed to the mobile couches of earlier periods, led the way to developments in the design of the bed and its appurtenances. They became ceremonial pieces with pillars, canopies and hangings of oriental or Italian silks, brocades and velvets. Some of them reached enormous sizes: Noel du Fail in his *Propos Rustiques* (1586) speaks of fifteenth century beds that were nine feet wide and nineteen feet long. Henri Sauval, the French historian who died in 1670, confirms that old beds were *extraordinairement grands* and mentions one that was eleven feet by thirteen feet. In 1520, Dürer saw an immense bed at Nassau which, it was claimed, could have held fifty people, in, presumably, conditions more crowded than that of the Great Bed of Ware where,

'Four couples might cosily lie side by side,
And thus without touching each other abide.'

In Italian Renaissance houses, the bed stood majestically on a dais, canopied and curtained and sometimes decorated on the corners with bunches of ostrich feathers. It was during the sixteenth century however, that the framework of the bed gained in importance when, for example, the bed of one Raoul de la Faye, according to an inventory made in Paris in 1544, had columns 'carved to represent Hercules.' The fashion spread and canopies or testers were variously supported by caryatids or figures

of Atlas or Telamon. While the bedroom remained a reception room, the bed of state retained its important position, but as the lay-out of the household changed and the reception of guests began to be confined to the drawing-rooms, the bed diminished in prestige. In more practical terms, its form was lightened. The pillars or posts became more slender, the hangings less confining. Its position within the bedroom changed too. In some cases it was set in an alcove; more generally it was set against the wall with the longer side next to the wall. New types of bed appeared – French beds, military beds, Chinese beds, Polish beds, Turkish beds. Finally, during the period of the French empire, we find the bed with a headboard and a footboard, very like – allowing for the recent popularity of the divan – the type of bed in use today. The double bed, that is, the bed one and a half times as wide as the single, appeared in France about 1900.

Screens

Screens are referred to at a very early period in China, and in terms which suggest that their purposes were other than those to which they were generally applied. Ancient Chinese texts such as the I-li, or Book of Ceremonies, speak of them as objects with a symbolic meaning. In the Han dynasty they were already made in every shape and size from small, light, table screens standing on a single foot, to tall, twelve-panelled screens nearly seven feet high. During the Ming dynasty we find the first lacquered screens which were copied in Japan and Korea and exported – via the Coromandel coast of India, hence the name by which they are often known – to Europe where they were greatly prized and admired.

The word *screen* may of course convey the rich lacquers of a tall Coromandel screen, the smaller fire screen set in the fireplace during the summer to conceal the empty grate or the very small, often embroidered fire screens used to protect ladies from any ravages to their complexion caused by the fierce heat of a fire. Fire screens and their taller brothers have a respectable ancestry. There is a small, round wickerwork one in the *Très Riches Heures* of the Duc de Berry. The screen constructed from a number of panels hinged

This Annunciation, probably by the Master of the Legend of St. Ursula, and painted about the end of the fifteenth century (Florence, Gallerie Statali) contributes to the history of furniture in that it is one of the first paintings in which a bedside cupboard is shown.

Jean-Baptiste Mallet, L'Amour au Petit Point (c. 1790: Paris, Musée Cognac-Jay). The title of the painting refers to the cupid in the embroidery frame being shown to the visitor, the design being one of the many consequences of the interest in antiquity that followed the rediscovery of Pompeii and Herculaneum. The painting also includes a folding screen, a particularly practical piece of furniture in the war against draughts. (Below) This painting by an unknown artist (about 1775) of the drawing-room of Prince Max in the palace at Dresden (Berlin, Haberstock Collection) shows two screens. One is placed in front of the door; the other, smaller but more elaborate, is a fire screen.

together is known from the twelfth century when it may have been used as a draught screen. In the sixteenth century, a screen was placed beside the altar to protect the priest from draughts. For the same reason, we find it in eighteenth century drawing-rooms. Embroidering screen panels provided occupation for the ladies of the household and painters as well-known as Watteau were not averse to painting the handles. Interiors of the neo-classical period show that the screen was still an essential piece of household equipment, especially in sitting-rooms and boudoirs. As long as draughts whistled through doors and windows, the screen remained in use; when they were conquered, it disappeared.

At table

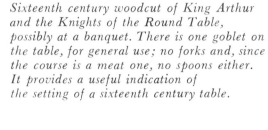

Sixteenth century woodcut of King Arthur
and the Knights of the Round Table,
possibly at a banquet. There is one goblet on
the table, for general use; no forks and, since
the course is a meat one, no spoons either.
It provides a useful indication of
the setting of a sixteenth century table.

Archaeological research tells us a little of the banquets, the fine dishes, the delicate glass and the table decorations of the civilizations of Egypt and Babylon and Nineveh. During one period in ancient Egypt, we find that, as in twentieth century fashion, it was the custom to set not a single long table but a series of small tables.

Greeks of the Homeric period may have sat on stools at banquets. By the seventh century B.C. the Asiatic custom of reclining began to spread. The Etruscans followed it and passed it to the Romans.

The reality was probably less appealing, though a Roman like Lucullus had some pretensions to the status of gourmet and the ordinary people of the Roman provinces almost certainly ate the kind of food, largely vegetarian throughout the Mediterranean world, that they ate until modern times and, in some areas, still eat today. The Middle Ages are associated with colossal feasts of meat and game, washed down with vast quantities of wine, beer or mead but these were certainly exceptional, even for the rich; when they did take place, chroniclers never fail to mention them – and the days of fasting that preceded them. For the rest, rich and poor probably ate the same kind of food, the same kind of stew whether it incorporated meat or not; the rich simply ate more often. The principal implements used were knives and fingers and, quite often, spoons.

The fork which was used in the Middle East was confined at first to the kitchen. In the eleventh century, however, Pietro Damiani referred, among the other luxuries imported to Venice by the Byzantine wife of the Doge Pietro Orseolo II, to some small implements for carrying food to the mouth. From the end of the thirteenth century, they are mentioned more and more frequently in domestic inventories; they are described as having two or three prongs or tines and as sometimes being made of gold with handles of rock-crystal or ivory. The tines were straight and remained so until about 1700. Forks were used for fruit; fingers still served for other foods and, in his advice to young gentlemen, Erasmus counsels that only three fingers should be used and that they should be quickly removed from the common dish. Some sixteenth century authors condemned the fork as soft and that great arbiter of elegance, Louis XIV, found it rather finicky.

In other words, food was for centuries conveyed from the dish to the mouth by the fingers or, at most, a spoon. Deep plates – for soup – were in use in Italy at the time of the Crusades though they did not become generally known in the rest of Europe until much later.

In attempting to picture a medieval table, one must remember that besides little cutlery there were no glasses on it. Anyone who wished to drink had to ask a servant to bring him a glass of water or

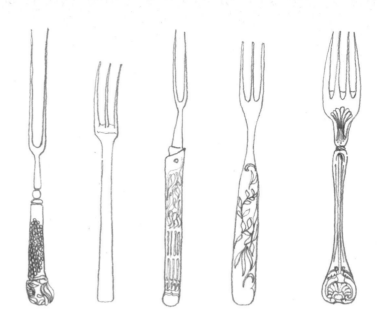

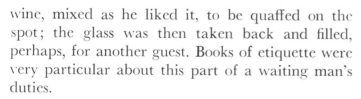

Forks: (from the left) Assyrian, in bronze; Roman (the next two), made of silver; fifteenth century Flemish and (the next two) sixteenth century Italian; seventeenth century Venetian; seventeenth century Italian with handle of gilded bronze; seventeenth century French in silver; (the next two) eighteenth century Italian (?) of which the first can be folded for travelling; eighteenth century French in silver.

Moreau le Jeune, Le Souper Fin (c. 1775). In this engraving we see not only forks but glasses, as many as there are diners. The table is decorated with small posies of flowers around the centre-piece, a refinement that has not appeared since classical times; small side tables hold other dishes for succeeding courses.

wine, mixed as he liked it, to be quaffed on the spot; the glass was then taken back and filled, perhaps, for another guest. Books of etiquette were very particular about this part of a waiting man's duties.

Only during the eighteenth century did the number of glasses begin to equal the number of guests. Carafes of wine and water stood on the splendid sideboards of the period but, just after 1750, it was discovered that it was convenient to have these too on the dining-table. In this as in other aspects of everyday life, change filtered down from the top. In his diary for the 27th. September 1760, the lawyer Barbier recorded that 'His Majesty had the goodness to serve wine to the Archbishop of Paris several times as the bottles were on the table.' In less eminent households, the old manners were retained.

During the eighteenth and nineteenth centuries the appurtenances of the table multiplied and silversmiths and goldsmiths were kept fully occupied with the production of cutlery and dishes of all descriptions in silver and silver-plate, the more so as there was a tendency to invent special dishes for specialized purposes; and so we have a proliferation of dish warmers, vegetable dishes, sauce boats, jugs, baskets, salt cellars, oil flasks and wine coasters. A Victorian dining-table in all its splendour of silver and porcelain and wreathed in flowers, decorated perhaps à la Russe, was an awe-inspiring sight.

385

The kitchen

(Above) Hearth
for cooking,
and latrine, found
in a small house
at Tel el-Amarna
in Egypt
(c. 1300 B.C.).
(Left) Rare
picture of
a medieval
kitchen in
Pietro Lorenzetti's
fresco of The
Last Supper
(Assisi,
San Francesco,
Lower Basilica).

This is probably the room of which, from the point of view of documentation, we know least; at the same time, it is one in which change must have taken place very slowly indeed until the recent revolution in the equipment of the kitchen.

To begin with, of course, it was not a separate room at all but merely the area round the central hearth of the house. The most important piece of kitchen equipment was the fire itself. When the house grew larger – both in Egypt and the classical world – it was separated from the principal rooms of the house, often on another side of the courtyard. Drains were constructed for the removal of water; the water closet placed next to it made use of the same amenities.

The utensils in a Roman kitchen consisted of iron or bronze pots, dishes and jars of baked clay, tripods, and knives and scrapers of iron. The *batterie de cuisine* was used on a dresser set in the wall convenient to the stoves and ovens; the Roman oven, one of the most distinctive of archaeological finds, has been uncovered from central Scotland to the frontiers of Persia.

In the Middle Ages, the kitchen reverted again to its position in the heart of the house where the cooking fire and stove warmed the entire family. The utensils were as before iron pots, clay vessels for dry goods and jars for liquids. Each kitchen would contain moreover a gridiron, a mortar and pestle for grinding spices, spoons, ladles and strainers of metal and wood. The dishes used at table were for the most part of wood or pottery and, later, pewter. Glass was rarely used and was a very fragile luxury. Iron pots were suspended above the fire with the help of tripods and, later, of chains and pothooks. Metal stoves were introduced late in the Middle Ages.

Pieter Aertsen, Christ in the House of Mary and Martha *(c. 1560: Rotterdam, Boymans-van Beuningen Museum). This presents a faithful inventory – in a series of still-lifes – of the contents of a very well-stocked sixteenth century kitchen.*
L. tom Ring the Younger, The Marriage at Cana *(Berlin, Kaiser-Friedrich Museum): here are the preparations for the marriage feast as they would have been carried out in a wealthy Renaissance household: the paintings on the wall are not, probably, typical of contemporary kitchens.*

During the Reinassance the kitchen was frequently consigned to the lower regions which, in a palace or mansion of the period, were ill-lit and damp as well as enormous. They were connected with the upper regions by back staircases and, later, by small lifts for carrying food. In his *Proprietario Architetto*, published in Venice in 1832, Urbano Vitry commented, however, that kitchens so disposed were unwholesome and responsible for the high mortality rate among cooks. It would be quite easy, he added, to improve this distressing situation. All that was necessary was to build the stove under the canopy of the fireplace. Mrs. Beeton was more practical about what she described as 'the great laboratory of every household'; she demanded plenty of light and air, and convenient fuel and water.

(Left) Philibert-Louis Debucourt, Interior of a Kitchen (1812). This engraving almost certainly shows a country kitchen though those in large town houses may not have been very different.
(Below, from the left) During the nineteenth century, the American stove ranged through an enormous variety of forms and functions. This one, featured in the American Woman's Home *in 1869 could – once stoked with sufficient anthracite for 24 hours – provide 17 gallons of hot water an hour, roast and bake bread, cakes and joints of meat; ashes were easily removed from the ashbox.*
The kitchen designed by Le Corbusier for the Villa Savoye (see pages 322-3).

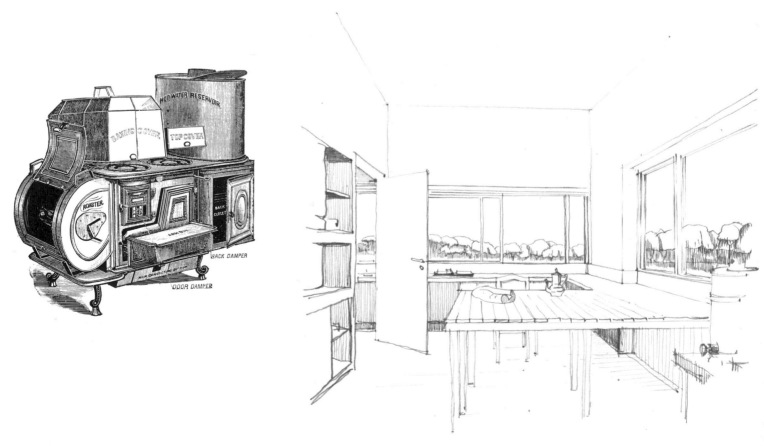

The water supply

Wood was probably the first material pressed into service for the conducting of water. Hollow tree trunks were doubtless used as primitive pipes and wooden pipes were used by the Romans; they were used in the Middle Ages too and have been found in sections nineteen feet long with a diameter of three to five inches. The Romans also used pipes of baked clay which were known in slightly different form to the Mycenaeans and to the peoples of the civilizations that flourished in the area between the Tigris and the Euphrates; some of these could still be used today. The Greeks fashioned water and drain pipes in such a way that one section fitted into the next, thereby sealing them more effectively. Pipes of hammered copper were used in ancient Egypt: in Tyre and Sidon the materials used were bronze or lead with carefully welded joints. The lead pipes manufactured during the period of the Roman Empire are an early example of industrial standardization. Since then the changes that have taken place in the construction of pipes have been those of material and method of manufacture.

Wells, often the subject of local folklore and superstition, were important to ancient, medieval, and comparatively modern communities. Early wooden linings to them were soon superseded by linings of stone or brick and, in Crete and Mycenae, of clay. Water was raised during the Roman Empire by buckets or, in the case of large wells, by a continuous chain of buckets kept in motion by slaves. In the Middle Ages, the bucket and chain or rope continued in use until, and indeed long after, the invention in Germany of the piston pump. But as early as 1420, the principle of using air pressure to raise water was implied in Giovanni Fontana's proposal for a machine operated by hot air to raise water. From these primitive beginnings the pressure pump developed – and with it the opportunity for endless variations on the original theme.

(From the left) Pipes of baked clay found in Crete; each section fits closely into the next. The Archimedes screw, operated by a slave, for raising water: from a mural at Pompeii, though not a particularly accurate one since the slave would have to be bending further forward.

(Above) Small opening in the wall communicating with the well, on one of the upper floors of the Palazzo Davanzati in Florence.
(Left) Well of traditional type in Venice in the middle of the nineteenth century. In towns of this period, water was led into the courtyards of houses or, at most, into the kitchen at ground level, where there were means of leading in water.

(From the left) Pump with cog-wheels providing the water supply for a house in the first half of the eighteenth century (From Grollier de Servière's Recueil d'ouvrage... de mécanique, Lyons, 1733). Hot water system for domestic use (United States, middle of the nineteenth century). English-speaking and western European countries legislated, from the middle of the nineteenth century onwards, for the control of water supplies and the quality of the water available.

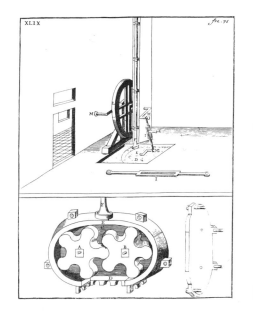

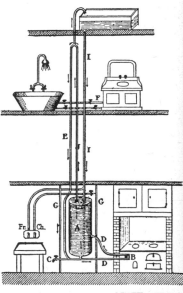

Women under the shower, from a Greek vase. Note the animal masks used to decorate the showers, and the towel rail.

The bathroom

In the Sumerian city of Eshnunna in the third millennium B.C. a bitumen coating on bricks was intended to waterproof the floors of the bathroom. Similar thought was devoted to the convenience of the bathroom as a whole. The Egyptians too made careful provision for bathing and in the Egyptian house at Tel el-Amarna, illustrated on page 35, allowance is made for at least one room for the bath, faced with stone; beside the bath was a bench for massage.

That cleanliness is next to godliness was not a widespread article of faith in the Middle Ages, and on occasion extreme cases of non-washing tended to be associated with sanctity. But those who possessed the money and the fortitude did bathe in tubs protected by curtains: some tubs were large enough to take both husband and wife together. And when she wished to refurbish her equipment for the toilette, Margaret of Flanders bought in 1403 about forty-four yards of *toille bourgeoise* to line two bathtubs and red Malines cloth for their canopies. Those families who did not have at their disposal the revenues of Flanders kept a basin with a spout in a corner of the kitchen or the main room of the house and with the water in it the whole family washed their faces and hands; the rest of the body was not exposed to this treatment.

Positive prejudice against washing was remarkably pertinacious. In 1635, the medical author, Théophraste Renaudot, solemnly assured his readers that 'except in cases prescribed by the doctor, bathing is not only unnecessary but very dangerous.' At the same time, a book of etiquette published in Paris was very precise in its advice: 'The

(Below) In this illustration, also taken from a piece of Greek pottery, the water pours from a mask into a basin which seems to anticipate the most modern pattern of wash-basin. On the floor is a comb, similar to that on page 395, and a flask for perfumed oil. (Botton of page) Fresco attributed to Memmo Filippuccio in the Palazzo del Populo in San Gimignano. Two or more people bathing together in a single tub was fairly common in medieval Europe. as in present-day Japan.

Portrait of Diane de Poitiers *by François Clouet (Washington, National Gallery, Kress Collection). Since the king's mistress commanded the most expensive of luxuries the preparations for her toilette are elaborate: the bath is not only lined but apparently curtained with heavy silks; and should she feel hungry in the bath, there is a bowl of fruit to hand.*

(Below) Bath of the second millennium B.C., found in the so-called inn at Knossos in Crete. It resembles the one discovered in the elaborately decorated 'Queen's bathroom.' (Bottom of page) Bain en forme de sopha (sofa), model of a bath designed by Jean Charles Delafosse (1734-1789): its manufacture would have been a combined operation for cabinet-makers, bronze workers and painters.

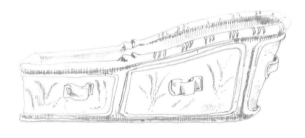

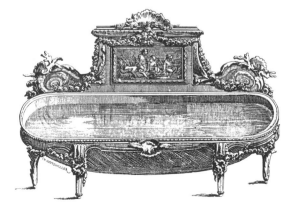

hands must be washed every day. In the same way, the face must be washed almost as often, the cheeks must be shaved, and the head washed occasionally.' Louis XIV suffered from a profound distaste for washing though at times he submitted to being sponged with tufts of cotton wool soaked in alcohol.

Modern prejudice against the drying properties of soap and water on the skin manifested itself as early as 1782 when one J.-B. de la Salle wrote in his *Règles de la Bienséance* that 'a respectable person must have his face cleaned every morning with a white cloth to take the grease off: it is not good to wash it with water because it makes it sensitive to the cold in winter and to dryness in summer.' This may explain the size of the basin and jug possessed by Marie Antoinette – only nine and a half inches high. The famous Percier designed those of Napoleon and Josephine but they were hardly more capacious.

But there were developments in the popularity of the bath. In the last half of the eighteenth century, a talented tinsmith called Level introduced a bath 'in which the person bathing sits down and is contained on all sides, as in an armchair'. It was an improvement on the tubs then in use and on the rare marble baths. The makers of this new bath had, however, to wait until the second quarter of the following century for it to become popular.

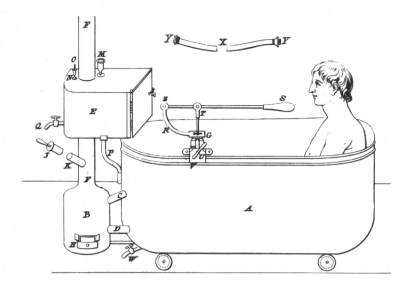

curiosity. It turns up now and again in letters and diaries. A letter from Madame de Pompadour discusses two *bidets* she is buying, from the famous dealer, Lazare Duvaux: one is 'decorated with flowering rose trees and mouldings, standing on feet embellished with bronzes and golden filigree'; the other is 'of walnut with a lid and back in red morocco leather studded with gilt nails'.

The perfumes of Arabia – which was, of course, the source of frankincense – aromatic oils, unguents and other cosmetics originated in the east and from there, their use was learned by the classical world. The ladies of Sumer and Babylon used combs and mirrors and exquisitely carved and fashioned hair pins and ornaments. Throughout the history of ancient Egypt it is possible to watch the flow of fashion, kept in motion by the use of wigs and other aids as well as a battery of cosmetics, spoons, spatulas and palettes. Cosmetics were kept in containers of alabaster, ivory and glass: an important and practical one was kohl for the eyes. Cosmetics were carried too by the Phoenicians in their trading ships.

Then, when most houses of any pretensions contained small bathrooms, the bath was accompanied by an armchair and even a couch, or a table with writing materials. There might be too – *pace* Seneca – a statue, Venus perhaps, on a pedestal. But the wash-stand with its equipment of basin and jug – and shaving mug, soap-dish and the rest – stayed in the bedroom, which was warmer. Eventually, of course, the wash-basin too moved out of the bedroom and into the bathroom.

With the barbarian invasions, the export and import of cosmetics from the east became more spasmodic. But the barbarians themselves had a weakness for them. The Saxons reddened their lips. The Burgundians were proud of their gleaming hair, the gleam being achieved by the liberal application of rancid butter, a common article of the toilette in Asia and Africa. Voices were raised in disapproval of such self-adornment: in the twelfth century, they condemned in particular women's attempts to lighten their skin and hair.

Concern for personal hygiene did persuade French society of the late Middle Ages to the use of an item of equipment that is hardly mentioned in histories and encyclopaedias though it has been described in all solemnity as 'an invention the social importance of which is equal to that of the arquebus' – though not, perhaps, in any Anglo-Saxon country where the *bidet* has been traditionally regarded, until recently, with a kind of scandalized

Neither then nor later did their condemnations obtain much of a hearing. The period of the

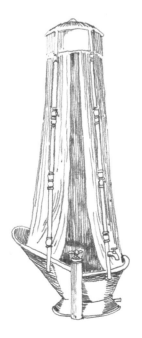

(Opposite page, top) A complicated heating system for bath water, illustrated in an Italian manual for architects published in the second half of the nineteenth century. The bath is on wheels and is used in the kitchen; the various gadgets have as their object the economical use of water and heat, both of which were hard to come by.

(Right) Basin and ewer in rock crystal which belonged to Marie Antoinette *(Paris, Louvre)*. There was no waste of water here: the ewer is no more than 10 inches high.

(Below) R. Buckminster Fuller, Dymaxim unit; a service block planned and moulded together, United States 1959.

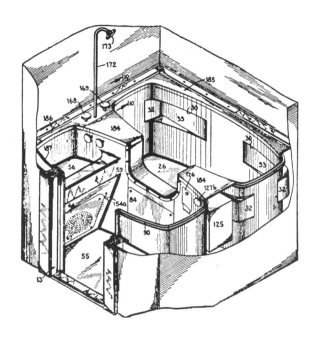

(Opposite page, from the left) Detail from a German woodcut of about 1500, which shows the commonest type of wash-basin in the Middle Ages. A small tank with a tap supplied the water to the basin; dirty water was emptied into the receptacle under the basin. The towel hung on a roller as it often does today.
The hip-bath: this version had a seat so that it allowed for little more than the bathing of the feet. The sabot, a version of the hip-bath in the form of a metal tube from which, presumably, water was less likely to spill than in the more open version. The bath-cum-shower. A water heater for the bath built by B. Waddy Maugham in 1868.

(Right, from the left) Wash-basin designed by Percier and Fontaine for Napoleon and the Empress Josephine about 1800: medallions of the imperial couple are on the base.
Biedermeier wash-basin, the medieval tank with tap but greatly refined; the towel holder is in the form of a garland.

Renaissance saw an increase in the use of cosmetics and Pietro Aretino is found, oddly, reproaching women for colouring their nipples. The quantity of implements required grew though their quality was often unsatisfactory. The mirror was still made of polished metal, as were those of the Etruscans and Romans, and the reflection was, accordingly, not very bright: glass mirrors were used in the Middle Ages but the glass itself was impure. The first 'silvered' mirrors were introduced to Europe via Venice and were very small and precious. When the Countess d'Aulnoy mentions in the story of Cinderella (in the reign of Louis XIV) that Cinderalla's sisters had mirrors so large that they could admire themselves from head to foot, she is clearly intent on astonishing her readers, for such mirrors did not appear until a century later.

Yet the seventeenth century dressing-table was elegant and well-stocked. After the death of Louis XIII, his widow, Anne of Austria, emulated the Grand and Petit Lever that had formed a part of the King's routine; that is, she took off her nightgown in private and completed her dressing in

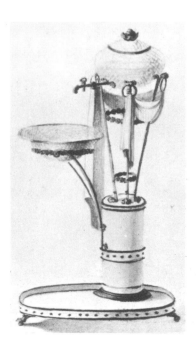

In the second half of the nineteenth century, increased efforts were made to concentrate hygienic necessities into as small a space as possible. One of the exhibitors at the Great Exhibition of 1851 in the Crystal Palace in London, G. Jennings, managed to combine a wash-basin, a bidet, a footbath and a toilet in this portable apparatus. The inventor was inspired, he claimed later, by the certainty that 'a people's civilization can be measured by its hygienic and sanitary arrangements'.

public. A complicated ritual developed, attended, in the case of the queen, by her ministers, diplomats, clerics and marshals of France; at a slightly less exalted level, her imitators had to make do with magistrates and minor officials. Not much soap and water but a great deal of powder and perfume were used. The furnishings of the bedchamber were designed to be worthy of so important a concourse.

Men too used pomades and perfumes and, later, powdered their hair. They were shaved by barbers. Louis XIV had eight in his service, which was not too onerous since he was shaved only once a week. In 1770, a M. Perrel published his *Pogonotomie* or *The art of learning to shave oneself*; at the time it seems to have been regarded as a mildly revolutionary publication which would bring undying glory to its author. It is unlikely that the barbers approved of it.

The demands of the toilette both for men and women gave rise to some exquisite and ingenious pieces of furniture with mirrors that rise into view when the lid is lifted, with accommodation for jugs and ewers, and a multitude of drawers, some fitted with silver and crystal boxes and bottles. For journeys, cases fitted to take similar boxes and bottles were made by the finest craftsmen. They turn up today in antique shops and salerooms, sometimes unrecognized for what they are, and, alas, more often than not devoid of their fittings.

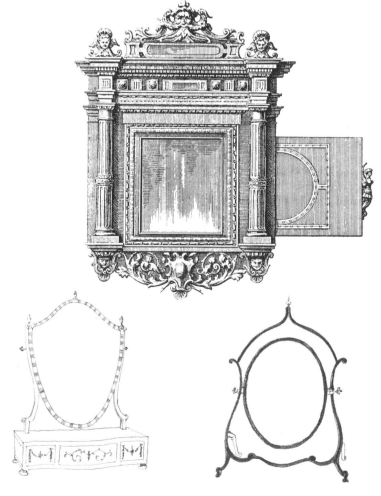

(Above, left) Sixteenth century Florentine mirror with a sliding door to protect the surface from oxidization.
(Above) The ivory back of a French mirror, exquisitely decorated with fascinating detail.
(Left) English eighteenth century mirrors for the dressing-table; the first is an elegant, functional piece in silver; the other is of wood, decorated with very fine inlays.

Su Han-Ch'ên, At the Dressing-Table *(Boston, Museum of Fine Arts). This painting on silk shows the variety and complexity of the equipment (much of it is in the box beside the vase of flowers) required for the maquillage and hairdressing of a Chinese lady in the twelfth century.*

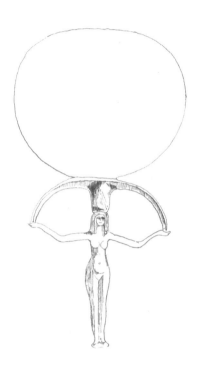

(Above) Egyptian mirror in bronze of a type found in tombs dating from 2500 B.C. During the period of the Middle Kingdom, they were very popular and were sometimes made of silver or gold. The disc, which had a single reflecting face, was often round, like this, in the shape of the sun. (Below) Assyrian comb in ebony (Paris, Louvre).
(Right) Painting attributed to F. Brunel (Lyons, Museum) which shows a household of considerable luxury. In the foreground, half masked by drapery, is a comb resembling the Assyrian one.

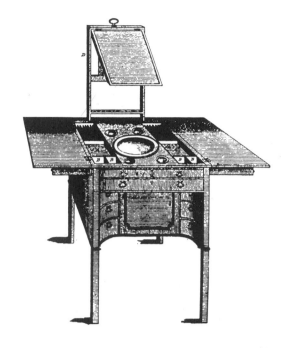

(Opposite page) Detail from a miniature illustrating a novella in the Decameron (II, 5) in a fifteenth century French codex (Paris, Arsenal). 'The sitting-place' was placed, according to Boccaccio, 'as we often see between two houses, on top of two joists, for the use of those living in both houses'.

(Left) The incredible array of vases, bottles, casts, pots, weapons, knick-knacks and antiquities disposed on and around the dressing-table of Gabriele d'Annunzio in his villa, Vittoriale, above Lake Garda.
(Right) Shaving table, a model published by Chippendale in 1754.

(Below) Small nineteenth century Cuban dressing-table.
(Right) In this painting by Jean-Baptiste Pater of the gallant spying on the lady (London, Wallace Collection), we see a bathroom of about 1730 with the bath and dressing-table: the mirror is still very small.

The toilet

The Egyptians, according to an apparently surprised Herodotus, ate and drank in the street and performed the consequently necessary function of relieving themselves indoors: it was the reverse of standard ancient practice as well as of modern practice among primitive tribes. The habit of answering the call of nature out of doors – undesirable in cities – was one that for centuries exercised the ingenuity of legislators. Montaigne, who judged Paris 'incomparable for the abundance of comforts' remembered with horror the acrid stink of its mud, for a succession of police orders – in 1522, 1525, 1539 and so on – enjoining the installation of drains and latrines had been ignored and the public continued to use the streets. Windows had to be kept closed during the summer because of the smell. In the eighteenth century, the governor of Versailles issued yet another order to forbid:

> à toutes personnes de jeter des matières fécales, eaux et autres immondices par les fenêtres.

The emptying of chamberpots was accepted practice in many cities and the cry of 'gardez l'eau', which became in English 'gardyloo', was calculated to disperse pedestrians. In Italy the cry from the pedestrian crouched at the side of the house was 'Take away your lantern!'

All this represented a serious falling off from the standards of Knossos where the people of Minoan Crete made special arrangements for ventilation as well as drainage; from those of Eshnunna in Sumer where the inhabitants enjoyed the advantages of something like a lavatory seat; or from the complex sanitary arrangements of Mohenjo-Daro in the valley of the Indus. These were, for the most part, amenities of the ruling class and we know very little of this as of other aspects of ordinary life.

The same is true of ancient Greece. In *Lysistrata* Aristophanes mentions that the street is used as a latrine but some houses almost certainly had special rooms, as did the houses of Egypt, among them the one at Tel el-Amarna to which reference has already been made; here there was a small, white-washed room immediately behind the bathroom, fitted with a stone seat set over a box in the wall containing sand. Roman houses had rooms similar to the Turkish style lavatory still in use today, usually close to the kitchen so that the same drain and water supply served both rooms.

In Roman cities the cesspools were emptied at night and their contents collected in carts. The same system operated in the Middle Ages in those cities where sewage disposal was organized even in rudimentary fashion. They were comparatively few as were houses with a water closet. A verse in Dante's *Inferno* mentions the 'private room' and in one of his stories Boccaccio refers to some rather temporary installations. Some latrines, decorated with the *graffiti* customary in these places, survive in such buildings as the Palazzo Davanzati in Florence. In the seventeenth century, a commentator on Lippi's *Malmantile* claimed that 'Every house has a loft, a lavatory, a cesspit and a kitchen sink.' Optimism had, however, got the better of him.

But if Roman and medieval householders did

The name often used in medieval England for the latrine or toilet was the garderobe. *In castellated architecture, it was most often placed in a tower, and there might have been three garderobes, one above the other. (Right) Front view and plan of the* garderobe *at Southwell Palace, Nottinghamshire; a 'four-seater', the seats are of stone.*

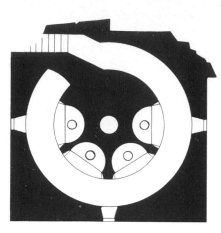

not always find it possible to install separate rooms, they did have what the Romans called a *sella pertusa* or a seat with a hole in it. Containers were placed under the seat which might be fixed or moveable. The practice survived into the Middle Ages when such contrivances were fashioned with a good deal of luxury. In the fourteenth century, John II of France commissioned the painter Girart d'Orléans to make a seat of this kind specifying that he should use velvet and that it should be painted. Montaigne complained of princes who settled the most urgent affairs of state while sitting on a *chaise percée* 'as if it were a throne'; the charming Duchess of Burgundy and other courtiers did the same. One of the officials of the court of Louis XIV was the gentleman who enjoyed the privilege of holding the king's sword while the king used his seat (in his case it was referred to as the *chaise d'affaires*). At Versailles, apart from the royal 'throne', there were another 274 close-stools, 66 of them upholstered in crimson damask or red or green velvet, and the rest simpler. During the succeeding century, the number seems to have increased so greatly as to be a source of anxiety to Marie Antoinette who refers to them in a letter to her sister. As well as multiplying, these close-stools became more elaborate and were decorated with gilt reliefs, bronze mounts, and painted with birds, landscapes and Chinese motifs. Madame de Pompadour bought a number from the cabinet-maker, Migeon, who asked three thousand livres for a single one. A description of one owned by Madame du Barry survives in the archives of the prefecture of Seine-et-Oise. It was 'inlaid with a white background, blue motifs, red stars and fine black tracery, trimmed with blue velvet embroidered in gold, with gold arms and feet, the hole covered with morocco leather, the container of heavy silver.' The colour of the upholstery usually matched that of the other furniture in the room. Sometimes it had a heraldic or symbolic significance; black was used for mourning.

The object of this piece of furniture was, obviously, not privacy but that its owner or occupant should not be obliged to leave the company or the comfort of the room in which the chair was placed.

Ingenuity as well as artistry and craftsmanship was also lavished on some of these close-stools and they were devised in different shapes. One was made to look like a pile of books with imaginary titles of a predictable nature such as *Journey into the Low Countries.* They are today much prized as antiques and some years ago in the Hotel Drouot, a Brazilian collector paid 700,000 francs for the close-stool which had belonged to Cardinal Richelieu. Since the franc was revalued at the end of the 'fifties, the price of the close-stool would today approximate to £5,000 ($12,000).

The middle classes made use of the plain chamberpot which dated back at least to the Middle Ages and allowed the householder to relieve himself without leaving the comparative warmth of his bedroom, or the room in which his bed happened to be, and facing the night chill in the state of nudity in which he customarily slept. Some such pots have been recorded; one is that owned by the Duc de Berry in 1416, made of decorated glass and hung with four gold chains: the rest of it, Viollet-le-Duc assures us, 'was the same shape as it would be now.'

During the eighteenth century, chamberpots were largely manufactured from zinc or pottery; grander ones were also made of silver. There were also bell-shaped ones of glass complete with a stopper. Complaints were made about them because of breakages and because of their unsteadiness and their general clumsiness.

The first patents for water closets appeared early in the seventeenth century in England but it was late in the nineteenth century before they began to be produced in quantity. The shape was similar to that of today and recently there has taken place too a reversion to the splendid decoration of those beflowered nineteenth century lavatories.

The chamberpot often appears in medieval miniatures, even in the noblest bedchambers: in more modern drawings it sometimes stands on a table beside the bed; in this print by J. de Brune from Emblemata of Zinnewerk *(Amsterdam, 1624), it is conveniently placed on a chair.*

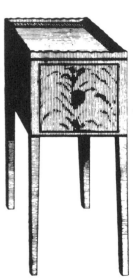

(Left) An eighteenth century chaise percée in the shape of a pile of books (from the Grand dictionnaire historique ou le Mélange curieux de l'histoire sacrée et profane, *published by Louis Moreri in 1674). A similar item of furniture, shown open.*
(Right) Night table or pot cupboard, included by Hepplewhite among the models published in 1787.
(Below, from the left) Toilet with a pedestal in the form of a lion (from the catalogue of E. John and Co., of London, about 1890). Another, entitled Epic Symphonic *decorated with floral motifs and slightly classical in style, also English, 1897. (There were others rich in acanthus leaves, and so on.) An Art Nouveau model, 1907.*

Doors

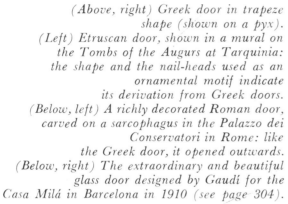

(Above, right) Greek door in trapeze
shape (shown on a pyx).
(Left) Etruscan door, shown in a mural on
the Tombs of the Augurs at Tarquinia:
the shape and the nail-heads used as an
ornamental motif indicate
its derivation from Greek doors.
(Below, left) A richly decorated Roman door,
carved on a sarcophagus in the Palazzo dei
Conservatori in Rome: like
the Greek door, it opened outwards.
(Below, right) The extraordinary and beautiful
glass door designed by Gaudí for the
Casa Milá in Barcelona in 1910 (see page 304).

The doors and windows of a house present, first of all, a technical problem: how is the wall above the opening to be supported? Two solutions have been evolved; one uses the lintel, the other the arch. The lintel imposes certain restrictions on the shape and, in earlier centuries, the size of the door, and the materials that may be used for a lintel are limited in nature. The arch does not in theory suffer from these limitations, though in practice some of the problems presented by it have only recently been solved.

In Egypt, the door of a tomb was the same as the door of a house. It was wooden, in two parts. Doors were closed from the inside with one or two crossbars. Outer doors possessed simple locks. If we read correctly the accounts that we have of the

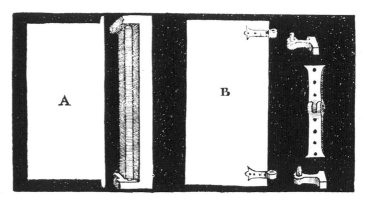

The Greeks used bolts operated by hooks; Roman smiths made locks and keys not unlike our own; the Normans secured their possessions with guards made for the most part of wood. The key and its lock shown here (Munich, Bayerische Nationalmuseum) were made in southern Germany at the beginning of the sixteenth century, a period of prosperity for German coppersmiths.

palaces of Assyria, it is possible that their entrances were protected by larger, more elaborate doors; larger because the doorways provided the lighting for the room behind. Entrances, especially inner ones, seem to have been screened by mats and curtains, but not, judging by the absence of cavities for hinges, by solid doors. In India and in the Moslem world, as we have already seen, solid doors were fitted only to the main entrance of the house; these were often intricately fitted together and decorated and, from the seventeenth century onwards, they were often lacquered. Other doorways in the house were usually screened by curtains.

Homer refers to gold and silver doors and the Greek doors of which we know were very elegant. For the most part, they were narrower at the top than the bottom. The threshold, lintel and doorposts were of timber or stone and the door itself was made of solid planks reinforced by crossbars held in place with nails the heads of which, arranged in decorative fashion, were the door's first ornament. Later refinements, both decorative and functional, were added; the keyhole, carefully shaped as was the knocker, formed like a leaf or a ring; the strip of leather to jam together the two sides of the door, which were afterwards shut securely with the help of heavy bolts pushed into holes in the framework of the door. Heavy and solid as they were, they provided a reliable protection against invasion from outside whether by stealth or during public disorders. They had no bells; visitors knocked loudly on the outside to attract the attention of the inhabitants and, since the doors opened on to the street, the residents coming out also knocked as a warning

(Above) Plan published by Sebastiano Serlio in his treatise on architecture in which he shows doors and hinges and makes it clear that in his day every smith could make them. 'All the same', he pointed out, 'the hinges which were used in ancient times and on which the door hung, as is shown in figure A, were less heavy and more easy to lock and open than those used today throughout Italy, as shown in figure B'.
(Below) Bronze door-knocker, probably sixteenth century Venetian (Washington, National Gallery, Kress Collection): a lively and delicate composition of cornucopias, dolphins and shells.

The luxury achieved in middle class Dutch houses in the eighteenth century is illustrated (left) in this double door in the Snouck van Loosen House in Enkhuizen, the furnishings of which date from about 1740. (Right) An equally impressive doorway to the 'pink room' in the eighteenth century house built by Abraham van der Hart on the Spaarne in Haarlem and now occupied by the Dutch Society of Science.

of their intentions. The half-door – that is the door the top part of which could be opened separately – seems to have been a Greek invention. The Greeks too used locks from about the fifth century B.C. and these, first of bronze and then of iron, and their keys, straight or curved, represented a considerable advance on the earlier wooden locks.

The Etruscans took over the Greek shape of the door, as did the Romans, and along the roads that led from Rome it was transported to every part of the empire. The doors were usually hung from hinges in the doorposts and closed with the help of bolts or crossbars. The shape gradually changed to become rectangular. Ornament became much more elaborate as the simple nail-heads were superseded by bronze studs or reliefs in a variety of materials. By the simple use of counterweights, the doors of baths and closets were ingeniously devised to shut by themselves.

Subsequent changes in doors and door furniture were of an ornamental and mechanical nature. They were not always for the better: according to Sebastiano Serlio, as far as hinges were concerned,

the doors made by the Romans were better than those being put together in the sixteenth century. In a style reminiscent of and probably inspired by the work of Moslem craftsmen, some Gothic doors were decorated with inlay. But fifteenth century doors were decorated, on the whole, with little more than a simple moulding. Carved and richly inlaid doors were a later development: in these inlays again the influence of Moslem or perhaps Moorish craftsmen is evident in the use of abstract design, as it is in the bronze plaques with their geometric decorations. An important part of a door's ornament, especially in Spain, was the coat of arms of the householder. During the late sixteenth and seventeenth centuries, we find doorposts in the form of *caryatids* or *atlantes*. In the following century, they were more soberly bedecked with stucco reliefs, mirrors and gilding.

An English adjunct to the door is the porch which protects the front door. The Greeks made use of the same device and, indeed, the protective portico with its columns was later reproduced in the Palladian architecture of England.

Windows

Monumental architecture of the kind found in Egypt, Greece and certain Central and South American civilizations may have no windows, but they are an essential part of the dwelling house. They betray much, indeed, about the occupants of the house and about the regard in which they hold the outside world – allowing always, of course, for the technical capacity of any given period.

There is little point, for example, in drawing attention to the small windows of early civilizations as an indication of suspicion of the outside world, since the builders of, for example, Sumer and Babylon could not build large windows and climatically it was undesirable that they should. In Egypt, windows were protected by shutters or screens which opened to let light in. Screens of plaster, stone, wood or brick, often very beautifully made, protected the windows of Moslem houses. The cost of glass meant that its use was limited until about the eighteenth century. Oiled or waxed paper was often used instead and occasionally strips of translucent marble or alabaster.

The eastern use of small windows as a protection against the heat passed to the Greeks and the windows shown on their vases – there are not many – cannot have been more than nineteen inches high and a little less wide. They too were often fitted with shutters. The Romans arched their windows in order the better to distribute the weight of the wall above the window. This allowed them also to enlarge the window openings which were then subdivided by small pillars. The use of glass, which was possible, was probably as limited as it was throughout the Middle Ages and those narrow lancet windows embedded in the thickness of massive walls were not glazed. Romanesque windows were decorated with slender columns and delicate traceries and the restrained ornament of their frames is delightful. The delicacy of their workmanship was shared by Gothic windows. Removeable panes

(From the top left) Grill of baked clay (eighteen inches wide) for a window of the third millennium B.C., found in Iraq.
Windows of Roman buildings in the Via della Fontana at Ostia.
Gallery in the Ca' d'Oro in Venice (see page 86).
(Above, right) Ground level window of the Palazzo Medici Riccardi, Florence, possibly the work of Michelangelo.
Window, from the interior, in the Zambert House in Delft (1537). French window in Havana, a mixture of baroque and rococo in cornices and ironwork.

Lucas Cranach, Cardinal Albert of Brandenburg as St. Jerome in his Study (1525: Darmstadt, Hessisches Landesmuseum). The cardinal's desk is carefully placed to catch the light from the wide window.

(Left) Windows with cloth panels which gave the name to the painting by Raphael, Madonna dell'Impannata (c. 1540: Florence, Pitti Palace).
(Below) Window in the shape of a mouth in the façade of the Zuccari house near the Spanish Steps in Rome.

of glass were fitted in the windows though waxed paper was always more widely used, even in the Renaissance, when the growing predilection for the antique encouraged the discovery of the virtues of the sober lightness of rectangular windows.

The function of the window as a means of conveying light to the interior of the house could and sometimes did, however, conflict with its part as an ingredient in the total exterior plan of the house. This was particularly true of baroque architecture in which house façades were garnished by many windows, the placing of which was dictated more by the external appearance than by their effectiveness. The comfortable mansions and villas of Georgian England avoided this conflict, on the whole, and the tall sash windows, admirably appropriate to the room behind and a pleasing part of the exterior, are one of the most delightful features of the Georgian manor.

Balconies

'An extension of the house into the street,' might be one description of the balcony. A similar extension is the bay, bow or oriel window, or the dormer window which projects from the roof of the house. Laws and bylaws have at various periods endeavoured to control if not prohibit what was in a sense a form of trespass on to the public street, without notable success.

It has been claimed that the history of the balcony begins in precisely 318 A.D. when the *praetor* Gaius Menius installed a number of loggias as theatre seats above the forum in Rome. This enterprising official was not, however, the first to realize the advantages of such a structure. Loggias are attached to some of the Etruscan burial urns shaped like houses and a reference in Aristotle to an Athenian law of 403 B.C. is probably to a prohibition of the building of balconies projecting over the street. More distantly in time and space, the palace of Gudea, the famous governor of Lagash in Sumeria, may have possessed open or closed projections which could have been balconies.

(*Above*) Renaissance house with a large balcony, shown by Fra Angelico in his predella of 'stories' of St. Nicholas of Bari (c. 1437: Rome, Pinacoteca Vaticana).
(*Below*) Balcony of the fourteenth century Palazzetto Balsano at Brindisi; the brackets are richly carved, each with motifs apparently different from the others.

(*Below*) Detail from The Miracles of St. Augustine, by Simone Martini (c. 1330: Siena, Sant'Agostino). The closed wooden balcony on the upper floor may have been derived from the temporary watch-towers found in medieval castles.

(From the left) House at Innsbruck with a covered balcony, the canopy of which was built in 1425 by Duke Frederick in order to prove that his enemies' gibe of 'Empty-pockets' was undeserved.

The central section of the façade of the house that to-day shelters the Royal Library in The Hague: it was designed by Daniel Marot about 1735.

Detail of the Palazzo Roverella at Ferrara (1508) showing the covered balcony over the front door.

(Right) Section and plan of the corner balcony of the house of the Sanabrias family at Trujillo in Extremadura (see also page 97): balconies of this design are fairly common in this region.

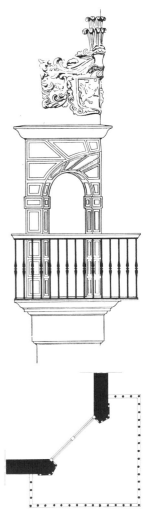

(Above) The delightful wrought-iron balcony of the seventeenth century house at No. 20 Via Durini in Milan which belonged to the conductor, Arturo Toscanini.

(Right) The distinction between balconies and windows is here reduced to a minimum by Gaudí's highly original treatment of the façade of the Casa Batlló in Barcellona.

The closed balconies which were common in Italy until the thirteenth or fourteenth centuries and then fell out of use there – though they continued in northern Europe – have been related to the temporary wooden structures that projected from castle walls for a number of reasons – local emergencies among them – but it is more likely that these enclosures are yet another architectural feature that Europe owes to Asia. In the region from the Mediterranean to the Ganges we find balconies, open and closed, of every shape and size, many of them very beautiful, with screens of intricately fretted and carved wood, stone or metal. They were attached to the palaces of the Turkish Sultans – the kiosk of Osman III in the palace of Topkapi in Costantinople is one – and of Mogul emperors in Agra and Delhi.

Loggias and covered balconies were fairly common in Roman buildings during the period of the Empire, as is shown in such wall paintings as this, part of a series found in a villa at Boscoreale, Naples, and partly removed to the Metropolitan Museum in New York.

A variety of covered balconies is found throughout India. This row of balconies (left) surmounted by small decorated cupolas occupies the façade of the Hava Mahal (Hall of the Winds) built in the middle of the eighteenth century in Jaipur, the 'pink' city of Rajasthan.
(Left, below) Covered loggias in a house in Katmandu, Nepal, probably eighteenth century.

(Right) Early fifteenth century French miniature (Geneva, Public Library) which shows features closely resembling mansard roofs.

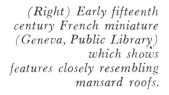

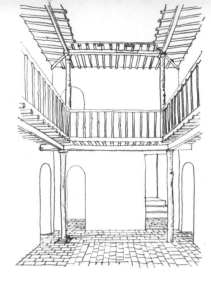

Reconstruction of the inner courtyard of a house at Ur (see page 32).

Gardens and courtyards

The ancient civilizations from Egypt to India, Mycenae to Columbian America, whether they developed in temperate, sub-tropical or tropical climates, had at least one architectural feature in common, the courtyard attached to the dwelling house. Around the *atrium* of the Roman house and the *hosh* of the Moslem house the life of the home circulated. The *peristyle* that enclosed them filtered heat and light to the house's interior. In certain areas – often, curiously, in inland regions – there was no *peristyle* though the courtyard existed. In the fortress houses of the Middle Ages, the courtyard retained its importance in the life of the household, securely gathered behind stout walls and in the shadow of the central tower or keep.

The Renaissance opened up new horizons, physical as well as mental and spiritual, and changes ensued in the form and purpose of the courtyard. A splendid central court was still part of the richer houses at least but the encircling columns were often placed on three sides only, the fourth side being that which incorporated the main entrance of the house. Room was made, moreover, for the staircases of increasing grandeur that became a part of such houses.

It was a pattern that was followed until at least the nineteenth century and the courtyard remained not merely the heart of the house but the coordinating element in its arrangement. In France a different pattern evolved in, for example, the *hôtels particuliers* built from the seventeenth century onwards. Here the grand courtyard separated the house from the street. A second service courtyard, communicating with the first and with the house, was sometimes added at the side of the house to accommodate servants' quarters, stables and stores.

Paintings and prints, documents relating to land registry and taxation, and literary references tell us the little that we know of the gardens of the past. Soon after the year 1200, the wealthier inhabitants of Florence were cultivating gardens around their houses. A century later, when the walls of the city extended over a wider area, these gardens were larger and more numerous. That of Durante Chiemontesi contained as many as 3500 orange and lemon trees; that of the Leoni family was only a little

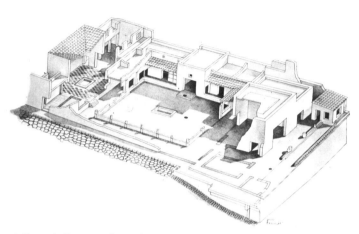

(Above) Restoration of a house known as 'the house of the atrium *with mosaic', one of the finest in Herculaneum. The main entrance is the small door on the left; in the centre is the courtyard; on the far side of it is the dining-room and the owner's rooms. The varying levels of balconies and windows ensured that the sea could be seen from the garden at the side of the residential part of the house. (Below) Courtyard of the house of Gamal ad-Din az-Zahabi in Cairo, built in 1637.*

smaller as were those of the Frescobaldi, the Rucellai, the Pandolfini, the Pitti, the Pazzi and the Puc-
ci. Venice too was a city of gardens by the end of
the fifteenth century despite the meagreness of the
site. Urban development has destroyed many of
these private gardens though city authorities make
strenuous efforts to maintain public gardens.

The earliest gardens were almost certainly utilitarian – as indeed would be that of Durante Chiemontesi, to which we have referred, with its thousands of orange and lemon trees. The garden of Al-
cinous in the *Odyssey* was a kitchen garden and
an orchard. But the Hanging Gardens of Babylon, one of the seven ancient wonders of the world,
were built by the king, probably Nebuchadnezzar,
to console his homesick Persian queen and it is
to this part of the world, to Babylon and later to
Persia, that we owe the idea of taming nature for
the pleasure of man. The Egyptians too were sensitive to natural beauty as one can see from their
wall paintings. Their gardens, planted in the rich
soil of the banks of the Nile with rows of vines and
lemon, orange and pomegranate trees, were tidily
laid out, but with an eye to the effect created by the
garden enclosed within a wall or palisade, with the
dwelling house on one side, a pond with water-lilies
floating on the water and some ducks in the middle,
and beyond, a canal or the Nile itself. Even where
space was precious, the Egyptians refused to be
parted from at least a fragment of garden and
greenery. Middle class houses in the city of Thebes
had precisely arranged clumps of trees before them
and in the small inner courtyard.

In China, the decorative garden is very ancient.
It contained, traditionally, a pool surrounded by
rocks but it was so arranged that its plan could
not be taken in at a single glance but unfolded
gradually as one walked along the paths. It is an
artistry comparable to that of the landscapes on
painted scrolls, which again require detailed examination and may not be appreciated in a single
glance. In China too, the plants had and have sym-

Background detail, showing a typical hortus conclusus, *from a painting of* The Virgin and Child *with a devout woman as Mary Magdalene, painted about 1480 and attributed to the Master of St. Gudule (Liège, Diocesan Museum).*

bolic values. The flexible bamboo signifies the man who bends beneath adversity but quickly rises after the storm; the plum tree, life which is not extinguished but is constantly revived; the lotus flower, the ability to rise above one's origin – the lotus grows out of the mud. The garden also contained pavilions, closed or open, circular or polygonal, according to their purpose. Narrow paths, along the side of the lake and over bridges reflected in the waters of a stream, connect the different areas.

'Harmony with things' – *mono-no-aware* – is the Japanese name for a garden in which the functional, the ritual and the traditional are combined. The inspiration of the Japanese garden is the love of nature not only as an external spectacle but as something of interior significance. The principles of the Japanese garden were set out between the fourteenth and the end of the fifteenth century and its constituents are still sea and river stones, corroded and wave-marked where possible; moss covered tree trunks, and in certain gardens, 'spread sand' or 'piled sand'. Water played an important part as did and do coniferous trees: deciduous trees were less highly valued. Where water is used, it should show its source in a spring or a small waterfall. Rocks and trees and the ubiquitous bamboo are arranged to create the impression of a broad

landscape within a little space. In this *tsukiyama* or hill garden, there are no lawns in the open spaces but azalea bushes where they catch the sun, or moss in the shade. The dry garden – the *kiraniwa* – makes use of trees and, above all, sand and rock: the garden in the grounds of Nijo Castle at Kyoto is a famous example. Here too are set out the dwarf trees, prized in Japan and Europe.

In Rome the garden was conceived as a decorative extension to a room enclosed by solid walls and shaded by arcades. As in Egypt, straight paths flanked by bushes of rosemary or myrtle, or by flowerbeds, met in the centre of the garden. Statues, fountains or vases with plants in them marked the intersection of the paths. The formality of this kind of garden was softened by the attempts their owners made to reproduce in them the Arcadian landscapes of poets and painters. Grottoes, pavilions and statues were shrouded accordingly in ivy, vines and maidenhair fern, in what at a later date was the best romantic manner. Admirers of the art of topiary trimmed their bushes and trees into spheres or prisms, or animals, buildings or figures. Statues of the gods concerned with the government of nature in all its aspects were popular – among them Priapus and assorted satyrs. Where there was no space for an extended garden, the Romans, like the Thebans, made the most of what space they had by having landscapes and other rustic scenes painted on the walls of *peristyles*. Examples of this adaptation to circumstances have been found in Rome and at Pompeii.

Throughout the Middle Ages, Roman formality governed the lay-out of gardens from Italy to Flanders. Flowerbeds were carefully outlined and planted though the accompanying statues were rarer. They probably contained lilies, hyacinths, and jasmine (brought to Europe during the Crusades), roses and gillyflowers. Exchanges of gifts between rulers might include rare plants: one such exchange took place between Charlemagne and Harun al-Raschid. Kitchen gardens probably featured more largely in the life of the household and with them that section devoted to herbs. The gardens near the Duomo in Padua, where Petrarch held Boccaccio in conversation until nightfall, were kitchen gardens.

In the Islamic world the development of gardens was much more advanced. It had, however, little effect on Europe outside Spain. There, during the Moorish occupation, ibn-Loyoun of Granada set down his advice on the subject. 'When building a house,' he wrote, 'choose that site which will assist you in caring for and watching over it. Set it facing south, with the door on one side, and raise the well and pool a little, or better still, instead of the well, channel the water so that it runs in the shade. Near the fountain, plant evergreens to gladden the eyes; and beyond them flowers of every kind and more evergreens. Train vines over the centre of the garden and construct pergolas to shade the paths round the open spaces. In the centre itself, set a garden house open on all sides and surrounded by flowering creepers, by myrtles and every flower that delights the eye in the garden. It should be longer than it is wide so that the eye is not tired. A part of the building should be reserved for guests, with its own doorway and pool secluded in a clump of trees. A dovecote and a small tower, habitable, would further improve the whole garden.' As one can detect from this, a reliable water supply was essential to the Moorish garden and in the richer Moslem houses the pools and channels were large enough to be described as lakes and canals and to be used by small boats.

In the fifteenth century in Europe, topiary caught the popular fancy. In the gardens of the Pazzi and the Medici in Florence, box-wood hedges were shaped to look like animals, humans and mythological figures. Fountains and statues reappeared and the fortunate and wealthy Florentine could enlist the aid of, for example, Donatello. As cities expanded beyond their medieval walls so did their gardens, and the *Italian* garden evolved in all its impressive precision and monumental formality. It evolved, however, in conjunction with the palace or the mansion: at a lower social level, the pattern remained that of the medieval enclosed garden.

Mannerist and baroque gardens matched the architecture of the period. They indulged the taste for fantasy on a spectacular scale with triumphal arches, pavilions, water displays and similarly theatrical conceits. The Italian garden was copied throughout western Europe. The ingenious also contrived gardens to be viewed from the balcony of a house, or from certain specific viewpoints. Where nature had failed to supply features suitable for exploitation, as on the plain of Lombardy and in the city of Cremona, artificial mounds were created in the gardens of some of the palaces and pools excavated – in which the Cremonese involuntarily anticipated in the sixteenth and seventeenth centuries the thirst for natural beauty of the romantic revival.

The natural garden was quintessentially the English garden. The return to nature was not achieved without a good deal of artifice. In his

Detail of a large painting of Venus and Cupid by an unknown painter of the school of Fontainebleau (c. 1570). The garden here is not unlike that shown opposite; it is still protected by a wall and formally laid out.

Epistle to the Earl of Burlington, Alexander Pope suggested the new concept of the garden. This, elaborated later by Lancelot 'Capability' Brown, became the *English* garden with miniature lakes, summer houses, classical temples, rustic pavilions, ingeniously contrived ruins (occasionally inhabited by a hermit – for a consideration) and, eventually, for they take a long time to reach perfection, lawns of velvet. The art that conceals art created these magnificent gardens and landscapes (for some are too extensive to be accurately described as gardens). It was, moreover, a highly sophisticated art, seen at its finest in England but exported even to the home of the Italian gardens, some of which fell victim to Anglophile passion.

And though the gardens and landscapes of William Kent and Capability Brown were immune, for reasons of the sheer size of the concept, to the vagaries of fashion, these did dictate during the nineteenth century a greater degree of intimacy between house and garden. Verandahs and conservatories brought nature, suitably tamed and no longer romantic, indoors. The gardens themselves, especially those attached to smaller houses, reverted to formal arrangements of flower beds and borders; sometimes even the weeds at the bottom of the garden were upgraded by the title of *wild* garden.

Below stairs

In the ancient civilizations and in the Middle Ages, the house of a family of means was a self-contained unit which employed servants whose duties were the same as those of today (or more accurately yesterday) and others who were craftsmen, that is, carpenters, potters, weavers, smiths and so on. This meant that the household consisted not only of the family – and the Roman and medieval family was a unit much larger than the father, mother, children unit of today – but of a large number of slaves or servants whose well-being was bound up with

Madame Geoffrin at Breakfast *by Hubert Robert (Paris, Veil-Picard Collection). An eighteenth century servant is here caught in morning dress, with an apron on, standing beside the broom he has propped for a moment against an armchair.*
(Left) Examples of mezzanines in fifteenth and sixteenth century Italian buildings. The first (left) is in a small house in Bologna: the arrangement of windows indicates the shifts to which householders were put to create such extra space.

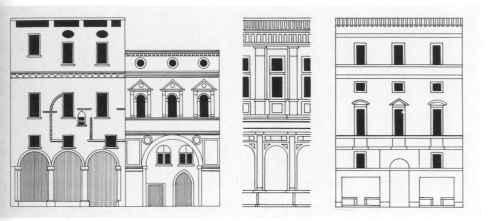

that of the family. The system lasted for a very long time and, even when craftsmen moved out from beneath the common roof and set up shop independently, their dependence on the patronage of the noble families still implied servant status. Famous artists and sculptors of the fifteenth and sixteenth centuries were as much the servants of the noble as his cook or his groom.

The living conditions of slaves varied, obviously, according to the character of their owner. There were those who treated them as, at least, valuable commodities and cared for them. Others regarded their slaves as useful but dangerous, an opinion in which they were confirmed by the slaves' rebellions. How they were housed depended on their duties and whether they worked in the house or on the land attached to it. And while it must be conceded that not all slaves in the classical world lived in conditions of abject misery, slaves had no legal rights and no freedom of action. Indeed slavery was so widely accepted as a factor in human life in the ancient world that suprisingly little reference is made to it.

Gradually, and in a way almost imperceptibly,

A Country Lady's Morning, *painted about 1823 by A. G. Venetsianov (Leningrad, Russian Museum), shows two Russian servants receiving instructions from their mistress.*

Detail from The Letter, *by Jan Vermeer (c. 1667: Amsterdam, Rijksmuseum). In this, one of Vermeer's finest paintings, we see a corner of the house while the housework is being done. The broom rests against the door; there is a basket of laundry in the background, and the maid has the front of her dress tucked up for work.*

A view of the fazenda Pau d'Alho *(already illustrated on page 219) and of the* senzala *or slaves' quarters: these consist of small rooms, each about six feet wide. It occupied one side of the complex and was built as far as possible from the owner's residence.*

it was eradicated from Europe under the influence of Christianity. By the eighteenth century, the African and oriental slaves acquired by wealthy noblemen were luxuries, expensive toys who might sleep in the same room as their master or mistress and who, suitably costumed, accompanied them when they went abroad.

In the medieval town house, the servants slept in attics, under the stairs and in whatever corner they could find. Kitchen servants curled up in the kitchen, grooms and stable boys in the stables, and the door-keeper beside the main door. Later in the period, they occupied the mezzanines constructed between the ground floor and first floor; this practice continued until the nineteenth century when regulations on the minimum height of rooms and on the proper housing of servants were framed.

As the better class of slave-owner had done, householders often felt some responsibility for the wellbeing of their servants; for, at least, their spiritual wellbeing. During the seventeenth century, wealthy French families were often careful of the state of their servants' souls and faithfully ensured that they went to the obligatory Mass on holidays

and recited the rosary in the evening: in this latter duty, the servants often joined the rest of the family. They seem to have given less thought to their physical welfare and, after family prayers, the servants might be consigned to two comfortless dormitories, one for men, one for women, under the roof of the house, where they slept several to a bed. The coachman remained in the stables and the cook in the kitchen which inconvenienced no-one, since the domestic day started at five in the morning and continued until just before midnight.

The servant's lot began to improve in the eighteenth and even more in the nineteenth century. The conditions of the house servants became more comfortable and the upper servants of each household – which included the personal servants of the master and mistress – were allotted their own quarters and, most important, their own dining-hall behind the green baize door that separated them from the rest of the house. Memoirs of life below stairs, whether written by the servants themselves or by their masters, indicate that in a prosperous and generous household the servants were eventually able to live nearly as well as the masters.

The nursery

Until very recently – until, indeed, this century – children were treated as miniature adults; their clothes were scaled-down versions of adult clothing. And while nurseries are not a modern invention, nursery furniture is. From past centuries, it is rare to find furniture adapted to less than adult-sized users. The little we know about medieval and later nurseries suggests that they were furnished with the rejects from the rest of the house.

In the ancient world, as in the east today, children lived in the women's part of the house. The practice continued during the Middle Ages in those households in which children were cared for by nurses or servant-girls. They did not, on the whole, live close to their parents, and the infant's cot was as likely to be close to the bed of the wet-nurse as the mother.

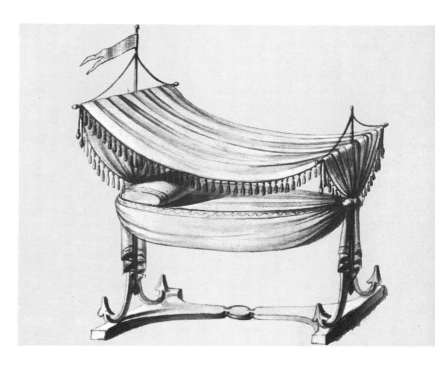

A Biedermeier cot (the drawing is one of the group on pages 274-5) for, presumably, a nautical infant, with pennant, awning and supports in the shape of anchors. (Left) This seventeenth century print (by J. de Brune, Emblemata, Amsterdam, 1624) depicts a familiar nocturnal scene in which father walks the floor with the fretful baby; the wheeled cot, made of rushes, indicates a middle class household. (Below) The cradle of the victor of Agincourt, Henry V, fourteenth century. A seventeenth century cot for rocking, ornately carved. Infant's chair used in ancient Greece (from a drawing on pottery) with two holes in it through which the child's legs were placed to prevent him from falling.

The cot on rockers is known from the Middle Ages: it was a modestly made and decorated piece of furniture. A cot made in 1392 for Giovanna, daughter of Amadeus II of Savoy, cost a trifling 15 *denari*. During the Renaissance the craftsmanship lavished upon it, in the shape of carving and inlays, made of it a luxurious piece of furniture. Famous artists designed, carved and painted cots and cradles. On a more modest scale, cradles of wickerwork were made. They were upholstered and draped with fabrics of varying degrees of costliness and when George Macdonald asked,

'Where did you come from, baby dear?

Out of the everywhere into here',

he was probably posing his question to the inhab-

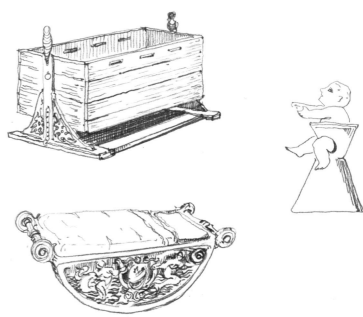

itant of a cot draped and flounced in white muslin.

There are large areas of the world, however, in which the cot or cradle is unknown. It is not found in most of Asia and Africa or among Eskimo tribes. In hot climates, it is unnecessary and in cold, beyond the Arctic circle for instance, the mother prefers to keep her baby warm inside her own furs.

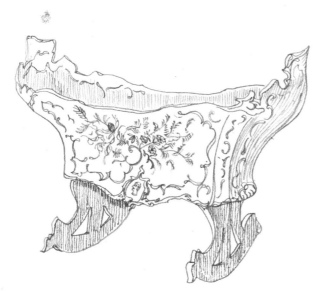

(Above, left) Venetian cradle, about 1750, in carved and lacquered wood.
(Above, right) This oleograph published at the beginning of this century shows the reason for the historic tendency to furnish nurseries with the rejects from other parts of the house.
(Below) Nursery in the Noordeinde Palace in The Hague, from a watercolour painted by Queen Sophia of the Netherlands in 1854 (The Hague, in an album in the Orange-Nassau Museum): it is furnished by solid but outdated pieces of furniture. The fireplaces are protected by fireguards.

Kennels and cages

When the Wild Dog and the Wild Horse joined the Man and the Woman in their cave in the *Just-So Stories*, they did so in order to serve them in return for food. The association of animals with domestic dwellings does probably derive from their usefulness for certain functions. The dog was almost certainly one of the first animals to throw in his lot with man: Kipling is probably wrong about the horse. Ducks may have been the first birds to be domesticated and they were a part of the domestic scene in Babylon and Egypt. The Egyptians also kept, or at least fed, crocodiles which were regarded as sacred animals, and hyenas: one of the tomb paintings from Sakkara depicts the hyenas' mealtime.

Homer mentions dogs more than once and they appear in other early texts. There is little information as to where and how they were housed but their predilection for the master's softest bed and armchair is obviously a very ancient one. At Tel el-Amarna the dogs were housed in the north courtyard of the richer houses. And the many treatises on hunting produced in the Middle Ages are most specific about the conditions in which dogs should be kept, that they should get as much sun as possible, that they should be provided daily with a thick layer of straw – which was more than their masters could expect – good drinking water, bread and meat.

The kennels in the palace at Tel el-Amarna were next to the stables which, until the advent of the motor car, were an important part of any establishment. Between the fourteenth and eighteenth centuries, it was reckoned, a rich man kept in his stables about 15 horses. In Paris in the reign of Louis XV, the Duc de Croy maintained 18 horses and 14 pack mules, which were also common items

of household equipment. Works on the care and maintenance of hounds were matched in quantity by those on the care and maintenance of horses and stables which, it was recommended, should be light, because a horse's eyesight was liable to deteriorate in the dark. The windows should be, ideally, behind the horse; the stable floor should be raised to guard against damp and the whole should be well ventilated.

Birds were kept for ornament, for hunting and for eating. Gothic miniatures show some of the decorative birds. Swans and peacocks appeared on platters at royal banquets and hunting birds were, like dogs and horses, the subject of an extensive literature. It is not certain at what point people began to keep birds for the sake of their songs; they were certainly caged for this purpose from the seventeenth century onwards and, in the nineteenth century, a cage with a singing bird in it was one of the most widespread of human pleasures, albeit a faintly dubious one. It might cheer a seamstress's attic or an emperor's study.

Seventeenth century Dutch paintings often show animals and birds indoors, especially dogs and parrots as in this detail (left) from The Parrot's Cage *by Jan Steen (Amsterdam, Rijksmuseum). or in the delightful* Lady and Parrot *by Frans van Mieris (above: London, National Gallery). It is rarer to find smaller cages like the one on the previous page, in the shape of a house with a stepped gable, in the small painting by Gerard Dou (Turin, Galleria Sabauda).*

'Beware of the Dog' in the first century A.D., in a mosaic from Pompeii (Naples, Museo Nazionale).

Domestic shrines

The shrines of the ancestors and household gods were probably the house's first decoration in the modern sense of the word, though to those who worshipped at them, they had a very definite function. In China the table of the ancestors was to be found in virtually every house. The household gods of the Romans occupied an equally important position. Other evidences of domestic piety are, for example, the innumerable statues of the Buddha that have been excavated in south-west Asia and that almost certainly came from private houses. The *kamidana* or 'holy shelf' of Japanese houses, with its miniature shrines, is used for religious purposes. In the Egypt of the Pharaohs, no rich house was without its chapel and, in some cases, the household might maintain their own priests and singers. To the Aztec, the hearth was the house of the fire-god himself. In Moslem houses, the *noguldūm* – niches – were often turned into chapels.

In medieval Europe, the woodcut, as we have seen, served as an aid to devotion in the houses of ordinary people. Where and how they were placed we cannot know. Such evidence as we do have as to the placing of paintings – whether religious or otherwise – is largely derived from other paintings of, obviously, households sufficiently prosperous to be able to commission them. These indicate, however, that medieval householders did not hang religious paintings or symbols on the wall above their beds. An exception is Rogier van der Weyden's *Annunciation*, painted about 1435 and now in the Louvre. Here a bronze medallion of the Holy Spirit hangs above Mary's bed; a circumstance so exceptional that it may rather be intended to suggest the presence of the Holy Ghost than to record the existence of the symbol. During the seventeenth and eighteenth centuries, moreover, pictures with secular rather than religious subjects were preferred and the gods of Olympus rioted over acres of baroque and rococo walls and ceilings. It was the piety of the nineteenth century – aided in practical terms by mass production techniques – that introduced holy pictures and symbols such as crucifixes on to the wall at the bedhead. Until then any aids to devotion were hung above the faldstool or *prie-dieu*. If they were absent, the reason may have been the custom of family prayers in the main living-room of the house: altarpieces are sometimes found in paintings of drawing-rooms.

(Above) The altar of the lares, *the household gods, in the house of the Vettii at Pompeii. In ancient Roman houses, the altar of the* lares *was associated with the cooking hearth. (Right) Altar of the ancestors in the house of Menander, also in Pompeii (first century B.C.).*

(Above) Domestic Japanese altar, open: an elaborate lacquered container holds both the sacred images and the religious objects needed.
(Left) Small altar with the figures of ancestors, probably nineteenth century, from Nias in Sumatra (Copenhagen, Nationalmuseet).

(Left) Carpaccio set his famous
Dream of St. Ursula (c. 1495: Venice,
Accademia Gallery) in a Renaissance room.
This detail indicates what was probably
a typical arrangement, a kneeling
stool with a small altarpiece above it,
a candleholder with a long arm, and a holy
water stoup with a sprinkler. The same
arrangement is found in another painting
(also in the Accademia) of roughly the same
period: here the devotional painting is
hung in a drawing-room where, possibly, the
family gathered to recite the rosary.

(Opposite page, above) Jan Steen, Vigil of the
Epiphany (1662: Boston, Museum of Fine
Arts); in the doorway on the left, the Three
Kings are arriving.
(Below) Also by Jan Steen, The Feast of St.
Nicholas (Amsterdam, Rijksmuseum): this
shows the northern European Christmas, or
rather the celebration of the feast of St. Nich-
olas of Myra or Bari, whose name changed
down the centuries into Santa Claus or Sinter
Claas.

(Left) F. Schrank, Family Portrait (c. 1810;
Cologne, Wallraf-Richartz Museum).
The room is dominated by the religious
painting over the fireplace; family prayers
were, presumably, conducted round the table.
(Below) Reconstruction of Christmas Eve
in a middle class Italian house about 1850
(room by G. Ragazzo, figures by A. Mazzeo:
Milan, Mostra del Presepio all'Angelicum,
no. 3). The crêche is on the left.

The ancestry of the Christmas tree goes back to pre-Christian tradition. From the Protestant north, from Germany in particular, it has spread throughout the world; it was a popular subject of nineteenth century postcards: this is dated 1888.

The pursuit of pleasure

Spanish miniature of 1283, now in the library of the Escorial. Chess, one of the most ancient of table games, had arrived in Spain, France and Italy by the eleventh century, introduced to Europe by the Arabs or Moors, who may have learned it from the Persians, who probably took it in the sixth century from India, where it may have begun – unless the Chinese invented it after all in the first century B.C. The change from chess in its oriental form to the form we know today seems to have taken place in the fifteenth century in France and Spain.

'At the height of his power,' Paul Valéry wrote, 'Louis XIV possessed not a hundredth part of the command of nature, of the means of enjoyment, of the opportunity for spiritual relaxation or stimulation, that many people in a middle condition of life enjoy today.' Agreed. Consider only the worlds of experience available to us by means of radio and television, literature and gramophone records. The pleasures of art and music and literature that are ours for the taking surpass those of Versailles.

In the space left to us we cannot, obviously, begin to describe these pleasures and the accommodation created for them in our houses: the libraries, music rooms, the equipment for parlour games – chess, cards, dice, and the rest – the development of musical instruments, the influence of universal – or almost universal – literacy. In the pages that follow, we shall content ourselves merely with illustrating a few aspects of this complex subject.

Reading chair shown at the Milan Exhibition of 1894: providing the means of reading in comfort was and is an aspect of what is today termed 'the leisure industry.'

A watercolour of 1905 of The Happy American Family, *with the pledge to temperance, duly signed by the household, on the wall. Children's games and hand-sewing are two of the activities shown which might be said to have suffered under the impact of television: reading too, perhaps.*

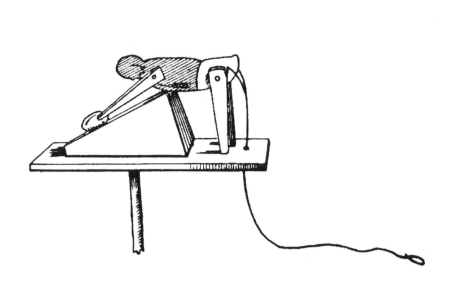

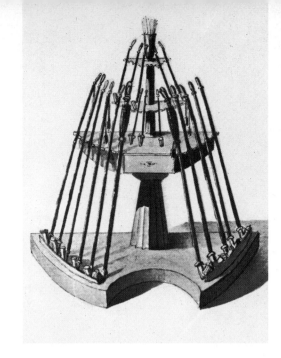

(Above, left) Egyptian toy
found in a tomb at Memphis
of about 2000 B.C.; a wooden
figure of a woman kneading
bread, moved by a string.
(Above) A piece of smoker's
equipment from Biedermeier
Germany: a stand
for long porcelain pipes.
(Left) In the Dining-room,
an engraving by Philibert-Louis
Debucourt from a painting by
M. Drolling (1821). Then
perfected, the pianoforte
was becoming the principal
source of music in the home.
(Below) The faintly guilty
enjoyment of French novels is
shown in this painting,
A Nobleman's Morning, by
P. A. Fedotov (1849,
Moscow, Tretyakov Gallery).

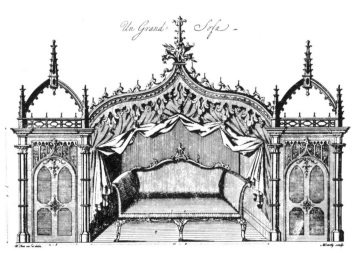

The sofa or day bed arrived in Europe from the east in the
eighteenth century. En route this one has clearly picked up
some Gothic accessories.

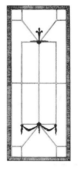 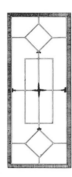 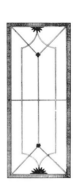  

In the eighteenth century, the upper part of a set of shelves of this kind (right), which happens to be English, was often used for books while the lower remained a cupboard. The secrétaire-bookcase first appeared in England (this page, below) in a form that was to remain unchanged for a long time. The books were stored behind glazed doors (below, and opposite page) while the lower part of the piece was fitted as a desk and cupboard.

(Above) The Greeks and Romans had no piece of furniture devoted exclusively to the storage of books: they used a small cupboard in which scrolls or volumes were laid one on top of the other in rows, as this fifth century mosaic from the Tomb of Galla Placidia in Ravenna – showing how the copies of the Gospels were stored – indicates. The custom of storing books in cupboards continued until the seventeenth century.

Books were placed in cupboards with their backs facing inwards and this meant that, until the sixteenth century or later, the title was written on the fore-edges, as in this volume of Aristotle, published in 1588: the fore-edge was further decorated by Titian's son, Cesare Vecellio, for the patrician, Pilone of Belluno.

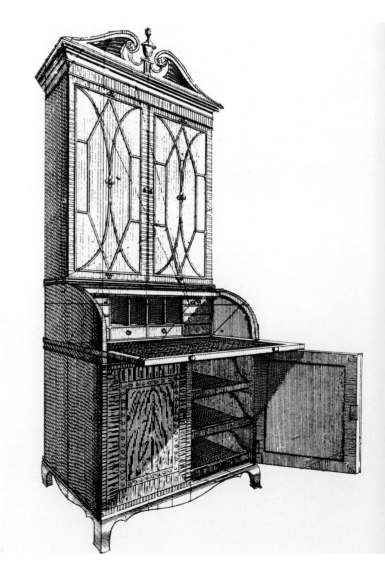

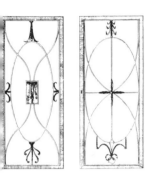

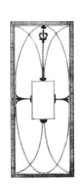
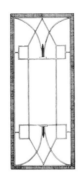

(Above, right) Johann Zoffany, Charles Townley in his Sculpture Gallery *(c. 1792: Burnley Art Gallery and Museum). This shows the famous collection of antiquities bought for £ 20,000 by the British Museum in the early years of the nineteenth century: Townley himself is shown with three friends, Charles Greville, Thomas Astle and M. de Hancarville. His collection occupied, in fact, several rooms in his house at No. 2 of what is now Queen Anne's Gate in Westminster though, by the exercise of artistic licence, it is here concentrated into one. The pursuit of antiquity could be, for an eighteenth century enthusiast, a way of life rather than a mere hobby.*

G.F. Kersting, Reading *(1812: Weimar, Schlossmuseum). In this interior, the reader is using an Argand lamp (see page 374). In the shadows on the right is a modest bookcase, the shelves curtained, as is fairly common during this period. The end of the eighteenth and the beginning of the nineteenth century saw impressive developments in the design of bookcases and very elaborate designs were available.*

L.-L. Boilly, Le Concert Improvisé (c. 1790-95: St. Omer, Musée des Beaux-Arts). The harp was known, in a rudimentary form, to the Egyptians; in its present form it dates from 1710 and the design of the Bavarian musician, Hochbruecker. Before the advent of the piano, all girls of good family were taught to play the harp.

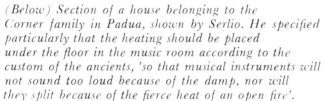

(Below) Section of a house belonging to the Corner family in Padua, shown by Serlio. He specified particularly that the heating should be placed under the floor in the music room according to the custom of the ancients, 'so that musical instruments will not sound too loud because of the damp, nor will they split because of the fierce heat of an open fire'.

The first attempts to record sound mechanically were those of Scott's phonoautograph (1857): Edison followed with his phonograph (1876), then Bell and Tainter with their gramophone. The apparatus (below), worked by a pedal, was made before 1888, the year in which the clockwork gramophone appeared. The recording disc dates from 1897 and was used on the horn gramophone (above).

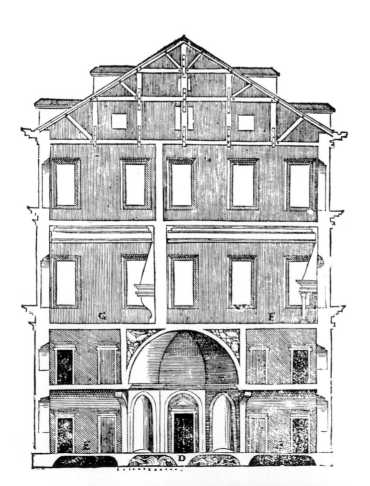

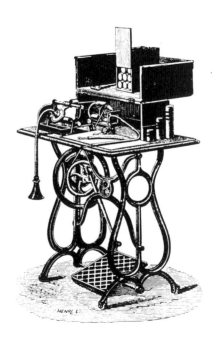

(Above) Music at home: a fortnightly magazine for amateur violin and guitar players, published early this century. This number of Il Concerto contains the tenor aria, Spirto gentil from Donizetti's La Favorita, transcribed for mandolin. Radio killed this kind of music-making.

Eishi, Taki-koto concert (twelfth century: Paris, Musée Guimet). The instrument in use was a kind of psaltery with thirteen strings which were plucked (the sound in the similar but smaller koto was made with a bow): it was very popular with Japanese ladies, and was often in itself an objet d'art, made of a precious wood inlaid with ivory or lacquered.

Petite Galerie in the Palace of Malmaison, watercolour begun in 1812 by Auguste Garnerey and completed in 1832 by his sister (now in the Malmaison collection). A harp, an indispensable adjunct to every polite nineteenth century drawing-room, stands at the end of the room which later became the music-room.

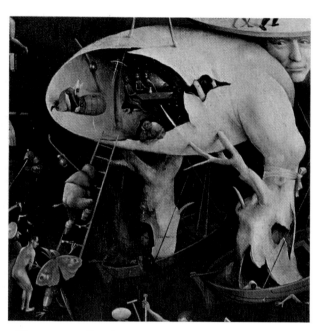

Hieronymus Bosch, The Garden of Earthly Delights, *detail from the right-hand of the three panels; it depicts the tavern inside the body of the monster from hell. (Madrid, Prado.)*

CONTRIBUTORS

DANIEL ALCOUFFE, Decorative Arts Department, Louvre, Paris, France.

P. M. BARDI, Museum of Art, São Paulo, Brazil.

ANNE BERENDSEN, Stedelijk Museum, Delft, Netherlands.

MARIO BUSSAGLI, University of Rome, Italy.

GIANFILIPPO CARETTONI, Department of Antiquities, Rome, Italy.

SERGIO CORADESCHI, Politecnico, Milan, Italy.

JOHN DRUMMOND, Rome, Italy.

JOSÉ GUDIOL RICART, The Amatller Institute of Spanish Art, Barcelona, Spain.

MIHAIL ILJIN, Moscow University, U.S.S.R.

WOJCIECH KALINOWSKI, University of Tórun, Poland.

GIANNI K. KOENIG, University of Florence, Italy.

ADAM J. MILOBEDZKI, University of Warsaw, Poland.

CHARLES F. MONTGOMERY JR., Former Registrar, Virginia Museum of Art, U.S.A.

MICHELANGELO MURARO, Curator of Galleries, Venice, Italy.

G. OPRESCO AND P. PETRESCO, Institute of the History of Art, Bucharest, Romania.

ACKNOWLEDGEMENTS

Where the names of the artists responsible for the drawings in the present volume are not indicated, these are the work of the architect Sergio Coradeschi. The originals of the black and white, and colour illustrations have been supplied by the collection to which the work belongs. Other illustrations have been supplied by the following agencies and photographers; Alinari, Florence; Alzati, Milan; Arborio Mella, Milan; Carraro, Venice; Cooper (Colour), London; Elettra Cliché, Milan; De Antonis, Rome; Gasparini, Gorizia; Gautherot, Rio de Janeiro; Germanisches Nationalmuseum, Nuremberg; Giraudon, Paris; Istituto Archeologico Germanico, Rome; Legrand et Mallet, Paris; Malvaux, Brussels; Mas, Barcelona; Mercurio, Milan; Novarese, Florence; Pineider, Florence; Positano de Vincentiis, Milan; Preti, Florence; Rozema, The Hague; Sandak, New York; Scala, Florence; Scheier, São Paulo; Stichting Lichtbeelden-Instituut, Amsterdam; Stichting tot bevordering van het kunsthistorisch Onderzoek in Nederland, The Hague. The remaining photographic originals have been taken from Rizzoli archives.

INDEX

In this index, the abbreviation H. or h. is used to designate House or house.

Figures in italics indicate illustrations.

431